How a Nation Grieves:
Press Accounts of the Death of Lincoln,
the Hunt for John Wilkes Booth,
and America in Mourning

Other Books by Glenn Alan Cheney

Love and Death in the Kingdom of Swaziland

Thanksgiving: The Pilgrims' First Year in America

Journey on the Estrada Real: Encounters in the Mountains of Brazil

Journey to Chernobyl: Encounters in a Radioactive Zone

Nuclear Proliferation: Problems and Possibilities

Neighborhood News

Frankenstein on the Cusp of Something

Passion in an Improper Place

Acts of Ineffable Love

They Never Knew: The Victims of Atomic Testing

Life in Caves

For Ian Alan

Published in 2012 by
New London Librarium
P.O. Box 284
Hanover, Conn. 06350
www.NLLibrarium.com

First Edition
Printed in the United States

Cheney, Glenn Alan
How a Nation Grieves: Press Accounts of the Assassination of Abraham Lincoln, the Hunt for John Wilkes Booth, and America in Mourning

Includes index

1. Abraham Lincoln 2. Civil War

ISBN: 978-0-9856284-2-0

How a Nation Grieves:
Press Accounts of the Death of Lincoln,
the Hunt for John Wilkes Booth,
and America in Mourning

Glenn Alan Cheney

New London Librarium

Table of Contents

Foreword

How a Nation Grieves offers a fascinating new perspective on the most written-about and analyzed figure in American history. The subject of an estimated 16,000 books, Abraham Lincoln has been written about from every angle imaginable. Historians have dissected every aspect of his personal, professional, and political lives. The proliferation of writers who have weighed in on Lincoln reflects the enduring power of his larger-than-life personality and the cataclysmic struggle that raged during each of his 1,503 days as President.

Previous Lincoln books include great works of American literature such as Carl Sandburg's *Abraham Lincoln: The War Years*, and historical triumphs like Eric Foner's recent *Trial by Fire*. They also include children's books, novels and regrettably even vampire stories. In all cases, these writings are influenced by the inescapable impact of the passage of time, subsequent events that flowed from the Civil War, and the evolution of public opinion. Edwin Stanton's famous observation when Lincoln's lifeless body was removed from the boarding house opposite Ford's Theatre, "Now he belongs to the ages," was not only a mournful cry, but also an astute observation that our understanding of Lincoln would be shaped by mores and sensibilities bound to evolve over time.

Glenn Alan Cheney's remarkable book, which recounts Lincoln's final days, his assassination, funeral, burial, and the subsequent manhunt and death of John Wilkes Booth, is a brilliant effort to set aside modern perspective and capture the days immediately before and after Lincoln's assassination. Unlike so many other efforts to capture an historic moment, Cheney's account is told with purely contemporary, primary sources. The compilation of press clips and speeches from all regions and opinion leaders across the United States is an extraordinary accomplishment. The writing is fresh with the thoughts and emotions of Lincoln's present, unfiltered by the passage of time or the aid of perspective. For example, the anger of northern newspapers, lashing out at Booth's crime, is raw and drenched with emotion. For even a casual historian, it is fascinating to see how anxious the reporting is about the meaning of Lincoln's death at such a fragile moment in the nation's existence. The writing is bursting with very real insecurity about the stability of the country that later historians, with the benefit of hindsight, cannot convey.

Even more powerful, the southern comment is a reminder of how bitterly divided the nation was during the days that followed the "end" of the Civil War. The loathing of Lincoln expressed in news accounts and the lionization of the murderer Booth vividly convey the poisonous political climate that was roiling during those momentous days. These toxic sentiments are a healthy reminder that as bad as contemporary politics may seem, the political discourse of 1865 was far more violent and threatening to the very fabric of our Republic.

Glenn Cheney's book is a useful and thorough contribution to our understanding of the days following Lincoln's death. Newspaper descriptions of the assassination and subsequent manhunt are reminiscent of contemporaneous clips of the Kennedy assassination and the live coverage of Jack

Ruby shooting Lee Harvey Oswald in 1963. Our understanding of the way the nation mourned Lincoln's death is limited to the written word, but thankfully, the style of reporting in 1865 is visual and textured, driven perhaps by the absence of accessible photography. As a result, in both instances the coverage is frighteningly fast-paced and violent, even though the journalistic medium in one case is uncut footage and in the other, it is column inches. These first, immediate accounts - the first drafts of history - are not the final word on Kennedy and Lincoln, but their existence deepens our understanding of who these men were and what they meant to our country.

How A Nation Grieves is a massive and ambitious undertaking that provides a rich new contribution to our understanding of the events of April, 1865. As future Lincoln historians add to the existing historical volumes, Glenn Cheney's work will provide a solid footing on which to stand.

U.S. Representative Joe Courtney
Washington, D.C.

Introduction

When I started compiling How a Nation Grieves: Press Accounts of the Death of Lincoln, the Hunt for Booth, and America in Mourning, I had little intention of pulling together a whole book. But I soon realized I was witnessing – not reading about but witnessing — the most traumatic moment in American history. The nation's most horrific war was just ending when one more bullet seemed to kill one too many. The assassination of Lincoln shocked North and South alike. War had gone one step too far.

Except for the people at Ford's Theatre on April 14, 1865, the American people witnessed the national trauma through newspapers, the only medium of information of the news of the day. Through words — without hearing the shot or seeing the blood, not even in a scratchy recording or black and white photograph — Americans shared the experience. They witnessed the cataclysm through language alone, and reading that language today is quite the same experience as reading it in 1865.

The nation's newspapers exuded passion as they struggled to report events and make sense of them. Journalism was a little different in those days. In that journalism had to do what television, radio, film, recordings, and the Internet do today, its practitioners were not restricted to today's dispassionate, professional voice. They were expected to provide details, and they were free to use language to connote the emotions that came with those details. If those journalists were anything like me, they were touched less by the actual events than by the details they chose to share and the words they used to describe them.

We do not know which reporter The Age of Philadelphia sent to Independence Hall on April 22 to witness the wake and open casket that bore the remains of the former president. The article on the event that appeared on April 25 had no byline, but it included the following:

> The flowers filled with dust,
> and their white and crimson mouths,
> instead of being filled with soft silver dew,
> were dry and parched and arid,
> sprinkled over with dust, as though
> it had been distributed by a dredger box.
>
> The wax tapers were discolored with it,
> and it seemed even to make the flames
> of the candles sputter.
>
> It had settled in thick layers
> upon the portion of the coffin lid
> which had not been removed, and,
> above all, on the features of the dead.
>
> This it was, the dusty accumulation
> of a whole day, which lent so leaden
> a cast to the face,
> and covered with an unruffled
> and unnatural veil the really
> genial and kind expression.
>
> But the undertaker's skillful brush,

long, thick, light, and flossy,
removed, with a few artistic touches,
the unseemly discoloration,
and a white cambric handkerchief,
delicately applied, transformed to itself
the last molecule lingerings.

That was a paragraph, not a poem. But when I compiled How a Nation Grieves: Press Accounts of the Death of Lincoln, the Hunt for Booth, and America in Mourning, I found myself reading articles that went beyond journalism and into the realm of literature and poetry. I decided to start each chapter with a few sentences broken up into the appearance of a poem. With that objective I looked at each sentence with a more careful eye.

Each chapter presented the reports and editorials appearing on one given day in cities across the nation, though the first chapter included reports appearing between April 10 and April 14. Those few days before the assassination brought the news that Lee had surrendered the Confederacy's largest army. The Southern cause was now hopeless. The war was over, the Union saved, the slaves freed. From The Sun of Baltimore I pulled a title, and from the Washington Chronicle I pulled two sentences:

The All-absorbing Subject of Remark

This news will go everywhere
like an angelic visitor.

It will heal the sick,
restore the drooping

and fill all the land
with thanksgiving.

The reporters who wrote those lines, of course, had no idea of the tragic irony that that awaited, that the thanksgiving that filled the land would soon be infused with pain and existential darkness. As I watched for more unintended poetry, my careful reading of each sentence gave me a new perspective on the history I was witnessing. These were newspaper reports, not retrospective analyses of events that had moved from current to historical. Every line was written with no knowledge of what would follow, how the events of the next day, the next year, and the next centuries would shed new significance on their observations.

The Hartford Courant ran an un-bylined article from the Springfield Republican, written by a reporter in Richmond, Va., who quoted a former slave. The New York Times provided me a title that lent the quote a chilling prescience:

A Quarrel in Embryo

Dey part us all.
Dey send us away from our family.
Dey send us jus whar dey please.

Dey han-cuff us.
Dey put us in jail.
Dey give us thirty-nine lashes.
Dey starve us.

Dey do ebery ting to us.

At the National Intelligencer, one reporter, writing during the hours between the shot at Ford's Theatre and the president's death just across the street, wrote a single, long, heavy sentence that must have brought him close to tears. During those same hours, an editor at the Daily Constitutional Union ended a sentence with three words of piercing irony:

April 10 - 14, 1865

Carnival of Blood

As to the awful catastrophe,
the drift of reliable information
is, that
when a pistol shot was heard
in the second box
of the right-hand side
of the stage of Ford's theatre,
persons in the theatre
imagined
that it was part of the play.

Newspapers reported that Abraham Lincoln went to that play with a certain lightness in his heart. The nation had been tearing itself apart on every one of his 1,503 days in office. Now the war was almost over, and the capital itself, once threatened by invasion but now safe, was in a lighter mood. The last sound that Abraham Lincoln heard was people laughing, and maybe he was laughing, too. The play, Our American Cousin, was a satire contrasting the cultures of England and its former colony. The last line spoken was "Don't know the manners of good society, eh? Well, I guess I know enough to turn you inside out — you sockdologizing old man-trap!" Half the joke was that silly-sounding word — sockdologizing. It was relatively new to the English language, and it hasn't been used much since. It comes from a combination of sock, meaning "to hit hard," and doxology, with its notion of finality. Historians have theorized that John Wilkes Booth, an actor who knew the play well, had been waiting for that line.

Just as we can link ourselves to the past through these newspaper accounts, the times they reported link forward to ours. The April 17 edition of the Philadelphia Inquirer gave its times and ours a rather long sentence whose rhythm and timing are impeccable. The title comes from Booth's dramatic declaration, spoken as he stood with a broken leg on the stage of a comedy, words that are still today in the motto of the state of Virginia:

> Sic Semper
>
> The art of misrepresentation
> has been, from the first,
> boldly resorted to
> in order to bolster up
> an unrighteous cause,
>
> and whether the effort was to show
> that a violation of the Constitution
> was constitutional,
> or that a war undertaken
> to establish slavery forever
> was a battle in behalf of freedom,
>
> whatever was the object to be gained,
> it has generally been
> that the common claims of the language
> were perverted.

If the perversion of language served the justification of slavery, war, and twisted notions of constitutionality, the reportage that followed the death of Lincoln was a victory of language — language beautiful, poetic, philosophical, and emotional. It reported tragedy, but it did so with dignity and honor. It reported the facts and struggled to articulate the incomprehensible. Language expressed the grief of a nation, and the underlying truth of it speaks to us still.

April 10 - 14, 1865

**Monday, April 10
through
Friday, April 14, 1865**

The All-absorbing Subject of Remark

This news will go everywhere
like an angelic visitor.

It will heal the sick,
restore the drooping

and fill all the land
with thanksgiving.

The Age
Philadelphia
Monday, April 10, 1865

THE LATEST NEWS BY TELEGRAPH — OFFICIAL GAZETTE — SURRENDER OF LEE AND HIS WHOLE ARMY TO GRANT.— A GREAT AND BLOODLESS VICTORY. — MAY IT BRING TRUE PEACE AND UNION.

War Department, Washington, D.C. April 9, 1865 — 9 P.M. Maj. Gen. John A. Dix[1], New York: The Department has just received official report of the surrender, this day, of General Lee[2] and his army to Lieutenant General Grant,[3] on the terms proposed by General Grant. Details will be given as speedily as possible.

Edwin M. Stanton[4]
Secretary of War

*　*　*　*　*

1　John Adams Dix (1798 - 1879) was a senator from New York, then postmaster of New York City, then president of Union Pacific, then Secretary of the Treasury, then a major general. In 1861, he prevented the Maryland legislature from voting to secede by arresting its pro-Confederate members. In 1873 he was elected governor of New York.

2　This was not a surrender by the Confederate government, but when the South's famously effective Army of Northern Virginia abandoned Richmond, the Confederate capital, and then surrendered, other Southern armies knew loss was inevitable. Mostly due to the limited communication, fighting would continue elsewhere in the South until June.

3　Hiram Ulysses Grant (1822 - 1885) renamed himself Ulysses S. Grant when he entered West Point, and he said the middle initial stood for nothing. His classmates dubbed it "Sam." He served in the Mexican-American War, then followed assignments that took him to Oregon, Panama, and California. He resigned from the army in 1854 but rejoined when the Civil War started. A brilliant tactician, he conducted several successful campaigns against the armies of the Confederacy. He was elected President of the United States twice despite widespread corruption in his government.

4　Edwin M. Stanton (1814 - 1869), an anti-slave democrat, was Secretary of War from 1862 through 1868.

The Sun
Baltimore
Tuesday Morning, April 11, 1865

The War News — Nothing later than the official dispatches of General Grant, published yesterday, have been received concerning the surrender of Lee's army. Telegrams from various points of the country, state that the rejoicings of the people over this most important event have been very general and

Gen. Ulysses S. Grant

highly enthusiastic. A steamer from New York was dispatched yesterday afternoon, one day in advance of her regular day of sailing, to take the news of General Lee's capitulation to Europe...[5]

GENERAL LEE'S SURRENDER

Views and Opinions of the Press — the Anticipation of Peace, etc.

The surrender of General Lee's army to Lieutenant General Grant, under the terms and conditions presented by the latter, is of course the all-absorbing subject of remark, so that the views and opinions of the press general will be read with more than usual interest.[6] We, therefore, subjoin a number of extracts:

---

5   News of the surrender would appear in the Times of London on April 25. News of the assassination would appear on April 27.

6   General Robert Edward Lee (1807 - 1870), commander of the Confederate Army of Northern Virginia, Lee was second in his class at West Point (where U.S. Grant had graduated 21st out of 39). There he studied engineering more than battle tactics, He supported the Union and to some extent opposed slavery, but he opted to remain loyal to his state — Virginia — and thus to the Confederacy.

[From the Washington Chronicle]

This news will go everywhere like an angelic visitor. It will heal the sick, restore the drooping and fill all the land with thanksgiving. It cannot be a voice of woe to the South, for there is no carnage and death in the terms, and no humiliation in a defeat which could not be resisted or longer delayed. Accepted in this sense, it will be good for those who have yielded too much to the rebel leaders; rejected or disregarded, it will only increase the tortures of which they are so profoundly tired. The surrender of Lee is the surrender of the whole rebel Confederacy. From the Potomac to the Nueces[7] — from the Mississippi to the Gulf— from the wilds of Texas to the morasses of Louisiana and the everglades of Florida — there will soon not be known or seen an alien flag, or an organized hostile column. The bolt that struck the head of the serpent paralyzed its extremities; and that which is now alive in the land of love of country — the exquisite sense of an established Union: the knowledge that we are free in all our borders; and, let us not forget our abiding gratitude to God, that he has led us through this bloody war and crowned us with these priceless blessings, by such a peace as becomes a Christian people.

[From the N.Y. News, anti-war dem.[8]]

The terms of surrender are honorable to both generals. As between soldier and soldier, General Grant has accorded to his fallen adversary such warlike honor as it is possible for the conqueror to concede to lessen the humiliation of defeat. May the political chief of the Republic follow his example. It is useless to deny that, by the rule of civilized warfare, the cause of the Southern Confederacy has received a blow that, by the usual sequence of such military fortune, should decide the contest. After such an overwhelming disaster in the field, peace between the contestants is the natural result. But peace may be forbidden even in this condition, by an unnatural policy on the part of the

---

7   The Nueces river flows southeast across the western part of Texas. It was the border between Texas and the rest of Mexico until the newly formed Republic of Texas claimed that the Rio Grande was the border.

8   Newspapers became unabashedly partisan as soon as distinct parties began to emerge in the late 18th century, some even serving as government organs. Anti-war democrats were a pro-Union faction that opposed secession but also opposed the war because it was being fought, in their opinion, primarily to end slavery, not secure the Union.

4

victors.

For the sake of republicanism, for the sake of the blood of common origin that pulses from the exultant hearts and the proud though stricken breasts of victors and of vanquished, for the honor of our country and for the peace of future generations, let Americans in their hour of victory be just, magnanimous, and generous to Americans in their hour of defeat. Peace, if honorable to both sections, would be the most welcome boon that could be vouchsafed to a people so visited with heavy burdens and afflictions.

[From the New York Tribune]

The rebels lost much in the loss of their capital. In the loss of Lee they lose everything. Lee, not Davis, is their leader[9]. He may be the heart of a faction, not of a people. Davis is a politician; Lee a soldier. The military head gone and there is nothing left. — If Johnston[10] is wise he will follow Lee's example. If he is not wise he will earn the execrations of the South for the useless waste of blood that must follow the necessity of his annihilation. With him it is a question of days. He must bow to fate and succumb or accept a swift destruction. There is no other alternative. The most faint-hearted, the most hopeless now at the North need waver or doubt no longer. The most desperate, the most determined at the South can no longer hope or struggle. The rebellion is over; suppressed — overwhelmed — destroyed — fought down — by strong arms, and stout hearts, and wise heads — ended — ended as rebellions should be by utter destruction.

[From the New York World]

The correspondence between Grant and Lee, by which this noble triumph

---

9   Jefferson Davis (1808 - 1889) was a West Point graduate, a colonel in the Mexican-American War, U.S. Representative and Senator from Mississippi, Secretary of War, and President of the Confederate States of America during its entire existence. He was against secession but defended the right of states to secede. He was married to Zachary Taylor's daughter until she died of malaria three months after the wedding.

10   General Joseph Eggleston Johnston (1807 - 1891) was a senior but generally unsuccessful Confederate general. Organizer of the Army of the Shenandoah, he later led three armies defending the South against General Sherman's March to the Sea. He was still fighting when Lincoln was assassinated, but hearing of Lee's surrender and its lenient terms, he surrendered his starving armies by April 26, 1865.

is achieved and attested, does honor alike to the head and the heart of the victorious commander and entitles the vanquished to all the respect which justly attends the frank and magnanimous abandonment of a struggle become visibly hopeless, and only to be prolonged at a hideous, because an utterly useless, waste of human life and human happiness. We cannot pause to dwell upon the work which may still remain to be done. Rebel armies are still in the field; the forms of a rebel government still nominally exist; but only the extremest unwisdom on our own part can galvanize into any sustained and formidable life the body whereof the heart has ceased to beat with the occupation of Virginia and the disbanding of the army of Robert E. Lee.

[From the N.Y. Herald]

Lee's army has been for six months the only respectable obstacle to our arms, and now, with seven or eight days, it has been completely wiped out of existence — not a man of the whole force that lately held Richmond remaining in arms. Within that short period the bravest, best organized and most successful army of the rebellion has been utterly swept away. Never was there a more decisive campaign than this last one of General Grant's.

Grant will now, no doubt, immediately turn his attention to another foe. It should be remembered that it is now six days since Lee was beaten at Petersburg and compelled to evacuate that place and the rebel capital. — Johnston was, in all probability, informed of that defeat on the same day that Davis was informed of it — the 2nd inst.[11] — and though he was then at Raleigh, it is not in the least likely that he is there now. He has had abundant time to reach Danville, and no one ought to be surprised to hear of his being there. — His presence would bring him within reach of Grant; and with Grant on one hand, Sherman[12] on the other and Stoneman not far from Danville, we might soon hear of another surrender as clean and complete as the one just made by Lee.[13]

---

11   *inst.* stands for *instant* in its definition as "the current month."

12   William Tecumseh Sherman (2/8/1820 - 2/14/1891) was a Union general most famous for capturing Atlanta and waging a scorched earth campaign through Georgia and the Carolinas until, shortly after Lee's surrender, Confederate armies in the southeast surrendered to him.

13   Major General George Stoneman, Jr. (8/8/1822 - 6/5/1894) was a Union general

The operations against Mobile will be greatly affected by this immense success in Virginia.[14] It has been a point of honor with the rebel officers defending that place to hold as long as Lee did, and that the last stronghold of the Gulf States should not be taken while a stronghold was still defended in Virginia.

Gen. Robert E. Lee

The news of the fall of Richmond and the surrender of Lee will therefore satisfy the honor of the men at Mobile, and their surrender will be, in all likelihood, the next news from the Gulf. This same glorious news will doubtless disperse the fifty-three thousand rebels on the other side of the Mississippi, who adhere so loosely to the rebellion that they would not cross the river to help it. And thus, in whatever way we look, we see daylight shining through this miserable remnant of rebellion.

*   *   *   *   *

whose roommate at West Point was future Confederate general Thomas J. "Stonewall" Jackson. During the war, Stoneman had his men give their rations to the starving army of General Johnston when he surrendered in Durham. Stoneman is mentioned in the The Band's song "The Night They drove Old Dixie Down," lyrics by Robbie Robertson:
Virgil Caine is the name, and I served on the Danville train,
Til Stoneman's cavalry came and tore up the tracks again.
In the winter of '65,
we were hungry, just barely alive.
By May tenth, Richmond had fell
It's a time I remember, oh so well.

Stoneman later resisted the so-called radical (i.e. less lenient) Reconstruction. In 1882 he was elected governor of California.

14   Word had not yet reached the North that Spanish Fort, at Mobile, Alabama, had fallen on April 9, the day before Lee's surrender. Nearby Fort Blakely would fall on the next day, allowing occupation of Mobile.

Macon Daily Telegraph and Confederate[15]
Wednesday Morning, April 12, 1865

HOLD UP THE HANDS OF THE PRESIDENT[16]

We copy from the message of Governor Allen[17] to the Legislature of Louisiana, the following beautiful extract. Oh! that our Governor had the patriotism to breathe such pure and beautiful language in aid of our noble President, who is striving so earnestly to hold up our sacred cause. Governor Allen says:

"I must, gentlemen, through you, bid my countrymen be of good cheer. We all have steadily hoped that this war would end — that this revolution would abate — that the mountain top might be viewed, and the dove of peace would at last go forth and return no more. I am firmly convinced that this is near at hand. In the meantime, let us do our duty under all circumstances. The Ruler of the Universe, who spoke peace to the troubled waters of Galilee, will not forsake us, but, in His own good time, will speak peace to us. When Israel warred with Amalek, Joshua was sent out to give battle.[18] Moses stood hard by and held up his hands. As long as they were up, Joshua prevailed; but, in course of time, they became tired, and fell to his side. Then Amalek prevailed. Upon seeing this, Aaron and Hur came to the assistance of Moses, and stayed up his hands till the going down of the sun. Joshua prevailed, and Israel was free. Let us all then rally around the chief magistrate of the Confederacy. He is our President, and this is our fight. He is a pure patriot. Let us hold up not only his hands, but those of all others in authority. We will prevail — we will win the fight — We will be free!"

---

15   The *Macon Telegraph* was established as a weekly in 1826, three years after the incorporation of the city. It merged with **the Macon Daily Confederate** in 1864. The paper was able to achieve prominence in 1848 when the world's longest telegraph line, from New York to New Orleans, passed through town, giving the paper access to national and international news. It was Democratic and favored Georgia's secession from the Union. Today *The Telegraph* is the third-largest newspaper in Georgia. (http://telegraph.galileo.usg.edu/telegraph/about/)

16   Confederate President Jefferson Davis

17   Governor Henry Watkins Allen (1820 - 1866) participated in the Texas uprising against Mexico and went to Italy intending to fight for its independence. He was a general in the Confederate army before being elected governor in 1864. After the war, he moved to Mexico City, where he died of digestive problems.

18   Exodus 17

8

* * * * *

The Philadelphia Inquirer
Friday, April 14, 1865

FROM RICHMOND

Special Correspondent of the Inquirer

Richmond, VA., April 12

General Ord Takes Command[19]

Major-General Ord arrived early this morning, and has taken command of the entire section of country around Petersburg, City Point, and Richmond. He left the extreme front on Monday night, and came by rail to City Point and thence by boat. From an officer who was present at the capitulation of Lee's army, the main features are gathered.

Particulars of Lee's Surrender

The spot designated by General Lee to receive General Grant was at the house of Wilmer McLean,[20] in a little country village of about four or five hundred inhabitants, called Appomattox Court House.

The Place of the Meeting

It is a large two-story brick-house, nearly square, rather old, but surrounded by a beautiful yard of shrubbery and flowers. Roses and violets were in full bloom, and the trees had just been decked in a coat of green.

Lee Arrives

As the clock struck two P.M., General Lee, accompanied by Gen. Marshall, his chief of staff, rode up and was at once shown into the parlor, a large

---

19   Edward Otho Cresap Ord (1818 - 1883) was a career officer who had served in California and the northwest. He hunted buffalo with George Custer, Buffalo Bill Cody, Wild Bill Hickock, and Russia's Grand Duke Alexei Alexandrovich. He retired from the Army in 1881 to work on building a train line from Texas to Mexico City. He contracted yellow fever in Mexico and died in Havana, Cuba, on the way home.

20   Wilmer McLean (1814 - 1882) was a wholesale food distributor with a farm. The First Battle of Bull Run — the first battle of the Civil War — was fought within cannon shot of McLean's farm in Manassas, Va. A Confederate sympathizer, he later moved south to the village of Appomattox Court House to avoid battles and Union troops. He is said to have said, "The war began in my front yard and ended in my front parlor."

room, neatly furnished. Its owner, a well to do farmer, was one of the "F.F.V's," located in the vicinity.[21]

Ulysses Up to Time.

Grant entered but a few minutes later, accompanied by Colonel Parker, Aide-de-Camp. (col. Parker, it will be remembered, was Chief of the Six Nations, and is a man of wonderfully acute mind, and a fast friend of General Grant).[22] Grant was dressed in a very modest suit of blue, a dress coat the worse for wear, no sword and no segar (sic).

The Momentous Conference

On his entering Lee arose, and, shaking hands, they introduced their respective Chiefs of Staffs, and, after a few common-place remarks, Lee said: — General, I have requested this interview to learn more fully the terms of you propose." To which General Grant replied: —"I will grant a parole to officers and men, and the officers may retain their side arms and personal effects."

Lee replied, "I do not see any reason for their modification," and the Army of Northern Virginia was surrendered to the old Army of the Potomac. Orders were then given for the necessary papers to be drawn up, and in the meantime an hour and twenty minutes were passed in recalling reminiscences of the past, events that transpired long before the war, no allusion being made by either to our present war, its causes or effects, or to the future.

McLean House, Appomattox Court-House, Va.

---

21   First Families of Virginia

22   Ely S. Parker (1828 - 1895) was a Seneca chief who studied engineering at Rensselaer Polytechnic Institute and here served as an engineer in the Union army. As military secretary to Gen. Grant, he penned the surrender documents that Gen. Lee signed.

The Articles of Surrender

At about 3-1/2 P.M., the articles were drawn up and signed. Lee then remarked, "Many of my cavalrymen own the horses which they ride, does the word personal effects include them?" General Grant answered, "I think they ought to be turned over to the United States."

General Lee: "I coincide in that opinion, as they have been used by the army."

Grant Magnanimous, as Usual

General Grant quietly replied, "But I will instruct the officers who are appointed to carry out the capitulation to allow those who have their own horses to return to their homes; they will then do for spring plowing." Lee, apparently struck by this liberal act of General Grant, and with considerable feeling, said, "Allow me to express my thanks for such consideration and generosity on your part. I think it cannot fail of having a good effect."

Lee's Apprehensive of Jeff.'s Conscriptions

General Lee then asked that each of his men might be furnished with papers to prevent them being forced into the Confederate service by the conscription officers until they are exchanged!

General Grant replied, "I will order such certificates to be issued to every man as soon as the preliminaries are settled."

General Lee said that he had not the slightest idea of the number of men composing his army, as he had received no returns since the fighting began at Hatcher's Run[23], since which the casualties have been large.

The Conference Closes.

The staff of General Grant were then invited in and introduced to General Lee, but after a few remarks about topics foreign to the occasion they all separated for the night.

Our "Erring Bretheren" Fed.

The army printing press was set in motion to print the paroles for Lee's men, and an order was given by General Grant to send twenty-five thousand

---

23   A back-and-forth battle fought in Dinwiddie Country, Va. before the siege of Petersburg. It was fought Feb. 5-7, 1865, as the Union attempted to disrupt supply lines and divert Confederate forces.

rations to the starving troops that represented the Rebellion.

Grant Gives Lee a Pass.

Before parting with General Lee he was furnished with passes for himself and staff, to go wherever they chose at any time.

Both Lee and Grant were very grave, and seemed to be fully aware of the important parts they were playing in the great tragedy, the final act of which was passing so rapidly.

Meeting of Lee with His Officers.

When Lee returned to his camp on Saturday evening, he found most of his leading officers awaiting his return, and on informing them of the result and the conditions they seemed astonished at the terms, and manifested great joy.

One by one they took him by the hand, and expressing their thanks for the many kind acts received at his hands, and their regret at their failure, and their having to part, several were affected to tears. Soon afterwards the surrender was announced to the Rebel army, and on General Lee appearing he was loudly cheered. He seemed very hale and rugged, and was not so bowed down with grief as one would expect, and rather seemed to have anticipated this end of affairs.

So ended Sunday, April 9, 1865 a day that will be remembered by all who had the glorious honor or participating, and who can say, "I was with Grant when we captured Lee and his entire army of twenty-five thousand men.

* * * * *

Daily Constitutional Union
Washington, D.C.
Friday Afternoon, April 14, 1865

Merciful Interposition Humanely but Imperatively Demanded!

The bugle blast of a ferocious and inhuman policy towards the South is blown from the North with a fury equal to its madness, and an intensity surpassed only by its own malignity. The New York Post, a journal that in better days was distinguished no less for its justice and its courtesy than for its ability, enters into the arena stripped to the waist, and prepares to wage war to the hilt on those whose mistaken convictions of right led them into grievous error. In a very elaborate editorial in which it endeavors to atone for the lack of brains by assuming an air of erudition, it gravely proceeds to quote that section of the Constitution defining treason! It commands the Attorney General to bring Judge Campbell[24] to the gallows. And it prates of "reconstructing" the Union in the same breath with a demand for vengeance on this man who is laboring earnestly to restore Virginia to her old position in the Union. This is a sample of the ferocious radicalism of the Black Republic miscegenationists.

Blind in its insane fanaticism it now says that "levying war against the United States" alone constitutes treason. And yet, with a malignity that would have been appalling had it not fortunately been impotent, this radical sheet filled its columns last Summer and Fall with charges of treason against the Democratic party. It charged Mr. Pendleton[25] with being disloyal — called him a traitor — and ferociously accused him of treason. Mr. Pendleton had not levied war against the United States, but yet he had committed treason! The New York Post here openly and shamelessly confesses that it will stoop to anything for partisan ends — even to the bringing of false charges, knowing them to be false, against those who differ from its political biases. Such a journalist is no honor to the fraternity. In trying to make out a good case for its cold blooded Puritan barbarity it acknowledges its one unworthy prevarication of truth. It, to define treason *now* by the Constitution, when for years past it has preached steadily to its readers that adherence to Democratic principles was the worst of treason! It, to talk of reorganizing the Union while urging the hanging of those who are practically engaged in the good work! Hang Jeff. Davis, it cries, and

---

24   John Archibald Campbell (1811 - 1889) graduated from the University of Georgia at 14 and was admitted to the bar at 18. By special request of a group of Supreme Court justices, Franklin Pierce appointed him to that court. He opposed the secession until he learned of Lincoln preparing for war. He resigned from the Supreme Court and became the Confederacy's Assistant Secretary of War. After the war, he opposed Radical Reconstruction.

25   George Hunt Pendleton (1825 - 1889), an attorney in Ohio, was elected to the House of Representatives and the Senate. He was an antiwar Democrat with links to the Copperheads. He ran as George McClellan's vice-presidential candidate in 1864 against Lincoln and Johnson, gaining 45 percent of the vote. He married Francis Scott Key's daughter.

restore the Union. Butcher Judge Campbell, and execute Senator Hunter,[26] and re-admit Virginia to the Union. Exterminate the Southern people, and then grant amnesty to our "erring brethren."

Such is its consistency, such its ability, such its humanity. Of like kind is the entire Radical element. If the good and conservative men of the country desire to see the nation once more in a happy and peaceful condition — if they with that order shall reign instead of anarchy, and Republicanism, instead of monarchy, to be our form of government, let them come up at once to the work of combatting this shameless, this senseless, this sanguinary radicalism. Irrespective of party let them all rally at once, or else they will behold a hideous and appalling Despotism, whose head will be as obstinately senseless as its heart is foully corrupt, ruling the land in all the tyranny of its uncompromising bigotry.

Ford's Theatre

It is the duty of every citizen in this crisis, be he high or humble to lend his hearty support, in season and out of season, to the work of conciliation and compromise, and the overthrow of this bitter, blind fanaticism. A great responsibility rests on every citizen. No one is too high to be above it — no one so obscure to be beneath its influence or its demands. Let immediate steps be taken — let every conservative man join his neighbors in effecting an organization which shall restore to the country the blessings of fraternal concord once more, and thereby rescue it from that state of inhuman barbarity in which it would be finally and forever plunged by the madness of these fanatical Radicals.

---

26   Robert Mercer Taliaferro Hunter (1809 - 1887), a Virginia attorney, was elected to the House and to the Senate. He opposed secession until it was inevitable, then urged Virginia to secede. He was the Confederacy's Secretary of State and later served in its senate. His portrait appeared on the Confederate $10.00 note. After the war, Lincoln worked with him to restore Virginia to the Union.

The Federal gunboat Rudolph has been blown up and destroyed by a torpedo in Mobile Bay. We have previously noted the loss of two other gunboats, also by torpedos, since the commencement of operations again Mobile. A general assault upon the Confederate works was to have taken place on the 4th instant.

———————

Ford's Theatre — His Excellency, the President of the United States, and family, together with Lieutenant General Grant and staff, will visit the Theatre this evening.[27]

27   Ford's Theatre, located at 511 10th St., NW, was built as the First Baptist Church of Washington in 1833. John Thompson Ford (1829 - 1894) bought it in 1861 and restructured it as a theater called Ford's Athenaem. It was damaged by fire in 1862 but renovated and reopened in 1863 with seating for 2,400 people. Following the assassination, the federal government bought it and used it as an office, library, and warehouse of the War Department. Part of it collapsed in 1893, killing 22 people. It was used as a government warehouse until 1931, then was closed until 1968, when it was reconstructed and reopened as a 661-seat theatre and National Historic Site.

Saturday, April 15, 1865

Carnival of Blood

As to the awful catastrophe,
the drift of reliable information
is, that
when a pistol shot was heard
in the second box
of the right-hand side
of the stage of Ford's theatre,
persons in the theatre
imagined
that it was part of the play.

National Intelligencer[28]
Saturday, April 15, 1865

CONSPIRACY AND MURDER
THE PRESIDENT ASSASSINATED.
ATTEMPT TO MURDER MR. SEWARD
THE ASSASSINS NOT ARRESTED, BUT BELIEVED TO BE KNOWN.

[The following is an Associated Press report.]

President Lincoln and wife, together with other friends, last evening visited Ford's Theatre, for the purpose of witnessing the performance of the American Cousin.[29] It was announced in the newspapers that General Grant would also be present, but that gentleman instead, took the late train of cars for New Jersey.[30] The theatre was densely crowded, and everybody seemed delighted with the scene before them.

During the third act, and while there was a temporary pause for one of the actors to enter, a sharp report of a pistol was heard, which merely attracted attention, but suggested nothing serious, until a man rushed to the front of

---

28   The *National Intelligencer,* founded by Samuel Harrison Smith, was first issued on October 28, 1800. The Capitol building was still under construction at the time. Smith's wife was Margaret Baynard Smith, who kept a diary of Washington social life for forty years. The paper served as the mouthpiece of the Jefferson and Madison administrations, and its editors served as the administrations' press secretaries. The paper also printed the proceedings of Congress, and it was through the *Intelligencer* that the country's other papers received news from Washington. The paper remained a stodgy supporter of the Whig party, and though its owners opposed slavery, the paper did its best to ignore the issue. After the paper was sold to business interests in 1864, it dropped its political leanings and directed its news toward the interests of readers. No longer a source of government information, its readership dwindled, and in 1869 it ceased publication. (Ames, William E. "The National Intelligencer: Washington's Leading Political Newspaper," Records of the Columbia Historical Society, Washington, Vol. 66/68, Historical Society of Washington, pp. 71-83)

29   *Our American Cousin*, by Tom Taylor, was a comedy about an American who goes to England to claim his inheritance from his aristocratic relatives. The last line spoken before Booth's shot rang out was "Don't know the manners of good society, eh? Well, I guess I know enough to turn you inside out — you sockdologizing old man-trap." The audience was laughing when Booth pulled the trigger. "Sockdologizing" is apparently a combination of "sock," meaning to hit hard, and "doxology," with its notion of finality. It has been theorized that Booth, an actor who knew the play well, waited for that lline before pulling the trigger.

30   An unknown assailant tried to break into Grant's railroad car on the day Lincoln was shot. The assailant failed to enter and escaped unidentified.

the President's box, waving a long dagger in his right hand, and exclaiming, "Sic Semper Tyrannis," and immediately leaped from the box, which was of the second tier, to the stage beneath, and ran across to the opposite side, thus making his escape, amid the bewilderment of the audience, from the rear of the theatre, and, mounting a horse, fled.[31]

The screams of Mrs. Lincoln first disclosed the fact to the audience that the President had been shot, when all present rose to their feet, rushing toward the stage, many exclaiming, "Hang him! hang him!" (sic)

The excitement was of the wildest possible character, and, of course, there was an abrupt termination of the theatrical performance.

There was a rush toward the President's box, when cries were heard, "Stand back!" "Give him air!" "Has anyone stimulants?" etc.

On a hasty examination it was found that the President had been shot through the head, above and below the temporal bone, and that some of the brain was oozing out. He was removed to the private residence of Mr. Ulke,[32] opposite the theatre, and the Surgeon General of the army[33] and other surgeons sent to attend to his condition.

On examination of the private box, blood was discovered on the back of the rocking-chair in which the President had been sitting, also on the partition and on the floor. A common single-barreled pocket-pistol was found on the carpet.[34]

A military guard was placed in front of the private residence to which the President had been conveyed. An immense crowd was in front of it, all

31   Thus Always to Tyrants! It was (and still is) the motto of the State of Virginia, displayed on the state seal beneath an image of Virtue with her foot on a dominated Tyranny.

32   Julius Ulke was a photographer living across the street at the Petersen House. He photographed the bed after Lincoln's body had been removed from it.

33   Charles Sabin Taft was in the audience at Ford's Theatre on the fateful night. Another, a young army surgeon, Charles Leale, was also present and was first into the president's box. U.S. Surgeon General Joseph K. Barnes (1817 - 1883) arrived at Ulke's room soon after the president was moved. Barnes named Leale lead physician for the dying patient.

34   It was a single-shot, muzzle-loading, percussion cap-fired Philadelphia Deringer (not Derringer, a misspelling now used for any small pocket pistol) pocket pistol made by the Henry Deringer Company. Its barrel was octagonal on top and round on the bottom. The barrel rifling was left-twist, i.e. counter-clockwise, unlike that of most Deringers. The pistol was 5.87 inches long and 2.79 inches high with a barrel diameter of 0.41 inch.

deeply anxious to learn the condition of the President. It had been previously announced that the wound was mortal, but all hoped otherwise.

The shock to the community was terrible.

At midnight the Cabinet, with Messrs Sumner, Colfax, and Farnsworth, Judge Carter, Governor Oglesby, General Meigs, Major Hay, and a few personal friends, with Surgeon General Barnes and his medical associates, arrived at his bedside.[35] The President was in a state of syncope totally insensible, and breathing slowly the blood oozing from the wound at the back of his head. The surgeons were exhausting every possible effort of medical skill: but all hope was gone.

The parting of his family with the dying President is too sad for description.

The President and Mrs. Lincoln did not start to the theatre till fifteen minutes past eight o'clock. Speaker Colfax was at the White House at the time, and the President stated to him that he was going, although Mrs. Lincoln had not been well, because the papers had advertised that Gen. Grant and themselves were to be present, and, as Gen. Grant had gone North, he did not wish the audience to be disappointed. He went with apparent reluctance, and urged Mr. Colfax to go with him, but that gentleman had made other engagements, and with Mr. Ashmun[36] of Massachusetts, bid him good bye.

When the excitement at the theatre was at its wildest height, reports were circulated that Secretary Seward had also been assassinated.

On reaching this gentleman's residence a crowd and a military guard were found at the door; and on entering it was ascertained that the reports were based upon truth.

---

35   Charles Sumner was a Massachusetts senator; Schuyler Colfax was a U.S. Representative from Indiana and would become vice-president under U.S. Grant; John F. Farnsworth was a U.S. Representative from Illinois and a Union general. Judge David Kellogg Cartter (1812 - 1887, appointed by Lincoln to the Supreme Court of the District of Columbia. (In some sources, including Inquirer article, spelled Carter.). Richard James Oglesby was governor of Illinois. General Montgomery Cunningham Meigs was from Atlanta but staunchly anti-Confederacy. John Hay was Lincoln's private secretary until 1864, then served in the Union army. Joseph K. Barnes, twelfth surgeon general of the United States, would also treat President James Garfield after his assassination in 1882.

36   George Ashmun (1804 - 1870), U.S. Representative and Senator from Massachusetts, a Whig until leaving Congress, at which time he became a Republican and party leader.

Everybody was so much excited that scarcely an intelligible account could be gathered; but the facts are substantially as follows: About ten o'clock a man rang the bell, and the call having been answered by a colored servant, he said he had come from Dr. Verdi,[37] Secretary Seward's family physician, with a prescription, at the same time holding in his hand a small piece of folded paper, and saying in answer to a refusal that he must see the Secretary, as he was entrusted with particular directions concerning the medicine. He still insisted on going up, although repeatedly informed that no one could enter the chamber. The man pushed the servant aside, and walked heavily toward the Secretary's room, and was there met by Mr. Frederick W. Seward, of whom he demanded to see the Secretary, making the same representation which he did to the servant. What further passed in the colloquy is not known; but the man struck him on the head with a billy, severely injuring his skull, and felling him almost senseless.[38] The assassin then rushed into the chamber and attacked major Seward, paymaster United States Army, and Mr. Hansell, a messenger of the State Department, and two male nurses, disabling them all.[39] He then rushed upon the Secretary, who was lying in bed in the same room, and inflicted three stabs to his neck, but severing, it is thought and hoped, no arteries, though he bled profusely.

The assassin then rushed down stairs, mounted his horse at the door, and rode off before an alarm could be given, and in the same manner as the assassin of the President.

It is believed the injuries of the Secretary are not mortal, nor those of either of the others, although both the Secretary and the Assistant Secretary are seriously injured.

Secretaries Stanton and Welles,[40] and other prominent officers of the Gov-

---

37   Dr. Tullio Suzzaro Verdi, (1829 - 1902).

38   Frederick William Seward (1830 - 1915), at the time assistant Secretary of State under his father, William Henry Seward, Sr. He was the brother of General William Henry Seward, Jr., who helped prevent an assassination attempt against president-elect Lincoln in Baltimore in 1861. Lincoln was to stop there on his way to Washington from Illinois, but warnings in the letter and from other sources led Lincoln to bypass that city.

39   Augustus Seward (1826 - 1876), oldest son of William Sr. Emerick Hansell, messenger. Private George F. Robinson, assigned as nurse to William Sr.

40   Gideon Welles (1802 - 1878), Secretary of the Navy. During his term (1861 - 1869)

ernment, called at Secretary Seward's house to inquire into his condition, and, learning there of the assassination of the President, proceeded to the house where he was lying, exhibiting, of course, great anxiety and solicitude.

An immense crowd was gathered in front of the President's house, and a strong guard stationed there, many persons evidently supposing that he would be brought to his house.

The entire city last night presented a scene of wild excitement, accompanied by violent expressions of indignation and the profoundest sorrow. Many persons shed tears.

The military authorities have despatched mounted patrols in every direction, in order, if possible, to arrest the assassins, while the Metropolitan Police are alike vigilant for the same purpose. The attacks, both at the theatre and at Secretary Seward's, took place at the same hour — ten o'clock — thus showing a preconcerted plan to assassinate these gentlemen.

Some evidence of the guilt of the party who attacked the President are in possession of the police.

Vice President Johnson is in the city, and his hotel-quarters are guarded by troops.

———

SATURDAY MORNING, 2 o'clock — The President is still alive, but growing weaker. The ball is lodged in his brain three inches from where it entered the skull. He remains insensible, and his condition is utterly hopeless.

The Vice President has been to see him, but all company except the Cabinet, his family, and a few friends are rigidly excluded.

Large crowds continue in the street, as near to the house as the line of guards allow.

———

The Tragedy of Last Night

Our heart stands almost still as we take our pen to speak of the tragedy of last night. We have no words at command by which to express what we feel.

---

he increased the size of the Navy tenfold. He was great-grandfather of Orson Welles.

Before this paper shall go to press, the fact may reach us that the President
has been assassinated! We already know enough to be compelled to record the
fact that he was shot in the Theatre, and that the ball entered his head. GOD
ALMIGHTY grant that his life may be preserved! Still we have but little hope.

And, horror upon horrors! It seems that the house of Mr. Seward was
entered on a pretext by a murderer or murderers, who, it is represented to us
on authority which we cannot doubt, beat and stabbed his son, the Hon. F.
Seward, wounded others in his household, and who finally succeeded in stabbing the Secretary of State. The fact seems to be that his throat is cut. Up to
this hour — 2 A.M. we have no assurance that the perpetrators of this terrible
crime have been arrested. Nor are we advised as to the condition of the Secretary and his son.

Rumors are so thick and contradictory, the excitement at this hour is so
intense, that we rely entirely upon our reporters to advise the public of the
details and result of this night of horrors.

Evidently conspirators are among us! To what extent does this conspiracy
exist? This is a terrible question! When a spirit so horrible as this is abroad,
what man is safe? We can only advise the utmost vigilance and the prompt
response by the authorities. We can only pray GOD to shield us, His worthy
people, from further calamities like these!

If the President is dead, a noble and good man has fallen at his post, and
the only one among us who had the power and the will to do as much as he
could have done, and, as humanely and liberally, for the whole country. A nation will weep for him. The loss of the Secretary of State would be irreparable.
But our heart is too full to say more.

———

The President was received with great furore on entering the theatre: his
reception was, indeed, extraordinary. One of the actors (Mr Hawk[41]) had made
the remark, (as "Dundreary,") this "reminds me of a story as Mr. Lincoln says,"
and was telling the story as the President entered. The enthusiasm of the audi-

41   William Henry Hawk (1837 - 1916) was an actor with Ford's company. He was alone
on stage when Booth pulled the trigger. Booth slashed at him with his knife, cutting his vest
but not injuring him.

ence interrupted the story for several minutes. After the President was seated the actor was forced by the people to tell the "story" over again.

As to the awful catastrophe, the drift of reliable information is, that when a pistol shot was heard in the second box of the right-hand side of the stage of Ford's theatre, persons in the theatre imagined that it was part of the play. Hence the confusion of the audience. Meantime, the assassin appeared on the edge of the box crying "Sic Semper Tyrannis," and flourishing a dagger, leaped to the state. He crossed the stage rapidly, exclaiming "Revenge," and again flourishing his dagger, disappeared, saying, "I have done it."

All started to their feet, and there being cries that the President was shot, the intimation of the danger was a call for a surgeon." the crowd exclaimed, "Secure the assassin!" "hang him!" &c.

Miss Laura Keene[42] appeared on the stage, and with great self-possession implored the audience to be silent.

The President was seen to turn in his seat, and persons leaped upon the stage and clambered up to the box. His clothes were stripped form his shoulders, but no wound was at first found. He was insensible. Further search revealed the fact that he had been shot in the head, as is described elsewhere. Major Potter, paymaster in the army, and Major Rathbone,[43] (the latter having been in the box,) assisted by others, carried the President from the theatre, the blood from the death-wound falling upon the floor, stairway, and sidewalks as he was borne to the nearest house opposite, which was that of Mr. Ulke. Mrs. Lincoln was assisted in crossing the street with the President in a frantic condition, at the same time uttering heart-rending shrieks. She was attended by Miss Laura Keene and others, at the house, and army surgeon being at hand, called for a small quantity of brandy, which was administered, and it

---

42   Laura Keene (1826 - 1873), born Mary Frances Moss in Winchester, England, was an actress and manager of a traveling company. She was acting in the play on the night of the assassination.

43   Henry Reed Rathbone (1837 - 1911) was a major in the Union army. He was the son of Albany mayor Jared L. Rathbone. After Jared died, his widow married a judge, Ira Harris, who was later appointed senator from New York after Senator William H. Seward became Lincoln's secretary of state. Harris's daughter, Clara Harris, became Henry Rathbone's step-sister and, later, his fiancé. They married, but in 1883, in declining mental health, he murdered her, then tried to stab himself to death.

was thereupon announced to the pressing and excited crowd that he was alive, and not dead, as Mrs. Lincoln, in her agony, insisted. It was then found that Major Rathbone had received a wound in the arm, which he had intentionally concealed to prevent excitement. He then fainted. The Surgeon General was sent for, and Drs. Hall and Verdi also arrived.

An immense crowd had now assembled, but a strong military force arrived and guarded the entire locality.

Crowds now gathered in all parts of the city. Nothing was talked of but the murder of the President, of Mr Seward, and of the members of Mr. Seward's family. Intense excitement was added to the already nearly wild masses by a rumor that Gen. Grant has been assassinated in the cars, en route for Philadelphia, and that Mr. Stanton had barely escaped with his life by being warned in time to exclude the conspirators from his house. (This is discredited.) It may be added that a person who was passing Mr. Seward's house saw the murderer mount this horse, pass up Fifteen-and-a-half street, where Mr. Seward resides, and thence rapidly to H street, where he disappeared.

The alarm of murder from Mr. Seward's house was frightful as the assassin passed out, and much space of time elapsed before pursuit was had. We forbear to give the name of one of the supposed murderers, about whom great suspicion gathers.

The long-roll was beaten all over the city, and every avenue was at once guarded. Such a night of horror has seldom darkened any community. The indefinite dread which conspiracy inspires seized on the public mind, and suspicion, apprehension, and agony pervaded the people.

At the police headquarters it is understood that Mr. Hawk of Laura Keene's troupe, has been held to bail to testify to the identity of the suspected assassin of the President who he is said to have recognized as a person well known to him.

LATEST — As we go to press at FIVE o'clock this morning the President is still alive, but was rapidly sinking.

* * * * *

The Sun[44]
Baltimore
Saturday, April 15, 1865

A Great National Calamity.
Assassination of President Lincoln!
Attempted Murder of Secretary Seward and his Son.

The startling, dreadful, absolutely paralyzing intelligence reached us last night, amid the gloom of midnight, that the President of the United States and his chief Secretary, and the latter's son, had all been stricken down by the hands of assassins, the President injured beyond possibility of recovery, and that the two latter dangerously wounded whilst totally unsuspecting and unconscious of danger.

The magnitude of these high crimes, the lofty position of the victims, and the grave consequences likely to flow from the diabolical deeds, affecting, it may be, the future destinies of the country, shock and appal (sic) us, and must awaken in every breast the most melancholy forebodings. Men will naturally ask themselves is it possible that a Republic, born, nurtured and reared in an age of civilization and Christianity can hold within its bosom men capable of the vilest crimes which blot and disgrace the pages of history during the worst epochs of the world?

But we have not, at the very late hour at which we write, time to say all that the momentous event demands, or to express fully that detestation all right thinking people must feel for these dastardly acts. All the horrible details, so far as ascertained, are fully set forth in our news column, and to them the reader will naturally turn with eager interest.

---

44   The *Sun*, or *Baltimore Sun*, was founded by Arunah Shepherson Abell in 1837. Its first edition was issued on May 17 of that year, quite likely with Abell himself setting the type. It had four pages and cost a penny. It was one of the first newspapers that did not serve the purposes of a political party and believed that it should present news that was of interest to its readers. Its first issue carried news of the Baltimore City Council, which none of the other six papers in town mentioned. Abell passed the paper to his sons in 1888, and it stayed in the family until 1910. The A.S. Abell Company was bought by the Times Mirror company in 1986. In 2000, that company merged with the Tribune Company.

We can only now express the earnest hope that this untoward and most unhappy event may not bring upon our already afflicted country fresh calamities, and that prudence and moderation may rule the hour.

By Constitutional provision, Hon. Andrew Johnson, Vice President, becomes President of the United States, and of him, under such extraordinary circumstances, the highest exercise of firmness and wisdom is demanded.

Official Bulletin from Secretary Stanton

War Department, April 15, 1865 — 3 A.M. — Major General Dix, New York: The President still breathes, but is quite insensible, as he has been ever since he was shot. He evidently did not see the person who shot him, but was looking at the stage, as he was approached behind.

Mr. Seward has rallied, and it is hoped he may live.

Mr. Frederick Seward's condition is very critical.

The attendant was stabbed through the lungs, and is not expected to live.

The wounds of Major Seward are not serious.

The investigation strongly indicates J. Wilkes Booth as the assassin of the President. Whether is it was the same or a different person that attempted to murder Mr. Seward remains in doubt.

Chief Justice Carter is engaged in taking the evidence, and every exertion has been made to prevent escape of the murderer. His horse has been found on the road near Washington.

Edwin M. Stanton [45]

Secretary of War

Proclamation of Gen. Morris — Precautionary Measures

General Morris,[46] commanding the Middle Department, has issued a proclamation suspending all travel, either by railroad, steamboat, or other water carriage, or by vehicle, from the city of Baltimore, in view of the assassi-

---

45   Edwin McMasters Stanton (1814 - 1869), Secretary of War under presidents Lincoln and Andrew Johnson. He was an anti-war democrat.

46   William W. Morris (1801 - 1865), brevet major general, was commander of Fort McHenry in Baltimore.

nation of President Lincoln. By this step it is hoped that if the murderer shall have taken refuge in Baltimore his escape will be surely estopped.

Com. Dornin has the harbor under his charge, and Major Weigel[47] has dispatched an armed tug to visit, in conjunction with the revenue cutters, different harbors on the bay to prevent egress of vessels. Market wagons will be allowed to enter the city, but no vehicles will be permitted to depart except under permit of the military authorities.

With a view to the preservation of order, all the military are put under arms, and the civil authorities are taking energetic steps for the same purpose. The citizens are requested to aid the authorities in this laudable design. Parties over three will not be allowed to congregate. All suspicious persons will be arrested by pickets who have been stationed on the roads, and military rule will be more vigorously enforced.

Generals Lockwood and Tyler are in the city co-operating with General Morris. The former has charge of the military forces. We trust that these energetic measures will suffice to maintain the public order. Col. Lawrence, chief of staff, is actively at work, and Marshals Carmichael and Mauly have the whole police force out. The Mayor was also promptly in attendance at his office as soon as the sad news was communicated to him.

Last night Marshal Carmichael received a dispatch from the marshal of police of Washington, notifying him to arrest J. Wilkes Booth where he may be found, and steps for that purpose were immediately taken. Major Wiegel received a similar notification from the provost marshal of Washington, and dispatches from Washington further state that suspicion rests upon Mr. Booth as the assailant of the President.

* * * * *

---

47   William H. Wiegel was acting provost marshal of Washington, D.C. (In this article, The Sun also spelled it Weigel.)

Daily Constitutional Union[48]
Washington
Saturday Afternoon, April 15, 1865

War Department — Washington, April 15

Major General Dix, New York:

The President continues insensible, and is sinking. Secretary Seward remains without change. Frederick Seward's skull is fractured in two paces, besides a severe cut upon the head. The attendant is still alive, but hopeless.

Major Seward's wounds are not dangerous. It is now ascertained with reasonable certain, that two assassins were engaged in the horrible crime — Wilkes Booth being the one that shot the president; the other, a companion of his, whose name is not known, but whose description is so clear that he can hardly escape.

It appears, from a letter found in Booth's trunk, that the murder was planned before the fourth of March, but fell through then because the accomplice backed out until Richmond could be heard from. Booth and his accomplice were at the livery stable at six o'clock, last evening, and left there with their horses about ten o'clock, or shortly before that hour.

It would seem that they had for several days been seeking their chance, but for some unknown reason, it was not carried into effect until last night. One of them has evidently made his way to Baltimore, the other has not yet been traced. Edwin M. Stanton, Secretary of War.

$10,000 REWARD

HDQR Dept. of Washington

April 15, 1865

A Reward of Ten Thousand Dollars will be paid to the party or parties arresting the murderer of the President, Mr. Lincoln, and the assassin of the Secretary of State, Mr. Seward and his son.

C.C. Augue

Major General, com'd'g Dept.

----

48   The *Constitutional Union* began publication in 1863, ceased in about 1870. It was a Democratic paper.

Important Police Order

The following order was issued by Superintendent Richards, at three o'clock this morning:

In view of the melancholy events of last evening, I am directed to close all places where liquor is sold, to be closed during this day and night. The sergeants of the several precincts will see that this order is enforced.

A.C. Richard, Superintendent.

A NATION BOWED IN GRIEF! — MURDER OF THE PRESIDENT! THE PEOPLE WILL AVENGE HIS DEATH!

An awful calamity has befallen the Nation! By the hand of a traitorous Assassin, Chief Magistrate has been MURDERED, brutally, cowardly, wickedly murdered, and hurried into ETERNITY. Words are entirely inadequate to express sufficiently severe our abhorrence and detestation of this most inhuman Act. The head which conceived, the heart which prompted, the hand which executed this most dastardly and infamous atrocity, with all who are in league, if any such there be, with the brutal patricide, deserve, and will receive, the execration of mankind, throughout the civilized world. We confess our inability to indite patiently our heartfelt and sincere regret at this terrible occurrence.

The President of the United States, the father of the people, the official head in and around whose person centered all our affection, all our respect, all our generation, and all our hopes, has in a moment been stricken to the earth, a cold, senseless, inanimate corpse. What punishment is too severe, to be visited upon the base man, who for any purpose or in view of any object, but with wicked, devilish, malfelous (sic) design, without the awful fear of God's vengeance or the terribly earned scorn of mankind has thus offended? At this important period pending this thrilling crisis in our country's history, what but barbarity, has dared to strike cold in death's embrace, at the very moment of the exercise of his highest benevolence and kindest sympathy in behalf of an erring and rebellious face of men, the chosen of the People under the very eaves of the National Capitol!

Besides, as if in defiance of the awful retribution over certain to follow such cowardly malignity, a base attempt has been made to murder the closest constitutional advisor of the President, the distinguished Secretary of State. This gentleman suffering from the effects of a recent accident, confined to his invalid couch, in the innermost privacy of his domestic surroundings, safe, all humane persons would believe, from the intrusive and sly approach of a sneaking assassin, he too has been cruelly cut and mangled, to end, it is apprehended, to his lamented death. God of justice — but we have fallen upon evil times!

The mind of every sound-thinking man in this stricken and mourning community is terribly excited over these sad and melancholy doings. The motive so wicked, and the end so terrible, has no palliation or shadow of excuse or justification. It is in its highest and broadest extent cold-blooded dual murder, and fiendish parricidal-fratricide. The hands of the assassin are dyed in the blood of the father of the people, and his nearest and most intimate official associate. Execrations not loud but deep are muttered in agony of heart against the fiendish perpetrators. God help those in our midst, if any such there be, which the Father of heavenly mercies earnestly forbid, who have any sympathy for the dastardly actors in the conspiracy which has so tragically ended in this carnival of blood.

What will be done now by the authorities in view of this terrible blow to the people's highest expectations? Vigilant and active efforts to arrest the daring offenders against the purest instincts of humanity and its inevitable requirements is of course their first duty in accordance with enlightened public opinion and to satisfy the outraged and violated law. When discovered, a thorough and searching investigation to probe deep down to its roots, the extent of, and participation in this damnable conspiracy against the peace, quiet, prosperity and happiness, of a highly outraged and justly excited, but patient people, whose highest and holiest aspirations were beating in unison, indulging the religiously inspired hope, the angel of peace was spreading her white wings in token of amity and goodwill, soon to restore quiet to our agitated, torn, and bleeding land, is imperatively demanded.

Is this cup of joy to be ruthlessly dashed from our lips? Was not our cup of misery filled to overflowing? Who can measure the extent of vengeance or retribution to be meted out by an offended and incensed people? We confess at this writing, we are lost in wonder and absorbed in mysterious wanderings in the very labyrinth of conjecture. With the contending armies who are yet facing each other, what is to occur there?

Will severe and speedy retribution be visited upon the head of those arrayed in armed hostility against us? The overwhelming battalions may be hurled in revengeful forces, sweeping all opposition and scattering it as chaff before the northwest blast. What ought to be the course of those yet arrayed in armed hostility against the Government? Instantly to lay down their arms, or be utterly destroyed and literally exterminated. These deadly assassins hovering around us have "sowed the wind" at our very hearthstones. Their aiders, sympathizers and abettors, especially if armed forces, "must reap the whirlwind."[49] May God, whose mysterious Providence is beyond our knowledge, enable us through his benevolence and mercy to bear the burdens of this terrible visitation, and to meet the stern duties so suddenly imposed upon us by the emergencies of this painful hour. GOD SAVE THE REPUBLIC!

JOHN WILKES BOOTH

Everything now pertaining to this notorious individual will be of interest to your readers. We met him yesterday, on the Avenue, and in a short conversation with him, he stated that a number of Canadian Theatrical managers were desirous of engaging him for a season. He also stated he had lost about $6,000 in oil by the recent floods at Oil City. He appeared to be perfectly sober, though we now recollect, that at times, he seemed abstracted, and to have a nervous movement of his arms and body, as if anxiously thinking of something. It is true that he drank and indulged in other excesses, but not to an extent to characterize him as reckless and dissolute — yet when aroused, he was vindictive and

---

49   Hosea 8:7 "They sow the wind and reap the whirlwind."

violent, and would go to any extreme for the sake of revenge. He was (we speak of him as dead,) a very handsome man, but we should hardly thought him possessed of sufficient nerve to execute the deed, that will forever render the name infamous. He has of late been dealing in petroleum, and has been in this city much of the time for the last two months. He is a native of Baltimore county, and the last time he appeared on the stage was at Grover's Theatre in the character of "Romeo," — he volunteering for the occasion of Miss Avonia Jones' benefit.[50]

*   *   *   *   *

50   Avonia Stanhope Jones (1839 - 1867), Shakespearean actress.

Sunday, April 16, 1865

The Dreadful Fact

It is a little strange that Mr. Lincoln,
on one such occasion,
should have twice read aloud,
and called the marked attention of those about him
to the well-known lines which MacBeth,
in his remorse, utters about
the traitorously murdered Duncan:
"Duncan is in his grave;
After life's fitful fever, he sleeps well;
Treason has done his worst; nor steel, nor poison
Malice domestic, foreign levy, nothing
Can touch him further."

Louisville Daily Journal[51]
Sunday, April 16, 1865

We deeply regret that the column rules of our paper are so formed that they cannot be reversed so as to display broad lines as a tribute of respect for the memory of our lamented President.

The New President. — The sudden and startling death of President Lincoln has devolved upon Andrew Johnson the chief executive office of the United States. On (sic) yesterday Chief Justice Chase administered to him the

Andrew Johnson

Presidential oath. Having sworn to "execute the laws," he said, "The duties are mine; I will discharge them, trusting in God." The ordinary solemnity of the occasion was immeasurably deepened by the peculiar circumstances attending this new inauguration. The form of the dead President, stricken down by assassination, was lying in state at the Capitol; the hearts of the people were melting with grief, and great perils were yet threatening the nation's existence. How incalculably important the duties thus assumed by Andrew Johnson! But he said, "The duties are mine I will discharge them, trusting in God."

Fervently do we pray that he may prove himself worthy of this mighty trust. We hope, for the nation's sake, for the cause of our bleeding Union, that

51   The *Louisville Daily Journal* was founded in 1832 as an organ of the Whig Party. Its founder, George D. Prentice, would edit the paper for 40 years. The paper was anti-slavery. The other main paper in Louisville, the *Courier*, was pro-Confederacy and fled to Nashville, Tenn. during much of the Civil War. After the war, the Courier returned and in 1868 merged with the Journal to form the Courier-Journal.

Andrew Johnson, forgetting party ties, and devoting himself with singleness of heart to the public weal, will exalt himself to the dignity of his great office. His vow is pledged to the whole country. He is now the President of the United States. And we hope that his administration of the Government will be such as we can sustain in consistency with our love for the country and the inestimable principles on which the Government is based. Prompted by a sense of patriotic duty, we shall pursue toward him the same course that we have pursued toward his lamented predecessor, supporting him in all that he shall rightly do, and kindly but earnestly opposing him in all that he shall wrongly do.

We reserve further remarks upon the new situation of affairs resulting from the death of President Lincoln and the inauguration of President Johnson.

Headquarters Department of Kentucky

Louisville, April 15, 1865

General orders, No. 23.

The telegraph announces that President Lincoln was assassinated last night. The purest man of the age has fallen, and the whole nation which was rejoicing over the prospects of speedy peace is mourning.

Let the people of Kentucky disappoint the miscreants who may involve them in bloodshed and strife, by conducting themselves with calmness and moderation. Avoid all heated conversation and imprudent expressions. Let all unite in every means for preserving order.

The wicked need not rejoice nor the patriotic despond. The Government will still go on, and as great as the calamity is, the country will accomplish its high destiny.

By command of Maj.-Gen. J.M. Palmer[52]

E.B. Harlan

Captain and Assistant Adjutant-General.

---

52   John McAuley Palmer (1817-1900). Like Lincoln, Palmer was born to a poor family in Kentucky but raised in Illinois. After considerable action in the war, he was named military governor of Kentucky, where he wiped out guerrilla resistance and enforced the liberation of blacks. In Illinois, where he was a lawyer, he switched political parties often, eventually becoming a Bourbon Democrat, i.e. one who supported business but opposed subsidies for companies, opposed imperialism, advocated the gold standard and small government. He was governor of Illinois from 1868 to 1873 and a presidential candidate in 1892.

**National Intelligencer
Washington, D.C.
Sunday, April 16, 1865**

EXTRA

He who was yesterday our good, gentle, wise, upright, Christian, affectionate President, is no more! Who *realizes* the dreadful fact that Abraham Lincoln was assassinated on Friday night? The tragedy overcomes and stupefies the community. All of us feel as if we were passing through a horrid dream, which is yet to have a bright awakening. But, alas! it (sic) is real; the late President has been butchered. The Great Hand still presses heavily upon us; our chastisement is not ended! In the midst of our exultation the nation is bowed down; another great example is furnished whose moral is humility; an earthly popular idol has been removed, and a stricken people feel that the Lord God Omnipotent reigneth.

The sad details are before our readers. How he died, when he died, where he died, is told with painful exactness. The harrowing particularities concerning the anguish and distress of his bereaved and devoted family are disclosed to us, and we can thus faintly comprehend how deep is their grief. A noble and great man, a loving and tender husband and parent, who or what can replace him to these sobbing and sorrowing ones? It is their consolation, as it is of the country, to know that no man since Washington has performed so great a mission as he; none has ever lived in all the tide of time who evinced more purity, or who was more largely trusted by a great nation in the issues of its life and its death. He did not have, he could not have among those worthy of consideration, a single enemy. The being does not live, himself a just and thoughtful man, who assailed his integrity. And this is saying enough for the personal character of him in whose hands such a people, at such a time, entrusted both the Sword and the Purse.

The life of Mr. Lincoln, in its details is too well known to require republication at this moment. Everybody is informed about him. All of us have read that he was essentially an American, and a representative of our institutions; because he was the child of poverty and industry; rough grown on our soil like its grand mountains; and because he was self-made by the force of his will, by the purity and religious convictions of his nature, and by that unrelenting industry and energy which has created us a great and powerful people. History, in this respect, furnishes us no stronger example in favor of true democracy than Abraham Lincoln.

The marked features of his political career are also fully comprehended. He rose into note by his moderate advocacy of the political necessity which he thought had arisen to limit the extent of slavery. To this he added always his *personal* opinion that, before God, all men are equal, according to what is given them of opportunity and minds, equal in responsibility and entitled to the right of seeking their bread and destiny in their own way, within the limits of the laws of the land. He hated slavery, but he respected the compromises of the Constitution. He was elected as a conservative Republican on an issue which simply involved the extension of slavery; and, during all the excitement which preceded his inauguration, he sought every opportunity to assure the people of the South that all their rights (including that of slavery, as defined by the guaranties, as he understood them, of the Constitution) would be protected by him an assurance which he hastened formally to announce in his first Inaugural, and which he endeavored to make good during all the early stages of the war. We have said this much about the political career of the late President simply as those who record what we believe to have been *his* convictions, and with no design ourselves to intimate any needless opinion of our own on issues which are of the past, and which we hope never to see reopened.

His conduct of the war generally is conceded to have been all that could have been expected of a statesman of limited experience, and of an unmilitary man, surrounded and distracted by such complications, and by so many jarring interests, as involved his Administration. We think that all loyal men will say that he intended for the best, and that he sought inspiration, strength, and direction from on high.

No man is known to history whose personal character was just *such* a "household word" as that of the late President. It was not a remote and dazzling character, admired and followed like that of a Napoleon, or of a Clay or a Jackson; but it was rather that of an honest neighbor or relative, in whose entire integrity, prudence, great patience, good humor, Christian purity, and well-balanced and far-reaching sense, his fellows had implicit reliance. While his friends supposed that there were many more brilliant and perhaps more able men, they felt that none was so *safe* as he; and so they overlooked what were called his mistakes, and ratified and endorsed all his official conduct, with almost total and fraternal confidence, trust, and hope. Certainly no man is known to the record of history, in a position so commanding and elevated, who, in the same degree, was rooted in the intimate and family affections of the large body of people.

Mr. Lincoln's statesmanship was rather great, perhaps, in what he forbore to do, than in what he did. His distinguishing mental trait was that of eminent common sense. To this he added wonderful individuality and great astuteness and shrewdness in reconciling or overcoming mere political intrigues and combinations. He was eminent in simplicity and directness of thought, and his grasp of mind and keenness of reasoning, his aptitude in illustration, his power of statement, and his peculiar talent for popularizing elevated topics were really wonderful. No man ever wrote who came nearer to the hearts as well as to the heads of the masses; his was the faculty of satisfying the millions who read him or heard him, that, if he was not right always in his positions, at all events that he was sincere and conscientious in what he said.

About the period of his murder, the late President was directing his heart, and soul, and mind to the great work of restoring the Union. His feelings towards the South, *we know*, were most charitable. His designs were most liberal; they went to such an extent as must have harmonized the sections, had they been properly seconded, which all the substantial reforms needed by the nation would have been embraced by his plans or plans. His extreme kindness of heart, in this regard, may be noted in the fact that his last official act (as we state on the highest authority) was to sign a permit to Jacob Buchanan, to leave this country for Europe.

Among those significant things, which often look like inspirations, that frequently attend the latter days of noted men, we will mention an affecting fact connected with the deceased President. While on his recent trip to Richmond, he amused himself with reading Shakespeare, and often to the friends about him. It is a little strange that Mr. Lincoln, on one such occasion, should have twice read aloud, and called the marked attention of those about him to the well-known lines which MacBeth, in his remorse, utters about the traitorously murdered Duncan:

> "Duncan is in his grave;
> After life's fitful fever, he sleeps well;
> Treason has done his worst; nor steel, nor poison
> Malice domestic, foreign levy, nothing
> Can touch him further!"

But we must close these crude remarks. It only remains to be said that on the night of the celebration of the crucifixion of our Saviour, on the night of the anniversary of the fall of Sumter, in the midst of the joy of the people over the prospect of peace and reunion, which he was laboring to promote, Abraham Lincoln was murdered. Man proposes, but God disposes. May His mercy not be withdrawn from us. May His spirit grace and strengthen the present incumbent of the Presidential chair! And kneeling around our country's altar, may the nation feel, that as God is above party, so should we accept his dispensation in such spirit as shall teach us, while we fear and serve Him, to remember that he has given us freedom and a country to transmit to future ages.

*   *   *   *   *

Monday, April 17, 1865

Sic Semper

The art of misrepresentation
has been, from the first,
boldly resorted to
in order to bolster up
an unrighteous cause,

and whether the effort was to show
that a violation of the Constitution
was constitutional,
or that a war undertaken
to establish slavery forever
was a battle in behalf of freedom,

whatever was the object to be gained,
it has generally been
that the common claims of the language
were perverted.

National Intelligencer
Washington, D.C.
Monday, April 17, 1865

The Late President and the New President

Abraham Lincoln was born in Hardin county, Kentucky, February 12, 1809, and consequently, at the time of his death, was in his fifty-seventh year. When he was eight years of age his father removed to Spencer county, Indiana, then an almost uninhabited wilderness. Here young Lincoln obtained the rudiments of an education, by industry and perseverence, almost unaided by tutors. In 1830 his father removed to Decatur, Illinois. In 1832 Mr. Lincoln raised a company for the Black Hawk war, and was made captain. After his military service was over he entered into business for himself, but did not succeed, and in 1834 commenced his political career in the Legislature.

After his first term expired he studied law; in 1836 was admitted to practice, and in April, 1837, removed to Springfield and commenced business in partnership with John T. Stewart. He was three times elected to the Legislature, and then remained six years in private life. In 1844 he stumped the State of Illinois for Henry Clay.[53] In 1847 he took his seat in the Congress as the only Whig Representative from Illinois. In 1848, Mr. Lincoln canvassed his State for General Taylor.[54] In 1849 he was the Whig candidate for United States Senator, but did not succeed. He took an active part in

The Lincoln cabin in Kentkucky

---

53   Henry Clay, Sr. (1777 - 1852) served as senator and U.S. representative from Kentucky and as speaker of the house and secretary of state. He supported the War of 1812 but opposed the Mexican-American War. He opposed slavery and supported Lincoln.

54   Zachary Taylor (1784 - 1850) served in the War of 1812, the Black Hawk War, the Second Seminole War before being elected president in 1848. He was the last president to hold slaves while in office, the last Whig president, and the second to die in office.

the politial campaign of 1854, stumping the State against Mr. Douglas.[55] In 1858 the State Convention nominated Mr. Lincoln for United States Senator. He was defeated by Mr. Douglas. In 1860 he was nominated, May 16, at Chicago, for President of the United States, and was elected November 6. On his arrival at Harrisburg a plot for his assassination, as he passed through Baltimore, was discovered, and he reached Washington in disguise. He was inaugurated March 4, 1861. He was re-elected November 8, 1864, and re-inaugurated March 4, 1865. Just when peace was dawning upon his country, just as he was about the enjoy the fruits of a wise administration of affairs, on the fourth anniversary of the surrender of Sumter, he falls by the hand of an assassin, and died this morning at twenty minutes past seven o'clock.

*　*　*　*　*

Andrew Johnson taking the oath of office.

55　　　Stephen Arnold Douglas (1813 - 1861), Democratic congressman and senator who lost the presidential election of 1860 to Lincoln.

The Daily Age
Philadelphia
April 17, 1865

Official Announcement of the Induction of President Johnson

Washington, April 15, 1865

Major-Gen. DIX, N.Y.: Official notice of the death of the late President, Abraham Lincoln, was given by the head of the Department this morning to Andrew Johnson, Vice-President, upon whom the Constitution devolved the office of President.

Mr. Johnson upon receiving this notice, appeared before the Hon. Salmon P. Chase, Chief Justice of the United States, and took the oath of office as President of the United States, and assumed its duties and functions.[56]

The President met the heads of Departments in a Cabinet meeting, at the Treasury Building, and among other business the following was transacted:

1. The arrangements for the funeral of the late President were referred to the several Secretaries, as far as relates to their respective departments.

2. William Hunter,[57] esq., was appointed the Acting Secretary of State during the disability of Mr. Seward and his son Frederick Seward, the Assistant Secretary.

3. The President formally announced that he desired to retain the present Secretaries of Departments of his Cabinet, and they could go on and discharge their respective duties in the same manner as before the deplorable event that had changed the head of the government. All business in the Departments was suspended during the day.

The surgeons report that the condition of Mr. Seward remains unchanged; he is doing well. No improvement in Mr. Frederick Seward. The murderers have not been apprehended.

Edwin M. Stanton, Secretary of War.

---

56   Salmon Portland Chase (1808 - 1873) served as Senator from and governor of Ohio, U.S. Treasury Secretary, and, from 1864 until his death, Chief Justice of the Supreme Court. He opposed slavery very strongly. Chase Manhattan Bank was named after him, but he had no participation in it.

57   William Hunter, Jr. (1805-1886) had already been acting aecretary of atate in 1853 and 1860. He had also served as assistant secretary of state.

April 17, 1865

* * * * *

Chicago Tribune[58]
Monday, April 17, 1865

THE GREAT CALAMITY
Sec'y Seward very Comfortable.
HIS SURGEONS SPEAK FAVORABLY OF HIS CONDITION.
Fred. Seward Remains Unconscious.
Narrow Escape of President Johnson from Assassination.
President Johnson's Inauguration Speech in Full.

THE CAPTURE OF BOOTH UNCERTAIN.

The President in Favor of Condign Punishment
on the Leaders of the Rebellion.

DEATH OF HON. RICHARD COBDEN[59]

Reported Surrender of Johnston's Army.

MOBILE CAPTURED ON THE 9TH.

FROM WASHINGTON

The Assassins believed to have Escaped — Several Parties in the Gang of Conspirators — Booth's Card to Vice President Johnson — His Narrow Escape — Prompt Action of ex-Governor Farwell.

[Special Dispatch to the Chicago Tribune.]

Washington, April 16

It is now the general impression that the murderer Booth and his accomplices have escaped into Virginia. It is unlikely that a person so well known would attempt to travel through the north. The contiguity of the debateable (sic) land occupied by guerillas (sic) outside of our lines, the theater of the

---

58   Founded in 1847, the *Tribune* was vehemently abolitionist and supported Abraham Lincoln. It filed for Chapter 11 bankruptcy in December of 2008.

59   Richard Cobden (1804 - 1865), British manufacturer, parliamentarian, widely respected in England and in the United States.

operators of Mosby,[60]White[61] and their gangs render escape in that direction comparatively easy. It is therefore most probable that they fled by a precon-certed route, where accomplices with horses or carriages would be found awaiting them, crossed the lower Potomac in a boat and were among friends at an early hour on the day of the President's death. Parties believed to be the guilty ones are said to have been traced to the vicinity of Piscattowag, on the lower Potomac, some fifteen or seventeen miles from Washington. Many peo-ple still believe, however, that Booth is concealed somewhere in this city or vicinity by his secession friends. It has been observed that for the last three months he has been spending money freely in this and other cities. There are

indications coming to light which point to the im-plication of some of the blockade running frater-nity in the assassination plot.

A rebel Assistant Adjunct General, who came up on the mail boat yesterday, on hearing the news at Fort Monroe, said the South had lost its best friend, and emphatically disclaimed the

Fortress Monroe

act in the name of the people, and attributed it to foreign monied interests.

Between 4 and 4:30 o'clock on the afternoon of the murder, J.W. Booth called at the Kirkwood House and left the following card for Vice-President Johnson:

"I don't want to disturb you. Are you at home?"

(signed) J.W. Booth

For several days previous a large, desperate looking man has been stop-ping at the Kirkwood.[62] He is now missing, and among the papers found in his

60   Col. John S. Mosby (1833 - 1916) led the 43rd Battalion Cavalry, a quasi-independent "partisan rangers" force attached to the Confederate Army, famed for its lightning raids on Union positions. Mosby's Raiders (or Rangers) were also reputed to be a rogue force of thieves. Highly educated in the classics, Mosby opposed slavery but felt obliged to defend Virginia.

61   Elijah Viers White (1832 - 1907) led the 35th Battalion of Virginia Cavalry, aka White's Battalion, White's Rebels, and, for their war cry, White's Comanches.

62   The man was George Andreas Atzerodt (1835 - 1865), a conspirator who had

baggage is a letter from Booth. These and other suspicious circumstances confirm the impression that the Vice-President was included in the hellish plan, and that this missing individual was allotted his death. The Vice-President retired to rest that Friday about 9 o'clock.

Ex-governor Farwell,[63] of Wisconsin, was at Ford's theater at the time of the assassinations. Suspecting that an attempt would also be made on the life of the Vice-President, he rushed from the theater to Mr. Johnson's room, which he reached within five minutes after the shooting of the President. He knocked at the door several times before receiving a reply. At length the Vice-President, who was asleep, awoke and said, "Who is there?" Gov. Farwell replied: "Let me in immediately," at the same time giving his name and saying he had important information to communicate. Mr. Johnson at once opened the door, and Mr. Farwell told him of the murder of the president. It fell like a thunderbolt upon Mr. Johnson, who at first refused to believe it. Upon being convinced, he manifested powerful emotion. Both gentlemen were so much affected that for the moment they were obliged to mutually support each other to avoid falling. Gov. Farwell soon recovered his presence of mind, and to guard against further calamities which be believed menaced the heads of the Government, took the precaution to lock the door and extinguish the gas. After giving warning below he went and procured a guard. Either the miscreant to whom this part of the work was assigned quailed when the time came, or the early retiring of the Vice President, or quick arrival of Gov. Farwell deranged the plan.

The Assassination — How It Was Accomplished

[Special Dispatch to the Chicago Tribune]

Washington, April 15

---

been assignd to kill vice president Andrew Johnson. He apparently he lost his nerve, drank quite a bit, and wandered the streets all night. He was born in Germany but came to the U.S. at the age of eight. He had a carriage repair business in Port Tobacco, Md..

63   Leonard James Farwell (1819 - 1889) was the second governor of Wisconsin. He abolished the death penalty in that state in 1853. He worked in Washington as principal examiner of the U.S. Patent Office.

Miss Harris,[64] who was in the box with the President at the time of murder, gives the following account of the affair:

Nearly an hour before the commission of the deed, the assassin came to the door of the box and looked in to take a survey of the position of its occupants. Supposing it to be a mistake, or the exercise simply of an impertinent curiosity, this circumstance at the time attracted little attention. Upon his entering the box again, however, Major Rathbone arose and asked the intruder his business. He pushed past him without reply, and placing the pistol close to the President's head — actually in contact with it Miss Harris thinks — fired, and instantly sprang upon the cushioned balustrade of the box, where he made a backward plunge with his knife, aimed at the face or breast of Mr. Lincoln. Major Rathbone, spring (sic) forward to protect the President, received the stab in his arm. The murderer then jumped upon the stage and effected his escape.

From a relative of the family of Secretary Seward, the following additional particulars of the murderous attempt at his residence are obtained. Mr. Fred. Seward attempted to prevent the miscreant, who is a very large, powerful man, from entering his father's chamber. The assassin[65] snapped his pistol at him twice, but did not succeed in discharging it. He then struck him two blows upon the head with it, crushing the skull and felling him to the floor. Immediately rushing into the room he attempted to cut the Secretary's throat, and succeeded in inflicting severe gashes upon his face, laying open both cheeks but was prevented by the bed clothing about his neck, and the fact that Mr. Seward rolled out upon the floor, from inflicting fatal injuries. A soldier by this time had entered the room and sprang upon the assassin's back. He stabbed him in the side, and succeeded in breaking loose, and after wounding Maj.

---

64   Clara H. Harris (1834 - 1883), fiancée of Henry Rathbone, daughter of N.Y. Senator Ira Harris. She married Rathbone, moved with him to Hannover, Germany, where he apparently became insane. He shot her, then stabbed her several times.

65   Lewis Thornton Powell, a.k.a. Lewis Paine and Lewis Payne (1844 - 1865), had been a soldier in the Confederate army. At Powell's hanging, his last words were, "I thank you. Good-bye." Though the location of his remains is unknown, his skull was found in the Smithsonian Institution in 1992. It was subsequently buried beside his mother's grave in Geneva, FL.

Seward, another son of the Secretary,[66] and an attendant,[67] reached his horse and rode away.

The pistol was a large navy revolver,[68] and was broken in pieces by the force of the blows. It is covered with blood. The knife used is some ten or twelve inches in length, and was also left in the house.[69] The attendant who was stabbed in the lungs died a few hours later.[70]

The Feeling in Washington — An Impressive Incident

A Citizen Shot for Rejoicing at Lincoln's Death.

[Special Dispatch to the Chicago Tribune]

Washington, April 15

The city is consumed with excitement. The all pervading gloom of last night has given place this morning, in a great measure, to desperate resolves to visit in active measure to all rebel participants, the utmost retributive vengeance. The slightest expression of secession sentiments are sure to be wiped out in blood. A few moments since a rebel resident inquired of a guard in front of the State Department, if it were true the President was dead. The soldier replied that it was. Whereupon the citizen replied, "I'm damned glad of it." He had scarcely concluded his utterance when the guard put a ball through his head, and lies now a corpse, execrated by all. The incident fairly illustrates the intensity of popular feeling. The reported capture of Booth, the supposed assassin of the President, is not confirmed. His trunk and personal effects were seized at the National Hotel last evening. In the trunk were two pairs of snap-handcuffs, a Colonel's uniform, and a large number of letters, the latter, it is claimed, clearly implicating him in a general plot of assassination.

---

66   Gus Seward. Also present, his sister Fanny Seward.

67   The attendant was probably Sgt. George Foster Robinson, an army nurse assigned to Seward, who was slashed in the face and forehead. The reference could also be to State Department messenger Emerick Hansell, who was stabbed in the back as the assassin fled out the door.

68   An 1858 Whitney .36 caliber six-shot revolver with a 7-1/2-inch barrel, produced by Eli Whitney.

69   It was a silver-mounted bowie knife with an alligator motif and engraved "The Hunter's Companion - Real Life Defender."

70   This item is misreported. Neither Robinson nor Hansell was stabbed in the lungs nor died within hours.

Yesterday he called at the Kirkwood House and obtained the number of the Vice-President's room. The horse found last night near the Lincoln Hospital, in the eastern suburbs of the city, was identified this forenoon by its owner, as the one hired to Booth. It was evident form the condition of the saddle, &c, that the horse had thrown its rider.

Secretary Seward and his son Frederick are sinking rapidly. The latter is reported dying by his physician.

The body of Mr. Lincoln has been removed to the White House.

The citizens of Illinois meet this afternoon at two o'clock to consent in regard to the removal of the President's remains to that State.

Andrew Johnson took the Presidential oath this forenoon. It was administered by Chief Justice Chase.

Immediately upon its being known that the President had been assassinated, the Secretary of the Navy telegraphed to the picket posts on the Potomac and in Chesapeake Bay to overhaul all floating crafts and arrest all suspicious persons. The city is draped in mourning.

*　*　*　*　*

The New-York Tribune
Monday, April 17, 1865

The New Vice-President

Special Dispatch to the N.Y. Tribune

Washington, April 16, 1865

The Governors of several States are in town, and a large number of United States Senators. Senator Foster[71] of Connecticut, now Vice-President, arrived this morning. He is pronounced by our ablest public debaters the utmost ac-

---

71   Lafayette Sabine Foster (1806 - 1880), born in rural Franklin, Conn., served as mayor of nearby Norwich, Conn. and then as a U.S. representative and speaker of the House. He was elected senator in 1854. In 1865 was elected president pro tempore of the Senate, six weeks before the assassination. He did not become vice president when Johnson became president, but he became president of the senate, making him next in the line of succession. Had George Atzerodt successfully followed through on the plan to kill Johnson, Foster would have become president.

complished Parliamentarian in the country.

A venerable Cabinet Minister, under a former Administration, who has recently returned from abroad, says that the quiet and harmonious movements of our Republican form of Government, under our appalling calamity, will be the greatest marvel among foreign nations.

The Messrs. Blair[72] have been indefatigable in their efforts to assist the Government in its hour of sublime trial. They have also the credit of having done much to temper the overwhelming grief of the President's stricken household.

Mrs. Montgomery Blair has delicately extended to Mrs. Lincoln an earnest and feeling invitation to make her private residence her home so long as she may remain in Washington.

* * * * *

The Philadelphia Inquirer[73]
Monday, April 17, 1865

"SIC SEMPER TYRANNIS."

When the miserable wretch who assassinated President Lincoln had accomplished his deed, for which bloody work he was prepared with a pistol and

---

72   Montgomery Blair (1813 - 1883) and his wife Mary [Woodbury] Blair. Though from a slave-owning family in Kentucky, Montgomery was steadfastly opposed to slavery and was a supporter of Lincoln, who made him postmaster general. Mr. and Mrs. Blair were the great-grandparents of actor Montgomery Clift. The Blair House on Pennsylvania Ave., the traditional guest house for visitors to the president, was at one point owned by Montgomery's father, Francis Blair, who later built a house next door for his daughter and to which the Blair residency was later attached. It was bought by the U.S. government in 1942 and retains the Blair name.

73   The *Philadelphia Inquirer* is either the oldest or third-oldest paper in the United States, depending on how its various incarnations and mergers are counted. It may go back to *The Pennsylvania Packet* of 1771, or maybe only to the *Pennsylvania Inquirer,* founded in 1829. The paper struggled against competitors until the Civil War, when its truthful and balanced reporting was respected by both North and South, including Confederacy generals who used it to glean information about battles. The founders of the *Pennsylvania Inquirer* dedicated the paper to represent all people, not just the upper class. The paper backed the Democratic party until 1836, when it switched support to the Whigs. Before and during the Civil War, it moved toward a Republican stance, supporting preservation of the Union but opposing abolition and emancipation.

a knife, he shouted, in melo-dramatic vehemence, as he left the crowded house, the motto of the State of Virginia, "Sic Semper Tyrannis." One of the most remarkable features of the Rebellion has been the facility with which words of well-settled meaning have been misapplied to assist the base purposes of treason. The art of misrepresentation has been, from the first, boldly resorted to in order to bolster up an unrighteous cause, and whether the effort was to show that a violation of the Constitution was constitutional, or that a war undertaken to establish slavery forever was a battle in behalf of freedom, whatever was the object to be gained, it has generally been that the common claims of the language were perverted, and the most sacred phrases which were moulded during the most alarming scenes of our political and national history were turned aside, and used to sanction [illegible], which they plainly condemned.

The wild exclamation of the assassin, to which we have adverted, shows how the remorseless passions engendered by slavery had poisoned his judgment, and how in the execution of an inhuman crime, he dared to pretend that his act was noble and his motives grand. To no man who has appeared in this exciting era of our history was the appellation "tyrant" less applicable than to Abraham Lincoln. He was the impersonation of goodness, of generous impulse, and of tender pity. His high office demanded of him certain duties and certain sacrifices. He endeavored to discharge them with fidelity, but he always hoped to be able to temper justice with mercy. His thoughts and hopes were that he might so conduct the nation through its perils that the dreadful necessities of action should be curbed so that they wrought no needless damage. His heart pulsated kindly, his aspirations were gentle. He endeavored, while firmly conducting the national affairs, to control justice so that it should not become vengeance.

He delighted not inscenes of blood, and his greatest error was that he was easily persuaded to pardon, where he should have sternly condemned. The Southern traitors, in their wild disregard of the meaning of words, called him "usurper" and "tyrant." His usurpation was occupation of an office to which he had been called by the voice of the people, with the sanction of the constitution and the laws, in no other mode than had been used to confer a great trust upon fifteen presidents who went before him. His tyranny was his fidelity to his oath of office, which bound him to maintain the integrity of the Union over all the States, to defend the national property, and to resist armed treason by armed loyalty. Every one of his predecessors had taken a similar oath, and every one of them was bound to observe it had there been necessity. The great and good Washington vindicated that oath against the Rebels of Pennsylvania who engaged in the "whisky insurrection." The stern and patriotic Jackson was ready to do so against the South Carolina nullifiers. Had James Buchanan the honesty or vigor of either, the egg of Rebellion would have been broken ere it was hatched, and his vindication would have been in his official oath.[74] That Mr. Lincoln performed a duty which his immediate predecessor avoided, is to be ascribed to the fact that with him honesty and fidelity were superior to convenience and timidity. To no man could the epithet "tyrant" be applied with less truth than to Abraham Lincoln. He was just, but he was also benignant. He discharged his solemn trusts because he understood the importance of what he assumed to do. It was not with savage vindictiveness or bitter malice that he fulfilled his duties, but frequently with a sorrowing spirit of regret that it had been his lot to do as an officer that which as a man he would have avoided. He was struck down in the exuberance of his lenient, merciful spirit; he prayed for a restoration of peace as the measure best calculated to heal the wounds of the South. His heart was given to a consideration of the means, how, whilst restoring the Union, he could best protect the South against the violence of the

---

74   Buchanan, elected in 1856, walked the fine line between maintaining federal power in the South and inciting the South to secede by force. He argued that the South had no right to secede but the federal government had no right to use force to prevent secession. After Lincoln's election in November of 1860, the South moved closer to secession. Buchanan offered no military reaction to South Carolina's declaration of secession on December 20 and six other states soon did the same, seizing federal property. The issue came to a head at Fort Sumter, located in Charleston, S.C. harbor, one of few federal properties still under federal control. Buchanan was reluctant to send reinforcements, fearing the "invasion" would lead more states to secede. When he finally sent a ship on January 5 (by which time the reinforcements were no longer requested), the South was prepared to resist. When Confederate forces fired on the ship, it retreated to New York. When Lincoln took office on March 4, Buchanan handed him a situation that inevitably lead to war.

radicals at the North. When the hand of a man, who acted for the cause of the Rebellion, struck him down, he removed from influence and power a mighty intercessor. The conquered South would have got better terms from Abraham Lincoln than it will from Andrew Johnson. It could have secured under the influence of the late President a kinder disposition in the loyal people of the North. It has rudely torn these sentiments from our breasts. It has chilled our generous emotions, and turned the tide of kindness into stern sorrow, which will seek its revenge. It was a rash act which struck down this noble hearted man in the wild impulses of a malicious disposition. John Wilkes Booth has not removed a tyrant, he has murdered a friend.

The New President

It has been the will of the Almighty to place the destinies of the nation in the hands of Andrew Johnson for nearly four years. It is the duty of the people to rally to his support, to strengthen his hands.

We believe that Andrew Johnson, as President, will endeavor to discharge his high trust with earnestness, resolution, and a judicious policy. He has been a stern and uncompromising opponent of the Rebellion, from the moment that it endeavored to stand up against the national government.

In the United States he was the only Southern man who boldly resisted the madness which was evinced by his colleagues in the winter of 1860-61. He denounced them boldly, and with vigorous prediction sketched the consequences which would follow their mad conspiracy. He was open strong and unreserved in his opinions, and incipient treason received from him more stirring rebukes than were pronounced against it by any northern Senator. All that Mr. Johnson then presaged has happened: the South threw down the gauntlet, and it was taken up by loyal citizens. The conflict has been long and bloody, but it has been won by the Union. In his own State Mr. Johnson never faltered in his allegiance, and never failed to contend against treason. His influence was great, his labors arduous. He had the happiness to see Tennessee restored to the Union by his own exertions, and the assistance of loyal men whose faith never deserted them, even under the most adverse circumstances. He was appointed the Military Governor of Tennessee during the most perilous period of its history.

His rigorous administration checked the mischievous efforts of the wicked sympathizers with secession, encouraged the loyal sentiment to assert itself, and from a condition of anarchy and chaos, brought back the State to peacefulness, order and law. He had the satisfaction when he left his station to hand over the Government to Union officers who were enabled to maintain their authority by the settled condition of affairs when they assumed power. To have done so much, required abilities of a high grade, strong determination in dealing with the defiant, and tact in encouraging the timid. The task was without parallel in our experience, and there was no precedent which would establish the method in which it should be executed. Governor Johnson was compelled to act upon his judgment, and to inaugurate a policy suitable to the exigencies of the occasion. The best qualities of a statesman were needed in the elucidation of the social and political problems which pressed upon the government of Tennessee. From the results, we know that every obstacle was overcome, and every difficulty promptly decided. We can point to these acts as the best evidence which can be adduced, to show the capacity of Andrew Johnson to discharge the greater duties which have devolved upon him, and in view of these circumstances, we can confidently ask that he shall be aided by the spirit of our loyal people with faith, sincerity and confidence.

There are important questions yet to be settled, and mighty interests yet to be secured. We are sure that they will receive proper consideration at his hands, because we believe that his heart is firmly set in the cause. While he will be assiduous in endeavors to bring back the erring, he will be firm and just with the defiant victims of the Rebellion, the oppressed people of the South, who have been sacrificed to the selfish ambition of their leaders, will be encouraged, but the wicked authors of all this woe will receive the strictest measure of justice. It was the part of Abraham Lincoln to conduct the Republic through many tribulations to the point final triumph; it will be the task of Andrew Johnson to insure a wise, permanent and speedy restoration.[75]

---

75   It was his efforts at Reconstruction that would lead to his impeachment. Attempting to continue the policy of leniency that Lincoln had advocated, he came under the ferocious

SUMMARY OF NEWS

- A nation mourns its honored President.

- Abraham Lincoln, at the time of his death, was aged 56 years, 2 months, and 2 days.

- President Johnson is said to be about to convene an extra session of Congress.

- General B.F. Butler[76] resigned his commission on Friday.

- President Johnson was born in Raleigh, N.C., December 29, 1808, and is consequently in the 57th year of his age.

- The citizens of Dayton, Ohio, have presented an elegant sword to Major-General Thomas J. Wood.

- The Rebel General Sterling Price,[77] with a mere handful of men, is cruising about on the borders of the Red River.

- Montrose, Pa. is a small place, but very patriotic, and has had a credible celebration over Lee's surrender.[78]

- The latest novelty in London is an electric toothbrush to cure the toothache. It is warranted infallible.

- In China, married men are at a premium. If a young man remains single after reaching the age of 20, he is drummed out of town.

- Since 1860 no less than seven thousand brigands have been killed, wounded or captured in Italy.[79]

---

criticism of Radical Republicans who demanded stricter federal control (and congressional rather than presidential control) over Reconstruction and the new governments of the South.

76   Benjamin Franklin Butler (1818 - 1893) resigned from the rank of general as Congress was investigating his incompetence. He later became a congressman from and governor of Massachusetts.

77   Sterling Price (1809 - 1867), 11th governor of Missouri, a brigadier general in the U.S. Army in Mexican-American War who sided with the Confederacy. Refusing to surrender, he took his surviving troops to Mexico, where he offered his services to Emperor Maximilian (who declined), then founded a Confederate exile colony. He returned after contracting painful intestinal problems, soon dying of "chronic diarrhea" in St. Louis, MO.

78   General Lee abandoned defense of Richmond, the capital of the Confederacy, on the night of April 2, 1865, and surrendered to U.S Grant on April 9, 1865. This was not a surrender by the Confederate government, but with the loss of its most effective fighting force, other Southern armies knew loss was inevitable. Mostly due to the limited communication, fighting would continue elsewhere in the South until June.

79   Until the Kingdom of Italy was founded in 1861, its independent principalities were

- There is a man in London who earns his living by waking sound sleepers early in the morning, at one penny per head per day.

- Gold ore, it is said, has been discovered in the town of Moscow, in Maine.

- A niece of General Wm. Tecumseh Sherman made her first appearance as an actress at one of the Cincinnati theatres, on Monday evening last.

- John Wilkes Booth, the dastard murderer of Mr. Lincoln, is the son of Junius Brutus Booth, the great tragedian, and a brother of Edwin and young J. Brutus Booth, all well known as actors.

- To kill a king is regicide. To kill the President of a free Republic, chosen by the voluntary suffrages of the people, is a crime without a name, a wickedness too great to be designated.

CITY INTELLIGENCE — PRESIDENT LINCOLN'S DEATH. — Reception of the News in this City — ITS EFFECTS ON OUR CITIZENS. — APPEARANCE OF THE CITY. — MEETINGS HELD IN VARIOUS PLACES. — PUBLIC AND PRIVATE BUILDINGS DRAPED IN MOURNING — LAMENTATIONS OF THE PEOPLE AT LARGE — Etc., Etc., Etc., Etc.

—

The murder of Abraham Lincoln, President of the United States, although telegraphed to this city about 11 o'clock on Friday night, did not become generally known until Saturday morning, when the news spread with lightning rapidity, and acted like an electric shock upon the minds of our community. We just say that, without distinction of party, all lamented the untimely death of this truly great and noble man. In a much less time than it takes to write these few lines, flags and public buildings were draped in mourning, and other demonstrations of grief were exhibited by our people.

Thousands flocked around the newspaper offices, with the faint hope that some later intelligence might contradict the sad news, and when the report of

---

infested with brigands who could flee from one state to another to escape capture. One of the most famous in that decade was Domenico Tiburzi, sometimes referred to as the Robin Hood of Maremma.

the assassination and its fatal termination was confirmed beyond doubt, old men bowed their heads in sorrow and wept like children. Untold grief was depicted in the countenances of every one, and notwithstanding the immense throng in our streets, great quiet and order prevailed, such as is not witnessed in ordinary times of excitement.

All business was immediately suspended: stores and workshops were closed and draped in mourning. The sight along Third and Chesnut (sic) streets, as far up as Thirteenth, was really sorrowful. The whole street as far as the eye could stretch, was wailing the loss of the Chief Magistrate of the nation. Besides, from every private dwelling were exhibited signs of lamentation. The bells throughout the whole city of Philadelphia were slowly and solemnly tolled for several hours. Numerous places of public worship were at once thrown open, and thousands assembled to participate in services appropriate to the occasion.

The public Courts, mercantile bodies, brokers, and other associations at once suspended business. With our whole city clothed in mourning, and our people depressed and sorrow-stricken, the scene was indeed a sad and impressive one. Such general affliction and tokens of respect were never before shown in this or any other city, upon the announcement of the death of the Chief Ruler of the Nation. The horrible assassination of President Lincoln greatly incensed the minds of the people, who, although not loud or boisterous in threats, plainly showed in their countenances the fearful feeling of revenge that was hid within. Many exciting and interesting scenes and incidents concurred during Saturday and yesterday, a full and correct report of which will be chronicled below.

DOES THIS ACCOUNT FOR IT?

The following advertisement was published in the Selma, Alabama, Dispatch in the month of December last; in consequence of recent events it is exceedingly suggestive —

ONE MILLION DOLLARS WANTED TO HAVE PEACE BY THE FIRST OF MARCH — If the citizens of the Southern Confederacy will furnish me with the cash, or good securities for the sum of one million dollars, I will

cause the lives of Abraham Lincoln, William H. Seward and Andrew Jackson
to be taken by the first of March next. This will give us peace, and satisfy the
world that cruel tyrants cannot live in a "land of liberty." If this is not accomplished, nothing will be claimed beyond the sum of fifty thousand dollars, in
advance, which is supposed to be necessary to reach and slaughter the three
villains.

I will give, myself, one thousand dollars toward this patriotic purpose.
Everyone wishing to contribute will address box X, Cahawba, Ala.
December 1, 1864

* * * * *

Louisville Daily Journal[80]
Monday, April 17, 1865

There can be no doubt that J. Wilkes Booth, the distinguished actor, if
guilty of having assassinated President Lincoln, should be hung. We would
gladly have him hung so high that our people would see him by telescopes from
all portions of the continent.

We have no doubt that John Wilkes Booth, though a man of great histri-
onic genius, has a broad streak of insanity in his nature; but the evidence of
his long-contemplated, deliberately-considered, and terribly-executed crime
exclude and make impossible all considerations or thoughts of mercy. Oh that
he had twenty million necks — one for the private thought and feeling of every
loyal man in the United States.

About thirty-three years ago, the elder Booth, the father of Wilkes, Edwin, etc., came to this city upon a theatrical engagement. He sent for us to
his hotel with many but queer compliments. We went. He received us kindly,
but strangely. In a little while, he asked us if we were "armed." "Not, much,"
we answered. "Well, how much," said he. We drew from our pocket a spring-
knife, presented to us two days before and gave it into his hands, showing
him how it was to be used. He instantly raised it on high and exclaimed in his

---

tragic style, "What is to save you now?" We retired a step and replied, "What is to save me is your fear of this pistol!" He responded in a most joyous laugh, "Oh I don't care for knives or pistols, as I know you don't, but I wanted to find you worthy to be my friend." We told him that we had not thus far found him worthy of our friendship.

He then asked us to go up to his room and see some of his departed friends. Having an awful prejudice against the sight of ghosts, we declined. He urged. We yielded. We went with him, and he introduced us to twelve or fifteen roosters, hens, and pullets, his travelling companions through the country, saying that they were his deceased friends, and telling us the name of each. His solemnity was evidence of his sincerity. There was no hypocrisy in his soul.

The next night he was advertised for his third appearance at the Theatre. An immense crowd assembled. He didn't show himself. Impatience became irrepressible, and the people in the house had their money returned at the door. As we passed down a cross-street, a well-known voice from a carriage exclaimed, "Halloo! Have you been at the Theatre?" "Yes," we said "What sort of an audience was there?" "A tremendous one." "Did they see Booth?" "No, and Booth treated them like — dogs!" "Ah, well, were they very much disappointed?"

Two days afterward we were sent for by the keeper of the city jail. Poor Booth was in his keeping. He had been taken in a state of unconsciousness from the streets, and he was still unconscious. He had blacked himself blacker than the blackest negro in Kentucky. We helped him away from the city, and when he came again he behaved better, and spoke his gratitude to us.

We do not mention these evidences of paternal insanity as the slightest reason for the sparing of President Lincoln's murder from the gallows. We mention them simply because, at a time like this, they may be interesting to many readers. As for the assassin, we repeat that he should, if possible, be hung higher than the clouds.

This morning we publish an accurate report of the last speech of the lamented President Lincoln, delivered in Washington on the 11th inst. The speech discusses the important subject of reconstruction, and expresses the view that the rebellious states are, in contemplation of the law, still members of the Union, and that the loyal people thereof have but to reorganize the suspended civil governments in them, electing Governors, and Legislatures, and representatives in Congress, to restore the proper practical relations between those States and the Union. This sound view of the subject is directly antagonistic to the theory announced by Senator Sumner which is that the so-called seceded States have lost their identity as States and, by rebellion, have been reduced to the conditions of unorganized territories. The enlightened view of the lamented President is the same for which we have contended all along, rendering, as it does, the important work of restoration comparatively simple. The radical theory on the subject is not only in violation of constitutional law, but fraught with endless complications, President Johnson, happily for the country, holds the same conservative position on this question as his predecessor. In a late speech he illustrated his idea by saying, "Tennessee is not out of the Union; she never was out of the Union, and no earthly power can take her out."

The Effect of President Lincoln's Assassination. — No less than fifteen persons were arrested on Saturday by the Provost Guards, for using disloyal language and rejoicing over the President's demise. Three Federal soldiers and three ladies are among the number. It is very probable that a few days of hard work on the fortifications will be the consequences in most of the cases. They were confined in the barracks to await an examination. We append their names: John Womack, company L, 4th Kentucky cavalry; Alex. Cissil, 52nd Indiana; Silas W. Veach, company B, 49th Indiana; Mrs. Anna Friend, late of New Orleans; Mrs. J. Clark, Mrs. Mary A. Burke, Wm. Steele, Chas. Burke, Thos. A. Morris, John Sparks, J.H. McAllister, Henry Earle, of this city, Frank Bache, of Jeffersonville; and Chas. Liney, of New York,

The Guerrilla Captain Marion Killed.[81] — Major C.J. Wilson telegraphed

81   Captain William Marion, Confederate guerrilla, associated with Quantrill's Raiders, the guerrilla forces of William Clarke Quantrill.

us yesterday from New Haven that the notorious guerilla leader Captain Marion was shot and killed at a still-house, near Manton [Kentucky], on Saturday evening, by one of Captain Terrell's Union Guards.[82] The body of the dead guerilla will be forwarded to this city to-day. Marion was one of the most bloodthirsty and desperate outlaw leaders operating in the State, and the news of his death will create intense delight. But a few days ago he threatened to avenge the death of Sue Mundy a hundred-fold.[83] Thanks to a Union guard, he will not be able to put his boasted threat into execution.

Jeff Davis's Valedictory Proclamation of April 1, 1865

Whereas, in the course of inhuman Yankee events the capital of the confederate States of American no longer affords an eligible and healthy residence for the members of the present Cabinet not to speak of the Chief Magistrate himself, the Vice-President, and the members of the two Congressional bodies; I do therefore, by virtue of the power vested in my two heels, proclaim my intention to travel instanter, in company with all the officers of the Confederate States Government, and to take up such agreeable quarters as may yet be granted unto me.

To such persons as are in arms against the confederate States of America, I do hereby tender absolute amnesty, on condition that they forthwith desist from annoying our patriotic population.

Under the circumstances, slavery had better be abolished.

The capital of the confederacy will henceforward be found "up a stump" on the picturesque banks of the celebrated "Last Ditch."[84]

---

82   Manton is a small town in central Kentucky just a few miles from the place where today Maker's Mark bourbon is produced.

83   Sue Mundy, a fictional Confederate guerrilla leader created by George Prentice, editor of the Louisville Journal. She and her supposed exploits were modeled on Marcellus Jerome Clarke, a guerrilla leader. Prentice created the persona of Sue Mundy to embarrass the military governor of Kentucky, Major General Stephen G. Burbridge, for his inability to eliminate guerrilla raids.

84   For years Southern leaders had promised a fight to "the last ditch." The promise eventually inspired a political cartoon, "The Sour Apple Tree, or Jeff Davis' Last Ditch," featuring Davis in a petticoat and shawl (which he was supposedly wearing when captured) running with a bag of gold toward a tree with a noose hanging from a branch. Another lithograph, titled "Finding the Last Ditch," shows a Union soldier hurling Davis over a cliff as a black man in broken shackles raises his arms in celebration. Note Booth's reference to the

To the foreign subscribers of the Confederate loan I return sincere thanks.

Lieutenant General Grant, United States army, will please see that they get their cotton.

All persons having claims against this Government will please present them to A. Lincoln, Richmond, by whom all such accounts will be most cheerfully audited.

It is not altogether improbable that the glorious experiment of a slave-

Jefferson Davis

holder's Confederacy may yet prove a delusion and a snare. I have often thought so. So has Gen. Lee, who has lately been fighting mostly for his last year's salary. The Confederate treasury being light, I think I will take it in my valise. Gen. Lee thinks that we have a good opening before us, and that we have seen the last of this fratricidal war. I hope so. Stephens[85] thinks peace more imminent than ever.

If the United States persists in refusing to recognize the Confederacy, on my return I shall again urge the arming of the negroes.

Office-seekers are respectfully solicited to cease their importunings. Genius is the beau ideal, but hope is the reality. Fellow-citizens, farewell.

J. Davis

President Confederate States of America

Done at Richmond, April 1, 1865.

The American citizens of African descent, of Columbus, Ohio, held a

last ditch in his letter published in the *Philadelphia Inquirer* on April 19.

85   Alexander Hamilton Stephens (1812 - 1883) was vice president of the Confederacy. Before and again after the war he was a U.S. representative from Georgia, where he was elected governor in 1882. Often at odds with Jefferson Davis, he pushed for a negotiated peace, a prisoner exchange, and an end to Davis's suspension of *habeas corpus*.

meeting on Tuesday night to make arrangements to join their white brethern, of the Republican party, in the partisan celebration of Good Friday. The
colored people appointed committees, &c., to go in. One of the committees
met with the committee appointed by the Jo. Sullivant-Jo.-Geiger-Julius-Wood
meeting; and, the Statesman [newspaper] says, had a long and stormy joint
session, and, finally decided that blacks must be excluded. It was urged on
their behalf, that the colored soldiers were the first Federal soldiers to march
into Richmond, and that the African race was immensely interested in the war,
and that therefore, they ought to be allowed to rejoice, but all of no avail. The
African "brethern and sistern" were ordered to stand aside and not rejoice by
the representatives of the party that put them into the army and promised them
social and political equality.

* * * * *

Macon Daily Telegraph & Confederate[86]
Macon, Ga.
April 17, 1865

Barnum, Shoddy, and New York

From the Freeman's Journal

Last Saturday, as the Fourth of March, was the day for the re-inaugu-
ration of Abraham Lincoln — endorsed, thereby, by a sufficient number of
bayonets and intelligent "ballot boxes," and with the tamest, if not the most
hearty acquiescence of all the people of North! Endorsed, we say, by a full
Vespasian license of a new lex regia![87] Endorsed in all he has done in violation
and destruction of the United States Constitution! Endorsed in everything else
he may hereafter do, as fully as if on each dumb rag taken from the immortal
and immaculate "ballot box," it had been inscribed, "Quod placest principi,

---

86   The *Macon Telegraph* was founded in 1826 and became a daily in 1831. In 1860 it
merged with the Macon Confederate to become the *Macon Daily Telegraph and Confederate*.
It reverted to *Macon Daily Telegraph* on April 20, 1865.

87   Royal or King's Law, a concept reputed to go back to Romulus's earliest
government of the Roman Kingdom.

legis habet vigorem. * * * populus ei, et in eum, omne suum imperius et pote-statem transfulerit!" "Whatsoever our President fancies shall henceforth have the force of law * * * the people have given over to him and lodged in him all their sovereignty and all their political power!" It is rather a large transfer — but then this is a great age! Men, now-a-days, are men of unusual greatness, and do great things!

This wonderful city of New York, which in 1860 and 1864 went almost crazy in the November elections in the effort to keep Lincoln from being Pres-ident, and from being re-elected has shown its high and honorable sense of consistency — its devotion to sentiment and to principle — its contempt for greenback gains — by having resolved to make a grand gala day of the Fourth of March.[88] The governing classes were resolved to link on to Lincoln all the woe and humiliation and suffering among those they lately honored as their "fellow citizens," and that has happened to the people of Georgia and the Carolinas. The abolition papers, Herald, Tribune, Times &c., have had glow-ing accounts of how the women and children and non-combatants of Savan-nah, Charleston and Wilmington are frightened and cowed in presence of the Yankees. These, be it remembered, are not the men who have made war for Southern independence of the Union. They are the simple unarmed people, who have lived as like classes live everywhere, floating along in communities they live in without taking part in public affairs. They speak the same language with the people of the North. They have been supposed to be parts of the one same people with the North — else this is clearly a war of invasion and aggres-sion! Here is how the "special" "own" correspondent of the New York Tribune speaks of their present position:

"The rebel families of Charleston are perfectly cowed. They live in terror of us. Thus far they are as well behaved as spaniels. It will depend on the ad-ministration here, whether this appropriate sentiment of subordination, (which they have taught is proper and necessary in an inferior race,) shall continue."

The cowardly and infamous character of this hireling of Greeley, the pol-troon of the Tribune, needs not to be explained. The fighting men of Charleston

---

88   The day of Lincoln's first and second inaugurations in 1861.

are not there. They are "rebel families!" Women and children — or people incapacitated from taking part in public affairs! Over there the venomous and skulking Puritan yankee exults! He would flee, howling and terrified, before the slap on the face and the kick, that any man would give him! But, he says, "I will revenge myself for your pulling my nose, by making faces at your sister!" Revenge in keeping with a Yankee, and a Puritan! Like a hyena, he revenges his miscreant feelings over the illustrious dead. — The scurvy spaniel boasts of his achievements over the simulacrum of a man whose fame is planted in history as one of the purest and greatest statesmen of this late federal Union gave birth to. The dog, waging (sic) his tail in the Tribune, thus talks of an image of the dead lion:

"In the front room, there were four busts of eminent Americans — one of them Calhoun. I hate him. I said to the negress who showed us into the room: "That man was your great enemy — he did all he could to keep you slaves — you ought to break his bust." She said nothing, and as I was occupied in examining manuscripts I did not notice that she left the room. After a while, having finished my search, I thought that the bust of Calhoun[89] would be a good trophy for the Tribune office, and made up my mind to "spoil the Egyptians" to that extent. The negro woman was there and I saw that the bust had disappeared. I asked her where it was. She had "gone done" and broke it!"

Last week, on the fifth column of our editorial, fourth page, we gave place to a satire, called the letter of a Massachusetts mother, to her son, a Quartermaster, or some other [illegible] making officer in a Yankee regiment. Perhaps some "moderate" reader of ours, may think that supposed letter was too hard on the Yankee genus. The mother was represented as urging her son to steal and rob all he could and to "read his Bible steddy!" She advised that the soldier should break and destroy the "marvel status and paters" and "send them the jawelry and slik dresses they tuk from the women!"

Now is there any appreciable difference between that picture of Yankee morals, in last week's Freeman, drawn by a master and that does not care to be

---

89   John Caldwell Calhoun (1782 - 1850) served as secretary of state and of war,
U.S. representative and senator from South Carolina, and vice president under John Quincy
Adams and Andrew Jackson. He defended slavery and secession.

known, and the story of his pimp and thieving vagabond, sent to the Tribune by a Yankee — for earth produces none else that could do such a thing.

We have given but specimens of the Puritan atrocities uttered by the chosen and hired underling of the heretofore beswitched and Horace Greeley. But we will not occupy space with more of his filth.

These are the trophies over which New York is called to rejoice. The granite and the marble palaces of New York — the crystal windows of her most showy shops — the pretentious equipages, and the "whole array of vulgar finery that made New York what she was, and what she had the power, of late years, to show herself to be, was drawn from the productions of the Southern States! Having got rich on this, New York claims her correspondents as her property, whether they will or no!

Anyway, she claims, now, a great gala day, to celebrate the accumulated miseries of the families of those men out of whose production she has heretofore made grand profits. New York is noble. New York is princely. New York deserves all the eulogies that the needy and shirtless Bohemians have ever written, to order, on her behalf.

Anyway, this magnificent New York, with an eye to business, proposed to unite in celebrating in one grand ovation, the reinauguration of Abraham Lincoln, the African, and the distress and sufferings of all the people, whites and negroes, in the South States. It would be vere dignum et justum![90] It would be altogether worthy of the honor, and the adherence to principle, of great New York — the city that cares nothing for profit, but is the soul of honor, in all its [illegible].

All this grand celebration was to have come off on the 4th inst. We would to God it had. It seemed to us that it had been meet and just that Lincoln's unlimited leave to do whatsoever, and these "triumphs" at the North have been all celebrated together! They are part and parcel of one same batch! It seems to us they ought to have gone off together.

But:

"God moves in a mysterious way!" If God was such a Being that a Yankee

---

90   truly fitting and just.

was made in his likeness — not perverted and marked with "total depravity," as condemned goods were the God of Heaven like the idols of the nations — a mere demon — He might have been frightened by the big [illegible] of the Yankees, into some change of principles that have been declared eternal! The afore cited cur which the Tribune hires to write from Charleston, says,

"Nearly all of the heathen temples, called churches here, in which they worship a God who instituted and ordained human slavery, have been smashed into by Gilmore's shells."[91]

That "slavery" was "instituted and ordained by God, any more than Justice of the Peace, or Constables, is a piece of Puritan nonsense. But that "slavery," having been instituted "by human law, for mutual advantage" (as the Angel of the schools says) is approved and sanctioned by God, has been the common opinion of all the great authorities of nominal Christendom. Not only Catholic, but Protestant authorities, Leibnitz[92] Grotius,[93] Puffandorf,[94] Noodt,[95] etc. etc., among the Protestant magnates, do not differ from the grand cotena of Catholic authorities that, from the Apostles' day to our own, have maintained this doctrine.

But the genuine Yankee seems to think the Almighty God rash and inconsiderate of His own interests, in view of Gilmore's shells! We are of an ancient opinion, that Gilmore and the Yankee Puritans, and the devil who fell with Lucifer may all explode their gas, and their shells, and that God, being Almighty, will, at last, laugh at them, and one day call them to a reckoning for

91   Quincy Adams Gilmore (1825 - 1888) innovated the use of a rifled cannon and used it and other cannon to breach Fort Pulanski, near Savannah, GA, thus rendering stone fortifications obsolete.

92   Gottfried Wilhelm Leibniz (1646 - 1716) was a German philosopher, scientist, and mathematician who devised a calculator that used a binary system that is used by modern computers. His rationalist philosophy infused his writing on politics and law.

93   Hugo Grotius (1583 - 1645) was a Dutch theologian, jurist, and philosopher. He established the concept of the seas as international territory. He died after being shipwrecked on a voyage from Sweden.

94   Samuel von Pufendorf (1632 - 1694) (not Puffendorf) was a German political philosopher, jurist, and historian who used the theories of Grotius, René Descartes and Thomas Hobbes to establish concepts of law. American constitutionalists, including Thomas Jefferson, James Madison, and Alexander Hamilton tapped his ideas for their defense of democracy.

95   Gerhard Noodt (1647 - 1725), Dutch jurist and writer of political thoughts on, among other things, freedom and conscience.

all that they have done!

As between the powerful explosion of Gilmore's shells, and the churches erected in honor of the Holy and Triune God, whose laws have sanctioned the condition of slavery, to say our eternal portion be with that side where Gilmore's shells exploded! Unlike the Yankee hound who is paid to write for the Tribune from Charleston, we do not believe the Almighty God will be frightened by the damage done to churches erected in His honor, into succumbing to either the devil or to Puritan Yankees!

All this terror and damage to a people lately claimed as "fellow citizens," was to have been celebrated in this city, by a grand display of all vulgar pretensions that money and Barnum, and people advertising their wares, could get up. It was to have been New York city (sic) showing its shameless self to itself — an out of-doors brothel. But it didn't come off.

The great paper, the leading paper, the representative paper, of this modern and so-called Union, is, without doubt, that buffoon sheet, Bennett's Herald[96]. The cannie old Scotchman knows the shallowness of the people he has to deal with, and the old man fools them "to the top of their bent." The Herald, buffoon sheet as it is, does most of the public thinking that is done in this city. Lawyers, and bankers, and merchants babble out its nonsense day after day, as their own thoughts. Poor goslings, they don't think at all! Old Bennett, or some hired Bohemian of his, does the thinking of the grave owls you meet, that you mistake for men. We glance over the fooleries of the Herald, to know what fooleries for the day we may expect to meet among men. Well, the Herald, on last Saturday morning, was as wise as ever. It said, "The weather * * * gives promise of bright skies to smile upon the patriotic exhibition of the nation's rejoicing over events which are to close up the rebellion!" etc. Oh, yes!

The celebration is to come off. Ever so many makers, or venders of wares, and goods in this honest city, have prepared for it, and it must come off! "It is the cheapest kind of an advertisement," says Peter Fack & Co. So it must come

---

96   James Gordon Bennett, Sr. (1795 - 1872) was editor and publisher of the *New York Herald*. (The paper would be handed off to Bennett's son in 1866 and in 1924 would merge with the *New York Tribune* to become the *New York Herald Tribune*, which ceased publication in 1966.)

off. Barnum's Giraffe and Judge Daily, and Barnum's Elephant and Judge Pier-repont, and ever so many eccentricities of nature, will put themselves up on exhibition.

Oh, if this could be for restoring the ancient relations between the States! To attain it, how gladly would we see Judge Daily and Barnum's dirtiest monkey embracing each other; and both jumping off the deepest wharf of the port. But, neither Barnum's dirtiest monkey nor Judge Daily, nor any other patriot, means anything of the kind.

* * * * *

The New York Times[97]
April 17, 1865

The Nation's Bereavement

Death, as the Northmen imaged him, is no dart-brandishing skeleton, but a gigantic shape, that inwraps mortals within the massive folds of its dark pigment. Long has it been since those dread robes closed upon a mightier victim than President Lincoln. It is like the earth's opening and swallowing up a city. The public loss is so great, the chasm made in our national councils so tremendous, that the mind, not knowing how to adjust itself to such a change, shrinks back appalled. It comes home to every bosom with the force of a personal affliction. There is not a loyal family in the land that does not mourn. It is as when there "was a great cry in Egypt, for there was not a house where there was not one dead."[98]

No public man has ever died in America invested with such responsibilities, and the mark of so much attention as Abraham Lincoln. The unprecedented manner of his death has shocked inexpressibly, but it is not that which

---

97   "The Grey Lady" was founded in 1851, when it declared that it would be both conservative and radical, as necessary, to defend the public good. It tended to support Republican candidates until 1884. Adolph Ochs bought the paper in 1896 and gave it the slogan that still appears on every front page: "All the news that's fit to print," establishing the *Times* as more serious than New York's several sensationalist papers.

98   Exodus 12:30

more harrows with anguish. It is the loss of the man himself — the privation of him when he seemed so peculiarly necessary to the country, and when the heart of the people was bound to him more than ever. Had he been taken by a natural death, the public grief would have been just as profound, though un-accompanied with the other emotions which his assassination has excited. All true men feel that they have lost a man of wondrous fitness for the task he had to execute. Few Americans have lived who had such a faculty of discovering the real relations of things, and shaping his thoughts and actions strictly upon them without external bias. In his own independent, and perhaps we may say very peculiar way, he invariably got at the needed truths of the time. Without anything like brilliancy of genius, without any great breadth of information or literary accomplishment, he still had that perfect balance of thoroughly sound faculties which gives an almost infallible judgment. This, combined with great calmness of temper, great firmness of purpose, supreme moral principle, and intense patriotism, made up just that character which fitted him, as the qualities fitted Washington, for a wise and safe conduct of public affairs in a season of great peril.

Political opponents have sometimes denied that Mr. Lincoln was a great man. But if he had not great faculties and great qualities, how happens it that he has met the greatest emergencies that ever befell a nation in a manner that so gained for him the confidence of the people? No man ever had greater responsibilities, and yet never were responsibilities discharged with greater acceptance. All disparagement sinks powerless before this one fact, that the more Abraham Lincoln was tried, the more he was trusted. Nobody can be so foolish as to impute this to the arts and delusions which sometimes give success to the intriguer and demagogue of the hour. It would be the worst insult to the American people to suppose them capable of being so cajoled when the very life of their country was at stake. Nor was it in the nature of Mr. Lincoln to act a part. He was the least pretentious of men. He never sought to win confidence by any high professions. He never even protested his determination to do his duty. Nor, after he had done his duty, did he go about seeking glory for his exploits, or asking thanks by his presence for the great benefits he had conferred. Sampson-like, he could rend a lion and tell neither father nor mother of it. He was a true hero of the silent sort, who spoke mostly by his actions, and whose action-speech was altogether of the highest kind, and best of its kind. He was not an adventurer, aiming at great things for himself and courting the chances of fortune; nor was he a great artist in any sense, undergoing passions and reflecting them; but he was a great power, fulfilling his way independently of art and passion, and simple, as all great powers are. No thought of self — no concern for his own repute — none of the prudish sensitiveness of his own good name, which is the form selfishness often assumes in able and honorable men, ever seemed to enter his mind. To him it was but the ordinary course of life to do that which has made him illustrious. He had a habit of greatness.

An intense, all-comprehensive patriotism, was a constant stimulus of all his public exertions. It grew into the very constitution of his soul, and operated, like a natural function, continuously, spontaneously and almost as it were unconsciously. It pervaded and vilified all that he said, and formed the prime incentive of all that he did. If he had ambition, it was to serve his country, and in that sphere where he might do it most effectually. In no way did he ever fail his country in the time of need. He was independent, self-poised, steadfast. You always knew where to find him; you could calculate him like a planet. A public trust was to him a sacred thing. Sublimer moral courage, more resolute devotion to duty, cannot be found in the history of many than he has displaced for the salvation of the American Union. It was the sublime performance of sublime duties that made him so trusted, and which has given him a fame as solid as justice, and as genuine as truth.

Abraham Lincoln had a heart full of all gentle and pure affections — a heart not prone to strong passion or tumultuous emotion, but ever glowing with a steady, warm, all-comprehensive sympathy. It was a large, equable, genial, tender heart, none the less delicately strung because its chords were deep laid. It was a heart that could not retain a single bitter or vindictive feeling. Public life has a tendency to chill the kindly and generous affections, and blight the sweet charities of life, but of President Lincoln it may be said as was said of Mr. Fox,[99] that his heart was a little hardened as if he had lived and died in a farm-house. No public power, no public care, no public applause could spoil him; he remained ever the same plain man of the people. It was this which peculiarly endeared him to the people, and makes the sorrow for him so tender as a personal feeling, apart from the sense of a national calamity. It is not simply because "he had been so clear in his great office," but because "he hath borne his faculties so meek"

> "that his virtues
> will plead like angels, trumpet-tongued, against

---

[99]   Charles James Fox (1749 – 1806), British parliamentarian renowned for brilliant oratory, contrarian ways, support of the American and French revolutions and objection to slavery. Foxborough, Mass. is named after him.

the deep damnation of his taking off."[100]

The Effect of President Lincoln's Death on National Affairs

The death of President Lincoln naturally excites universal and profound solicitude as to the immediate future of the country. He has been so marked a figure in the terrible events of the last four years, the action of the government in its contest with the rebellion has been so stamped by the impress of his personal character, and he had some to have so strong a hold on the confidence and love of the whole people, without distinction of party, that his sudden removal from the state of events naturally excites anxiety and apprehension on the public mind. He does, indeed, seem to have been needed to close the great work of pacification which he had so well begun.

Nevertheless, it is well to remember that the peculiar nature of our institutions makes it impossible that any one man should be absolutely indispensable to their preservation and successful working. Our government is of the people. They not only elect our rulers, but their spirit, their temper, their will pervade and control all the acts and all the measures of government. Whoever died, the people live, and the government lives also. If the emperor Napoleon had been assassinated, all France would have been in revolution before twenty-four hours had passed away. President Lincoln's death, sudden and awful as it was — though it removes him in an instant from the most important and conspicuous position held by any living man — does not interrupt for an instant the grand movement of our republican government. So far from exciting revolution, it only unites the whole people, more thoroughly than ever, in a common sentiment of devotion to the country and of profound grief for the great calamity that has fallen upon it. All party rancor is hushed. Political strife has ceased. All men of all parties, feeling a common interest and a common grief, stand together in support of the nation and of the man thus suddenly charged

100   From Macbeth's soliloquy of Act I, scene 7, which begins "If it were done when 'tis done, then 'twere well/ It were done quickly. If the assassination/ Could trammel up the consequence, and catch/ With his surcease success; that but this blow/ Might be the be-all and the end-all here,/ But here, upon this bank and shoal of time,/ We'd jump the life to come."

with the execution of the people's will.

The current of events will continue to dictate the policy of the government, as it had done hitherto. The rebellion is already substantially crushed. The war, to all intents and purposes, is closed. There is nothing in the death of Mr. Lincoln which can raise new armies for the rebel service or inspire new hopes for the rebel cause. No portion of the Southern people will be stimulated by it to renew the struggle. The same great Generals who have given our flag victory are still at the head of our armies and the act of an assassin has so fired the loyal heart of the nation, that those armies can be doubled in number if the necessity should arise. But it will not arise. The blow which has aroused the North will paralyze the South. The rebellion will see in it nothing encouraging to their cause, nothing inciting them to new exertions of its behalf.

In President Johnson, moreover, the country has a man of courage, of sound judgment and of a patriotism which has stood the test of the most terrible trials. His sympathies are with the people, and all his action will be for their good. He will respond to their sentiments and will execute their will. Nor will he be unmindful of the fact that the general line of policy which Abraham Lincoln was carrying out, when attested by the murderer's blow, commanded the hearty and universal approbation of the great mass of the American people. No man ever came suddenly to power with a plainer path before him than that which lies before the new President. And no one need fear for a moment that the rebellion is to gain anything by the death of President Lincoln or by the accession to power of Andrew Johnson as his successor.

The Second Inaugural Address of the Late President[101]

Fellow Countrymen:

At this second appearing to take the oath of the presidential office, there is less occasion for an extended address than there was at the first. Then a statement, somewhat in detail, of a course to be pursued, seemed fitting and proper. Now, at the expiration of four years, during which public declarations have been constantly called forth on every point and phase of the great contest

---

101   Delivered March 4, 1865 outside the U.S. Capitol.

which still absorbs the attention and engrosses the energies of the nation, little that is new could be presented. The progress of our arms, upon which all else chiefly depends, is as well known to the public as to myself; and it is, I trust, reasonably satisfactory and encouraging to all. With high hope for the future, no prediction in regard to it is ventured.

On the occasion corresponding to this four years ago, all thoughts were anxiously directed to an impending civil war. All dreaded it-- all sought to avert it. While the inaugural address was being delivered from this place, devoted altogether to saving the Union without war, insurgent agents were in the city seeking to destroy it without war-- seeking to dissolve the Union, and divide effects, by negotiation. Both parties deprecated war; but one of them would make war rather than let the nation survive; and the other would accept war rather than let it perish. And the war came.

One-eighth of the whole population were colored slaves, not distributed generally over the Union, but localized in the Southern part of it. These slaves constituted a peculiar and powerful interest. All knew that this interest was, somehow, the cause of the war. To strengthen, perpetuate, and extend this interest was the object for which the insurgents would rend the Union, even by war; while the government claimed no right to do more than to restrict the territorial enlargement of it.

Neither party expected for the war the magnitude or the duration which it has already attained. Neither anticipated that the cause of the conflict might cease with, or even before, the conflict itself should cease. Each looked for an easier triumph, and a result less fundamental and astounding. Both read the same Bible, and pray to the same God; and each invokes his aid against the other. It may seem strange that any men should dare to ask a just God's assistance in wringing their bread from the sweat of other men's faces[102]; but let us judge not, that we be not judged.[103] The prayers of both could not be answered--that of neither has been answered fully.

The Almighty has his own purposes. "Woe unto the world because of

---

102   Genesis 3:19

103   Matthew 7:1

offenses! for (sic) it must needs be that offenses come; but woe to that man by whom the offense cometh."[104] If we shall suppose that American slavery is one of those offenses which, in the providence of God, must needs come, but which, having continued through his appointed time, he now wills to remove, and that he gives to both North and South this terrible war, as the woe due to those by whom the offense came, shall we discern therein any departure from those divine attributes which the believers in a living God always ascribe to him? Fondly do we hope--fervently do we pray--that this mighty scourge of war may speedily pass away. Yet, if God wills that it continue until all the wealth piled by the bondsman's two hundred and fifty years of unrequited toil shall be sunk, and until every drop of blood drawn by the lash shall be paid by another drawn with the sword, as was said three thousand years ago, so still it must be said, "The judgments of the Lord are true and righteous altogether."[105]

With malice toward none; with charity for all; with firmness in the right, as God gives us to see the right, let us strive on to finish the work we are in; to bind up the nation's wounds; to care for him who shall have borne the battle, and for his widow, and his orphan--to do all which may achieve and cherish a just and lasting peace among ourselves, and with all nations.

*　*　*　*　*

Second Inauguration of Abraham Lincoln, March 4, 1865

104　　Matthew 18:7
105　　Psalm 19:9

Tuesday, April 18, 1865

If Only Strength Were All She Had to Pray For

Every one of us feel that the President died
because he was where we put him.

Had he been a hereditary sovereign
we should have no such feeling.

Had he been a usurper like Mr. Davis,
we should not have felt so.

It is because, by our votes,
we placed this man where he was,
that we feel responsible for his fall.

Philadelphia Inquirer[106]
April 18, 1865

THE GREAT TRAGEDY!
THE MOVEMENTS OF BOOTH ON THE FATAL DAY.

President Johnson also to Have Been Massacred!
SEC'Y SEWARD OUT OF DANGER.
THE PROBABLE ARREST OF THE DASTARD ASSASSIN.
National Grief for Mr. Lincoln — The Funeral to Take Place on Wednesday
Official Order for the Ceremonies

IMPORTANT FOREIGN NEWS!
The Late Insult to Our Flag.
PORTUGAL BACKS DOWN AND APOLOGIZES!!

Arrival of Gen. Lee in Richmond. — Meeting of Congressmen in Washington.

THE CAPTURE OF MOBILE!
Forts, Guns and Prisoners Taken

[Special Despatches to the Inquirer.]

Washington, April 17, 1865

The Assassination of the President

Every hour passing goes to prove that the assassination of President Lincoln and Cabinet associated with the Knights of the Golden Circle,[107] the same plotters who designed last fall to revolutionize the great West by murdering the Governors of the States of Indiana, Illinois, Iowa, &c.

---

106   Also in this edition: Front-page map of Mobile and report on its fall to Union troops on April 9; false report of Booth's arrest; biographic sketch of Lafayette S. Foster, new president of the Senate; plague in Siberia; Portugal's apology for accidental cannon discharge that killed an American sailor.

107   The Knights of the Golden Circle was the country's largest anti-war/anti-abolition/anti-Lincoln Copperhead group. It was formed in Ohio in the 1850s. It later morphed into the Order of the Sons of Liberty.

Further About Booth's Movement on Friday.

On Friday last Booth was about the National Hotel as usual, and strolled up and down the avenue several times.

He Tries to See Mr. Johnson.

During one of his strolls he stopped at the Kirkwood House, and sent in to Vice President Johnson a card upon which was written —

"I do not wish to disturb you. Are you in?

"J. Wilkes Booth."

A gentleman of Booth's acquaintance at this time met him in front of the Kirkwood House, and in the conversation which followed made some allusion to Booth's business, and in a jesting way asked, "What made him so gloomy? Had he lost another thousand in oil?" Booth replied that he had lost considerably by the freshet; that he was about the leave Washington, never to return.

At seven o'clock on Friday evening he came from his room at the National, and was spoken to by several concerning his paleness, which he said proceeded from indisposition. Just before leaving he asked the clerk if he was not going to Ford's Theatre, and added, "There will be some very fine acting there to-night" Mr. Lessford, the ticket agent at the theatre, noticed Booth as he passed in, and shortly after the latter entered the restaurant next to the theatre, and in a hurried manner called for Brandy, brandy, brandy," rapping at the same time on the bar. Judge Carter[108] and a Mr. Ferguson[109] saw Booth loitering about the entrance to the President's box, and just previous to the fatal shot lost sight of him.

---

108   Judge David Kellogg Cartter (1812 - 1887) was appointed by Lincoln to the Supreme Court of the District of Columbia. (In some sources, including Inquirer article, spelled Carter.)

109   James P. Ferguson, owner of the restaurant next to the theatre. But it was possibly William J. Ferguson (1845-1930), a stage hand at the theatre who witnessed the shooting (same encyclopedia) p. 206

The Plot One of Long Standing

For two months he has appeared to be greatly occupied with something, something that weighed heavily upon his mind, and of so large a magnitude that he would not disclose it to his most importunate and intimate friends. Among his companions he was often silent, and when talking frequently absent-minded and wandering. The hideous crime he had in contemplation and which he had sword to accomplish, was the cause.

The Murder Fixed for the 4th of March

The fourth of March was fixed originally for the assassination, and Booth was on the ground, but either through fear of not being able to effect his escape because of the failure of his accomplice to meet him at that time, the attempt was not made.

The Assassin Lies in Wait.

He is now known to have waited for the President on that day, on the embankment near the north wing of the Capitol, close to which Mr. Lincoln would pass.

His Appearance.

He was dressed shabbily in a slouchy suit, his pantaloons crammed into his boots, and an old felt hat pulled down over his face. One of his acquaintances passing, hailed him, but Booth pretended not to hear and refused to speak until closely approached.

George Atzerodt

When the President passed him he hurried away, evidently disappointed, and through the day was gruff and moody to all who addressed him. Being a coward, he hesitated to strike the blow then, since he knew that he would have instantly been torn to pieces by the thousands present to witness Mr. Lincoln's inauguration.

The more investigation pries into the murder the more dastardly it appears. It was as cool and deliberate an assassination as the world ever knew.

His Movement on Friday Evening.

During Friday Booth had visited Ford's Theatre and examined carefully the position of the box, and ascertained how he should enter and escape from it when his purpose was accomplished.

More Proof of the Fiendishness of the Crime.

Behind the door of the passage a hole had been made in the wall, in which, at night, Booth inserted the end of a board, as a brace against the door, thereby precluding anyone from following from the dress circle. The screws were next removed from the lock of the further door, opening into the double box. The thread of the screw-holes was broken and the lock and screws replaced, so that should the inmates of the box fasten the door by which they entered, the other door might be easily pushed open.

Judicial Visit to the Theatre.

Judge Olin[110] and others visited the theatre, and satisfied themselves by actual experiment, that the door ostensibly locked could thus be pushed in with the greatest ease. The aperture in the panel of the door, which was thought to have been a bullet hole, and thus formed a contradictory feature in the chain of evidence, it now appears was made with a knife, and was designed to enable the assassin to survey the position of the occupants of the box previous to entering himself.

The President's Arm Chair.

The large arm chair always used by the President at the theatre, had been removed from its usual position, thereby enabling the murderer to carry out his design more readily, as he passed through the box. A pocket knife, the one probably with which the hole was cut in the door, was found lying on the cushion of the balustrade when Mr. Lincoln's party entered the box. Most of

110   Abram Baldwin Olin (1808 - 1879), had been a U.S. Representative from New York state, nominated by Lincoln to the Supreme Court of the District of Columbia in 1863.

this work must have been done previously by the assassin or by some confederate knowing the premises; probably during some portion of the day when the theatre or that part of it is unoccupied. It would appear, too, from the ease with which the somewhat difficult jump and rebound was made, a leap forward and obliquely to right, that it had been practiced previously, at some favorable opportunity, by the assassin.

History does not record a more willful, deep-studied plan to take the life of a ruler than that so faithfully executed by Booth on Friday night. His preparations for flight were equally well made, and the failure yet to capture him shows how certain he was of escape when he committed the crime. The rewards offered for the arrest of the assassins reach thirty thousand dollars. Philadelphia and New York should each offer a reward of twenty-five thousand dollars, and Baltimore and Boston should make up the other twenty thousand dollars. Such a sum of money would tempt any man who might be called upon to harbor and aid the villains, and they would soon be surrendered to the hands of justice.

Traces of Sec'y Seward's Assailant

On Sunday evening, a grey coat, stained with blood, and which had evidently been worn as an overcoat, was found near fort Bunker Hill,[111] just back of Glenwood Cemetery. In the pocket was a false mustache, a pair of riding gloves, and a slip of paper upon which was written Mary F. Gardner, 419. This is supposed to have been worn by the man who attacked Secretary Seward. Although the weight of evidence indicates that all the conspirators took the same route, that of the Navy Yard Bridge.[112]

General Arrests Made.

This morning detective Kelley and a detail of patrolmen of the Second

---

111   The earthenwork fort was built during the Civil War to guard the northeast of Washington, D.C.. After the war it was no longer used. The site is preserved today but little remains of the fort.

112   The bridge crosses the Anacostia River just upstream from the Potomac, connecting southeast Washington to Unionville, MD.

Ward, by order of Judge Olin, proceeded to the house of Mollie Turner,[113] on the corner of Thirteenth street and Ohio avenue (sic), and arrested all the inmates, from the mistress to the cook, eight in all, and carried them to the police head-quarters, to be held as witnesses. This is the house where Booth spent much of his time with Ella Turner,[114] the woman who attempted suicide on Saturday morning.

A Man Mistaken for Booth

A man was captured about fifteen miles this side of Baltimore, who answered almost identically the description of Booth, and the authorities were telegraphed to make due preparation for the safe-keeping of the assassin. Such preparations were accordingly made, but it was subsequently ascertained that the person arrested, though bearing so singular a resemblance to the criminal, was quite another party.

Mr. Lincoln's Remains.

Many Philadelphians at present in Washington are anxious that the committee from Springfield, Illinois, should pass through Philadelphia on their way west with the remains of our late beloved and lamented President. When the committee arrive, it will probably be decided at once whether they will go via Philadelphia. Meanwhile it would be but proper for some steps to be taken by the authorities of the city of Philadelphia and the Baltimore Railroad and the Pennsylvania Central railroad to secure the opportunity or Philadelphia to pay her tribute of respect to the mortal remains of him whom she honored and

---

113   a.k.a. Nellie and Ellen Turner. See footnote on Ella Turner below.

114   Ella Turner was one of many women who loved John Wilkes Booth, who was naturally and effortlessly attractive to women. She was the daughter of a brothel madam, Mollie Turner, who operated a house on Ohio Avenue. Turner, whose real name was Ellen or Nellie Starr, said she was "nineteen or twenty years of age" when she testified to police on April 15. She said she hadn't seen Booth in about two weeks and hadn't been on good terms with him for over a year. She was pregnant when she attempted to kill herself with chloroform. The fetus survived and was born Mary Louise Turner, later named a beneficiary of Booth's estate. Booth also left Mary Katherine Scott pregnant with Sarah Katherine Scott, who would be born on December 8, 1865.

loved as the advocate of universal freedom.

Order of Secretary McCulloch[115]

An order was issued to-day, by the Secretary of the Treasury, for the clerks in his Department to meet, at three o'clock, at the Treasury building, to proceed to the Presidential mansion for the purpose of viewing the remains of the President Lincoln. Mr. McCulloch also extended an invitation to the other departments to join the procession.

Mr. Lincoln's Coffin

The coffin in which the late President is to be buried is a magnificent affair indeed, costing above one thousand dollars. It is of mahogany, lined with lead, and covered with the finest black cloth.

The outside of the coffin is festooned with massive silver tacks, representing drapery, in each fold of which is a silver star. There are eight massive handles to the coffin, being placed on each side; the outer edges of the coffin are tastefully gilded with silver braid, to which are attached three tassels of five inches each in length.

A row of silver tacks encircle the entire top of the coffin, being places two inches from the outer edge, which a silver plate, encircled by a shield formed of tacks of the same material, occupies a central position on the top of the lid with a start at the head and foot of the coffin on the outside.

The inside of the face of the lid is lined with white satin, the centre piece being trimmed with black and white silk braid, fastened down with sixteen silver stars, four to each corner. The face, lid and top of the coffin is fastened together with five silver stars. The inside of the coffin is superbly lined with box[wood], plaited with satin, the bottom and pillow being of finest white silk, which rich three-inch chenille satin fringe encircles the entire inside.

---

115   Hugh McCulloch (1808 - 1895), was appointed treasury secretary by Lincoln on March 9, 1865. On the morning of the assassination, he said, "I never saw Mr. Lincoln so cheerful and happy." He finished his term under Andrew Johnson, then was appointed again under Chester A. Arthur.

Suspicious Circumstances

About three weeks ago a man named Atzerard,[116] represented as being a merchant at Briertown, Charles county, Md., went to the stables of Thompson & Naylor, corner of Thirteen-and-a-half and E streets, for the purpose of selling a stallion and a brown horse, blind in one eye. Atzerard made several attempts to sell the horses to the Government, but without success, and he finally disposed of the stallion to a Mr. Thompson, stage contractor to Port Tobacco. He continued to visit Mr. Naylor's stables, and in a short time reported that he had sold his brown horse.

On Friday afternoon a man named Havid (sic), who appeared to be intimate with Atzerard, came to the stable and hired a roan pacing horse, and shortly afterwards Atzerard appeared with a bay horse, which he left, telling the hostler to have it ready for him at 10 o'clock that night.

Upon calling for the horse at the appointed time, the hostler asked what had become of his friend Havid and the roan, to which Atzerard replied, "Has he not returned yet? He will be here directly." Some time after the hostler heard the pace of the roan coming down from the direction of the Treasury and went out to meet him, but the rider, apparently, wished to avoid the hostler and turned up Fourteenth street and down F. Hostler immediately went back to the stables, and fearing that Havid intended to make off with the horse, saddled another and followed him to the Navy Yard Bridge, where, in answer to his inquiries, the guard stated that a man riding such a horse had passed over, and was probably about a quarter of a mile in advance. John was also told that he might go over, but could not return before morning. He then came back to the stable, and hearing that a horse had been taken up in the street by the detectives, made some inquiries, and, after giving his statement to the Provost Marshal, was shown a saddle, which he identified beyond a doubt as the one used upon the brown horse when at Naylor's stable, and which he afterwards said he had sold.

---

116   George Atzerodt

Mrs. Lincoln

Mrs. Lincoln bears up under her terrible bereavement with becoming fortitude. The families of the members of the cabinet have paid her every attention, and many of our citizens have tendered her their sincerest sympathies, and striven to alleviate the fearful agonies of mind which she has endured for three days past. Mrs. Welles, wife of the Secretary of the Navy,[117] has been with her most of the time since the terrible tragedy occurred.

*   *   *   *   *

Daily Constitution Union
Washington, D.C.
April 18, 1865

AFFIDAVIT OF MAJOR RATHBONE

District of Columbia, City of Washington

Henry R. Rathbone, brevet major in the army of the United States, being duly sworn, says — that on the 14th day of April, instant, at about 20 minutes past 8 o'clock, in the evening, he, with Miss Clara H. Harris, left his residence, at the corner of Fifteenth and H streets, and joined the President and Mrs. Lincoln, and went with them, in their carriages, to Ford's Theatre, in Tenth Street the box assigned to the President is in the second tier, on the right hand side of the audience, and was occupied by the President and Mrs. Lincoln, Miss Harris, and this deponent, and by no other person; the box is entered by passing from the front of the building in the rear of the dress circle to a small entry or passage-way about eight feet in length and four feet in width. This passage-way is entered by a door, which opens on the inner side. The door is so placed as to make an acute angle between it and the wall behind it on the inner side. At the inner end of this passage is another door, standing squarely across, and opening into the box. On the left-hand side of the passage-way, and very near the inner end, is a third door, which also opens into the box. This latter door was closed. The party entered the box through the door at the end of

---

117   Mary Jane (Hale) Welles (1817 - 1886) was married to Gideon Welles (1802 - 1878).

the passage-way. The box is so constructed that it may be divided into two by a movable partition, one of the doors described opening into each. The front of the box is about ten or twelve feet in length, and in the centre of the railing is a small pillar overhung with a curtain. The depth of the box, from front to rear, is about nine feet. The elevation of the box above the stage, including the railing, is about ten or twelve feet.

When the party entered the box, a cushioned arm chair was standing at the end of the box farthest from the stage and nearest the audience. This was also the nearest point to the door by which the box is entered. The President seated himself in this chair, and except that he once left the chair for the purpose of putting on his overcoat, remained so seated until he was shot. Mrs. Lincoln was seated in a chair between the President and the pillar in the centre, above described. At the opposite end of the box — that nearest the end of the stage — were two chairs. In one of these, standing in the corner, Miss Harris was seated. At her left hand, and along the wall running from that end of the box to the rear, stood a small sofa. At the end of this sofa, next to Miss Harris, this deponent was seated. The distance between this deponent and the President, as they were sitting, was about seven or eight feet, and the distance between this deponent and the door was about the same. The distance between the President, as he sat, and the door, was about about four or five feet.

The door, according to the recollection of this deponent, was not closed during the evening. When the second scene in the third act was being performed, and while this deponent was intently observing the proceedings upon the stage, with his back towards the door, he heard the discharge of a pistol behind him, and looking around saw through the smoke a man between the door and the President. At the same time, deponent heard him shout some word which deponent thinks was "Freedom!" The deponent instantly sprang towards him, and seized him; he wrested himself from the grasp, and made a violent thrust at the breast of the deponent with a large knife. Deponent parried the blow by striking it up, and received a wound several inches deep in his left arm, between the elbow and the shoulder. The orifice of the wound is about an inch and a half in length, and extends upwards towards the shoulder several inches. The man rushed to the front of the box, and deponent endeavored to seize him again, but only caught his clothes as he was leaping over the railing of the box. The clothes, as deponent believes, were torn in this attempt to seize him. As he went over upon the stage deponent cried out with a loud voice, "Stop that man!" Deponent then turned to the President; his position was not changed, his head was slightly bent forward, and his eyes were closed. Deponent saw that he was unconscious, and supposing him mortally wounded rushed to the door for the purpose of calling medical aid.

On reaching the outer door of the passage-way as above described, deponent found it barred by a heavy piece of plank, one end of which was secured in the wall, and the other rested against the door. It had been so securely fastened that it required considerable force to remove it. This wedge or bar was about four feet from the door. Persons upon the outside were beating against the door for the purpose of entering. Deponent removed the bar, and the door was opened. Several persons who represented themselves to be surgeons were allowed to enter. Deponent saw there, Colonel Crawford, and requested him to prevent other persons from entering the box. Deponent then returned to the box, and found the surgeons examining the President's person. They had not yet discovered the wound. As soon as it was discovered it was determined to remove him from the theatre. He was carried out, and this deponent then proceeded to assist Mrs. Lincoln, who was intensely excited, to leave the theatre. On reaching the head of the stairs, deponent requested Major Potter to aid him in assisting Mrs. Lincoln across the street to the house to which the President was being conveyed. The wound which deponent had received had been bleeding very profusely, and on reaching the house, feeling very faint from the loss of blood, he seated himself in the hall, and soon after he fainted away, and was laid upon the floor. Upon the return of consciousness, deponent was taken in a carriage to his residence .

In review of the transaction, it is the confident belief of this deponent that the time which elapsed between the discharge of the pistol and the time when the assassin leaped from the box, did not exceed thirty seconds. Neither Mrs. Lincoln nor Miss Harris had left their seats.

H.R. Rathbone

Subscribed and sworn before me this 17th day of April, 1865.

A.B. Olin.

Justice of the Supreme Court, D.C.

THE LATEST DEVELOPMENTS
The Assassin at Mr. Seward's Arrested and Identified

Booth's Late Agent Attested, Etc.

The Assassin at Secretary Seward's Arrested

About three o'clock this morning, a man clad in coarse clothes, covered with mud and having a pick-agxe on his shoulder, was arrested entering a house occupied by members of the Suratt family on H streets, between 9th and 10th. On removing the mud from his person he turned out to be of much more genteel appearance than his disguise indicated.

He has since his arrest been confronted with those at Secretary Seward's, who saw the Secretary's assailant on Friday night, and he was at once identified as the man.

He said that his name is Paine, but the full particulars are not yet known. Surratt,[118] it is thought, was not a direct actor in the assassination, but seems to have been in some way accessory.

Upon the prisoner being brought to Gen. Augur's[119] headquarters this morning, Mr. Seward's colored servant, who was at the door at the time the assassin applied for admission, was sent for. The servant had no knowledge of the arrest of the prisoner, but upon entering the room in which the prisoner and a number of persons were, instantly exclaimed, "Why, here is the man that

---

118   John Harrison Surratt, Jr. (1844 - 1916) was one of Mary Surratt's three offspring. A Confederate spy and courier to Canada, he had been conspiring with Booth since late 1864. He was in Elmira, N.Y. on the day of the assassination. He fled to Montreal and then to England, then to the Vatican, where he enlisted in the papal guards known as Zouaves. He was identified by a former classmate also in the Zouaves but escaped arrest by fleeing to Egypt, where he was arrested upon arrival. During this time abroad, his mother was put on trial for conspiracy and executed. John was tried but released after a jury, heavy with Confederate sympathizers, failed to reach a verdict.

119   Christopher Columbus Augur (1821 - 1898) led the 22nd Army Corps that defended Washington, D.C.

cut Mr. Seward.''

Mysterious Movements

We received considerable information yesterday relative to the movements of several suspected parties, and refrained from publishing them, at the request of our own detectives and also those from New York; but the Herald of yesterday contained most of the matter, and of course the news cannot now be contraband, and we give it.

On Friday morning early, a man came to the Kirkwood House and entered his name on the register as "G.A. Abyeradt, Charles county," and after paying his day's board in advance to the book-keeper, he was assigned to room No. 126. On Saturday afternoon suspicions were aroused that something was wrong about that room, from the fact that the key had not been left at the office, and there was no other key that fitted the lock. Mr. John Lea, a government detective, was sent for, when he burst open the door, and there found an army revolver, a large dirk, and a bank book belonging to J. Wilkes Booth, with a bank credit of some $400. The knife was found secreted under the bed. The name on the register is written in a very bungling style, as though the party desired to disguise the handwriting; thus this is not so as the name on another hotel register is in the same style. This man, no doubt, was the party detailed to murder Andrew Johnson, now President. Occupants of the room adjourning No. 126 heard parties talking in that room up at 9 o'clock on Friday evening. It is hard to tell why this man or men did not execute their hellish designs. No doubt they were frightened off from the commission of their crime by a friend early informing Mr. Johnson of the assassination of the President, who at once put out all lights in his room, thus thwarting the murderers.

MYSTERIOUS HORSE — WAS IT BOOTH'S?

Last evening, a colored man named Adams saw two men drive down to the river on Buzzard's Point in a buggy and leading a led horse tied behind the carriage. On arriving at the river, they took the horse into the water and shot it over the left eye, leaving it for dead. The colored man thought he would get the carcass this morning for the skin, but on going for that purpose found the horse alive and able to walk. He accordingly gave information to the tenth precinct station, and Sergeant Hepburn had the horse taken to the police headquarters with a view to ascertain if it was the horse used by Booth.

Mr. Pumphrey[120] was sent for. The latter sent up a gentleman connected with his stables, who decided the animal was not the one hired by Booth.

The animal found is a dark bay mare, with black tail and mane.[121] It was at first supposed that the horse might be glandered or otherwise diseased, affording a cause for the attempt to kill it; but good judges of horses say that she shows no signs of disease, and is far too valuable an animal to kill.

P.S. — It is now reported that the horse was a glandered animal, which the owner, Mr. S. Fowler, had paid a man to take away from the city and shoot.

ARREST OF BOOTH'S LATE AGENT

Mr. Matthew Canning, formerly J. Wilkes Booth's business agent, and who previous to the war was the lessee of the theatre at Montgomery, Ala., and has since been acting for Mad. Vestvalli, has been arrested and brought to this city. Several years ago, Canning shot Booth in the neck, by accident, while on the stage at Montgomery, and the ball remained in his neck until 1863, and while performing at Grover's Theatre was extracted, leaving an ugly scar on the back of the neck. Canning is a Philadelphian by birth, and practiced law there previous to his engaging in theatricals. His first essay in this business was with the late lamented John Drew, as treasurer of the old Continental Theatre. He has always been noted for his quiet and gentlemanly demeanor, both in public and in private.

TRANSPORTATION OF MR. LINCOLN'S REMAINS.

The Hon. G.W. Cass, president of the Fort Wayne and Chicago Railroad;

---

120   James W. Pumphrey (September 12, 1832 - March 16, 1906), owner of the livery stable at C St. and 6th St. He would be arrested (along with every other conceivable suspect) but soon released.

121   Booth did indeed hire a bay mare with black tail and mane, but she had a star on her forehead. Booth would ride the horse as far as the Potomac, where he and accomplice David Herold shot both their horses before crossing the river into Virginia.

Robert H. Berdell, President of the Erie Railroad, and A. Stone, Jr. President of the Cleveland, Painesville and Ashtabula Railroad, have volunteered to transport the remains of President Lincoln over their respective roads to their final resting place.

SECOND EDITION — LATEST BY TELEGRAM — IMPORTANT FROM BALTIMORE — ARREST OF BOOTH'S HOOKSTOWN CORRE-SPONDENT "SAM." — HE MAKES A FULL CONFESSION OF THE DE-SIGNS OF THE CONSPIRACY. — BOOTH REPORTED IN MARYLAND WITH AN ARMED PARTY — CAVALRY ATTACK AND REPULSE — THE PARTY SURROUNDED — $10,000 ADDITIONAL REWARD OFFERED

BALTIMORE, April 18, — A highly important arrest has been made here; the name of the party is for the present witheld, though it is rumored to your correspondents that he has made a free confession as being one of the conspirators against the life of the President, and acknowledges himself to be the "Sam"[122] which was signed to the letter found in Booth's trunk.

[Second Dispatch]
BALTIMORE, April 18, — It is understood that the party alluded to as under arrest here, states that the original design of the conspirators was merely to capture the President, sometime back, make him a prisoner, and thus com-pell (sic) a general release of all rebel prisoners then held by us, that when the general exchange commenced this project was abandoned by him and others as no longer necessary. He says he refused to have anything further to do with it, and endeavored to induce others to give up their designs upon the life of the President.

This is substantially a correct statement of what the prisoner has so far divulged.

122   Samuel Bland Arnold (1834 - 1906) joined the conspiracy in sympathy for rebel prisoners, hoping to use the planned kidnapping of Lincoln to barter the release of prisoners. He abandoned the conspiracy after Lincoln began exchanging prisoners. Arnold would be sentenced to life imprisonment but was pardoned by President Andrew Johnson in 1869.

He is a well known resident of Baltimore.

[Third Dispatch.]

BALTIMORE, April18, — A gentleman who was at Point Lookout yesterday morning, was informed by an officer of one of our gunboats that Booth and other conspirators, about thirty in number, were in St. Mary's county, heavily armed, and endeavoring to make their way across the Potomac which was strongly picketed, and no one allowed to pass.[123] He also stated that on Sunday morning a small squad of our cavalry had a collision with them and had been repulsed, but succeeded in capturing one of them. In the meantime our cavalry were reinforced, and yesterday morning were understood to have them completely surrounded, and their escape was deemed impossible.

BALTIMORE, April 18, — The City Councils have offered a reward of $10,000 for the arrest of the assassin of President Lincoln. The feeling here against Booth is greatly incensed by the fact that he is a Baltimorean, and our loyal people trust that one who has so dishonored the fair fame of Baltimore should meet with speedy justice.

THE GREENSBURG ARREST.

PITTSBURGH, April 17, — The person arrested at Greensburg, supposed to be the murderer Booth, is reliably stated not to be him.

AGITATION IN MEXICO — A letter from Mexico states that Maximilian's[124] subjects are much agitated over rumors that the empire is shortly to

---

123   There was no such band of conspirators. Booth and Herold were alone.

124   Maximilian I (1832 - 1867), born Archduke Ferdinand Maximilian Joseph, was proclaimed Emperor of Mexico by Napoleon III in 1863. He is commonly believed to be the illegitimate son of Napoleon II (the son of Napoleon Bonaparte). He was supported by Mexican monarchists and opposed by the liberal forces of Benito Juarez. Maximilian was executed in 1867.

be invaded by large numbers of soldiers who have heretofore been fighting for Jeff. Davis' confederacy. Gen. Price is said to be one of the leaders in this movement, and it is expected that during the coming summer an immense force of our rebels will cross the Rio Grande, provided with arms, ammunition and other necessary supplies, and march to the assistance of President Juarez,[125] for the purpose of expelling the Europeans from the country.

* * * * *

The Age[126]
Philadelphia, April 18, 1865

THE LATEST NEWS BY TELEGRAPH. — THE GREAT CRIME.
THE ASSASSINS.

WASHINGTON, April 17, — Every effort that ingenuity, excited by fervor, can make is being put forth by all the proper authorities to capture or trace the assassins of Mr. Lincoln and Mr. Seward.

The Common Council of this city have offered a reward of $20,000 for the arrest and conviction of the assassins. To this sum another of $10,000 is added by Colonel L. C. Baker, Agent of the War Department, making the whole reward $30,000. To this announcement are added the following descriptions of the individual accused:

The description of J. Wilkes Booth, who assassinated the President on the evening of April 14, 1865: Height: 5 feet 8 inches; weight, 160 pounds, compactly built; hair jet black, inclined to curl, medium length, parted behind; eyes black and heavy, dark eye brows; wears a large seal ring on the little finger; when talking, inclines his head forward and looks down.

Description of the Person who Attempted to Assassinate the Hon. Wm.

---

125   Benito Juárez (1806 - 1872) served five terms as president of Mexico from 1858 to 1872. He resisted and ousted the forces of Maximilian I. He died of heart attack as his fifth term of office was ending.

126   Also in The Age this day: things settling down in in Richmond as all agree "the jig is up"; Rochester, N.Y. fears Confederate raid out of Canada; Mobile and Selma reported captured; a tale of blackmail and suicide.

H. Seward, Secretary of State:

Height, 5 feet, 1 inch; hair black, thick, full, and straight; no beard, nor appearance of beard; cheeks red on the jaws; face moderately full; 22 or 23 years of age; color of eyes not known, large eyes, but not prominent; brows not heavy, but dark; face not large, but rather round, complexion healthy; nose straight and well formed, medium size; mouth small; lips thin, upper lip protruded when he talked; chin pointed and prominent; head medium size; neck short and medium thickness; hands soft, and small fingers tapering, show no signs of hard labor; broad shoulders, taper waist; straight figure, a strong-looking man; manner not gentlemanly but vulgar; dress overcoat with side pockets and one on breast with lappels (sic); black pants of common stuff; new heavy boots; voice small and thin; inclined to tenor.

All the theatrical and concert saloon proprietors announce that their establishments will be closed until further notice.

Meetings are called for this evening of Pennsylvanians, Missourians, Ohioans, who are residents of this city and Georgetown, for the purpose of giving expression to their feelings on the late sad affliction of the country in the death of Mr. Lincoln, and to make arrangements for his funeral.

A meeting of the New York Club, for the same purpose, will also be held to-night.

Capture of Mr. Seward's Supposed Assailant

WASHINGTON, April 17, — A man said to be Surratt, the supposed assassin of Secretary Seward, has just passed up the avenue surrounded by a large cavalry guard, and followed by an immense crowd. Major Seward will be sent to identify him. As far as can be ascertained he is the man.

[Second Dispatch]

WASHINGTON, April 17, — Three men have reached headquarters who were arrested on suspicion in Prince George county, Md.

Neither of them proves to be Surratt, though it is regarded as quite certain that they know something of the conspiracy.

There are as yet no tidings of Booth.

* * * * *

Boston Daily Advertiser
Tuesday Morning, April 18, 1865

In the midst of profound grief, and even because of profound grief, the nation feels stronger, as a nation, than ever before.

Every calamity of war has undoubtedly increased the national strength. The nation had no conception of the loyalty that it could rely upon, when its flag was fired on at Fort Sumter and sadly sank before its enemies.[127] The nation had not the strength therefore, as a nation, which it had afterwards. The misfortune did not merely reveal to it the loyalty of its citizens, — it gave it a new force for attack and defence. It increased their willingness to bear and to suffer. The reverses at Bull Run,[128] at Red River,[129] at Chancellorsville,[130] all wrought similar results. It was observed even in the recruiting offices, that disaster, sufficiently marked to arrest universal attention, and to ripple for a moment the smooth surface of superficial prosperity, increased the number of

---

127   Fort Sumter was built to guard Charleston (South Carolina) Harbor shortly after the War of 1812. It was near the smaller and more weakly defended Fort Multrie, which commander Robert Anderson abandoned in late 1860 under threats by South Carolina, which had by then declared its secession from the Union. President Buchanan, feared that reinforcement of Sumter and other forts in the South would rile rebels, leading to further secession or even military aggression. But he dispatched a relief ship to Sumter on the last day of the year, and indeed the move sparked resistance across the South. The first shots of the Civil War were fired on January 9, 1861, by cadets from The Citadel, who succeeded in preventing the ship from entering the harbor. Buchanan did little else to prevent or impose federal control over Southern states. Lincoln took office on March 9.

128   The First Battle of Bull Run, fought near Manassas, VA on July 21, 1861, was the first major battle of the war. It was bungled and bloody, and in the end, the Northern forces retreated in panic. It was in this battle the Confederate officer Thomas J. Jackson and his Virginian brigade held their ground, earning Jackson the nickname "Stonewall."

129   A series of battles along the Red River in Louisiana in May 1864. The objective was to surround a Confederate army, capture Shreveport, and capture a large supply of cotton. Though several times larger than the Confederate defenders, the Union forces failed to achieve any of their objectives

130   A battle fought near Chancellorsville, VA on May 1-3, 1863 in which Confederate General Robert E. Lee's outnumbered forces defeated those of Union General Joseph Hooker. Losses were heavy on both sides, and Confederate Lieutenant General Thomas "Stonewall" Jackson was mortally wounded.

volunteers who offered themselves for service.

With every other great calamity, therefore, endured in a just cause, the death of the President would have made determination more stern and loyal more true, — and would thus have added to the strength of the nation. But it is not in this way only, that by this cruel death he serves the country which he so purely loved. The confederacy has personally attacked every citizen of America in this assassination. Every one of us feel that the President died, because he was where we put him. Had he been a hereditary sovereign we should have no such feeling. Had he been a usurper like Mr. Davis, we should not have felt so. It is because, by our votes, we placed this man where he was, that we feel responsible for his fall, — and responsible that such baseness shall reap no permanent success. The inevitable feeling of every heart in a republic therefore, is that assassination is a crime which belongs to despotism, — that with us it is a crime as aimless as it is wicked. If the Emperor Napoleon should be killed, we can conceive that there might be anarchy, but with us, every citizen is bound only the more closely to the cause of law and order the moment when it is felt that a drunken fool, acting under the inspiration of a barbarous system, can in a moment plunge a nation into mourning.

The distinction between a republic and a monarchy has been often illustrated as this war goes on. It is not understood in Europe. It will not be, outside of Switzerland, while Europe is the Europe of today. So much the worse for Europe. The people being sovereign, the sovereign is weakened when the President dies, by the loss of a most faithful servant, of the sovereign's best counsellor, who always gave true advice without fear or favor, and often could speak the sovereign's mind more closely than the sovereign himself could do. Over the corpse of such a servant, such a sovereign may well weep. But after his death, such a sovereign will be more sadly resolute against the revels who have given such a sign of their barbarism. The nation will not be more disposed to lay down the sword. It will not be more disposed to chatter about terms of amnesty. It will not be prone to sue for peace to what is left of a cabinet of perjurers, whose only friends are now engaged in proving that they are not the assassins the world supposes them to be. The sovereign feels the loss of his best counsellor. But he knows he can rely on all his other counsellors as never before. He has lost his strongest right arm, nay, his most chivalrous nobleman, who, beneath the simplest clothing of our common life, carried the heart of most sensitive honor, beating for friends and for enemies. But in the moment when his chief falls, — first among equals, — the spectator of the host looks round to see that every soldier left has new strength in his arm, new courage in his heart and new devotion to his country. For there is not one soldier in her host but himself has worked, by vote, by wish, by prayer, or by gallantry in the field, that there may be such a constitution and such a law, such a system and such a government, as placed this Chief Magistrate where he fell.

It is this principle which recruits our armies by millions. Despots never dreamed of calling forces thus into the field. It is the sovereign who takes the field in person. Such a system makes assassination to be the most stupid of blunders. For under such a system, assassination abolished every party, and, for a solemn year of truce, makes the nation absolutely one. If Mr. Davis has a secretary left him to counter-sign the proclamation, he may well proclaim for the wreck of his followers a day of fasting and penitence, when he notes the consequence of this last blow.

Had he himself died suddenly of a broken heart, — of some vision of coming vengeance, — of some sudden glimpse into Belle Isle or Salisbury, — or had some prophet said to him "thou art the man," so that he could not live a moment longer in the full consciousness of what he was, — the confederacy would have died with him. In an oligarchy like that there is no self-continuing life.

But in the murder of the people's friend, of the Chief Magistrate of a re-public, the republic feels, in the midst of tears, that she is stronger than ever. If only strength were all she has to pray for! If her strength would make her grief the easier to bear!

FROM WASHINGTON

Riotous proceedings — Arrests

WASHINGTON, April 17, — This forenoon several persons from Prince

George County were brought to Washington. As they were being taken to the Old Capitol prison a large crowd followed, increasing in number at every corner, although as a precautionary measure, the route taken was down back streets. The crowd was a motley one of all ages and colors. It being represented that the parties were Booth and Surrat (sic), and the report gaining credit as they reached the vicinity of the Baltimore depot, the cry was raised, "Hang them!" "Kill them!" and at the same time the prisoners were attacked with stones, and were struck several times, as were also the guard. Some orderly persons attempted to quiet the crowd by remonstrating with them, and assuring them that they were mistaken, but they failed to stop the riotous proceedings, which, however, were soon quieted. After the guard were struck a number of times, they faced about and made ready to defend themselves with their muskets. The prisoners were delivered to the superintendent of the prison, each of them having been somewhat bruised by the flying missiles.

Among other arrests today were several men in female apparel.

* * * * *

Wednesday, April 19, 1865

Every Person a Dear Relative

A colored woman, bowed with years
and clad in the habiliments of mourning,
obstructed the narrow passage
on the right of the coffin,
and with her faced bandana to her eyes,
with tears and sobs bewailed the Nation's loss.

For several moments did she tarry,
alternately gazing and sobbing,
until at length she was gently
reminded by an official
that other were waiting.

She stepped aside as we passed,
but remained to weep
as the cortege reluctantly
wended its way from the room.

The New York Tribune
Wednesday, April 19, 1865

The Booths

It is stated that on Saturday Ella Turner, a mistress of John Wilkes Booth, attempted suicide by taking chloroform. Booth, himself, was in Boston last Thursday, having previously made over his property to his mother, and said he was about to join the Confederacy cause. Persons of his acquaintance in Boston are confident that he has committed suicide. The following letter was written by Edwin Booth[131] on Saturday:

Edwin Booth as Iago

Franklin Square, Boston, April 15, 1865

[To] Henry C. Jarrett, Esq., of the Boston Theatre:

My Dear Sir: With deepest sorry and great agitation I thank you for relieving me from my engagement with yourself and the public. The news of the morning has made me wretched indeed; not only because I have received the unhappy tidings of the suspicions of a brother's crime, but because a good man, and a most justly honored and patriot's ruler, has fallen in an hour of national joy by the hand of an assassin.

Edwin Booth as Hamlet

The memory of the thousands who have fallen on the field in our country's defence during the struggle cannot be forgotten by me, even in this, the most distressing day of my life. And I most sincerely pray that the victories we have already won may stay the brand of war and the tide of loyal blood. While mourning, in common with all other loyal hearts, the death of the President, I am oppressed by a private woe not to be expressed in words But, whatever calamity may befall me or mine, my country, one and indivisi-

---

131   Edwin Thomas Booth (1833 - 1893) was John's older brother. He was considered one of the great actors of the 19th century, most famous for playing the title role of *Hamlet*. Shortly before the assassination, Edwin saved LIncoln's son, Robert, from serious injury, possibly death, by pulling him from the gap between a moving train and a station platform in Jersey City, N.J. Though Robert recognized the famous Edwin, the latter did not know the identity of the stranger he had saved until some months after the assassination.

ble, has my warmest devotion.

Edwin Booth

* * * * *

The Age[132]
Wednesday, April 19, 1865

The News of the Assassination in Richmond

General Ord Announces the Fearful Story at 9 o'clock on Saturday Night — Fears of the Rebels in the City — Mr. Hunter Leaves the Town — Flags at Half-Mast along the River

[Correspondence of the World]

RICHMOND, Saturday night, 12 P.M. — The terrible news from Washington has been received by only a few leading officers of the army, and government. It has just began (sic) to circulate in the city, but to morrow (sic) will be known far and near, by the trembling and alarmed Virginians, by the victorious soldiers, by the sailors in the river, by folks on lonely farms, who will ask, with foreboding, what it may mean to them. To us who have had it confirmed by a double telegram, giving so many details that it must be true, the horror of the intelligence has struck profound dismay and grief.

Lincoln in Richmond after it falls to the Union.

---

132   Also in The Age today: Massachusetts has 48,757 excess females; sectarian riots in Belfast; oil well fraud in Franklin, Pa.; governor of West Virginia recommends a day of fasting and prayer for his state.

There could be no canard upon such a story. Mr. Lincoln is dead. Sad be that sentence in the starred North, but ten times sadder for the crushed South, whose best friend in the administration lies in his coffin with the kindly measures he proposed.

How the News Came to Richmond

This evening, at 9 o'clock, General Ord, commanding this department, and Generals Ord and Mumford, rebel and Federal commissioners of exchange, were sitting in the room of Col. John W. Forney, in the Spottswood Hotel, when a telegram message was handed in conveying the intelligence of the President's death. The three Northern gentlemen were demonstrative in alternate bursts of incredulity, anguish, and indignation: but Ord said:

"That is the worst blow the Confederacy has yet had: Lee's surrender is nothing to it."

General Ord with wife and daughter on porch of Jefferson Davis residence, behind them the table where Lee had signed his surrender. Ord purchased the table, a marble-topped antique, for $50.

Soon afterward the company departed, but at this writing the news is diffused throughout the city. A vague sense of coming calamities oppresses the people like a cloud. Some say that the loss of the President sets back the war to Sumter. The people here are already anxious to express their disapprobation of the assassination, while the more radical officers are over-zealous to saddle upon the State, in advance of fuller corroboration, the whole responsibility of the deed. Mr. Hunter, ex-senator, I hear, left the town post-haste, and Judge Campbell also expresses a desire to be out of the lowering atmosphere. It is not the best news in the world for General Lee, who galloped into Richmond to-day with full staff, and has spent the night in close reticence. A thousand vague and conflicting rumors, sentiments, and deductions, are afloat, but we are waiting, hoping, desponding. Would that the morning were come!

OLD POINT, Sunday afternoon. — This whole day has been like one spent in a Morgue. Only rumors and testimonials of blood have marked our whole route down the river. Every flag is at half-mast except that of a French man-of-war off Fortress Monroe which may not have known that the head of the country is departed.[1] At City Point the news was pretty generally known this morning, and has just begun to agitate the camp. I fear some violence, and that in the first flush of indignation the innocent will be involved with the guilty.

Coming down the river to-day we passed a steamer filled with recruits,who exposed upon the upper deck a great placard, which would be read from either shore, saying: "President Lincoln assassinated!"

As this ominous announcement steamed by, the men displaying it standing uncovered, every piece of bunting on the river dipped to half-mast, and soon the broad river, far and near, was funereal with humiliated colors. The flag at the fort was depressed as well; we doubt no longer that Mr. Lincoln is dead.

No boats have come through to the fort since Friday, and there is not a journal of any kind to be bought at Old Point. This uncertainty and mystery increases the general awe and confusion. The City Point, on which I descended the James, will be permitted to go to Washington. The rest of my dispatches I shall send you from the national capital.

George Alfred Townsend[2]

Further Particulars — A Reign of Terror — The Rebel Prisoners declare they are soldiers, and applaud no assassins — How General Less received the news — He shukts himself up and refuses to listen to the details of the terrible tragdy — Marshall Law to be enforced with Strictness.

---

1   Fort Monroe guards the channel between Chesapeake Bay and three rivers flowing out of Virginia. Though in a seceded state, the fort was held by the Union throughout the war.
2   George Alfred Townsend (1841 - 1914), renowned correspondent for the Philadelphia Inquirer, then the New York Herald, then the New York World. His reports of April 17 - May 17 were published as *The Life, Crime, and Capture of John Wilkes Booth.*

WASHINGTON, D.C. April 17 — 7 P.M. — The reception in Richmond of the news of Mr. Lincoln's sudden death, regarding which I have sent you a despatch by mail, admits of further elucidation. Two steamers left City Point simultaneously — the City Point and Thomas Collyer. By conference with passengers by both of these boats, I am able to add some interesting items.

Libby Prison

At 11 o'clock on Saturday night the troops at Richmond and Manchester, as well as at the Libby Prison, Castle Thunder, and other guarded jails, were apprised of the country's loss. For some time there was every indication of a terrible riot. Those of the troops who had retired to their beds were awakened, and gathered in groups before the jails. Their indignation bade fair at least to lead to violence. The well-known turnkey, Dick Turner, was named as a candidate for the rope, and there was a general movement to burst through the guards and take him from his cell; but prompt action on the part of the commandants suppressed these endeavors.

A paroled officer at the Ballard House who explained that he was "damned glad Lincoln was dead," was set upon by the negro waiters and tossed into the street. He ran for his life. A young lieutenant on the City Point boat "thought that Mr. Lincoln ought to have been killed four years ago." He was with difficulty released from a crowd of passengers who meant to lynch him.

Many arrests have taken place in Richmond and the environs of parties who could ill conceal their satisfaction at the loss of their best friend in the councils of the nations. The authorities have declared that the disposition of the citizens warrants more stringent regulations. Passports, paroles, and safe-conduct have therefore been revoked in many cases, and the released rebels from Lee's army are forbidden to assemble or to go at large. Great terror exists in the Libby Prison,[3] and the inmates on one of the floors held a meeting,

3   A Confederate prison for Union officers in Richmond. It was known for its inhuman conditions. The Confederates later used it to hold their own military criminals. When the

and passed resolution that "they were soldiers and applauded no assassins."

When General Lee was told of the news, he shut himself up, and refused to hear any of the details. He said that he was already too fagged and weary to be unnerved with the terrible history.

Northern men of timid natures are hurrying away from Richmond, afraid that assassination will become fashionable. More intelligent rebels are frightened, and begin, for the first time, to do justice to Mr. Lincoln's sterling virtues. They urge that his life was in less danger in Richmond, among enemies, than in Washington, among his friends.

Booth, the assassin, is well known in Richmond, and an officer of Mosby's command is said to have been his old and favorite "chum." He used to date his nativity to Richmond, as if anxious to be considered a Virginian.

It is feared that the troops in the camps will vent their ire upon the paroled prisoners yet straggling through the country. Everybody is either in gloom or terror; there is no more thought of war. This private crime has absorbed all attention.

A town meeting is to be called, if the military authorities permit it, to express disapprobation of the murder and respect for the President's memory. Governor Pierpont is hourly expected in Richmond. The leading generals of the city have doubled their guard, and the picket lines around the town are strengthened. Rigid martial law will be the rule hereafter.

Geo. Alfred Townsend

* * * * *

Union captured Richmond, it used the prison to hold Confederate officers. After the war, a candymaker bought it, dismantled it, and moved it to Chicago.

The Ohio Statesman[4]
Columbus, OH
April 19, 1865

A False and Dastardly Charge

The [Ohio State] Journal of Tuesday morning, in an article headed, "The Rule of Secession," says, referring to the assassination of President Lincoln and the attempt to assassinate Secretary Seward:

"Those not actively engaged in the rebellion, but who, from partisan ties or other considerations, have been inclined to apologize for those engaged in it, and palliate their offense, should now feel themselves called upon to come over from those associations and renounce all fealty to a party having such proclivities. For although Democrats, as a party may disclaim the act, and but very few of the party are probably directly responsible for the enormity in which it has culminated, yet it is a fact that the assassination is distinctly traceable to the teachings of that party, and it behooves all honest men who are disinclined to share in such grave responsibility, to separate from the association of those who are to a greater or less degree answerable for the act aimed, as well, at the life of the nation as at that of the President."

Here are two distinct and explicit charges brought against the Democratic party as a class of citizens, and against every man belonging to it:

1. That Democrats are inclined to apologize for those engaged in rebellion, and palliate their offense;

2. That the assassination of the President is DISTINCTLY traceable to the teachings of the Democratic party.

As to both these charges, and other malicious insinuations contained in

---

4   A Democratic paper, the *Ohio Statesman* was founded in 1837 by Samuel Medary, an editor known for his acerbic pen. A *New York Times* article reporting his retirement in 1853 said, "Never were the flowers of rhetoric so systematically surrounded with thorns as in the columns of the *Statesman*. It is a study in that branch of letters; a department of its own.... No more shall we consult the current file of the *Statesman*, to refresh our gall-bladders and recruit our objurgatory vocabulary." The *Statesman* opposed the war and in 1863 supported a Peace Democrat for governor though the candidate was in hiding in the South. The newspaper's office was destroyed by a rogue mob of soldiers from a nearby military base.

the foregoing extract from The Journal, we brand them as false and infamous, and charge that the editor of The Journal knew them to be such when he wrote them down. They originated in a soul as corrupt as that of Judas, and were published from the basest motives.

It is utterly false, as the editor of The Journal, and every other intelligent man knows, that Democrats as a party are inclined to apologize for revolutionists or rebels, North or South, or to palliate their offense. On the contrary, the Democratic party, by its steady and determined opposition to, and denunciation of conspiracies, revolution and rebellion, wherever, and with whomsoever originating, has excited ire and incurred the bitter hatred of such principles partisans as he who now controls the editorial columns of The Journal.

But equally false and still more infamous is the base and dastardly charge that the assassination of President Lincoln is DISTINCTLY traceable to the teachings of the Democratic party. Nothing can well exceed the falsehood and atrocity of this charge. It is made by a man who knows, if he knows anything, that the Democratic party has been ridiculed, maligned and persecuted by him, and his political associations, because it taught implicit obedience to the Constitution and laws and a sacred regard for the rights of person and property.

But who is this that disturbs the funeral solemnities in which a great nation is engaged, with shouting at the top of his voice, that one-half of her citizens have been accessories to the assassination of her Chief Magistrate? It comes from a very small man — small in mental and moral stature — who has, for his political associates, men who have been engaged for at least four years, in fanning into greater violence the flames of disunion and civil war, reckless of the consequent bloodshed and slaughter - reckless of the wail of the widow or the cry of the orphan.

More than this, this malignant partisan charge comes from a man whose political associates sing alleluias to a conspirator, a murderer and a traitor to the Government of the United States — one who levied war against them, denied their authority, and resisted unto blood the officers of the national Government; and to their other crimes, he and his hand added the double one of murder and treason. Yet this is the man whom the editor of The Journal and his fellow-maligners of the Democratic party, hold up as an example, great and illustrious, and worthy of imitation, and call upon the people to sing anthems in his praise.

We do not charge that Mr. Coggeshall[5] and his political associates who thus elevate John Brown[6] to the rank of a martyred political saint, present an example for imitation and teach things to which the assassination of president Lincoln is DISTINCTLY traceable; but we do say, that it would be becoming in such men to withhold their malignant slanders of their fellow-citizens, till at least the funeral cortege has passed, conveying the remains of our late lamented President to their final resting place.

*   *   *   *   *

The Daily National Intelligencer[7]
Washington, D.C.
April 19, 1865

Intelligence from Richmond

We have advice and communication from Richmond to Monday last. The Whig of that day has the following expressive comments on the great crime which has convulsed the land:

ASSASSINATION OF PRESIDENT LINCOLN

The heaviest blow which has ever fallen upon the people of the South has descended. Abraham Lincoln, the President of the United States, has been

---

5   William Turner Coggeshall (1824 - 1867), editor of the Ohio State Journal, Ohio State Librarian, author, and U.S. Minister to Ecuador. He died of consumption in Quito, and his daughter, who served as secretary of legation in Ecuador, died four months later in Guayaquil.

6   John Brown (1800 - 1859), ardent abolitionist who started a militant liberation movement that culminated in his attack at Harpers Ferry, after which he was tried and hanged. Lincoln considered him a "misguided fanatic."

7   Also in the *Intelligencer* this day: Citizens of several states meet to express their states' condolences; Custer's address to his cavalry; a hymn by Rev. T.N. Haskel, of Boston, for Lincoln's funeral; Raleigh is occupied, the North Carolina governor captured.

assassinated! The decease of the Chief Magistrate of the nation at any period is an event which profoundly affects the public mind, but the time, manner, and circumstances of President Lincoln's death render it the most momentous, the most appalling, the most deplorable calamity which has ever befallen the people of the United States.

The thoughtless and the vicious may affect to derive satisfaction from the sudden and tragic close of the President's career, but every reflecting person will deplore the awful event. Just as everything was happily conspiring to a restoration of tranquility, under the benignant and magnanimous policy of Mr. Lincoln, comes this terrible blow. God grant that it may not rekindle excitement or inflame passion again!

That a state of war almost fratricidal should give rise to bitter feelings and bloody deeds in the field was to be expected; but that the assassin's knife and bullet should follow the great and best-loved of the nation in their daily walks, and reach them when surrounded by their friends, is an atrocity which will shock and appall every honorable man and woman in the land.

The secrecy with which the assassin or assassins pursued their victims indicates that there were but few accomplices in this inhuman crime. The abhorrence with which it is regarded on all sides will, it is hoped, deter insane and malignant men from the emulation of the infamy which attaches to this infernal deed.

* * * * *

Albany Evening Journal
April 19, 1865

The Nation's Grief

As these lines are being penned, a nation pays the last honors of affection to the mortal remains of the slaughtered President. The obsequies of the funeral are celebrated in Washington. But every city, village and hamlet in the land takes part in the imposing ceremonials of the hour. A Nation mourns; for the blow which has fallen upon it struck the fibres of every loyal heart. It is as when the destroying angel of the Lord passed in one night over Egypt, and there was no house found in which was not one dead.

Abraham Lincoln was emphatically a Man of the People. By the exhibition of qualities alike rare and honorable, he had endeared himself to the masses, until almost every citizen felt for him a personal regard and an individual interest. His perfect and almost childlike simplicity and unostentatious character; his earnest solicitude for the welfare of his fellow-countrymen; his heroic consecration to the duties of his position; his purity of Christian character; his freedom from any of those pomps and vanities which so often disfigure persons in exalted station, had won him a hold upon popular esteem unparalleled in the history of any of his predecessors since Washington. The remark was everywhere made when intelligence of the murder came: "I feel as I had lost a near and dear relative."

There is no partisanship in this grief. It is not merely sorrow for the loss of a great leader, but affliction because of the removal of an illustrious friend. They only refuse to join in its expression whose hearts are dead alike to patriotism and to principle. No sincerer or warmer tributes of regard have consecrated the memory of the great and good martyr, than those expressed by the lips and through the pens of men who opposed his election. Such universal commendation could have been won only by the most spotless virtue. In every home, every heart, rests the shadow of the mourning pall with which the land is draped.

The comparison is suggested between George Washington and Abraham Lincoln. Both were men of irreproachable personal character. Both were almost idolized by the people. Both led the Nation through a great crisis of suffering to victory. Both stamped themselves ineffaceably upon the thought and action of the times in which they lived. The work of one was a supplement to that performed by the other. Washington's mission was to instill into the hearts of his fellow-countrymen a love for Union – to create and fix the spirit of Americanism — to lay the bases of that compact democracy which has been able to withstand, unimpaired, the mightiest whirlwind of Revolution. Lincoln's task was to purify the Government, and remove from its escutcheon the dark stain of Slavery — to bring its life into harmony with the great principles of human Freedom — to establish justice and promote equality. We cannot think of Washington without remembering that his sword saved the infant Republic, and his wise statesmanship laid the foundation of "a more perfect Union." Future generations will immortalize Lincoln as the Great Emancipator, who struck the hateful chains of bondage from the limbs of the Nation; who gave emphasis in policy to the declaration of our forefathers, that "all men are created free and equal."[8]

Henceforward, the tomb of Abraham Lincoln will be, like Mount Vernon, a Mecca to the American people. As peace returns — as the furrows of sanguinary war are covered with the ripened growths of already up-springing industries — as the teeming millions who throng to our shores from every foreign clime, add strength to our sinews and energy to our character — as the fruits of this wonderful work are developed in the blessings the land will be permitted to enjoy — then, in the white light of history, when all differences are forgotten and the asperities which even still exist have passed into the gloom of oblivion — they who love best the cause of humanity, will make haste to inscribe upon the tablet of fame, beside the name of the father of his country, that of the Saviour of its Liberties.

* * * * *

Gazette & Republican
Trenton, N.J.
Wednesday, April 19, 1865

PROCLAMATION BY THE GOVERNOR[9]
To the People of New Jersey

The President of the United States is dead; he was murdered by an assassin.

---

8   The last line of a speech Lincoln gave in Springfield, Ill. on July 17, 1858: "I leave you, hoping that the lamp of liberty will burn in your bosoms until there shall no longer be a doubt that all men are created free and equal."

9   Joel Parker (1816 - 1888), governor of New Jersey twice (1863-66 and 1871-74), a Democrat supporting the war but critical of Lincoln's suspension of *habeas corpus* and perceived unconstitutionality of the Emancipation Proclamation.

The crime has no parallel in our history. Its enormity has astounded and almost paralyzed the nation.

At this crisis the death of the Chief Magistrate in such manner and through such means is peculiarly a national calamity. After four years of terrible war, the sunlight of people began to glimmer through the dark clouds, and while a joyful people hailed the brightening prospect, the blow fell. The ways of God are above our comprehension, yet in Him will we put our trust. "The Lord is high above all nations."[10]

In view of the sad and appalling event which engrosses the public mind, it is right and in consonance with the feelings of all good citizens that some general manifestation of sorrow should be made.

Therefore, I, Joel Parker, Governor of the state of New Jersey, do hereby recommend the people of this State to observe the day appointed for the obsequies of the late President of the United States, to wit,

WEDNESDAY, the 19th day of April instant,

By closing all places of business, by draping all public buildings in mourning, by assembling at the hour of 12 o'clock, noon, in their usual places of worship, and by such other demonstrations of grief and respect as are fitting to the occasion.

Given under my hand and privy seal, at Trenton, this seventeenth day of April, A.D. eighteen hundred and sixty-five.

JOEL PARKER

Attest: S.M. Dickinson, Private Secretary

April 18th

THE FUTURE

To-day the nation joins in the solemn expression of its sorrow over the sudden and violent death of its chosen chief. Terrible as the blow is, and painfully as it affects all true hearts, we are not destitute of consolation.

The attempt to paralyze the government of the nation by the simultaneous assassinations of its principal officers failed, and the constitutional successor

---

10   Psalm 113:4

of Mr. Lincoln assumed his place without shock or disturbance to the well balanced machinery of government. In the monarchies of Europe, the assassination of the reigning monarch is the signal for serious disturbance if not of bloody revolt. Here we lament the death of a great and good man, and execrate his assassins and those whose teachings led to the commission of the awful crime, but we feel no fears for the safety of the Republic.

No government except a government of the people, by the people and for the people, could so calmly bear so rude a shock. But by the wisdom of our laws, the succession to the Chief Magistracy is so simply provided for that no massacre — however widespread — could leave the government without a visible head. It was the confidence in a government of law, that enabled the people to bear the terrible blow without panic or despair. While all gave way to the natural emotions of sorrow and indignation, all felt that, terrible as the blow was, it had still left us the country, the Union, the constitution and the laws, and that the blow of the assassin — although destroying our greatest and best — could inflict no harm to the nation. Even that most sensitive barometer of public feeling — the gold market — showed no loss of confidence. On the contrary, through all these last awful days it has remained steady, showing the faith of the people in our great fortune.

For the great crime committed in the nature of the rebellion, justice demands the punishment — not only of the wretched instrument that aimed the blow, but of the traitors who incited and directed it. Mercy to the leaders of the secession rebellion would be cruelty to all true men. They have richly earned condign punishment, and must receive it. But this last desperate effort of treason, like those which preceded it, will fail to destroy the Union, which crushing all its enemies, is destined to centuries of a prosperity to which not even our former progress can furnish a parallel.

*　*　*　*　*

The New York Tribune
Wednesday, April 19, 1865

THE NATIONAL LOSS.

SECRETARY SEWARD AND SON IMPROVING. — The Would-be Assassin of Secretary Seward Secured. — BOOTH BROUGHT TO BAY — PREPARATIONS FOR THE FUNERAL — Delegations Wait Upon President Johnson — HE ADDRESSES THEM. — Lying in State.

Special Dispatch to the N.Y. Tribune

Washington, Tuesday, April 18, 1865

At an early hour this morning Pennsylvania ave. (sic) was thronged with people of both sexes, white and black, pouring toward the White House in order to avail themselves of the privilege of beholding for the last time the remains of the Nation's former chief.

The city — which, ever since the assassination, has been darkened with funeral decorations — still retained its mournful aspect; both citizens and soldiers generally wore badges of crape (sic); and, as the procession waited for admission to the western avenue leading to the White House, the minute-guns at long intervals boomed in respect to the memory of the sixteenth President.

Notwithstanding the preparations made, there seemed to be a great lack of officials to stem and regulate the masses moving toward the entrance to the Presidential Mansion. At 10 o'clock the gates were thrown open, and the vast crowd by half dozens admitted between the bayonets of soldiers of the Reserve Corps, stationed at the west entrance.

As last time the rear of the procession rested on fifteenth-st. nearly down to the avenue, and occupied the whole breadth of the walk to the gate, where it culminated in one vast, swaying, surging mass, which, as the bayonets of the guards were elevated for a moment, made frantic rushes to gain admittance to the avenue leading to the White House.

A large number, perhaps a majority, of those forming the procession were colored men and women of all ages and sizes, which had been drawn thither to look upon the inanimate form of one who, in the last four years of life, of perplexing cares, anxiety and turmoil, intensified by a war for the nation's existence, proved himself their's (sic) and humanity's friend.

Although the morning was cloudy a sultriness like that of Summer oppressed everyone, but, notwithstanding, the long column extending the length of nearly four blocks, remained sweltering yet patiently awaiting their admission to the presidential grounds. Every countenance bears evidence of sympathy in the nation's sorrow and every low toned voice referred in heartfelt words to our great calamity. As the main column neared the gate it was beset on either flank by the crowd which had there accumulated, and the struggle at this point for the position opposite the crossed bayonets was eagerly but not noisily contested.

"It isn't dat I car' for Massa Linkum more'n for any odder man," says an old gray-haired negress, who, with the sweat-drops standing on her ebony

Mary Surratt's House

brow, is holding her little grandchild over the heads of the people to prevent it from being smothered; "but I wants dis little chile to see de man who made her free." "Truly de good Lord has open de eyes of the nation," says another, "though dey kill Massa Linkum, wese got Massa Johnson and Butler left."

As the procession slowly moved through the entrance of the Presidential Mansion to the East room, where lay the body, the scene was one of the greatest solemnity. Many an eye was wet with tears from both sexes, and a stranger to the circumstances might have easily imagined, as the crowd filed by on either side of the coffin, every person a near relative of the deceased.

When the writer passed, a colored woman bowed with years and clad in the habiliments of mourning, obstructed the narrow passage on the right of the coffin, and with her faced bandana to her eyes, with tears and sobs bewailed the Nation's loss. For several moments did she tarry, alternately gazing and sobbing, until at length she was gently reminded by an official that others were waiting. She stepped aside as we passed, but remained to weep as the cortege reluctantly wended its way from the room.

Several naval and army officers were standing or seated around the room, which was draped appropriately in the robes of mourning. The expression of the face was serene and lifelike, but the skin was discolored, and appeared of a greenish yellow — probably recently made so by the embalmers.

The huge columns of the White House were completely enveloped in mourning, and all surroundings were in keeping with the solemnities of the occasion.

A number of persons suspected of complicity in the crime of assassination have been arrested to-day, and the scenes of yesterday repeated. Large crowds have been drawn together by rumors of the capture of Booth and abortive attempts made to rescue the prisoners, most of whom were arrested for the expression of traitorous sentiments.

How the Game was Bagged

Special Dispatch to the N.Y. Tribune

Washington, Tuesday, April 18, 1865

Late last night R.C. Morgan of New-York made a lucky strike in working up the assassination plot. Acting as one of the Special Commissioners of the War Department, under Mr. Orcutt,[11] he visited the residence of Surratt on H-st., between Ninth and Tenth.[12]

---

11   Not Orcutt but Col. Henry S. Olcott (1832 - 1907) was assigned by Secretary of War Edwin Stanton to manage and organize the flood of evidence that was flooding into the War Department. Also assigned: Lt. Col. John A. Foster and Col. Henry H. Wells.

12   This was the house of Mary Elizabeth Surratt (1823 - 1865), mother of conspirator John, who was in or on his way to Canada. she was the mother of three by John Surratt, Sr., an alcoholic who died in 1862. She managed her children and the family's tavern with great difficulty. John, Jr. failed to help much as he was busy as a Confederate spy and courier. In 1864, she moved to the house at 541 H St., where she rented rooms to boarders. Booth and

The women were put under arrest and sent to headquarters for examination. Then a search of the house was made. Papers and correspondence of a most important character were found, but the most important even transpired while search was being made in the garret.

A peculiar knock was heard at a lower outer door. The expert at once entered and opened the door, when a large man confronted him with a pick-ax in his hand. Stepping aside, the man entered rapidly and unbidden. Morgan then closed the door upon him, and quickly locking it, put the key in his pocket.

The stranger, here discovering that something was wrong, turned and remarked that he had made a mistake — was in the wrong house, &c. "Who did you wish to see," was asked. "I came to see Mrs. Surratt," said he. "Well, you are right, then — she lives here," was replied.[13]

He nevertheless insisted upon retiring, but a pistol was pointed at him and he was ordered into the room adjoining. His pick-ax was taken from him and he was ordered to sit down. Here a lengthy questioning and cross-questioning took place.

He stated that he was a refugee from Virginia; was a poor man's son; had been brought up on a farm; did not know how to read; had always been kept hard at work, because his father was poor, and then showed his oath of allegiance which he had in his pocket, and said he had worked on the horse-railroad here.

When asked where he lived, he boggled a little. When asked where he slept last night, he said, Down to the railroad. (sic) When asked where the night before that and Friday, he was still more embarrassed, and equivocated considerably. He said he came to this house to dig a drain for Mrs. Surratt; that he was to work at it early in the morning, and thought he would come up before he went to bed, as she would not be up in the morning.

It is proper to state that up to the question of where he stayed, no suspicion had been excited that he was other than a veritable laborer; but the fact

other conspirators visited often.

13   Mary Elizabeth Jenkins Surrat (May/June 1823 – July 7, 1865) would be convicted of conspiracy. She guarded firearms in her boarding house, where she conspired with accomplices. She and they, with the exception of her son John, would be tried, convicted and hanged.

of his coming at so late an hour led to suspicion that he might know something of the family connections.

Surratt himself having disappeared with Booth,[14] a glance at his boots covered with mud disclosed them to be fine ones; his pants, also very muddy, were discovered to be of fine black cassimere. His coat was better than laborers usually wear, and nothing but his hat indicated a refugee.

He was still further questioned, and on saying that he had no money he was searched and twenty-five dollars in greenbacks and some Canada coins found on his person, a fine white linen pocket handkerchief with a delicate pink border, a tooth and nail-brush, a cake of fine toilet soap and some pomatum, for all of which he tried to give a plausible account, though bothered a good deal about his taste for the white handkerchief in his possession.

Here his hat was explained, and found to have been made of a fine gray or mixed undershirt of his own, which he had taken off to make a cap of, cut out in Confederate soldier style, and not sewed up but pinned. This led to the conviction that he had lost his hat, and other circumstances fixed suspicion that he was the assassin of the Seward family.

The Secretary's negro doorkeeper[15] was sent for without the knowledge of what was wanted, came into the room and was seated, the gas having been turned down previously. After he was seated the gas was turned on brightly, and, without a word being spoken, the poor boy started as if he had been shot and the pseudo-laborer started also and turned deadly pale.

The recognition was instantaneous and mutual. On being asked why he seemed to affected, the negro immediately answered, "Why, dat's the man wot cut Massa Seward," and moving for a moment uneasily and with his eyes fixed on the prisoner, he continued, I don't want to stay here, no how."

Major Seward and sister were sent to identify him this morning and did so completely. His identification is absolute and he is now a prisoner on board a monitor. All of the circumstances connected with his arrest and detection are of the more marvelous character.

The detectives would not have been at the house but for the fidelity of a

14   John Surratt was in Elmira, N.Y. when the assassination occurred.

15   The doorkeeper, or "second waiter," was William H. Bell.

freedman, a poor colored woman, and the merest accident divested him of his well-assumed character of a poor laborer.

Other evidence makes it probable that he is one of the St. Albans raiders. He gives his name as James Paine, and is known here by several aliases. We hear his supposition is that, finding himself unable to get out of the picket lines he had returned to Surratt's house for succor.

An Important Arrest

Special Dispatch to the N.Y. Tribune

BALTIMORE, Md., Tuesday, April 18, 1865.

A young man named Samuel Arnold[16] in the employ of J.W. Wharton, a store-keeper at Fortress Monroe, was apprehended yesterday morning at that place on suspicion of being implicated in the assassination of President Lincoln and Secretary Seward, and brought to this city arriving here this morning in custody of two Government officers. Arnold denies any knowledge of the plot to assassinate the President, but confesses that he was concerned with

Samuel Arnold

Booth and other parties, about seven in all, in a plot to kidnap the President and deliver him to Richmond authorities previous to the arrangement of the cartel for exchange of prisoners by Gen. Grant.

He says he withdrew from the gang when Booth threatened to shoot him. An altercation ensued, but the difficulty was settled by Booth apologizing. Since then Arnold says he had had nothing to do with Booth; but letters and other documents found in his possession, signed "Sam," prove to the contrary. The prisoner was taken to Washington.

The steamer Arago arrived at Fortress Monroe from Charleston last eve-

---

16   Samuel Arnold (1834 - 1906) had been involved in the conspiracy to kidnap Lincoln but backed out when the conspiracy turned to assassination. He would be sentenced to life in prison but pardoned by Andrew Johnson.

ning at 4 o'clock, and sailed for New York soon after. Assistant Secretary of War Charles A. Dana   left Fortress Monroe on the steamer City of Hudson, direct for Washington, last evening.

The News in San Francisco — A Riot

San Francisco, April 16, 1865

The destruction of the Democratic newspaper last evening was not the result of any recent offensive utterances, but the sudden outburst of long pent indignation at their opposition to the Government all through the war. It was effected with such rapidity, and was so unexpected, that the authorities were able to do nothing to prevent it. At nightfall the military were in possession of the whole length of Montgomery St., the principal thoroughfare, and all approaches to it, thus preventing further violence in the quarter of the city where it was most to be apprehended.

The French organ L'Echo de Pacifique, was threatened, and is now under guard. The L'Union and American was destroyed. Intense excitement prevailed all night. Memorial services were held to-day in all the churches. Public meetings were held to express the public feeling, and the Mayor called one for this afternoon to prepare for the obsequies.

It is stated that the Democratic papers at Marysville and Grass Valley have been mobbed.

Two French men-of-war that have been lying off Santa Barbara, arrived in port to-day.

Arrived. Pacific Mail steamer Golden City, from Panama, with the mails and passengers that left New York March 23.

[Second Dispatch]

San Francisco, Monday, April 17, 1865

A large meeting of citizens was held at Platt's Hall on Sunday, the Mayor presiding. A series of resolutions were passed, among which was the following, which amply expresses the general feeling on this coast:

"The great, capacious, manly heart of Abraham Lincoln was generous enough to have embraced all within the forgiveness of its loving nature. And in their madness they have killed him. Before his death peace was possible. All the atmosphere was filled with generous emotions and kind sympathy. Now peace means subjugation or annihilation. God have mercy on the souls of the Rebel chiefs!"

When this was read there was a great excitement, and the people cheered over and over again. A committee of fifty citizens was appointed to make preparations for the obsequies of the President. All loyal citizens are requested to wear crepe for thirty days.

No disturbance of the public peace has occurred since the last dispatch. The military are still under arms, and patrols the streets at intervals. But there is no probability of further disturbance.

Dispatches from Nevada and Oregon show that those States are moved equally with California.

From Cincinnati.

Cincinnati, Tuesday, April 18, 1865

In response to the call of a number of prominent citizens, a large meeting was held at Pike's Opera House last evening. Mayor Harris was chairman of the meeting. He said there had been a disposition prevailing among some persons to use the terrible calamity which had befallen us as a pretext to raise disturbance. Up to the present time, although some property had been destroyed and no lives lost, he favored law and order, and would enforce them at all hazards. He hoped the people in Cincinnati had sufficient confidence in Gen. Hooker,[17] and himself to know that they would arrest and punish any one who would now utter a disloyal statement.

Gen. Joseph Hooker

Appropriate resolutions were passed, after which speech-

17   Major-General Joseph Hooker (1814 - 1879) was generally successful as a military leader but was defeated by Gen. Lee at Chancellorsville. He was known for his wild headquarter parties.

es were made by Judge Stover, Messrs. Perry, Shalfont, Gaddis, Noyes and Gen. [illegible].

The city is still draped in mourning. Business has not yet fully revived, but confidence is almost restored, and a better feeling prevails.

A Committee of six gentlemen were appointed to communicate with the proper authorities in Washington, for the purpose of having the remains of the president pass through the city when en route to Illinois.

The Lost Chief
by
Charles G. Halpine [18]

He filled the Nation's eye and heart,
as honored, lover, familiar name;
So much a brother, that his fame
Seemed of our lives a common part.

His towering figure, sharp and spare,
Was with such nervous tensions strung,
As if on each strained sinew swung
The burden of a people's care.

His changing face what pen can draw —
Pathetic, kindly, droll or stern:
And with a glance so quick to learn
The inmost truth of all he saw.

Pride found no idle space to spawn
Her fancies in his busy mind;

---

18   Charles Graham Halpine (1829 - 1868) was an Irish writer who immigrated in 1851. He reported for various newspapers and served in the Union army. He wrote humorous pieces, poems, and satire, sometimes under the pseudonym Miles O'Reilly. He died of a chloroform overdose.

April 19, 1865

His worth — like health or air — could find
No just appraisal till withdrawn.

He was his Country's — not his own!
He had no wish but for her weal;
Nor for himself could think or feel
But as a laborer for her throne.

Her flag upon the bights of power,
stainless and unassailed to place —
to this one end his earnest face
was bent through every burdened hour.

The vail that hides from our dull eyes
A hero's worth, Death only lifts;
While he is with us, all his gifts
Finds hosts to question, few to prize.

But done the battle — won the strife,
When torches light his vaulted tomb,
Broad gems flash out and crowns illume
the clay-cold brows undecked in life.

And men of whom the world will talk
Forages hence, may noteless move;
And only, as they quit us, prove
That giant souls have shared our walk;

For Heaven — aware what follies lurk
In our weak hearts — their mission done,
Snatches her loved ones from the sun
In the same hour that crowns their work.

O, loved and lost! Thy patient toil
Have robed our cause in Victory's light;
Our country stood redeemed and bright,
with not a slave on all her soil.

Again o'er Southern towns and towers
The eagles of our nation flew;
And as weeks to Summer grew
Each day a new success was ours.

'Mid peals of bells, and cannon bark,
And shouting streets with flags abloom —
Sped the shrill arrow of they doom,
And, in an instant, all was dark!

Thick clouds around us seem to press;
the heart throbs quickly — then is still;
Father, 'tis hard to say, "Thy will
Be done!" in such an hour as this.

A martyr to the cause of man,
His blood is freedom's eucharist,
And in the world's great hero-list
His name shall lead the ban!

And, raised on Faith's white wings, unfurled
in Heaven's pure light, of him we say:
"He fell upon the self-same day
A GREATER DIED TO SAVE THE WORLD."

* * * * *

The New York Times [19]
Wednesday, April 19, 1865

Programme of the Transportation of the President's Remains

The programme for the transportation of President Lincoln's remains from Washington has been issued. The railroads over which the remains will pass are declared military roads, subject to the order of the War Department, and the railroads, locomotives, cars and engines engages on said transportation will be subject to military control of Brig-Gen. McCallum.[20] No person will be allowed to be transported on the cars constituting the funeral train save those who are specially authorized by the orders of the War Department. The funeral train will not exceed nine cars, including baggage and hearse car, which will proceed over the whole route from Washington to Springfield.

The remains will leave Washington at 8 A.M. of Friday, the 21st. and arrive at Baltimore at 10.

Leave Baltimore at 3 P.M., and arrive at Harrisburgh at 8:20 P.M.

Leave Harrisburgh at 12 A.M., 22nd, and arrive at Philadelphia at 6:30 P.M.

Leave Philadelphia at 4 A.M. of Monday 24th and arrive at New-York at 10.

Leave New-York at 4 P.M. of the 25th, and arrive at Albany at 11 P.M.

Leave Albany at 4 P.M. of Wednesday, the 26th, and arrive at Buffalo at 7 A.M. of Thursday, the 27th.

Leave Buffalo at 10:10 the same day, and arrive at Cleveland at 7 A.M. of Friday, the 28th.

Leave Cleveland at midnight same day, and arrive at Columbus at 7:30 A.M. of Saturday, 29th.

---

19   Also in the *Times* that day: Raleigh captured; Jefferson Davis and family join Gen. Johnston at Hillsboro, N.C, as Union troops approach.

20   Daniel Craig McCallum (1815 - 1878), a Scottish immigrant, had been general superintendent of the New York and Erie Railroad before being appointed military director and superintendent of the Union railroads.

Leave Columbus 8 P.M. same day and arrive at Indiannapolis (sic) at 7 A.M. of Sunday, the 30th.

Leave Indianapolis midnight of the same day, and arrive at Chicago at 11 A.M. of Monday, May 1.

Leave Chicago at 9:30 P.M. of May 2, and arrive at Springfield at 8 A.M. of Monday, May 3.

At the various points on the route the remains are to be taken from the hearse car by state or municipal authorities to receive public honors according to the foresaid programme, the authorities will make such arrangements as may be fitting and appropriate to the occasion, under the direction of the Military commander of the division, department or district; but the remains will continue always under the special charge of the officers and escort assigned by the War Department.

The route from Columbus to Indianapolis is via Columbus and Indianapolis Central Railway, and from Indianapolis to Chicago via Lafayette and Michigan City. In order to guard against accidents, trains will not run faster than twenty miles per hour.

THE FEELING IN CANADA

Opinion of the Leading Canadian Journal — The Deep Regard and Affection Felt for the President — the Secessionist Carousing in Honor of the Assassin — A Plea for the Murderer — His Crime Justified.

From the Toronto Globe. [21]

ABRAHAM LINCOLN

At twenty-two minutes after seven o'clock, on Saturday morning, about nine hours after he had received the shot of an assassin, Abraham Lincoln drew his last breath, surrounded by members of his family, his Cabinet, and leading political and personal friends. His death would, under any circum-

---

21   The *Toronto Globe*, today called The Globe and Mail, was founded in 1844 by George Brown, a liberal who initially used the paper as the voice of the Reform Party, which he himself had started. He and the paper advocated the Canadian Confederacy which in 1867 established four provinces as the Dominion of Canada.

stances, have produced an extraordinary sensation, but accompanied by murderous violence, the feeling which has been created has been the most intense. No single event of the present century in America can at all compare with it in effect on the popular mind, and we think that in England the shock will be nearly as deeply felt.[22]

The grief which is expressed has two very distinct origins, the stronger of which seems to arise from personal sympathy and regard for the deceased. We hear in all quarters the strongest expressions of admiration of the character of Mr. Lincoln, and deep sorrow that his noble career should have been brought to an untimely end. His simplicity of character, his straightforward honesty, his kindliness, even his bluntness of manner, seem to have won the popular heart, even among a foreign, and, in matter of opinion, a hostile nation. We may judge by the fact of his popularity among the citizens of the Northern States.

Almost all of us feel as if we had suffered a personal loss. Mr. Lincoln is spoken of in the same terms as are used toward a familiar friend. All mourn his untimely fate. He had arisen by industry, ability and integrity to the great position of a Chief Magistrate of his country. He found it in the most imminent danger, and his power to control the elements which were sweeping over the land were far from generally acknowledged. He was regarded with fear and trembling by the friends of his government, and with contempt by his opponents. But steadily he made his way.

He was not the best man who could have been imagined for the post of Chief Magistrate in a great civil war. He had not the commanding force which infuses energy into all around him, and his public appearances were often lacking in dignity. But he was sagacious, patient, prudent, courageous, honest and candid. If he did not inspire great Generals, he gave every man in the army an opportunity of developing the talents within him. He recognized merit and rewarded it. He placed confidence, as a rule, where it was due, and he had his reward in great military successes.

Some say that he has been cut off at a favorable moment for his reputation, but we cannot accept this view. It seems to us that he had gone through his worst trials, that his patience, sagacity and honesty would have borne even better fruits in the settlement of affairs of the South than during the wild commotion of the war. He has been cut off at a time when, certainly, he had accomplished a great deal, but leaving much undone which he was well qualified to do. A naturally strong man, of only fifty-six, he might have hoped to live many years after finishing his work as President, in the enjoyment of the respect and admiration justly due to one who had saved the life of his country he will be held, we think, by Americans, if not equal to Washington, second to none but he. But he had not the gratification of his great predecessor, of seeing his work completed and enjoying for a long period the gratitude of his countrymen and the admiration of strangers. There are few so hard of heart as to not shed a tear over the sudden and bloody termination of so bright a career. As great as Washington is in many moral and mental qualities, his genial character was calculated to win far more popular sympathy than his predecessor. Ability and honesty all admire, but when to them are added kindliness, simplicity and freedom from selfishness, haughtiness and pride in high position, they win love as well as respect.

THE MURDER JUSTIFIED

From the Toronto Leader[23]

A man may, on the spur of the moment, be so maddened with rage as to strike another down to the earth; but if the accounts which come to us of the distressing affair are correct, the attack upon both Mr. Lincoln's and Mr. Seward's lives were concocted some time prior to the inauguration ceremony on the 4th of March, and only failed of accomplishment because one of the parties in the plot lost heart to carry out the scheme at that time. Would that he had never found it again! The act was not committed without due time for reflection as to its awful nature. For over a month the plan remained unacted

---

23   Founded by Irish immigrant James Beatty Sr. in 1852, the *Toronto Leader* expressed conservative and reform opinions. Beatty was elected to Parliament as a Conservative in 1867.

upon in the bosom of its author, and time seems to have added to the burning desire to carry it out. There must have been a strong feeling on the part of the person who committed the crime that a grievous wrong had been done, either to himself or to his country, by the President or the government he represented. Had a Southern man, during the four years of the war, taken the life of the President, there would be no difficulty in tracing it to a cause. We cannot so soon forget the numberless acts of wickedness committed in the South by servants and emissaries of the Northern Government; the beautiful homesteads leveled to the ground with demoniacal fury; the fair women violated by a ribald soldiery; the brave men shot down in the coldest blood on the insane plea of retaliation — all this and much more is still fresh in our memories, and serve to remind us that if the assassination had been committed in the heat of the war by a Southern man, who had so much to drive him to desperation, a reason for his conduct could readily be found. In the present instance these considerations do not help us to discover the cause of the assassination. That the deed was committed by John Wilkes Booth, a brother of Edwin Booth, the celebrated actor of the present day, there seems to be little doubt. But why should he make himself the champion of the Southern people or the Southern cause? He must have been goaded almost to the verge of madness. No man of ordinary nerve or trivial impulse could have jumped into a private box at the theatre, as he did, calmly shoot down the object of his wrath, then spring on the stage uttering words which serve to give a clue to the act of assassination, and ultimately find his way through the theatre to a place of escape. The man who could have done all this, must have considered that his chances of escape were very few indeed, and that, if the need were, he was ready to give up his own life for that which he had taken. There is desperation in such a thought —such a desperation as is caused by a deep consciousness of wrong-doing on the part of the persons against whom it is conceived.

* * * * *

Louisville Journal
Wednesday, April 19, 1865

President Lincoln's Death — The Spirit and Comments of the Press

To-day the burial ceremonies over the remains of Hon. Abraham Lincoln, late President of the United States, will take place in Washington City. The whole nation is humbled at his untimely grave, and as a befitting tribute to his memory we forego the discussion of ordinary events, and surrender our usual editorial space to extracts from various public journals touching the sudden and terrible calamity which has overtaken the nation.

The New York World,[24] of Saturday morning last, in the course of the leading editorial on the Presidential assassination, says;

"Our history has no parallel to this. Such grief as ours to-day is new to this nation's heart. Other Presidents have died while holding the same high place — Harrison and Taylor; but both died in the ordinary course of nature and the nation's grief then had no such pang in it as this which is now given by the shot of an assassin.

"The cry of the murderer as he leaped from the President's box and ran across the stage, 'sic semper tyrannis,' betrays no madman's frenzy. The plot included the murder of Secretary Seward also, and all the circumstances show that the same political fury and hate which lit the flames of the great rebellion inspired these hellish deeds; and by so much as these detract from the splendor of our triumph in its utter subjugation, by so much do they brand with a deeper and more damning infamy its plotters, its leaders, its abettors, its sympathizers, its character in impartial history.

"Let every city, town, and street, and lane, and house, and farm of the whole North become to-day but the wards of an infinite prison to shut in and

---

24   The *New York World* was published from 1860 to 1931. Under Joseph Pulitzer from 1883 to 1911, the paper gained popular appeal, especially among immigrants, not only through illustrations and sensational stories but also exposés of life in tenements, the Ku Klux Klan, and other worthy topics. In 1890, he built the New York World Building, the tallest in the world. Nellie Bly was a famous *World* investigative reporter. The paper published *The World Almanac*. It was known as a Democratic paper.

secure the villains who have done this thing. Let every man be an officer of the law to search them out and bring them to summary and condign justice. The machinery of government has already been set in motion, but let there be no escape for them if that fail.

"Into what proportions this calamity will yet develop, no human eye can now foresee. Its effect upon the political future of the nation will at least not be such as when a dynasty is overthrown. Our laws provide for the succession to such remote degrees that even assassination cannot leave the nation without a visible leader and head.

"Andrew Johnson to-day becomes the President of the United States, and the chief political consequences which will follow from this tragedy will be mainly such as his personal character and political opinions, especially on the subject of reconstruction, shall determine. May God give him wisdom to discharge worthily the duties of his great office.

The New York Times, on the morning succeeding the fateful evening when the intelligence of the deed reached that city, and as if too full of grief for utterance, contains only the following brief allusion to it:

"The events of last night in Washington will strike with profound horror the whole American people. At this moment of writing, we have only a partial announcement of the facts, and have neither the data nor the spirit for comment."

The following is an extract from the leading editorial of the Philadelphia American and Gazette on the 17th inst.:

"There is a singular array of circumstances connected with this murder which are well calculated to confound us — the manner in which it was executed, the strange impunity enjoyed by the assassin in his escape, as though the plan had been deeply laid and skilfully carried into effect. Perhaps the most painful feature of the event is that the murder took place in the presence of Mrs. Lincoln. The exclamation of the wretch after the deed was done, indicates that he is a Virginian, the Latin quotation being the motto of that State. It seems unacceptable that the assassination should not have been attempted during Mr. Lincoln's sojourn in Richmond, and still more so that it occurs at the moment when Virginia has submitted to the authority of the Union, and the armies have all surrendered or been dispersed.

"The act will, unfortunately, have the tendency to create a wide-spread and determined desire to put a stop at once to any disposition to deal leniently with rebels and traitors. This manifestation of reckless and instance malignity will engender a prevalent belief that with such a spirit abroad in the South magnanimity is a crime and a blunder. The result, therefore, will be not less a terrible calamity to the South than to the Nation.

"The Hon. Andrew Johnson, of Tennessee, the Vice-President, who becomes President by the death of Abraham Lincoln, is a man of whom no fear need be entertained in regard to his firm and unyielding devotion to the great cause. He stood true in the senate when all around were false, and in the hour when treason seemed to be an epidemic among the Representatives of the South. Throughout the whole of the war he has never for a moment hesitated to give him cordial support to the measures and policy of the Administration. By those who have known him longest at home he is regarded with attachment of the most remarkable description. We, therefore, entertain no fears for him whatever, and believe that he will be just as staunch a man as we need in this emergency."

The following touching references to the melancholy event are from the Chicago Journal [25] :

"The bells, toll they ever so solemnly, are totally inadequate to express the solemnity of the hour — a vain attempt to utter the unutterable woe. The weeks of sombre and white that clothe the city do not, cannot give any but a very trifling intimation of the city's sorrow.

"The tolling bells, the weeds of mourning, the bowed heads, the streaming eyes, the choked speech, the salient salutation how idle, after all, are all these to tell the story of our affliction, and to speak what we feel, as we sink overcome, overmastered, overwhelmed by this, the Republic's unprecedented

---

25   The *Chicago Evening Journal*, published 1844 to 1929. It first published the rumor that the Great Chicago Fire of 1871 was started by Catherine O'Leary's cow. The paper morphed and merged to become today's *Sun-Times*.

bereavement.

"We can but lay our faces on the earth in recognition of Him who holds the nations in the hollow of his hand, and turning an eye upward, mean the words that we cannot speak. Farewell to the good and faithful servant, to the second Father of his country, "with all kind love, good thoughts, and reverence." Farewell, Abraham Lincoln!

"Sleep in dust, with kindred ashes
of the noble and the true,
Hand that never failed its country,
Heart that baseness never knew."

The Philadelphia Age, the Democratic organ of that city says,:

"The country will be more than startled — it will be appalled by the announcement that President Lincoln was last night mortally wounded. Such an event would have been deplorable at any time, but at this juncture it is, humanly speaking, the greatest misfortune that could befall the country. He had shown recently so manifest a desire and intention to act with magnanimity and moderation in adjusting our difficulties, that there was a good reason to look for the speedy advent of a just and lasting peace; and it is the possible frustration of this hope that will at once suggest itself to every patriot. We are assured that there is every reason to fear that the wound may prove fatal. May heaven avert such a calamity!"

The Buffalo (New York) Courier[26] says:

"We have no words in which to speak of the awful crime, the appalling calamity, of which the telegraph brought us news last night. President Lincoln is murdered. Secretary Seward has, in all probability, received his death wound at the assassin's hand. We need not here recount the slender details given elsewhere.

---

26   The *Buffalo Daily Courier*, published 1846 to 1888, eventually becoming the *Courier-Express*, of which Samuel Clemens was an editor. The *Courier-Express* published until 1982, when its guild voted that it would rather go out of business than let the paper be bought by Rupert Murdoch's News America Publishing Co.

"This is a horror unspeakable, and the mind staggers in the attempt to contemplate either the fact itself or its possible results. Not this country alone but civilization received a shock from the blow by which our President has fallen. To find a parallel for the hideous event we must go back a thousand years, and seek for it in the annals of the most barbarous nations. It must needs be a calmer moment than this in which the people shall attempt an observation of their new and sorrowful situation. Let it suffice for the present to say that the hand of the fiend incarnate who smote down President Lincoln last night has been guided by a hellish inspiration of sagacity. God save the Republic in this its dark hour."

The St. Louis (Missouri) Democrat[27] says:

"Of all the occurrences within the range of possibility, the assassination of our President in Washington, at this triumphant stage of the war, and while he was devoting himself in the most liberal spirit to an adjustment with the rebels, was perhaps the one event never thought of, still less looked for. The intelligence of it came with a force the more astounding and appalling because the land was just then decking herself in the riches regalia of joy — a joy in which gratitude and esteem toward the President were largely intermingled. The intense and universal expression of profoundest mourning testifies how deeply, in the hour of our country's deliverance, the personal and official worth of Abraham Lincoln have enshrined him in the hearts of his countrymen.

"He is dead. It is now a poor satisfaction to pour courses on the head of the wretch who perpetrated the strange crime. The severest punishment will avail little to repair the immense mischief wrought, and nothing to assuage the nation's sorrow. The assassin may well be left to a calm investigation of the motives which influenced him, and to dispassionate justice. There is too much deep grief for hate. The heroic statesman to whom has been twice confided the ark of our political salvation, on whom all eyes have been fixed, whom form and lineaments, and character have become indelibly engraven upon the popular mind, and endeared to the popular heart, is suddenly cut down at the helm of

27   The *Missouri Democrat,* founded in 1852, eventually merged with the St. Louis Globe. It was conservative but anti-slavery. The *Globe-Democrat* closed in 1982.

affairs. Worthy honors are to be paid to his high merit and historic name. This is a great work, but it is one which the hearts of the people and the genius of the nation will well perform. His patriotic influence will continue and become invested with a moral power which it never before possessed. The holy cause of the union will only be the holier and dearer because Mr. Lincoln has crowned his labors for it with his blood. The popular devotion to liberty and nationality was never lessened, and never will be, by the martyrdom of their champions. From his official and personal influence over his countrymen, he has passed to a grander and loftier sphere, from which, with Washington and Jackson, he will wield a more potent scepter through all coming time. If doomed rebellion could have added a final seal to its infamy and damnation, it has affixed that seal to the assassination of the nation's twice chosen leader."

The Chicago Times (Democratic) says on the 17 inst.:

"It is yet to be known whether Mr. Lincoln and Mr. Seward were the victims of a rebel conspiracy or of drunken insanity. We can understand why desperate rebel leaders should wish to strike them down. Events of the two days prior to the occurrence of the tragedy disclosed the adoption by Mr. Lincoln of a conciliatory policy toward the rebellion, under which Virginia, by the action of her leading public men, had inaugurated a movement toward reconciliation; and it is very well known that this policy had something more than Mr. Seward's concurrence. Virginia thus withdrawn from the rebellion, what ground of hope would remain for it? What, in the minds of desperate rebel leaders, more likely to change this conciliatory policy and defeat the Virginia movement than the death of Mr. Lincoln and Mr. Seward? If the assassinations were the result of conspiracy, this is the solution. If they were the work of insanity only — and it is to be hoped, for the credit of human nature, that they were — then rebellion has not crowned its crimes with an unpardonable sin.

"There are not on this day mourners more sincere than the Democracy of these Northern States. Widely as they have differed with Mr. Lincoln — greatly as their confidence in him had been shaken — they yet saw in the indications of the last few days of his life that he might command their support in the close of the war, as he did in its beginning. These indications inspired them with hope, and confidence, and joy, which are now being dashed to the ground. The Democracy may well mourn the death of Abraham Lincoln.

"The country may be happily disappointed in his successor. This is a possibility, though not a probability. At this writing, the Intelligence is that Mr. Seward is still living, and that he may recover. We pray God that he will. His life has a new value now, since the chief command has fallen into so uncertain hands."

The Chicago Tribune (Republican) says:

"No man but Abraham Lincoln could restrain the American people from visiting righteous wrath upon the heads of the wicked leaders of the accursed rebellion. No living man possessed the confidence and affection of the people and army as he. To the judgment of no other man would they defer to cheerfully and willingly. He possessed a marvellous power over the minds of the people; they reposed unlimited faith in his sagacity, integrity, honesty, and soundness of judgment. He could do almost whatever he pleased, because he never abused the confidence of the people, never betrayed their trust — because he was solely actuated by a sense of duty and patriotism. He ever tried to do what he conscientiously believed to be right. Right was his polar star; conscience was his monitor, and he tempered all his dealings with the rebels with forbearance and mercy. He harbored no particle of animosity. He never felt that sensation of revenge in his life; he never hated a human being. His millions of admirers and friends never found but one fault, and that was with his excess of lenity and kindness toward public enemies. It made his heart bleed to sign the death warrant of the worst guerilla assassin or rebel spy; he thought no evil, he wished no human being harm; he was the embodiment of Christian precepts and virtues the Chair of State, made vacant by his death, there is none in the land — no, not one, able to fill it as he filled it. An age produces but one Washington. Abraham Lincoln was the Washington of this generation — the second Father of his Country. In his untimely death a heavy calamity has fallen upon the American people."

The Chicago Post (Democratic) expresses itself in the following appropriate terms:

"The American people have cause for grief such as no other people have ever had. A nation mourns not alone for her Executive and her Minister of State, but for the shame that any one who has ever borne the name of American should sully the pages of history with such an atrocious deed.

"The rebellion has added another to its long record of bloody crimes. Treason stalked with fire and sword through the land, carrying desolation and ruin in its progress. Its four years of existence have been four years of blood — of blood spilled under the flimsy pretext of belligerent rights, and under the forms of war. But now, when its armies have been overcome, and its powers of armed resistance destroyed, it resorts to the assassin's pistol and the knife. Woe be to that man who took upon himself the bloody office of assassin! Woe be to those men, North or South, who may be found counsellors, advisors, or approvers of the deed! Woe be to that rebellion in whose behalf and in whose interest this fearful tragedy has been enacted. When the present profound grief shall have in some degree lost its intensity, the American people will demand a retribution equal in magnitude to the calamity that has been wrought. Where that retribution will end, and where it will be visited, it is not difficult to imagine.

"The present and future effect of this horrible affair upon the country it is impossible to predict. It may revolutionize for a while the country, or, more properly speaking, may paralyze it temporarily; but let us hope that the awful occurrence will duly impress the public mind with the fearful character of the present condition of affairs.

"Mr. Andrew Johnson has already been inaugurated as President. Let us hope that the country will unitedly give him that support and that encouragement that will enable him to bring the country forth from the fearful and appalling circumstances which now surround it.

"We have faith that Andrew Johnson will prove equal to the duty before him. If he be weak, the greater the reason for supporting him. Let us forget the past, and clinging to the one great end, the rescue of our country, let us stand by the Government, because that Government is all that stands between us and utter ruin, desolation, anarchy, and assassination."

The Cincinnati Commercial[28] of the 17th says:

"The bullet that pierced the head of President Lincoln touched the heart of the nation. No event since the death of Washington has so filled the land with sorrow.

"Added to the grief that would have been felt at the death of one so well respected as President Lincoln, is the unspeakable indignation and horror at the manner of his taking off, which we cannot help ascribing to a fanatical sympathy with the blackest and bloodiest treason that the world ever saw.

"Then it is a reflection, full of mournfulness that words are weak to tell, that after a life of such hard labor, and years of such harassing anxieties, seasons of the deepest gloom, and no intermission in the heaviest cares, President Lincoln should be struck down just as he had gained the public confidence and appreciation — in the blaze of victory and the dawn of peace.

"We can only trust that in his case, as in that of the assassination of William of Orange,[29] the passionate grief of the people will strengthen their public spirit, animate every bosom to serve the country with a higher devotion than ever, and that thus, under Divine Providence, whose mysterious ways to perform wonders the ages testify, as the poet sings, good may be wrought out of calamity, that, to the finite senses, seems almost unbearable."

The Cincinnati Times, in the course of a very fine editorial, speaks as follows:

"Booth — a name henceforward to be mentioned in hours of darkness as a sound of terror — to be whispered for all ages in the ears of children, as hideous gnomes and ghouls are whispered — to be our Guy of Faux,[30] with

---

28   Published 1846-1883 (and later under different banners), the *Commercial* was the first place "copperhead" was published with the meaning of "anti-war democrat."

29   William I, Prince of Orange, a.k.a. William the Silent (1533 - 1584) led the Dutch against the Spanish, which was occupying part of Holland. He was assassinated by Balthasar Gérard.

30   Guy Fawkes, the infamous English Catholic who planned the Gunpowder Plot to

hues of murder for the old traditional picture under the vaults of the Commons which stills the babes of England — was but an instrument, such as his pistol and his dagger. The real ruffian is the rebel chief. Place his features upon the shoulders of his emissary, and we shall have an epitome of the great tragedy.

"The world will read it so. Ever will men see a double figure stalk at midnight, with blood upon its garments. Ever will they shrink before the brandished steel held by the burly hand of Booth, bearing the countenance of Davis. Ever will their hearts chill at the thought of a little sharp report, a cruel puff of smoke, and the prostrate form of a great and good man, who would not have harmed a fellow-being in the world. And ever will they cry for vengeance. Vengeance! Why, what have these to pay for their dark deed? Can they render back this pure life by their's of perjury and murder? Can such as they pay down the price of the treasure they have stolen, or mend the golden bowl that's broken at the fountain, or twist again the silver cord that's loosed?

"Yet retribution is a goodly thing,

And it were well to wring the payment from them

Even to the utmost drop of their heart's blood."[31]

"They cannot escape. The gyves are already on their wrists. The earth dare not conceal them. They may not hide themselves upon the multitudinous seas incarnate.[32] The very rays of light, the stars, the quiet beams of the moon will point them out; and speedily the cause which this vile murder was meant to prop will sink into the bowels of that sacred soil which will never cast it up again."

The Baltimore American[33] says:

"The President has been murdered. At the time when he had become most endearing to the nation, at the moment when the war was of the past, and

---

blow up Parliament and assassinate King James in 1605.

31   From *MacBeth,* act 2, scene 2: "Will all great Neptune's ocean wash this blood Clean from my hand? No; this my hand will rather/ The multitudinous seas incarnadine..."

32   The *Enquirer* has been published continuously since 1841. During the Civil War, it was owned by a "copperhead" (anti-war) Democrat.

33   The paper's roots go back to the *Maryland Journal* of 1773. It was published continuously until 1986, when it was the *Baltimore News-America*.

he was bending the energies of his mind and the kindly feelings of a character more than usually forgiving toward the pacification of the country, Mr. Lincoln has been basely, cowardly and traitorously assassinated. Whilst surrounded by hundreds who would have given their lives to save his, with his wife by his side and his friends around him, the ball of the assassin, directed by that foul and traitorous spirit which has brought so many woes upon the country, reached his brain, and the President of the nation, the friend of the people, is no more.

"We have no words to express the feelings which this terrible event will excite. Its awful suddenness has overwhelmed us as it will overwhelm the country today. No language can adequately depict the sadness with which our people will turn from their rejoicings to mourning over an event that will stir up their deepest and most mournful feelings. Abraham Lincoln is dying. What more can we say." (sic)

The Cincinnati Enquirer (Democratic) says:

"This is one of the most awful pages in the dread history of the last four years, sustained as it is with horrors, and rendered bloody with crime. The hand of affliction has indeed been laid heavily upon our people, and we have been visited with the most dreadful ills that can scourge a nation, or render ill its tenure of existence painful and insecure.

"Fondly do we express a hope that the history is near its conclusion, and that the murder of our chief rulers in high places is the culminating leaf of an atrocious record, and that our darkest hour has passed, soon to be succeeded by a brighter dawn.

"In this connection we regret to hear or see a political allusion, for we scorn the thought that there is or can be any politics that will not detest and ab-hor the act of private murder, or any party that will not vie with its antagonists in condemning the first and great primal crime of our nature. It is the duty, as it should be the aim, of all to use their influence in calming passion to oppose hatred and prejudice, and to exercise the simplest act of believing without the strongest proof to the contrary, that there are men amongst us so base that they deplore with all their heart and soul this dark shadow of death that now rests upon the land."

The Nashville Union[34] says on the 16th inst.:

"Abraham Lincoln was a great and good man, and his administration of the Government, whatever may be the future career of our nation, will ever be regarded as one of the extraordinary sagacity, vigor, and efficiency. And he will always be regarded as a public benefactor, our second Washington.

"Penetrated with grief by the nation's great affliction, we have no heart to go into an investigation of the probable motives which impelled the assassin to fire the fatal shot. We bow in deep humiliation, amazed that any one with a human heart could be found to perpetrate so dastardly a crime, and trust to the justice of God for its punishment."

The above extracts from the press, both Democratic[35] and Republican,[36] indicate to the reader the profound public grief which the death of Abraham Lincoln has carried to the nation's heart.

INCIDENTS OF ARMY LIFE
SAD SCENES IN THE LIFE OF A CHAPLAIN
Trials and Executions for Desertion

Executions for desertion are common nowadays in the Armies of the Potomac and the James. As many as sixty of the captured runaways have been confined at one time in the provost marshal's prison camp of a single division. The "bull pen" as this enclosure is universally called, is a collection of tents

34   The *Nashville Union* published in 1862 as the *Daily Nashville Patriot*, changing its name to the *Nashville Daily Union* in 1864. A pro-Union paper, it was one of few southern papers to survive the war. It closed in 1866.

35   The Democratic Party, originally called the Democratic-Republican Party, came to power in the election of 1800. It advocated strict adherence to the Constitution, states' rights, and Jeffersonian principles. The party split over the nomination of James Monroe, becoming the Democratic Party, though no Republic Party was created at the time. The other main party at the time, the Whigs, would become divided on the slavery issue, and as it split up, the Lincoln's Republican Party emerged. During the Civil War, the Democrats of the North were divided into War Democrats and Peace Democrats. (The Confederate States had no political parties.)

36   The Republican Party was founded in 1854 by ex-Whigs who had disagreed with their party's pro-slavery stance, ex-Free Soilers (of a party that had opposed slavery), abolitionists, and others who saw a need for radical changes in government. Lincoln was the first Republican president, and Republicans held the majority in Congress during his terms.

surrounded by a close stockade of pine logs twenty feet high, guarded on all sides. Just at the right of the entrance, outside of the walls, is a small log cabin, used as the condemned cell. The man who enters that goes out only to his execution.

Sad stories of remorse and agony the walls of that low, dark, gloomy cabin could tell. As soon as convenient after a deserter is arrested on his way to the enemy or to the rear, and charges are preferred against him, he is tried before a general court-martial. The decision in his case is not promulgated until it has received approval at department headquarters. If a man is sentenced to death he knows nothing of the verdict until the order comes for his speedy execution. His suspense meantime is often terribly trying. Recently seven men who had deserted together, and against whom the evidence was clear, were suddenly ordered back to their regiment, when they anticipated death. The commanding General had noted a fatal error in the proceedings of the court, and had disapproved of its findings. These acts of leniency gave encouragement to many a prisoner who had before then been despondent. But the next move changed the current of feeling.

A soldier arrested one day was tried the next, and shot the third. Again, two men who had been tried four weeks before, and from the long delay now

Procession of Deserters

felt quite easy as to their prospects, were taken to the condemned cell, and thence to the gallows. Two or three days later, another, whose trial had been long previous, was out under guard cutting wood in the forest when a provost's deputy came, and putting handcuffs on him, led him back to that dreary cabin. Then the remaining inmates of the pen trembled. As the new victim was led out to be shot the provost called a bright-faced lad from the gazing throng at the entrance of the bull pen to enter the condemned cell. The lad's face blanched as he obeyed the summons, but he was only ordered to carry back the blanket of the culprit leaving for the field of death, and it was with a flushed face of grateful joy that he bounded back to the guarded pen, saying, as he drew a long breath, "I tell you! I thought they'd got me then." He was probably awaiting the promulgation of his sentence.

The Evil Work of the Bounty-Broker

Although desertion is one of the gravest crimes known in military law, and from its frequency merits extremest penalty, yet it does not follow that a soldier convicted of it is a vile and abandoned wretch. There are so many now at the North to advise and encourage desertions, and so many to entrap and swindle the ignorant and the unfortunate, that many an officer here at the front wishes that the broker or the provost, or the State agency, might be shot, instead of the deluded victim. Now and then a man is caught who richly deserves his punishment. One of the two hung as above mentioned was a professional bounty-hunter. He confessed to having deserted twice before, and to the third attempt he had planned the addition of robbery, and, if the necessity arose, murder.

On the other hand, the lad shot so soon after his arrest was a green Irish boy of nineteen but weeks in the country. His sister came to America several years since, and he had now toiled to find her. A substitute runner met him on the dock in New York, and offering him work, hurried him off to Bridgeport, enlisted him after getting him half drunk, took most of his money — the remainder being stolen at New Haven; and the lad reached here penniless, homesick, bewildered. Hearing of his sister's whereabouts, he was told he could easily go find her, and was advised to start. His shrewd comrades escaped. He was taken, and his life was the forfeit.

* * * * *

Macon Daily Telegraph & Confederate[37]
Macon, Ga.
Wednesday Morning, April 19, 1865

SEND IN YOUR NEGROES.

Owners of slaves in the vicinity of Macon are earnestly requested to notice the call of Lieutenant Colonel R.W. Frobel, for negroes to work on the fortifications around the city. There should be no resistance — no delay. They are wanted — and wanted at once. And let each one who sends a negro send with him a shovel, spade, or pick, or other suitable tool.

The fortifications are in a tolerable good condition, and, with a few days' labor such a force as the city and neighborhood can send, can be put in such a condition that a very few determined troops can successfully defend the city against the force which took Columbus.

Citizens of Macon! We appeal to you to send your servants with working tools, and aid in making a gallant defense of your families and hearth stones. You can save the one from insult and the other from spoilation if you will. Let not the disgraceful surrender of Montgomery be reenacted at Macon. Let it not be published that a mere handful of Yankees trotted unmolested through Georgia as they did through Alabama.

You can save the city if you but try.

Then send your slaves with working tools to Col. Probel at once — don't wait until morning — but send them this afternoon that they may be put to work.

———

Religious Notice

In view of the near approach of the enemy, and of the possibility that our opportunities for prayer may never hereafter be as they have hitherto been, the praying people and the believers in prayer in the city of Macon, are invited to unite in one more prayer, for our country, at 4 o'clock this afternoon (19th inst.) in the basement of the Presbyterian church.

---

37   Ecclesiastes 3:1 "To every thing there is a season, and a time to every purpose under the heaven."

BARRICADE THE STREETS.

There is considerable amount of cotton in Macon, which, as it cannot be destroyed where it is, or hauled now in time to a place where it can be destroyed without endangering the city, could be made to answer a valuable purpose in a military point of view.

We would suggest that all, or as much of it as possible, be used at once to barricade the streets. This is the best use it can be put to, and can be made serviceable. Let it be done at once, and if the enemy make a break in the outer defenses, this will prove a serious barrier to his entrance to the city, and, with trusty sharpshooters behind, might possibly defeat the enemy at last.

Let the cotton be thus used. We should avail ourselves of every means of defense at our command.

RANAWAY

From the subscriber, on the 9th inst., a negro man, named Charles, 25 years of age, dark complexion, about 5 feet 11 inches high, said negro was bought by me of Col. R.A. Crawford, of Macon, and may be trying to be back to that place. I will pay $100 reward for the negro, delivered to me, or lodged in jail so I can get him.

C.C. Brown

Morgan, Calhoun Co., Ga.

* * * * *

North American and United States Gazette[38]
Wednesday Morning, April 19, 1865

A Time to Every Purpose.

So said the wise man.[39] Allow one who remembers the sable drapery of churches and public buildings when Washington's life ended in perfect peace, to give utterance to a few thoughts which the present hour suggests.

A bereaved nation is now following the remains of its noble and beloved Chief Magistrate to the grave. A nation's tears will fall upon his unconscious body, and a nation's heart will embalm his precious memory. He lived and gladly died for his country, and will never — never be forgotten.

He occupied the Executive chair by the will of the people of the United States, and in him were embodied the national power and dignity. We, the citizens, of all ranks, conditions and circumstances, thought in him, acted through him, felt with him. We put our sword into his hand. We clothed him with the authority of his sovereign people, and when he spoke it was our voice. We did not put a crown on his head, nor a sceptre into his hand, to proclaim his power and dignity, because it was our power and dignity that he bore so meekly and so nobly.

In hereditary governments, the sovereign may be the depository of power by treaty stipulations or legislative enactments, but the people acquiesce in the arrangement; they do not make it. Of course they must be reminded of their duty as loyal subjects by the pageantry of Courts and the grandeur of palaces,

---

38   The *North American and United States Gazette* began as the weekly *Pennsylvania Packet*, founded in 1771 by the same John Dunlap who had printed the first 200 broadsides of the Declaration of Independence shortly after it was written. The **Packet** became The **American Daily Advertiser** in 1784, which would become the first successful daily in the country. That paper would morph and merge with and emerge from a number of other papers, including the *Gazette of the United States* in 1789, the *United States Gazette* in 1804, and the *North American* in 1839. The *North American and United States Gazette* itself was founded in 1847. [Journalism in the United States from 1690 to 1872, by Frederic Hudson, LoC, and Wikipedia.]

39   The wise man was Ecclesiastes, son of David, who said, in Eccesiastes 3:1, (King James Version) "For every thing there is a season, and a time to every purpose under the heaven:" (And in Ecclesiastes 1 he said, according to the New International Version, "'Meaningless! Meaningless!,' [says the Teacher, son of David, 'Utterly meaningless! Everything is meaningless.' What do people gain from all their labors at which they toil under the sun? Generations come and generations go, but the earth remains forever."

and the bristling bayonets of bodyguards. If the "succession" brings to them a tyrant, they must accept their destiny or change it by violence. No one can sit on our throne, for we occupy it ourselves. Every four years we call a servant to represent us and act for us, in certain prescribed forms, and for certain appointed ends. He is our prime minister, and respect shown to him is shown to us, while contempt or abuse of him we take to ourselves.

The fell deed of darkness and cowardice that extinguished the life of our beloved President speaks of another power, embodied in another form, but not less real and active. When that manly form sank down under the blow of the assassin,

"Then I and you, and all of us fell down."[40]

In that demoniac arm was represented the foul spirit of treason and disloyalty. It was the self-same spirit that nerved the arm of nullification in 1832[41]; it has threatened and browbeaten the friends of liberty and good order wherever and whenever opportunity favored; that locked devoted Christian missionaries in a gloomy southern prison, robbed the "poor, untutored Indians" of their houses and lands, and successfully defied the power of government to check them. It was the self-same spirit that trampled the ensign of our country's glory in the dirt, and sought an alliance with European despotism and aristocracy.

These two ideas or principles we behold struggling in that fearful tragedy of the 14th of April. They had been struggling in the open field for four years. Torrents of blood has been poured out on hundreds of battle fields, and hundreds of thousands of hearts had been wrung with anguish under sacrifice unparalleled in human history. Loyalty at last became triumphant. The dishonored flag was restored to its position. The foul spirit seemingly bowed to the national authority.

Then it was that it suddenly transformed itself into the person of a dastardly assassin, and under cover of darkness stole secretly toward its unsuspecting

---

40   From Julius Ceasar, Act III, Scene 2 (the "Friends, Romans, countrymen, lend me your ears" scene): O, what a fall was there, my countrymen/ Then I, and you, and all of us fell down,/ Whilst bloody treason flourish'd over us.

41   In 1832, South Carolina issued the Ordinance of Nullification, which declared the federal Tariff of 1828 and a compromise version of 1832 void in the state. The U.S. Congress authorized the use of force to enforce the tariff, but it also approved a lower tariff, which South Carolina accepted.

victim, took his life and fled! That was neither more nor less than the natural fruit of a tree planted in southern soil, and nurtured by southern principles and institutions. Involuntary servitude, with all its horrible accompaniments, has disclosed its revolting features in a thousand forms, but it has now revealed itself to every eye as the deadly foe of all liberty, order, and social existence.

If ever a nation mourned our nation mourns to-day; and though its revered and noble Chief Magistrate is dumb and motionless, his mortal wound is eloquent, and his open grave speaks to us with an emphasis that should send its echoes over all our mountains and vales, from sea to sea, and from shore to shore: Wipe slavery from every foot of American soil — Wipe it, as a man wipeth a dish, wiping it and turning it upside down." (2 Kings, xxi, 13.)

* * * * *

The National Intelligencer[42]
Washington, D.C.
Wednesday, April 19, 1865

Speech of President Johnson

In accordance with the resolutions passed at the meeting of the citizens of Illinois, held at the National Hotel yesterday, the citizens of the State assembled at Willard's Hotel, preparatory to paying their respects to His Excellency Andrew Johnson, President of the United States. Governor Oglesby[43], accompanied by Senator Yates, Gen. John N. Haynie, ex-Senator O.A. Browning, Hon. D.L. Philips, Gen. J. Farnsworth, Hon. Isaac N. Arnold, Hon. John Wilson, col. John L. Loomis, Col. Jas. H. Bowen, Gen. Julius White, Hon. J.M. Hannah, Major s. Wait, Major W.C. Carroll, Major P. Flynn, and large

---

42   Also in this edition: Article on assassinations, the poem "Hymn for the Funeral of Abraham Lincoln, April 19, 1865," a letter from Edwin Booth, General Custer's address to his troops regarding the assassination, Fifteen hundred barrels of whisky seized in fraud discovery, reports on occupations of Mobile and Raleigh.

43   Illinois Gov. Richard J. Oglesby (1824 - 1899) served in the Mexican-American War and with the Union in the Civil War as a major-general. Though he led well in many battles, he is most remembered for action in Mexico, where he captured part of General Santa Ana: his wooden leg. He served four terms (none consecutive) as governor of Illinois and also served as senator from that state.

concourse of citizens, repaired to the rooms of President Johnson, in the Treasury building.

Governor Oglesby presented the delegation and addressed the President as follows:

Mr. President: I take much pleasure in presenting you this delegation of citizens of Illinois, representing almost every portion of the State. We are drawn together in this city by the mournful events of the past few days to give some feeble expression to the feelings we, in common with the whole nation, realize as pressing us to the earth, by appropriate and respectful ceremonies.

We thought it not inappropriate before we shall separate, even in this sad hour, to seek this interview with your Excellency, that while the bleeding heart is pouring out its mournful anguish over the death of our beloved President, the idol of our State, and the pride of the whole country, we may earnestly express to you, the living head of this great nation, our deliberate, full, and abiding confidence in you as the one who in these dark hours must bear upon yourself the mighty responsibility of maintaining, defending, and directing its affairs. In the midst of this sadness, through the oppressive gloom that surrounds us, we look to you and to a bright future for our country.

The assassination of the President of the United States deeply depresses and seriously aggravates the entire nation, but under our blessed Constitution, it does not delay nor for any great length of time retard its progress; does not for an instant disorganize or threaten its destruction. The record of your whole past life is familiar to us all; the splendor of your recent gigantic efforts to stay the hand of treason, and restore the flag to the utmost bounds of the Republic, around that noble State we represent, and we believe the people of the United States; and to this end we come in the name of the State of Illinois, and we confidently believe fully and faithfully expressing the wishes of our people, to present and pledge to you the cordial, earnest, and unremitting purpose of our State to give to your administration the strong support we have heretofore given to the administration of our lamented late President the policy of which we heretofore, do now, and shall continue to endorse.

The President said:

Gentlemen: I have listened with profound emotion to the kind words you have addressed to me. The visit of this large delegation, to speak to me through you, sir, these words of encouragement, I had not anticipated. In the midst of the saddening circumstances which surround us, and the immense responsibility thrown upon me, an expression of the confidence of individuals, and still more of an influential body like that before me, representing a great commonwealth, cheers and strengthens my heavily-burdened mind.

I am at a loss for words to respond. In an hour like this, of deepest sorrow, were it possible to embody in words the feelings of my bosom, I could not command my lips to utter them. Perhaps the best reply I could make, and the one most readily appreciated, to your kind assurance of confidence, would be to receive them in silence. The throbbings of my heart since the sad catastrophe which has appalled us cannot be reduced to words; and oppressed as I am with the new and great responsibility which has devolved upon me, saddened with grief, I can with difficulty respond to you at all.

But I cannot permit such expressions of the confidence reposed in me by the people to pass without acknowledgement. To an individual like myself, who has never claimed much, but who has, it is true, received from a generous people many marks of trust and honor for a long time, an occasion like this, and a manifestation of public feeling so well timed, are peculiarly acceptable. Sprung from the people myself, every pulsation of the popular heart finds an immediate answer in my own.

By many men in public life such occasions are often considered merely formal; to me they are real. Your words of countenance and encouragement sink deep into my heart, and were I even a coward, I could not but gather from them strength to carry out my convictions of right. Thus feeling, I shall enter upon the discharge of my great duty firmly, steadfastly, if not with the signal ability of my predecessor, which is still fresh in our sorrowing minds. Need I repeat that no heart feels more sensible than mine at this great affliction?

In what I say on this occasion I shall indulge in no petty spirit of anger, no feeling of revenge; but we have beheld a notable event in the history of mankind. In the midst of the American people, where every citizen is taught to obey law and observe the rules of Christian conduct, our Chief Magistrate, the beloved of all hearts, has been assassinated. And when we trace this crime to its cause — when we remember the source whence the assassin drew his inspiration — and then look at the result, we stand yet more astounded at this most barbarous, most diabolical assassination. Such crimes as the murder of a great and good man, honored and revered, the beloved and the hope of these people springs not alone from a solitary individual of ever so desperate wickedness.

We can trace its causes through successive steps, without enumerating them here, back to that source which is the spring of all our woes. No one can say that if the perpetrator of this fiendish deed be arrested he should not undergo the extremest penalty law knows for crime. None will say that mercy should interpose. But is he alone guilty?

Here, gentlemen, you perhaps expect me to present some indication of my future policy. One thing I will say. Every era teaches its own lesson. The times we live in are not without instruction. The American people must be taught, if they do not already feel, that treason is a crime and must be punished, [applause] that the Government will not always bear with its enemies; that it is strong not only to protect but to punish. [Applause.]

While we are appalled, overwhelmed at the fall of one man in our midst by the hand of a traitor, shall we allow men — I care not by what weapons — to attempt the life of the State with impunity: While we strain our minds to comprehend the enormity of this assassination, shall we allow the nation to be assassinated? [Applause.] I speak in no spirit of unkindness. I leave the events of the future to be disposed of as they may arise, regarding myself as the humble instrument of the American people. In this, as in all things, justice and judgment shall be determined by them. I do not harbor bitter or revengeful feelings towards any. In general terms, I would say that public morals and public opinion should be established upon the sure and inflexible principles of justice. [Applause.] When the question of exercising mercy comes before me, it will be considered calmly, judicially, remembering that I am the Executive of the nation. I know men love to have their names spoken of in connection with acts of mercy — and how easy it is to yield to this impulse! But we must not forget that what may be mercy to the individual is cruelty to the State. [Applause.] In the exercise of mercy there should be no doubt left that this high prerogative is not used to relieve a few at the expense of many. Be assured I shall never forget that I came not to consult my own feelings alone, but give an account to the whole people. [Applause.]

In regard to my future course, I will now make no professions. I have been connected somewhat actively with public affairs, and to the history of my past public acts which is familiar to you. I refer for those principles which have governed me heretofore and will guide me hereafter.

In general, I will say, I have long labored for the amelioration of mankind. My opinions as to the nature of popular government have long cherished; and constituted me as I am, it is now too late in my life to change them. I believe that government was made for man, not man for government. [Applause.] This struggle of the people against the most gigantic rebellion the world ever saw has demonstrated that the attachment of the people to their Government is the strongest national defence human wisdom can devise. [Applause.] So long as each man feels that the interests of the Government are his interests; so long as the public heart turns in the right direction, and the people understand and appreciate the theory of our Government, and love liberty, our Constitution will be transmitted unimpaired. If the time ever comes when the people shall fail it, the Government will fail, and we shall cease to be one of the nations of the earth. After having perceived our form of free government, and shown its power to maintain its existence through the vicissitudes of nearly a century, it may be that it was necessary for us to pass through this last ordeal of internecine strife to prove that this Government will not perish from internal weakness, but will ever stand able to defend itself against all foes, and punish treason. [Applause.]

In the dealings of an inscrutable Providence, and by the operation of the Constitution, I have been thrown unexpectedly into this position. My past life, especially my course during the recent unholy rebellion, is before you. I have no principles to retract. I defy anyone to point to any of my public acts at variance with the fixed principles which have guided me through life. I have no professions to offer — professions and promises would be worth nothing at this time. No one can foresee the circumstances that will hereafter arise. Had any man gifted with prescience four years ago, uttered and written down, in advance, the events of this period, the story would have seemed more marvellous than anything in the Arabian Nights. I shall not attempt to anticipate the future. As events occur, and it becomes necessary for me to act, I shall dispose of each as it arises, deferring any declaration or message until it can be written, paragraph by paragraph, in the light of events as they transpire.

The members of the delegation were then severally introduced to the President by Gov. Oglesby.

* * * * *

Philadelphia Inquirer[44]
Wednesday, April 19, 1965

LETTER OF JOHN WILKES BOOTH
Proof that he Meditated his Crime Months Ago

Confesses that he was Engaged in a Plot to Capture and Carry off the President — His Excuses for the Contemplated Act — His Participation in the Execution of John Brown — A Secession Rhapsody.

The following verbatim copy of a letter, in writing which is the hand-writing of John Wilkes Booth, the murderer of President Lincoln, has been furnished us by the Hon. Wm. Millward, United States Marshal of the Eastern District of Pennsylvania. It was handed over to that officer by John S. Clarke,[45] who is a brother-in-law of Mr. Booth. The history connected with it is somewhat

---

44   Also in the news: The fall of Raleigh, Booth brought to bay, preparations for the funeral, England mourns the loss of Richard Cobden, English parliamentarian.

45   John Sleeper Clarke (September 3, 1833 - September 29, 1899), a classmate and theater partner of Edwin Booth, married John and Edwin's sister, Asia. After turning in this and another letter, Clarke was arrested and held for a month.

"John Brown. Meeting the slave-mother and her child on the steps of Charlestown jail on his way to execution." Currier & Ives, circa 1863.

peculiar. In November, 1864, the paper was deposited with Mr. Clarke by Booth in a sealed envelope, "for safe keeping," Mr. Clarke being ignorant of the contents. In January last Booth called at Mr. Clarke's house, asked for the package and it was given up to him. It is now supposed that at that time he took out the paper and added to it his signature, which appears to be in a different ink from that used in the body of the letter, and also from the language employed could not have been put to it originally. Afterwards he returned the package to Mr. Clarke again for safe keeping, sealed and bearing the inscription "J. Wilkes Booth."

The inclosure was preserved by the family without suspicion of its nature. After the afflicting information of the assassination of the President, which came upon the family of Mr. Clarke with crushing force, it was considered proper to open the envelope. — There was found in it the following paper, with some thirty-seven United States bonds and certificates of shares in oil companies. — Mr. Clarke promptly handed the paper to Marshal Millward, in whose custody it now remains. From a perusal of this paper it seems to have been prepared by Booth as a vindication of some desperate act which he had in contemplation; and from the language used it is probable that it was a plot to abduct the President and carry him off to Virginia. If this was meditated, it failed, and from making a prisoner of the President to his assassination was an easy step for a man of perverted principles. It also appears that Booth was one of the party who was engaged in the capture and execution of John Brown, of Ossawattomie, at which time he doubtless imbibed from Wise and his as-

155

sociates those detestable sentiments of cruelty which have culminated in an infamous crime. The letter is as follows:

———, ———, 1864.

My Dear Sir: You may use this as you think best. But as some may wish to know when, who and why, and as I know not how to direct, I give it (in the words of your master) "TO WHOM IT MAY CONCERN."

Right or wrong, God judge me, not man. For be my motive good or bad, of one thing I am sure, the lasting condemnation of the North.

I love peace more than life. Have loved the Union beyond expression. For four years have I waited, hoped and prayed for the dark clouds to break, and for a restoration of our former sunshine. To wait longer would be a crime. All hope for peace is dead. My prayers have proved as idle as my hopes. God's will be done. I go to see and share the bitter end.

I have ever held the South were right. The very nomination of Abraham Lincoln, four years ago, spoke plainly, war — war upon Southern rights and institutions. His election proved it. "Await an overt act." Yes, till you are bound and plundered. What folly! The South was wise. Who thinks of argument or patience when the finger of his enemy presses on the trigger? In a foreign war, I, too could say, "country, right or wrong." But in a struggle such as ours (where brother tries to pierce the brother's heart,) for God's sake, choose the right. When a country like this spurns justice from her side she forfeits the allegiance of every honest freeman, and should leave him, untrammeled by any fealty soever, to act as his conscience may approve.

People of the North, to hate tyranny, to love liberty and justice, to strike at wrong and oppression, was the teaching of our fathers. The study of our early history will not let me forget it, and may it never.

The country was formed for the white, not for the black man. And looking upon African slavery from the same stand-point held by the noble framers of our Constitution, I, for one have ever considered it one of the greatest blessings (both for themselves and us) that God ever bestowed upon a favored nation. Witness heretofore our wealth and power, witness their elevation and enlightenment above their race elsewhere. I have lived among it most of my life, and have seen less harsh treatment from master to man than I have beheld in the North, from father to son. Yet Heaven knowns, no one would be willing to do more for the negro race than I, could I but see a way to still better their condition.

But Lincoln's policy is only preparing the way for their total annihilation. The South are not, nor have they been fighting for the continuance of slavery. The first Battle of Bull Run did away with that idea. Their causes since for war have been as noble and greater far than those that urged our fathers on. Even should we allow they were wrong at the beginning of this contest, cruelty and injustice have made the wrong become the right, and they stand now (before the wonder and admiration of the world) as a noble band of patriotic heroes. Hereafter, reading of their deeds, Thermopylae would be forgotten.[46] When I aided in the capture and execution of John Brown, (who was a murderer on our western border, and who was fairly tried and convicted before an impartial judge and jury, of treason, and who, by the way, has since been made a god,) I was proud of my little share in the transaction, for I deemed it my duty, and that I was helping our common country to perform an act of justice. But what was a crime in poor John Brown is now considered (by themselves) as the greatest and only virtue of the whole Republican party. Strange transmigration! Vice to become a virtue, simply because more indulge in it.

I thought then, as now, that the abolitionists were the only traitors in the land, and that the entire party deserved the same fate of poor old Brown; not because they wished to abolish slavery, but on account of the means they have ever endeavored to use to effect that abolition. If Brown were living I doubt whether he himself would set slavery against the Union. Most, or many, in the North do, and openly curse the Union, if the South are to return and retain a single right guaranteed to them by every tie which we once revered as sacred. The South can make no choice. It is either extermination or slavery for them-selves (worse than death) to draw from. I know my choice.

I have also studied hard to discover upon what grounds the right of a State

---

46   The classic battle fought in 480 BC between Greek forces of about 3,000 men, including a reknowned group of 300 Spartans, and Persian army of well over 70,000. Greece lost.

to secede has been denied, when our very name, United States, and the Declaration of Independence both provide for Secession. But there is no time for words, I write in haste. I know how foolish I shall be deemed for undertaking such a step as this, where, on the one side, I have many friends and everything to make me happy, where my profession alone has gained me an income of more than twenty thousand dollars a year, and where my great personal ambition in my profession has such a great field for labor. On the other hand the South have never bestowed upon me one kind word; a place now where I have no friends, except beneath the sod; a place where I must become either a private soldier or a beggar. To give up all of the former for the latter, besides my mother and sisters, whom I love so dearly, (although they so widely differ with me in opinion,) seems insane, but God is my judge. I love justice more than I do a country that disowns it; more than fame and wealth; more, (Heaven pardon me if wrong,) more than a happy home. I have never been upon a battle-field; but Oh, my countrymen, could you all but see the reality or effects of this horrid war, as I have seen them, (in every state, save Virginia.) I know you would think like me, and would pray the Almighty to create in the Northern mind a sense of right and justice, (even should it possess no seasoning of mercy,) and that He would dry up this sea of blood between us, which is daily growing wider. Alas! poor country, is she to meet her threatened doom?

Four years ago, I would have given a thousand lives to see her remain (as I had always known her) powerful and unbroken. And even now I would hold my life as naught, to see her what she was. O, my friends, if the fearful scenes of the past four years had never been enacted, or if what has been had been but a frightful dream, from which we could now awake, with what overflowing hearts could we bless our God and pray for his continued favor. How I have loved the old flag can never now be known. A few years since and the entire world could boast of none so pure and spotless. But I have of late been seeing and hearing of the bloody deeds of which she has been made the emblem, and would shudder to think how changed she had grown. — O how I have longed to see her break from the mist of blood and death that circles round her folds, spoiling her beauty and tarnishing her honor. But no, day by day has she been dragged deeper and deeper into cruelty and oppression, till now (in my eyes) her once bright red stripes look like bloody gashes on the face of Heaven. I look now upon my early admiration of her glories as a dream. My love (as things stand to-day) is for the South alone. Nor do I deem it a dishonor in attempting to make for her a prisoner of this man to whom she owes so much of misery. — If success attends me, I go penniless to her side. They say she has found that "last ditch" which the north have so long derided, and been endeavoring to force her in, forgetting that they are our brothers, and that it's impolitic to goad an enemy into madness. Should I reach her in safety and find it true, I will proudly beg permission to triumph or die in that same "ditch" by her side.

A Confederate, doing duty upon his own responsibility.

J. Wilkes Booth.

From Harrisburg

INSULT TO THE AMERICAN FLAG — REWARD OFFERED FOR THE TRAITOR — MISS LAURA KEENE — MISTAKEN ARREST OF A MAN SUPPOSED TO BE BOOTH.

[Special Despatch to the Inquirer.]

Much indignation was manifested here this morning at finding a large and beautiful American flag, the handiwork of school girls, lying on the steps of the Girls' Grammar School in State Street. It had been shrouded in mourning, and hung in graceful folds over the door. During the night some traitor, unknown, tore it down and cut it almost to shreds with a knife, of the use of which the flag bears evidence. After the monster had ruined it, he trampled upon and other wise defaced it. Crowds of people assembled to see the ruined flag, and all expressed their abhorrence in unmeasured terms.

A man was arrested on the Pennsylvania train, bound West, near Greensburg, this morning, who was supposed to be Booth, the murderer of the President. It turned out, however, that the man's name was Davis.

Thirteen hundred and fifty dollars is offered for the detection of the party or parties who tore down, mutilated and insulted the flag in State street last night.

Miss Laura Keene and Messrs. Dyott and Hawk, have been released, by order of General Augur.

* * * * *

The New-York Tribune
April 19, 1865

For The Tribune.

A.L.

In Memoriam.

I.

But yesterday — the exulting Nation's shout
    Swelled on the breeze of victory through our streets.
But yesterday — our banners flaunted out
    Like flowers the South wind woos from their retreats;
Flowers of the Nation, blue and white and red,
    Waving from the balcony and spire and mast;
Which told us that War's wintry storm had fled,
    And Spring was no more than Spring to us at last.
To-day — the Nation's heart lies crushed and weak;
    Drooping and draped in black our banners stand.
Too stunned to cry Revenge, we scarce may speak
    The grief that chokes all utterance through the Land.
God is all. With tears our eyes are dim.
yet strive through darkness to look at Him!

II.

No, not in vain he died — not all in vain,
    Our good, great President! This people's hands
Are linked together in one mighty chain
    Drawn righter still in triple-woven bands
To crush the fiends in human masks, whose might

We suffer, O too long! No tongue, nor truce

Save men with men! The devils we must fight

    With fire! God wills it in this deed. This use

We draw from the impious murder done

    Since Calvary. Rise, then, O countrymen!

Scatter these marsh-light hopes of union won

    Through pardoning clemency. Strike, strike again!

Draw closer round the foe a girdling flame;

We are stabbed when'er we spare — strike in God's name!

C.P. Cranch

New-York, April 18, 1865

*   *   *   *   *

Daily Evening Bulletin[47]
San Francisco
Wednesday Evening, April 19

Personal Remembrances of the Late Abraham Lincoln

A number of years ago the writer of this lived in one of the judicial circuits of Illinois in which Abraham Lincoln had an extensive, though not very lucrative practice. The terms of the court were held quarterly, and usually lasted about two weeks. The occasions were always reasons of great importance and much gaiety in the little town that had the honor of being the county seat. Distinguished members of the Bar from surrounding and even from distant counties - ex-judges and ex-members of congress attended, and were personally, and many of them popularly known to almost every adult male and female, of the limited population. They came in stages and on horseback. Among them the one above all whose arrival was looked forward to with the most pleasurable anticipation, and whose possible absence — although he was never absent — was feared with the liveliest emotions of anxiety, was "Uncle Abe," as

---

47   The *Daily Evening Bulletin* was founded in San Francisco in 1855 by James King. When King criticized a city supervisor, the official shot King dead and was subsequently lynched.

he was loving called by us all. Some times he might happen to be a day or two late, and then, as the Bloomington stage came in at sundown, the Bench and the Bar, jurors, and the general citizens would gather in crowds at the hotel where he always put up, to give him a welcome if he should happily arrive, and to experience the keenest feelings of disappointment if he should not. If he arrived, as he alighted and stretched out both his long arms to shake hands with those nearest to him, and with those who approached — his homely face, handsome in its broad and sunshiny smile, his voice touching in its kindly and cheerful accents, — everyone in his presence felt lighter in the heart and became joyous. He brought light with him. He loved his fellow-men with all the strength of his great nature, and those who came in contact with him could not help reciprocating the love. His tenderness of the feelings of others was of sensitiveness in the extreme. It was that which caused him to go to the theatre on last Friday night. Public announcement had been made that Gen. Grant was to be present. Gen. Grant had left the city. In order that the audience might not be too much disappointed, Mr. Lincoln would go himself with his wife, although his wife was somewhat unwell. It was the same sensitiveness as to the feelings of others, whether before a jury or on the stump, or in the circle where his apt and illustrative stories were the entertainment of all, that created much of his popularity. He had so few personal enemies, that, although I knew him in his intercourse with men in several counties of the State, I cannot name one.

His political antagonists — and his political opinions, which had then long been unpopular, he maintained with exceeding earnestness — were among the warmest of his friends. Nearly all the practitioners in the circuit were of the Democratic party. The judge — David Davis, now of the United States Supreme Court — ran through the changes of party, from Whig to Anti-Nebraska, and from Anti-Nebraska to Republican, with Mr. Lincoln. The judge, as was then known, was held by Mr. Lincoln in higher personal esteem than any other judge before whom he has cases. But Mr. Lincoln did not stand at the head of the Bar, except as a jury lawyer. Before the Court he was inferior, both in argument and influence (if I may use the latter word in a legal sense) to such men as Judge Manning, Judge Parpie, and Mr Powell, now judge. Yet Mr.

162

Lincoln, as though aware of his inferiority as a lawyer in the highest meaning of the term, always recognized, with a [illegible] or a good natured remark that could not but touch the affections, the corrections, or the adverse decisions of the Court, and conceded, with genial and graceful heartiness, the more subtle legal acumen of his Democratic compeers at the bar. This wrought him in their hearts. They loved him as a superior man, one just and without envy. They loved him as Judge Douglas loved him, and Judge Douglas loved him as all who knew him did.

The term of the Court, as I have stated, generally ran through about two weeks. At the expiration of it two little [illegible] were invariably expected, one by the citizens, and one by a select circle of the attorneys and others. The former was a political speech by "Uncle Abe" — I indulge in the amiability over his new made grave in gentle remembrance of the days when I believe he was the most happy — and the latter a social gathering at the residence of some one of the citizens. The political meeting — and during a number of years we never knew a failure of the occurrence — was held in the Court-house on the evening after the adjournment of the court. He was always formally invited by the attorneys of all political persuasions, and all attended, because everybody delighted to hear him "speak." No one else, except in times of a general election, was so noticed. No one except himself, with his enunciation of what was then a very radical dogma, could have been listened to without manifestations of disapprobation.

I am writing of times prior to the passage of the Kansas-Nebraska bill in 1854.[48] The integrity of his opinions, the hold that he had upon the popular heart, his humor, sometimes genial and sometimes broad; the vigor, at times homely, of his language — the emphasis of his gestures, and the remarkable aptness of his illustrations, secured to him attention and applause. His eloquence was attractive, and, for aught that any of us can now tell, his arguments

---

48   The Kansas-Nebraska Act of 1854, supported primarily by Illinois Senator Stephen A. Douglas, opened those territories to settlement. When they became states, they would be able to vote on whether to allow slavery. This effectively nullified the Missouri Act of 1820, which had prohibited slavery in new states. Pro-slavery and anti-slavery advocates flooded into the territories so as to eventually gain more votes in Congress. The Republican Party was formed to oppose not only slavery but the Kansas-Nebraska Act. Kansas entered the Union as a free state before the war; Nebraska became a state afterward.

may have been convincing. He was not more radical before the passage of the Kansas-Nebraska bill than he was after, and his radicalism when he was a practicing attorney was conservatism when he became a President. His political standard then, as the political standard of a majority of the people to-day, at least of the loyal states. His own State has adopted the political creed that he advanced to it fifteen and more years ago. Then, in the days and on the occasions of which I am writing, he never neglected to dwell upon the iniquity of slavery, to denounce the Democratic party for upholding the institution, and almost, perhaps quite, to predict the lamentable result that followed upon his election to the Chief Magistrate of the Republic. His subsequent declaration that the country could not survive, half slave and half free, he foreshadowed those days. He was a politician, and ambitious, too; but his sincerity was deeper and purer than a common politician's. His sincerity was his own nature. He had occupied a seat in Congress during a portion of a broken term. He had voted against the opinions of his constituents in some matters relating incidentally to the annexation of Texas as a slave State. He had introduced a bill providing for the abolition of slavery in the District of Columbia. His course in Congress had been a dangerous one for a political aspirant from a State of the political proclivities of Illinois. It had been a ruinous one for a member from the Springfield district, that was largely populated by Kentuckians and Tennesseans. He could obtain no nomination. He could expect no further political confidence or advancement from his constituents unless he recanted and yielded up his political heresies. That he would not do, because he could not without violating that simple and innate integrity of his whole being that bye-and-bye (sic) made him President. He longed for political distinction, but he would not, even if he could, secure it by departing from the honesty of his opinions. So he was forced to content himself with his legal practice and his opportunities, that would hardly have been allowed to another, of telling the people what they did not like to hear for itself, but did not like to hear from the earnest lips and sincere heart of Abraham Lincoln, and these "talkings" of his, in those quite, inland towns, where, during the sessions of the Court, the intelligence of the county centered; where the grand and petit jurors, the supervisors of the country, the professional men, the farmers and litigants of all classes gathered together — may, as I have intimated, been more convincing than any of his listeners were then ready openly to acknowledge. The speeches of Mr. Seward, delivered during the same period of time, but for more general effect, we all know carried a powerful influence with them. And why may we not have Mr. Lincoln's in a more humble sphere? It is true that he then seldom, if ever, heard of a convert to his political doctrines. It is true that the Democratic party, triumphant at every election, continued to rule the State, and that in those congressional districts that were held by the Whig party, no one could look to preferment who even favored the Wilmot proviso.[49] But a political revolution began to take place in the State in 1854, after the annulling of the Missouri Compromise Act[50], and who, except themselves, can tell how well the numbers who took part in the change has (sic) been prepared for it through Mr. Lincoln's pleasant and vigorous harangues in the little county seats of the interior? The change came, and the influence of his somewhat earlier courts may be recognized in the fact that he was at once hailed as the chief of the party in Illinois.

* * * * *

---

49   The Wilmot Proviso was an amendment attached to an appropriations bill in 1846 by U.S. Rep. David Wilmot (D-PA) that was to have banned slavery in any territory acquired in the Mexican-American War. It passed in the House but failed in the Senate, where Southern states were more powerful. Subsequent attempts in 1847 and 1848 also failed. The issue was resolved by the Compromise of 1850.

50   The Missouri Compromise Act of 1850 a) allowed California to enter the Union as a Free State and Utah and New Mexico to decide for themselves whether to allow slavery. It also settled the borders of Texas, allowing New Mexico as a separate territory. It also strengthened the Fugitive Slave Act, requiring the return of slaves who had fled to the North. Slavery was allowed in Washington, D.C., though slave trading was prohibited.

April 19, 1865

The Liberator[51]
Boston
April 19, 1865

Arrest of a Pittsburgh Merchant as Accessory
to the Murder of President Lincoln

About seven o'clock Saturday afternoon, while in the saloon at No. 41 Congress street, J.H. Borland, a boot and shoe dealer on Market street, Pittsburgh, made the assertion that eight or ten days since he heard John Wilkes Booth declare that he would put the President through within eight days. Borland was under the influence of liquor at the time of making the assertion, and continuing to repeat it, other persons who were present informed the police of the fact, and detective Curtis with officer Task of the Second Police visited the saloon and arrested the man and committed him to the Toombs on the charge of being accessory to the murder of President Lincoln.

Borland repeated his assertion to the officers after his arrest, and added that Booth also said, "I am insane on the subject of putting the President through, and will do it within eight days."

Borland was in this city for the purpose of purchasing goods, and stopped at the Parker House. He desired that the fact of his arrest might be telegraphed to Pittsburgh.

Riotous Proceedings in Fall River. A Venomous Copperhead Mobbed. Fall River, Mass., April 15. On receipt of the melancholy news of the assassination of the President this morning, and while a large crowd of citizens were gathered around the bulletin boards reading the dispatches and giving ex-

---

51   Founded by William Lloyd Garrison in 1831, The *Liberator* was a well regarded Boston weekly dedicated to abolishing slavery. Garrison closed the paper at the end of 1865 with the passage of the Thirteenth Amendment, which ended slavery in the United States.

pression to their deep and heartfelt sorrow, a notorious Copperhead[52] secesh[53] sympathizer and liquor dealer, named Leonard Wood, was heard to declare that it was the best news he had heard for forty years. He had no sooner uttered this atrocious sentiment than he was seized by the indignant bystanders, struck, booted about the streets, and compelled to go into a store and procure an American flag, unfurl it and salute it with three cheers. He then rushed to his store and locked himself in, but the crowd surrounded his place and were making preparations to break in, when the Mayor and City Marshal appeared and escorted him to the lockup, where he is now confined. The crowd then returned to his store, stove in the windows and smashed things generally. They then visited other Copperheads, compelling them to show the American flag.

A Friend of the Assassins Tarred and Feathered at Swampscott. On the reception of the news at Swampscott, one George Stone said in public it was the best news we had received for four years, and gave three cheers. The citizens and soldiers of Swampscott took him by force, tarred and feathered him, dragged him through the town in a boat, compelling him to hold the American flag over his head, and upon promising to buy an American flag and keep it up during the mourning for the President at half-mast, he was then set at liberty.

Punishment of Secessionists. George Wells, John Gallagher, Wm. Fanring, and Peter Britton, the latter treasurer of a theatre, were, in New York, on the 17th, sentenced to six months in the Penitentiary, for uttering treasonable sentiments.

A number of persons in that city who have presumed to express satisfaction of the assassination of President Lincoln, have been roughly handled.

In Trenton, N.J., a rebel sympathizer was mobbed on the morning of the

---

52   Copperheads were radical Northern Peace Democrats who opposed the war, blaming it on abolitionists. They also opposed the draft and vilified Abraham Lincoln as an unconstitutional despot. Their message was often racist, and their tactics were sometimes violent. Republicans derived the name from the poisonous snake, but the Copperheads co-opted the word to refer to the portrait of Lady Liberty on the copper penny, which they used as a badge of pride. The Knights of the Golden Circle, the Order of American Knights, and the Order of the Sons of Liberty were the largest Copperhead organizations.
53   A secesh was a secession sympathizer.

fifteenth, and in various other places, persons who have had the audacity to express their satisfaction at the diabolical act of Booth and his associate ruffian, have been made to feel the heavy hand of popular indignation.

* * * * *

Chicago Tribune
April 19, 1865

The Last Hour sof the President.
His Condition Throughout the Night

The following mionutes taken by Dr. Abbott, show the condition of the late President throughout the night after his assassination:

11:00 o'clock—Pulse 46.[54]

11:05 o'clock—Pulse 45, and growing weaker

11:10 o'clock—Pulse 45.

11:15 o'clock—Pulse 42.

11:20 o'clock—Pulse 45; respiration 28 to 29.

11:25 o'clock—Pulse 42.

11:30 o'clock—Pulse 48, and full.

11:40 o'clock—Pulse 48.

11:45 o'clock—Pulse 45; respiration 22.

12:00 o'clock—Pulse 48, respiration 22.

12:15—Pulse 48; respiration 21; echmos both eyes.

12:20—Pulse 45.

12:32—Pulse 60.

12:35—Pulse 66.

12:40—Pulse 69, right.

12:45—Pulse 70; eye much swollen and echmoses.

12:55—Pulse 80, struggling motion of the arms.

---

54   Normal pulse for an adult would be 60 - 100 per minute. Respiration would be 12 - 20. "Echmos," below, would be ecchymosis, which is bruising from broken blood vessels.

1 o'clock—Pulse 86, respiration 30.

1:30—Pulse 95, appearing easier.

1:45—Puse 86, very quiet, respiration irregular. Mrs. Lincoln present.

2:10—Mrs. Lincoln retired with Robert Lincoln to an adjoining room.

2:30—President very quiet, pulse 54; respiration 28.

2:52—Pulse 48, respiration 30.

3 o'clock—Visited again by Mrs. Lincoln.

3:25—Respiration 24 and regular.

3:35—Prayer by Rev. Dr. Gurley.

4 o'clock—Respiration 26 and regular.

4:15—Pulse 60, respiration 25.

5:50— Respiration 28, regular sleeping.

6 o'clock—Pulse falling, respiration 28.

6:30—Still falling and labored breathing.

7 o'clock—Symptoms of immediate dissolution.

7:22—Death.

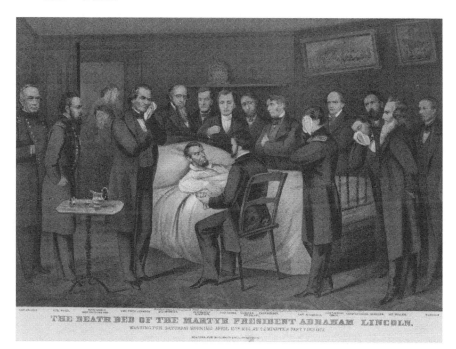

THE DEATH BED OF THE MARTYR PRESIDENT ABRAHAM LINCOLN,
WASHINGTON, SATURDAY MORNING APRIL 15TH 1865, AT 22 MINUTES PAST 7 OCLOCK

Thursday, April 20, 1865

Bowed Heads and Aching Hearts

We might hoe cotton for a peck of corn
and a couple pounds of bacon per week,
with a few cuts of a horsewhip thrown in at intervals;

we can certainly chop cord-wood
or dig potatoes for a living,
but we have not tried;

but to *represent* public opinion
in the editorial columns of a newspaper
is a task quite outside of our capacity.

The Farmers' Cabinet[55]
Amherst, N.H.
Thursday Morning, April 20, 1865

LINCOLN IS DEAD!

The sad news has reached all our readers, and all hearts are doubly-draped in sorrow and gloom. Be it ours rather to administer consolation and relieve the gloom, than to add poignancy to the national grief.

Lincoln has fallen by the assassin's hand! But let us remember that not a sparrow falleth to the ground without the notice of the Great Father. The same hand that raised up Abraham Lincoln and brought him to the Presidency at such a time has with no less wise and benevolent designs, removed him, and it becomes us, as a nation and as individuals, to bow in humble resignation to the Divine purpose and will. "Be still and know that I am God."

Clouds and darkness of awful depths surely are round about the throne of Heaven, but justice and judgment are still its habitation.

LET US TRUST GOD! This is one great lesson of the house — of the war! How often has the arm of flesh failed us —BUT GOD NEVER! — Through six troubles He has safely brought us, and in the seventh He will not fail us, if we trust Him!

God's ways are not our ways. Moses was to see the promised land, but not to enter it. His work was done in the wilderness. God knows through what a wilderness Lincoln has led the people, and how He took him up to Nebo and shew him the goodly land the people were to possess, and then gathered him, awfully, mysteriously, to his people.[56] His work was done; his mission ended.

Lincoln is dead but God lives! The man of His choice the leader whom His providence has placed at the head of the nation, shall be a life at His control and fulfill His purposes. The land in rebellion shall be subdued. Not one

---

55   The *Farmer's Cabinet* was founded by Joseph Cushing in 1802 and sold to Richard Boylston in 1809. It was published under that name until 1900 and through various incarnations was owned by the Boylston family until 2005.

56   Deuteronomy 34, The Death of Moses, in which God takes Moses up Mt. Nebo and said "This is the land I promised on oath to Abraham, Isaac and Jacob, when I said 'I will give it to your descendants.' I have let you see it with your eyes, but you will not cross over to it."

of God's purposes shall fail. Iniquity shall yet hide its head, and our nation, purified as by fire, shall in His hands fulfill its high destiny, and become the glory of the whole earth! THANK GOD FOR ABRAHAM LINCOLN!

DIRGE FOR THE DEAD

I.

Weep, Columbia! Weep thy son!
Weep thy second Washington!
Weep the noble and the brave!
Weep, O land, that knows no slave!

II.

Murderous hand has done the deed.
God allowed it to succeed.
O, Columbia, trust His power
In this dark and dreadful hour!

III.

Grateful be that life so pure.
Was through Him so long secure
Till that life's work had been done,
and God's purpose in it won.

IV.

By the noble Lincoln's word,
As God's double-cutting sword,
Slavery, Columbia's stain,
Lies, like him, among the slain.

V.

Bear him to a martyr's tomb!
His the glory! Ours the gloom!
Historic pages where nowhere keep
Such bright glory! gloom so deep

VI.

Weep, Columbia, weep the brave!
Shed warm tears over Lincoln's grave!
Like bright stars of purest light,
Shine his deeds in this our night!

VII.

Scatter garlands on his breast!
Rest, proud Lincoln, sweetly rest!
Gem his name with starts of light,
Hang it ever in our sight.

VIII.

Patriot, statesman, martyr'd dead!
For us they noble blood was shed.
Heaven accept the sacrifice,
Bid us from the dust arise!

The sad news of the fall of our noble Chieftain was received in our quiet village, as everywhere, with every appropriate demonstration of sorrow. Our bells were tolled through Saturday, our beautiful flag waved mournfully at half-mast, and distress was depicted on every countenance. On the Sabbath, the Congregational Church was heavily draped, and the services opened by a solemn dirge. A most appropriate and beautiful discourse was preached by the Pastor, Rev. J.G. Davis, from 2d Samuel, 3, 38-39: "Know ye not that there is a prince and a great man fallen, this day in Israel. The Lord shall reward the doer of evil, according to his wickedness." After an affecting allusion to the loss of the nation, and the esteem in the deep sorrow and gloom that rested upon the national heart, the speaker proceeded to draw a beautiful picture of that life which had so evenly flowed, and so richly, for the healing of the nation during these terrible years of war, and the early training by which the good man had been fitted for the crowning work of his useful and noble life. The picture was drawn in all the simplicity and truthfulness of the original and was listened to with deepest attention by a large congregation.

* * * * *

The New Hampshire Sentinel[57]
Keene, N.H.
Thursday Morning, April 20, 1865

THE NATION'S BEREAVEMENT.

A great sorrow has seized the hearts of the loyal American people, and the nation weeps as it has never wept before. Its Chief Magistrate has been murdered by the hands of an assassin, and that assassin an instrument of a cold blooded conspiracy which aimed at the lives of the President, members of the Cabinet, the Chief Justice, and commander-in-chief of our armies. But the president, beloved and confided in by the loyal millions, alone falls a victim to the madness of treason, when the madness of treason reaches its climax, and despair shadows the brow of the defeated and baffled traitor.

---

57   Founded in 1799 by 21-year-old John Prentiss and still published in Keene, N.H.,taking the name Keene Evening Sentinel in 1957.

But there is no bitter without its sweet — no sorrowing but has its gleams of light to illume the countenance darkened by anguish. As if there were yet something wanting to complete the universal conviction of the utter folly and wickedness of the rebellion, a blow that comes like a thunderbolt from a clear sky and strikes down the nation's noble chieftain in the midst of the nation's rejoicing in victories over treason, and when thousands of Southern people, deceived and betrayed by artful conspirators, were about to offer him their confidence and loyalty.

There is a God in history, says the intelligent and devout Christian, and we shall be much mistaken if we do not see the evidence of the Omniscient presence in this great tragedy. The nation now sees and feels more fully the great crime that has been at the bottom of this war against the nation's life. Those who now see the murder of the President, will the more keenly recognize the character of the blows that have been dealt during the past four years for the murder of a whole nation.

That the best friend of the Southern people has been murdered at the insistence of Southern treason; and the very kindness of heart which has enabled our much beloved President, so many times to temper justice with mercy, has only provoked the wrath of the mad conspirators who have sought the nation's life; and who, failing in that, have sought revenge in a moment of despair by taking the life of the nation's representative hand.

The armies of treason are everywhere scattered and defeated, and the proud old flag of our fathers waves in triumph over all the seaports, cities and strongholds of the seceded States; and now that the time has come for reconstruction and bringing back into the Union the states whose people have been forced into rebellion against their clearly expressed will, northern people will be all the more united, and will see all the more clearly their duty in the great work before them.

A Proclamation from Gov. Gilmore[58]. — Gov. Gilmore has issued a proclamation calling upon the people of this State to set apart Wednesday the

---

58   Joseph Albree Gilmore (1811 - 1867), Republican governor of New Hampshire, 1863-65.

19th of April, for the funeral obsequies of Abraham Lincoln. The authorities of towns and cities are requested to cause the bells of all the churches to be tolled, and minute guns to be fired from 11 to 12 o'clock. The people are requested to close their places of business — to drape their stores and dwelling houses with the appropriate emblems of grief, and to assemble in their accustomed places of worship, &c.

———

Encouraging Signs. — It is a most gratifying sign to witness the kindly tone, since the death of our late lamented President, which pervades many papers that bitterly opposed his whole administration and his war policy. One of the bitterest sheets of this class has been the Manchester Union. That paper now speaks of Mr. Lincoln's kindness of heart, and says high hopes were entertained that he would bring the war to an early and honorable end. The Boston Post, always more loyal than most democratic papers, most deeply mourns the President's death, and claims for President Johnson the public confidence, as an able statesman, patriotically devoted to his country's interest.

* * * * *

The Daily Courant[59]
Hartford
April 20, 1865

Obsequies of President Lincoln

Wednesday, April 19th, will long be remembered as one of he most sorrowful in the history of the American people. On that day, thirty millions, with bowed heads and aching hearts, united in paying the last tokens of respect to the remains of Abraham Lincoln. In every city and hamlet of the union, business was suspended, all mourning for the noble and generous leader whom the

---

59   The oldest continuously published newspaper in the country — today's *Hartford Courant* — the *Courant* was first a weekly founded in 1764 by Thomas Green. To keep the paper solvent, Green sold spices, stationery and hardware in the front office. He sold the paper to Ebenezer Watson, who died in 1777. His widow took over the business, becoming one of the first women publishers in the Americas. Before and during the Civil War, the paper was a strong supporter of Lincoln and the Republican Party.

hand of an assassin had murdered. The grief which overspread the land came to every household as if one of their own number had been taken. In the death of him who had become profoundly endeared to all lovers of humanity, each felt that he had sustained an irreparable personal loss.

Mr. Lincoln's public life was stormy in the extreme. Called from the seclusion of a remote town to the chief magistracy of the Republic at an hour when treason was dragging one half of the country with savage momentum into the vortex of revolt, and when a large minority in the other half openly justified acts of the secessionists, he took the helm, guiding the ship with heroic courage and far-sighted wisdom, through the horrors of the tempest to the very borders of peace. Under his guidance the military power of the fiercest of all rebellions was crushed, the most stupendous war in the history of the world was pushed to a successful close, liberty was given to four millions of bondmen, and our country for the first time was made truly free. From the first he strove to lift the oppressed, and to carry hope to the down-trodden. His acts were inspired by humanity, and even in dealing with the worst of criminals could never be divested of clemency. Through all the vicissitudes of the war he retained to a remarkable degree the confidence of the people, and at the moment of his death, probably no man was ever more profoundly or universally beloved by his countrymen. All rejoiced in the prospect that the leader who had served them so faithfully, was at length about to enjoy that repose in office which he had so richly earned.

While the murderous act of the assassin has robbed the nation of its chief, and liberty of a favorite apostle, the deed will not interrupt for a moment the successful progress of our cause. The existence of the republic does not depend upon the life of one man or a thousand. It goes on this week as it did the last, only with an intensified horror of the barbarism of slavery. Mr. Lincoln, having fought the good fight, is beyond the malice of treason. But the blow which prostrated him will pursue the leaders of the rebellion with avenging fury from the face of the civilized word. It will add another mill-stone to the neck of slavery, deepening still further the detestation in which all good men hold it. The fiendish outrage will turn pity to wormwood, and mercy to gall. The air of America can no longer give life to Davis, Breckinridge,[60] Benjamin,[61] and other leaders, whose diabolism instigated the tragedy of Friday night. The only alternative now left them is flight or the halter. Treason will be extirpated by the roots. Mr. Lincoln might have screened the devil's plottings led to his assassination from the arm of justice, but Mr. Johnson will not. The government is now in a position to dictate terms. The choice it will present to offenders will speedily disarm them of all power to injure the republic. There will be no trifling in settling accounts with the rebel leaders.

* * * * *

Baltimore Sun[62]
Thursday, April 20, 1865

LOCAL MATTERS

The Obsequies of President Lincoln — The Day in Baltimore

The weather yesterday was decidedly pleasant, having more the appearance of summer than early spring. There was an entire suspension of business during the day, and citizens of all classes joined in the general manifestation of sorrow for the untimely passing of the late President. Public buildings and private houses continued draped in mourning, flags were universally displayed at half-mast, the bells tolled forth a mournful dirge, minute guns were fired from different quarters of the city, and every mark of respect and veneration was paid to the memory of the deceased head of the nation. Appropriate reli-

---

60   John Cabell Breckinridge (1821 - 1875), vice president under Buchanan at age 36, a Democratic congressman and senator from Kentucky. He served with the Confederate army during the war.

61   Judah Philip Benjamin (1811 - 1884), senator from Louisiana, the second Jewish senator in American history, formerly a British citizen. Jefferson Davis appointed him Attorney General of the Confederacy, later Secretary of War, then Secretary of State. He tried to win British support for the South. At the end of the war, he fled to England. He was rumored to have conspired with Booth.

62   Also in the news: Booth rumored to be in Pennsylvania; Texas to secede from the Confederacy; Napoleon will put a marble bust of Richard Cobden in the museum at Marseilles; plague continues in St. Petersburg, Russia; two men commemorating the assassination were killed by a cannon known as "Old Sal" that fired prematurely at the foot of Third St. in the Williamsburg section of New York.

gious services were conducted in all the churches as well as in the three Hebrew synagogues, the ministers all passing high eulogies on the deceased. As
a general thing the congregations were quite full, and in most of the churches
the services were deeply interesting and solemn in the extreme. The mayor and
City Council, together with a large number of citizens, visited Washington, for
the purpose of joining in the funeral cortege, and returned late last evening.
The day bore the appearance of being Sunday, every movement being quiet
and orderly, as if each citizen had suffered a sad bereavement in his own family, and after nightfall the streets were almost entirely deserted.

Special military Order. — Yesterday General Wallace[63] issued the following order:

"Headquarters Middle Department, Eighth Army Corps, Baltimore, Md.,
April 19, 1865. — General Orders, No. 86 — The gray uniform worn by certain young men, said to be students, has become so offensive to loyal soldiers
and citizens, that it is prohibited in this Department.

"This order will take effect from and after the 25th of the present month.

"By command of

"Maj. Gen. Wallace.

"George H. Hooker, Assist. Adjt. Gen.

"Official: D.P. Thruston, Capt. and A.D.C."

———

Monument to the Late President. — After appropriate funeral services
yesterday at the Har Sinai Synagogue, in High street, (the Israelite Reform
congregation,) Rev. Dr. S. Deutsch, made a few remarks calling upon the members of the congregation, stating that it was contemplated to erect a monument
to the memory of our lamented President, and as part of the Israelites of this
city, they ought to take the first step in this undertaking. — Contributions were
at once offered, amounting to over $1,200. Considering that the congregation is
but a small one, counting but about about seventy members, this is an example

---

63   Lew Wallace (1827 - 1905) is best known for his defense of Washington, D.C. as
it sat vulnerable in July of 1864. He was on the military tribunal that rendered verdicts on the
conspirators. He later became a writer and authored the novel *Ben-Hur.*

which may well be emulated. It is expected that the amount will be increased, as a number of the congregation were not present.

Serious Charge. — Yesterday William Burke, Francis Conway, John Key, John S. Conway, Richard Thomas and Lewis Bobeth were arrested by order of Col. Woolley, and locked up in the military prison to await trial upon the serious charges of having entered a private dwelling on West Lombard st. on Sunday evening last, and there compelled the lady of the house to tear down a national flag, hanging from the wall; they then tore up the flag. It is also stated that they tore from the wall a likeness of the Late President Lincoln, broke it up, and then stamped upon it, and that, during their proceedings, they threatened to shoot the lady and the domestics of the house. The affair will be thoroughly investigated by Col. Woolley.

* * * * *

The New-York Tribune
New York City
April 20, 1865

THE PRESS AND THE PUBLIC

One of many letters of similar tenor recently received say, in perfect simplicity, "I assure that what you say in favor of Peace and lenity to Rebels does not *represent* the sentiments of your subscribers in this quarter." We haven't the least doubt of it. Representing — that is, reflecting, conforming to — the changing opinion of the hour, may not be difficult; but it surely cannot be achieved by those who do not try; and we never attempted the task, finding it unadapted to our mental habits and tastes. We might hoe cotton for a peck of corn and a couple pounds of bacon per week, with a few cuts of a horsewhip thrown in at intervals; we can certainly chop cord-wood or dig potatoes for a living, but we have not tried; but to *represent* public opinion in the editorial columns of a newspaper is a task quite outside of our capacity. The physical possibility of doing it may or may not inhere in our faculties; the moral does not.

179

We are sometimes inspired with intense disgust for a vocation whereof the popular estimate appears to be so sordid and low. We have quite often received epistles gravely informing us that what we think and say on a certain topic is unpopular, in the evident presumption that we only need to know this to make us wear ship[64] at once, and come short round on the other tack. The notion that a writer should ever undertake to resist, correct and improve public sentiment seems as inconceivable to our mentors as that a man should practice law with a view to the promotion of justice rather than for the sake of the money he might earn by it.

If the public is to be made any better, it must have instructors who do not "represent" its average views, but are wiser, better, profounder than they are. A journalist who uniformly "represents" the popular opinion may make his newspaper profitable to its publishers; but what can he possibly have done for his readers? As a vehicle of news, his sheet may be valuable; but his editorials, considered as lamps along the public highway and guides to correct thinking, can be of no use whatever.

The idea which seems to lie at the bottom of the degrading conception of our calling which we find prevalent seems to be not far from this: An editor is an intellectual gladiator, whom we hire or pay to find or invent reasons for the course which we have predetermined to take. He is like the lawyer who, being paid his fee, does his best for his client, whether that client's case be good or bad. He cannot always win; but he must ascertain what his clients want and "represent" it as well as he can.

Now we know and could name journals that always mean to "go with the tide," and generally succeed in this: We presume that they also succeed in making money; but they have no more influence on public opinion than the weathercock has on the direction or force of the wind. They may be consulted as evidence of what is popular, and may, in that view, have a certain value, but in no other are they worth a straw.

Sometimes we are addressed by a person who says, "I have taken your paper fifteen or twenty years, and have never disagreed with it till now." We

---

64   To "wear ship" is a nautical term meaning to turn and go with the wind.

are very sorry to hear it; for, in the course of so many years, we must have been many times wrong, and you ought to have detected some of those errors. The end and aim of this journal are, not to make its readers think in all cases as we do, but to teach them to think for themselves. We state our own opinion freely and frankly; we ask for them a fair consideration and candid judgment; but we never dreamed that everyone would make them his own. In fact, if we supposed every one united in the belief of a certain proposition, we should waste no words in its defense. it is precisely because we presume an opinion not generally entertained that we show cause for cherishing.

On a single point, we insist on being better understood. Several have written us, protesting against 'sentimentality," "tenderness to criminals," &c. They entirely mistake our position. It is in the interest not of the criminal but of the undepraved that we resist penal inflictions that tend to barbarize the community. It is in the interest of Human Liberty that we resist all that tends to invest the defeated champions of Slavery with the honors of martyrdom. We cannot well agree with those who hold that a great criminal escapes punishment unless the law takes his life or inflicts on him some kind of physical torture: for our respective stand-points are not within hail of each other; but we can possibly make students of history and of human nature comprehend that no party triumphant in a great civil war ever yet suffered from treating its vanquished opponents with too much lenity. The danger is all the other way: for there will always be a hundred voices crying Smite!" for every one which pleads "Spare!" In fact, they who would silence the one only evince an uneasy consciousness that their side of the question can not abide discussion. Better let all be fairly heard, and believe that they who "bear the sword" in such a crisis are most unlikely, even if unprompted to vigor, to "bear it in vain."

The President's Murderer

To the Editor of The N.Y. Tribune:

Sir: It is earnestly to be hoped that the American people in their hour of sorrow and indignation for the dastardly and hideous assassination of the kind-hearted, good and noble Abraham Lincoln, will not make too much of a hero of the assassin. His crime is gigantic; and it is unfortunately in the nature of gigantic crimes to excite morbid feelings in the minds of the insane or semi-insane, and cause them to emulate the deed that fills all men's minds and occupies all men's tongues. Some years ago, several attempts were made to assassinate the harmless and estimable lady who sits on the throne of England.[65] The attempts succeeded each other so rapidly that there seemed an epidemic of madness and assassination in the air — as difficult to explain as the cholera morbus. It was suddenly suggested by a student of human nature, that the desire of being spoken of, of being made the main actor in a great tragedy, had charms enough in the imagination of people of diseased intellects, to compel them to commit atrocious crime; and that the best way to render attempted assassination unpopular was to flog the bare back, every morning for a month or six weeks, the first wretch who should thereafter attempt to play the Brutus. The suggestion was acted upon; and since that time the life of Queen Victoria has been safe from the fanatics and lunatics. These people have no fear of the gallows; but they vehemently abhor a whipping. Preparatory to the hanging of the monster J. Wilkes Booth, a vigorous daily application of the whip on his naked carcass, on the night and morning of every day intervening between his capture and execution, would perhaps act as a wholesome corrective to the aspirations of any other fools and villains, who may think that there is heroism in murder. Believe me, yours respectfully,

April 18, 1865.

Chas MacKay.

Busts of Mr. Lincoln

To the Editor of The N.Y. Tribune.

Sir: I notice in your issue of this date an article regarding Mr. T.D. Jones'[66] bust of our lamented President, in which it is stated that Mr. Lincoln never sat

---

65   Queen Victoria (1819 - 1901), took the throne 1837 after her three older brothers died without producing an heir. She married a first cousin, Prince Albert, who died in 1861. The couple produced 9 children. Ruling until her death, she was the last monarch of the House of Hanover and until then the longest reigning British monarch.

66   Thomas Dow Jones (1811 - 1881) sculpted busts of Lincoln, Henry Clay, Daniel Webster, and Salmon P. Chase, among others.

for any other bust than that made by Mr. Jones. I feel it my duty to correct this statement immediately. I am the owner of a bust of Mr. Lincoln, presented me in Chicago by the artist Volk,[67] for which the late President sat within a few days of his nomination in 1860.

In this connection it may not be improper to mention an incident that took place at Mr. Lincoln's residence in Springfield at the time mentioned. Mr. Volk desired to make a cast of the President's hand, and in making the preparations Mr. Lincoln went into his back yard, took an old broom-stick, whittled off the end, and grasped it in his hand for the cast. I have a copy of this cast (a few of which the artist made for his friends.) which I will exhibit to you with pleasure, if you wish it. The marks of Mr. Lincoln's knife are plainly to be seen on the cast of the stick, and the hand is represented with perfect fidelity in its large muscular proportions.

Very respectfully,

William Wirt Sikes.

New York, April 19, 1865.

*　　*　　*　　*　　*

---

67   Leonard Wells Volk (1828 - 1895) cast a face mask of Lincoln when he was still a state senator. Shortly after Lincoln was nominated for the presidency, Volk sculpted his hands, one of them holding a broomstick. He also sculpted several large firgures for monuments. .

April 20, 1865

Daily Ohio State Journal[68]
Columbus, Ohio
Thursday, April 20, 1865

A dispatch from Gov. Brough[69] to Adjt.-Gen. Cowen[70] yesterday morning, and a special to the Journal from Washington, received last evening, state that the arrangements for the transportation of the President remain contemplated making Columbus one of the points on the route, and that the escort would arrive with the body on Saturday the 29th.

An official order from the Secretary of War announces that this arrangement has been changed and that the escort will move direct from Harrisburg to Springfield via Fort Wayne and Chicago.

A Scene in Wall Street

A remarkable exhibition of the temper of the people was given shortly after ten o'clock this morning in front of No. 44 Wall Street [New York City].

It appears that a man named Charles Anderson, who was known to Mr. Vermilye, a broker and banker of that number, approached Mr. Vermilye, while he was talking with two or three friends.

After some remarks had been made, Mr. Anderson said he did not think men who had sympathized with the secession movement, should be held responsible for the assassination. Mr. Vermilye differed with him, and in his reply said he did not think any sympathizer with the rebels could feel right to-day and that he (Mr. Vermilye) did not wish to continue a conversation with such a person. He then left Mr. Anderson and went into his place of business.

---

68   The *Daily Ohio State Journal* emerged in1848 after an ancestry that dates back to 1809. By mid-century it was representing the positions of the Republican Party.

69   John Brough (1811 - 1865) was governor of Ohio from January 11, 1864, to August 29, 1865, when he died of gangrene after a fall that bruised his arm and sprained his ankle. He was a War Democrat who supported the Union on anti-slavery grounds.

70   Benjamin Rush Cowen (1831 - 1908) had been Ohio Secretary of State before enlisting, first as a colonel in one Union army, then as a private under another, where he rose to adjutant-general. Among his several government positions was assistant secretary of the interior, in which capacity he helped establish Yellowstone National Park. He was editor of the *Ohio State Journal* from 1882 to 1884

A few persons who had overheard what had been said, gathered in front of the building, and Mr. Anderson saw that a storm was coming. It is reported that he ran into the office behind Mr. Vermilye, and escaped through the back part of the building.

The crowd gathered and became more and more excited. It was reported that Anderson had defended the assassination. There were frequent cries, "Bring him and let's have him." Some men demanded that he should be hanged.

Finally the crowd filled the street, vehicles which were compelled to stop were covered with men and the excitement became intense. The police were scarcely able to restrain the crowd and the determination to seize Anderson and to treat him as it was held deserved became fully apparent.

Afterwards it was decided to enter the building and find him. Just then, however, a squad of police appeared, and for the time prevented this movement.

As this point Moses H. Grinnell[71] appeared on the steps of the Bank of North America, which is the building, No. 44, and after some investigation as to the cause of the excitement, and an explanation, he addressed the crowd, by request of the police.

Mr. Grinnell spoke of the gathering and the cause of it and said he did not wonder at the intense excitement that was occasioned by the rumor that the murder of the chief magistrate had been defended by any man who had according to the rumor, taken refuge in the building around which so many men were not assembled. [Cries of "Bring him out" "Hang him."]

Mr. Grinnell then repeated the words used by Anderson, and said there was a vast difference between the expressions actually made and those that had been reported.

Mr. Grinnell then exhorted the crowd to act in a considerate manner, and like wise citizens.

Though all hearts, he said, were overwhelmed with sorrow, all men should stand for the right. If, however, our rulers were to be assassinated for doing the

---

71   Moses Hicks Grinnell (March 3, 1803 - November 24, 1877), a U.S. Representative (1839-1841) and later Commissioner of Central Park, had been a Democrat and a Whig before becoming a Republican.

right, traitors must understand that the time has come for every man to buckle on his armor. [Vehement cheering.]

Mr. Grinnell then alluded to Mr. Johnson, who was to take the place of the Chief Magistrate. [Cries, Nobody can take it.]

Mr. Grinnell continued, saying that he firmly believed that the nation would find that it possessed in Mr. Johnson a jewel whose worth could not be overestimated. [Great applause and cries, "We will support him — Let him hang the traitors."]

Mr. Grinnell concluded his remarks by advising the crowd to disperse. The street was soon cleared by the police — N.Y. Post

---

A Historical Clock

There is a clock in the Union Volunteer Refreshment Saloon, Philadelphia, made by soldiers who have just returned from its prisons. The mainspring is made from the blade of a saber which once belonged to "Stonewall" Jackson. The bands are made from a toasting fork taken from the kitchen of Vice President Stephens. The wheels are made from the mountings of carriages that belonged to rebels. The pillars holding the frame together, are made of ramrods. Nearly all the parts are taken from some article or other picked up in the so called Southern confederacy.

* * * * *

The New-York Times
April 20, 1865

THE OBSEQUIES — FUNERAL OF ABRAHAM LINCOLN — Solemn and
Imposing Ceremonies — A Day of Deep and Impressive Sadness
THE FUNERAL SERMON.
Just Tribute to the Virtues and National Services of the Late President.
[Official]
FROM SECRETARY STANTON TO GEN. DIX.

War department, Washington

April 19 — 1:30 P.M.

Maj. Gen. Dix:

The arrangement for conveying the President's remains to Springfield, Ill., has been changed this morning. They will go direct from Washington to Philadelphia, Harrisburgh, Fort Wayne, and thence to Springfield.

EDWIN M. STANTON, Secretary of War.

SECOND DISPATCH

WAR DEPARTMENT

WASHINGTON, April 19 — 11 P.M.

Maj. Gen. John A. Dix, New York:

It has been finally concluded to conform to the original arrangement made yesterday for the conveyance of the remains of the late President, Abraham Lincoln, from Washington to Springfield, viz.: By way of Baltimore, Harrisburgh, Philadelphia, New York, Albany, Buffalo, Cleveland, Columbus, Indianapolis and Chicago to Springfield.

EDWIN M. STANTON, Secretary of War

THE FUNERAL

Special Dispatch to the New-York Times.

Washington, D.C., Wednesday, April 19

THE FUNERAL CEREMONIES

The solemn and imposing funeral ceremonies of the day are over, and in point of sad sublimity and moral grandeur, the spectacle has been the most impressive ever witnessed in the national capital. The unanimity and depth of feeling, the decorum, good order, and complete success of all the arrangements, and the solemn dignity which pervaded all classes, will mark the obsequies of Abraham Lincoln as the greatest pageant ever tendered to the honored dead on this continent. The day has been delightfully warm and pleasant, and thus contributed to swell the throng of spectators, which was by the greatest that ever filled the streets of the city.

As early as 8 o'clock, people began to throng the avenue, and by 11 o'clock many thousands were assembled in the vicinity of the departments and the Executive mansion. The avenue, between Fifteenth and Seventeenth streets was kept clear by a strong guard of cavalry, for the purpose of forming the procession, though many of the societies had to wait on the side streets for hours. The arrangements made by the committee were carried out with a far greater degree of accuracy and comfort than is usual on occasions of this magnitude. No one was allowed to enter the grounds of the Executive mansion save such as had been provided with tickets, which included enough, however, to fill the great east room, where the body lay in state. It was intended that the attendance upon the funeral services should be of a highly representative character, and the intention was carried out with great success.

Lincoln with John Nicolay (seated) and John Hay.

At about 11 o'clock the various distinguished bodies and committees began to arrive, and to be ushered into their appropriate positions in the east room. This room has already been described in the Times, but since yesterday several tiers of low seats, or standing places, elevated one above another, just sufficient to give all a good view, had been erected on the east side and both ends of the room, and all covered with black muslin. On the west side of the room, against the door leading to the main corridor, were placed fifteen chairs, all draped, which were especially reserved by Secretary Harrington, of the Arrangement Committee, for the use of the press, a courtesy which was so completely arranged as to draw forth the commendation of every representative there. This grand east room presented a solemn appearance. It was hung with black everywhere. All glitter and gay color, save in the carpet beneath our feet, had been covered with the emblem of grief. The only relief from the mournful shade which met the eye everywhere were the white silk sashes of the marshals and committees, the rich silver ornamentation of the coffin, and the beautiful white japonicas, roses and green leaves which shed their perfume as incense over the dead.

The first to enter were the officiating clergymen, Rev. Dr. Hall, Rector of the Epiphany, Bishop Simpson, of the Methodist Episcopal Church, Rev. P.D. Gurley,[72] of the New-York Avenue Presbyterian Church,[73] the President's Pastor, and Rev. E.H. Gray, Chaplain of the Senate and Pastor of the E. street Baptist Church. Soon after came the Merchants Committee of New-York, whose names I sent you yesterday, followed by the Committee of the Union League. They took position on the platform at the north end of the building.

At 11:25, the Mayor of Washington[74] and the Common Council entered, escorting the Committee of the New-York Common Council, of which Alderman Bryce is Chairman; also mayor Lincoln and a committee from Boston, and a like committee from Philadelphia. Then came the officers of the Senate and House of Representatives, who took appropriate stations; the officers and members of the Christian and Sanitary commissions, the Assistant Secretaries, the Delegations from Kentucky and Illinois, the States of the President's birth and residence, who were designated as mourners, Govs. Fenton of New-York,[75]

---

72   Phineas Densmore Gurley (1816 -1868) was a close advisor of the Lincoln family. The Lincon's rented a pew at his church. The two often discussed theological questions. Gurley consoled Mrs. Lincoln and led prayers at Lincoln's deathbed.

73   From the church's website, nyapc.org/history: "The New York Avenue Presbyterian Church of 2010 embodies a rich history built on the very foundations of the Reformed tradition in this country. We were formed in 1859-60, but trace our roots to 1803 as the F Street Associate Reformed Presbyterian Church and another congregation founded in 1820 on our current site, the Second Presbyterian Church.

"The powerful story of these two early congregations and the merged church that welcomed President Abraham Lincoln and his family as pew holders on the first Sunday following his inauguration in March 1861—just six months after the dedication of the newly constructed church—is a story fully intertwined with the history of our denomination, the capital city, and this country.

"Reverend George Dogherty preached a Lincoln Day sermon on February 7, 1954 to a congregation that included President Dwight David Eisenhower. The sermon, titled 'One Nation Under God,' prompted the U.S. Congress to amend the Pledge of Allegiance to the Flag, inserting the phrase 'under God.'"

74   Richard Wallach (1816 - 1811) was on the City Council when the former mayor refused to take a loyalty oath to the United States. Wallach was appointed and reelected three times. He opposed emancipation and suffrage for freed slaves but led the building of the Lincoln Memorial.

75   Reuben Eaton Fenton (1819 - 1885) was elected to the House of Representatives as a Democrat, then was defeated, then was reelected three times as a Republican. He was

Andrew of Massachusetts,[76] Parker of New-Jersey, Brough of Ohio, Oglesby of Illinois, Buckingham of Connecticut,[77] and their staffs; the diplomatic corps in full court dress, the members of the Senate and House of Representatives, Admirals Gregory, Porter, Shubrick and Goldborough, the Supreme Court in the persons of Chief Justice Chase, Nelson, Davis, and Wayne, Ex-Vice-President Hamlin, the pall-bearers, twenty-two in number, then Grant and Farragut, arm in arm, Burnside and Hunter, Gen. Dyer of the Ordnance department, six lady mourners, the only ladies present, save one or two of the nurses of the household, Mrs. Sprague, Miss Nettie Chase, Mrs. Stanton, Mrs. Usher, Mrs. Welles and Mrs. Dennison.

At just 12 o'clock President Johnson, escorted by the venerable Preston King and the members of the Cabinet, entered and took their places on the right of the coffin. Private Secretaries Nicolay and Hay, and Capt. Robert Lincoln, the President's oldest son and only member of the family present, then Gen. Todd, of Dakotah, and relative of the family who were seated near the foot of the catafalque.

The room was now full, but no crowding, no disorder of any kind. The attendants upon the ceremonies had all arrived, and the scene in the room was of a very imposing character. A gentleman who had attended the funerals of three Presidents, assures me that this was the most imposing of all. The pall of black which met the eye everywhere, was suggestive of grandeur rather than gloom. The representative men from every part of the country impressed the beholder with the vastness of the power and influence of the form that lay cold in death, and the services which followed, the earnest prayer and eloquent sermon impressed upon all minds the virtues and great national services of Abraham Lincoln.

At ten minutes past 12, Rev. Mr. Hall opened the services by reading

---

governor from 1865 to 1868, then a senator. Opposing U.S. Grant, he joined the Liberal Republican Party.

76   John Albion Andrew (1818 - 1867) was an active abolitionist. As governor (1861 - 1866) during the war, he organized early regiments of black soldiers. He was a distant cousin of Lincoln.

77   William Alfred Buckingham (1804 - 1875) was governor (1858 - 1866) and then senator (1869 - 1875).

from the Episcopal burial service from the dead as follows:

"I am the resurrection and the life, saith the Lord; he that believeth in me, though he were dead, yet shall he live, and whosoever liveth and believeth in me shall never die." John 11th chap. 25th and 26th verses.

I know that my Redeemer liveth, and that He shall stand at the latter day upon the earth, and though after my skin worms destroy this body, yet in my flesh shall I see God, whom I shall see for myself, and mine eyes shall behold, and not another. — Job, chap. xix, 25th, 26th and 27th verses.

We brought nothing into this world and it is certain we carry nothing out. The Lord gave and the Lord hath taken away. Blessed be the name of the Lord." First Timothy, chap. vi., 7th verse, and Job, chap. i, 21st verse.

Lord, let me know my end and the number of my days, that I may be certified how long I have to live. Behold, Thou hast made my days as it were but a span long, and mine age is even as nothing in respect of Thee. And verily every man living is altogether vanity; for man walketh in a vain shadow, and disquieteth himself in vain. He heapeth up richest, and cannot tell who shall gather them. And now, Lord, what is my hope? Truly my Hope is ever in Thee; deliver me from all my offences, and make me not a rebuke unto the foolish. When Thou, with rebukes, doth chasten man for sin, Thou makest his beauty to consume away, like as

Funeral Procession down Pennsylvania Ave.

it were a moth fretting a garment. Every man is, therefore, but vanity. Hear my prayer, O Lord, and with Thine ears consider my calling. Hold not Thy peace at my tears, for I am a stranger with Thee, and a sojourner, as all my fathers were. O, spare me a little, that I may recover my strength before I go hence

Rev. Phineas Gurley

and be no more seen. Lord, Thou has been our refuge from one generation to another. Before the mountains were brought forth or even the earth and the world were made, thou art God from everlasting and world without end. Thou turnest man to destruction again, Thou sayest, come again ye children of men, for a thousand years in Thy sight are but as yesterday, seeing that it is past as a watch in the night. As soon as Thou scatterest them, they are even as sheep and fade away suddenly like the grass. In the morning it is green and groweth up, but in the evening it is cut down, dried up and withered.

For we consume away in Thy displeasure, and are afraid at Thy wrathful indignation. Thou hast set our misdeeds before Thee, and our secret sins in the light of Thy countenance; for when Thou art angry all our days are gone. We bring our years to an end as it were a tale that is told. The days of our age are threescore years and ten, and though men be so strong that they come to fourscore years, yet is their strength then but labor and sorrow, so soon passeth it away, and we are gone. So teach us to number our days that we may apply our hearts unto wisdom. Glory be to the Father and to the Son and to the Holy Ghost; as it was in the beginning, is now, and ever shall be, world without end. Amen."[78]

Then was read the lesson from the 15th chapter of St. Paul to the Corinthians,[79] beginning with the 20th verse. Right Rev. Bishop Simpson, of the Methodist Episcopal Church, then delivered a most eloquent and affecting prayer, after which Rev. Dr. Gurley, of the New-York-avenue Presbyterian Church, in which the deceased President had worshipped, delivered the following funeral sermon:

---

78   From The Book of Common Prayer, Hymn 79
79   On the resurrection of the dead.

Dr. Gurley's Sermon.[80]

As we stand here to-day mourners around this coffin and around the life-less remains of our beloved Chief Magistrate, we recognize and we adore the sovereignty of God. His throne is in the heavens, and His kingdom ruleth over all. He hath done and he hath permitted to be done whatsoever he pleased. Clouds and darkness are round about him; righteousness and judgment are the habitation of His throne. His way is in sea and His path in the great waters, and His footsteps are not known. Canst thou by searching find out God? Canst thou find out the Almighty unto perfection? It is as high as heaven — what canst thou do? Deeper than Hell — what canst thou know? The measure thereof is longer than the earth and broader than the sea. If He cut off and cut up, or gather together, then who can hinder him — for he knoweth vain men. He seeth wickedness: also will he not then consider it?[81] We bow before His Infinite Majesty

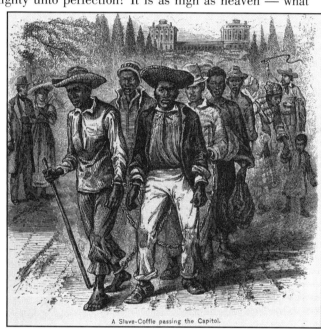

A Slave-Coffle passing the Capitol.

A coffle of slaves passing the Capitol.

— we bow, we weep, we worship. There reason fails with all her powers — there faith prevails and love adores. It was a cruel, cruel hand, that dark hand of the assassin, which smote our honored, wise and noble President, and filled the land with sorrow. But above and beyond that hand there is another, which we must see and acknowl-

---

80   This sermon was printed in a few long paragraphs, here broken up for ease of reading.

81   Job 11-11

edge. It is the chastening hand of a wife and faithful Father. He gives us this bitter cup, and the cup that our Father has given us shall we not drink it?

God of the just, thou givest us the cup,

We yield to thy behest and drink it up.

Whom the Lord loveth he chasteneth.[82]

Oh, how these blessed words have cheered and strengthened and sustained us through all these long and weary years of civil strife, while our friends and brothers on so many ensanguined fields were falling and dying for the cause of liberty and Union. Let them cheer and strengthen and sustain us to-day.

True, this new sorrow and chastening has come in such an hour and in such a way as we thought not, and it bears the impress of a rod that is very heavy, of mystery that is very deep, that such a life should be sacrificed at such a time, by such a foul and diabolical agen-

New York Ave. Presbyterian Church circa 1913

cy that the man at the head of the nation, whom the people had learned to trust with a confiding and loving confidence, and upon whom more than upon any other were centered under God our best hopes for the true and speedy pacification of the country, the restoration of the Union and the return of harmony and love -- that he should be taken from among us, and taken just as the prospect of peace was brightly opening upon our torn and bleeding country, and just as he was beginning to be animated and gladdened with the hope of ere long enjoying with the people the blessed fruit and reward of his and their tolls, care and patience and

---

82   Hebrews 12:6

self-sacrificing devotion to the interests of liberty and the Union.

Oh, it is a mysterious and a most afflicting visitation. But it is our Father in Heaven, the God of our fathers and our God, who permits us to be so suddenly and sorely smitten, and we know that his judgments are right, and that in faithfulness he has afflicted us in the midst of our rejoicings. We needed this stroke, this dealing, this discipline, and therefore he has sent it. Let us remember our affliction has not come forth of the dust, and our trouble has not sprung out of the ground. Through and beyond all second causes, let us see the sovereign permissive agency of the great First Cause. It is His prerogative to bring light out of darkness and good out of evil. Surely the wrath of man shall praise Him, and the remainder of wrath He will restrain. In the light of a clearer day, we may yet see that the wrath which planned and perpetrated the death of the President was overruled by Him whose judgments are unsearchable and His ways past finding out, for the highest welfare of all those interests which are so dear to the Christian patriot and philanthropist, and for which a loyal people have made such an unexampled sacrifice of treasure and of blood.

Let us not be faithless, but believing. "Blind unbelief is prone to err and scan His work in vain. God is His own interpreter, and he will make it plain." We will wait for His interpretation; and we will wait in faith, nothing doubting. He who has led us so well, and defended and prospered us so wonderfully during the last four years of toil and struggle and sorrow, will not forsake us now. He may chasten, but he will not destroy. He may purify more and more in the furnace of trial, but he will not consume us. No, no. He has chosen us, as He did his people of old, in the furnace of affliction, and He has said of us, as He said, of them, these people have reformed. For myself they shall show forth my praise. Let our principal anxiety now be that this new sorrow may be a sanctified sorrow, that it may lead us to deeper repentance, to a more humbling sense of our dependence, upon God, and to the more unreserved consecration of ourselves and all that we have to the cause of truth, and justice, of law and order, of liberty and good government, of pure and undefiled religion. Then, though weeping may endure for a night, joy will come in the morning. Blessed be God.

Despite of the great and sudden, and temporary darkness, the morning has began to dawn, the morning of a bright and glorious day such as our country has never seen. That day will come, and not tarry and the death of a hundred Presidents and their Cabinets can never, never prevent it. While we are thus hopeful, however, let us also be humble. The occasion calls us to prayerful and tearful humiliation. It demands of us that we lie low, very low, before him who has smitten us for our sins.

O! that all our rulers, and all our people, may bow in the dust to-day beneath the chastening hand of God, and may their voices go up to Him as one voice, and their hearts go up to Him as one heart, pleading with Him for mercy, for grace to sanctify our great and sore bereavement, and for wisdom to guide us in this our time of need. Such a united cry and pleading will not be in vain. It will enter into the ear and heart of Him who sits upon the throne, and He will say to us, as to His ancients. "In a little wrath, I hid my face from thee for a moment, but with everlasting kindness will I have mercy upon thee, saith the Lord, thy Redeemer."[83]

I have said that the people confided in the late lamented President with a full and a loving confidence. Probably no man since the days of WASHINGTON was ever so deeply and firmly imbedded and enshrined in the very hearts of the people as ABRAHAM LINCOLN. Nor was it a mistaken confidence and love. He deserved it; deserved it well; deserved it all. He merited it by his character, by his acts, and by the tenor and tone and spirit of his life. He was simple and sincere, plain and honest, truthful and just, benevolent and kind. His perceptions were quick and clear, his judgments were calm and accurate, and his purposes were good and pure beyond a question, always and everywhere. He aimed and endeavored to be right and to do right. His integrity was thorough, all-pervading, all controlling and incorruptible. It was the same in every place and relation, in the consideration and control of matters great or small, the same firm and steady principle of power and beauty, that shed a clear and crowning lustre upon all his other excellencies of mind and heart, and recommended him to his fellow-citizens as the man who, in a time

---

83   Isaiah 54:8

of unexampled peril, when the very life of the nation was at stake, should be chosen to occupy in the country, and for the country, its highest post of power and responsibility.

How wisely and well, how purely and faithfully, how firmly and steadily, how justly and successfully, he did occupy that post and meet its grave demands, in circumstances of surpassing trial and difficulty, is known to you all -- known to the country and the world; he comprehended from the first the perils to which treason had exposed the freest and best government on the earth -- the vast interests of liberty and humanity that were to be saved or lost forever in the urgent impending conflict.

He rose to the dignity and momentousness of the occasion, saw his duty as the Chief Magistrate of a great and imperiled people, and he determined to do his duty, and his whole duty, seeking the guidance and leaning upon the arm of Him of whom it is written — He giveth power to the faint, and to them that have no might He increaseth the strength.

Yes, he leaned upon His arm.

He recognized and received the truth that the kingdom is the Lord's, and He is the governor among the nations.

He remembered that God is in history, and he felt that nowhere had His hand and His mercy been so marvelously conspicuous as in the history of this nation.

He hoped and he prayed that that same hand would continue to guide us, and that same mercy continue to abound to us in the time of our greatest need.

I speak what I know and testify what I have often heard him say, when I affirm that guidance and mercy were the props on which he humbly and habitually leaned. That they were the best hope he had for himself and for his country. Hence when he was leaving home in Illinois and coming to this city to take his seat in the Executive Chair of a disturbed and troubled nation, he said to the old and tried friends who gathered tearfully around him, and bade him farewell, I leave you with this request — pray for me. They did pray for him, and millions of others prayed for him.

Nor did they pray in vain. Their prayers were heard, and the answer appeared in all his subsequent history. It shines forth with a heavenly radiance in the whole course and tenor of his administration from its commencement to its close. God raised him up for a great and glorious mission, furnished him for his work, and aided him in its accomplishment.

Nor was it merely by strength of mind and honesty of heart and purity and pertinacity of purpose, that He furnished him. In addition to these things He gave him a calm and abiding confidence in the overruling providence of God, and in the ultimate triumph of truth and righteousness through the power and the blessing of God.

This confidence strengthened him in all his hours of anxiety and toil, and inspired him with calm and cheering hope when others were inclined to despondency and gloom.

Never shall I forget the emphasis and the deep emotion with which he said in this very room, to a company of clergymen and others who called to pay him their respects in the darkest day of our civil conflict:

"Gentlemen, my hope of success in this great and terrible struggle rests on that immutable foundation, the justice and goodness of God, and when events are very threatening and prospects very dark, I still hope that in some way which man cannot see, all will be well, in the end, because our cause is just and God is on our side."

Such was his sublime and holy faith, and it was an anchor to his soul both sure and steadfast. It made him

Thomas "Tad" Lincoln

firm and strong. It emboldened him in the pathway of duty, however rugged and perilous it might be. It made him valiant for the right for the cause of God and humanity, and it held him in steady, patient and unswerving adherence to a policy of administration which he thought and which we all now think, both

God and humanity required him to adopt. We admired and loved him on many accounts, for strong and various reasons. We admired his child-like simplicity; his freedom from guile and deceit; his staunch and sterling integrity; his kind and forgiving temper; his industry and patience; his persistent, self-sacrificing devotion to all the duties of his eminent position, from the least to the greatest; his readiness to hear and consider the cause of the poor and humble, suffering and oppressed; his charity His inflexible purpose, that what freedom had gained in our terrible civil strife should never be lost, and that the end of the war should be the end of slavery, and as a consequence of rebellion, his readiness to spend and be spent for the attainment of such a triumph, a triumph, the blessed fruits or which should be as wide-spreading as the earth, and as enduring as the sun.

All these things commanded and fixed our admiration, and the admiration of the world, and stamped upon his character and life the unmistakable impress of greatness.

But more sublime than any or all of these, more holy and influential, more beautiful and strong and sustaining was his abiding confidence in God and in the final triumph of truth and righteousness through Him and for His sake. This was his noblest virtue, his grandest principle, the secret alike of his strength, his patience and his success. This, it seems to me, after being near him steadily and with him often for more than four years, is the principle by which more than by any other, he being dead yet speaketh.

Yes, by his steady enduring confidence in God, and in the complete ultimate success of the cause of God, which is the cause of humanity, more than in any other way does he now speak to us and to the nation he loved and served so well.

By this he speaks to his successor in office, and charges him to have faith in God.

By this he speaks to the members of his Cabinet, the men with whom he counciled so often and associated with so long, and he charges them to have faith in God.

By this he speaks to all who occupy positions of influence and authority in these and tumultuous times, and he charges them all to have faith in God.

By this he speaks to this great people as they sit in sackcloth to-day, and weep for him with a bitter wailing, and refuse to be comforted, and he charges them to have faith in God, and by this he will speak through the ages, and to all rulers and people in every land, and His message to them will be, Cling to liberty and right, battle for them, bleed for them, die for them if need be, have confidence in God.

O, that the voice of this testimony may sink down into our hearts to-day and every day, and into the heart of the nation, and exert appropriate influence upon our feelings, our faith, our patience and our devotion to the cause, now dearer to us than ever before, because consecrated by the blood of its conspicuous defender, its truest and most fondly trusted friend.

He is dead. But the God in whom he trusted lives, and He can guide and strengthen his successor as He guided and strengthened him.

He is dead. But the memory of his virtues; of his wise and patriotic counsels and labors; of his calm and steady faith

The funeral car at Alexandria.

in God, lives as precious, and will be a power for good in the country quite down to the end of time.

He is dead. But the cause he so ardently loved; so ably, patiently, toward those who questioned the correctness of his opinions and the wisdom of his policy: his wonderful skill in reconciling differences among the friends or the Union, leading them away from abstractions and inducing them to work together and harmoniously for the common weal; his true and enlarged philanthropy, that knew no distinction of color or race, but regarded all men as brethren, and endowed alike by their creator with certain inalienable rights, amongst which are life, liberty, and the pursuit of happiness; faithfully represented and defended, not for himself only, not for us only, but for all people in all their coming generations till time shall be no more.

That cause survives his fall and will survive it. The light of its brightening prospects flashes cheeringly to-day athwart the gloom occasioned by his death, and the language of God's united providences is telling as that though the friends of liberty die, liberty itself is immortal. There is no assassin, strong enough and no weapon deadly enough to quench its inexhaustible life or arrest its onward march to the conquest and empire of the world.

This is our confidence and this is our consolation, as we weep and mourn to-day; though our beloved President is slain our beloved country is saved; and so we sing of mercy as well as of judgment. Tears of gratitude mingle with those of sorrow, while there is also the dawning of a brighter, happier day upon our stricken and weary land. God be praised that our fallen chief lived long enough to see the day dawn, see the day star of joy and peace arise upon the nation.

He saw it and was glad. Alas! alas! (sic) He only saw the dawn when the sun has risen full orbed and glorious, and a happy reunited people are rejoicing in its light. It will shine upon his grave, but that grave will be a precious and a consecrated spot. The friends of Liberty and of the Union will repair to it in years and ages to come, to pronounce the memory of its occupant blessed, and gathering from his very ashes, and from the rehearsal of his deeds and virtues, fresh incentives to patriotism, they will there renew their vows of fidelity to their country and their God.

And now I know not that I can more appropriately conclude this discourse, which is but a sincere and simple utterance of the heart, than by addressing to our departed President, with some slight modification, the language which TACITUS, in his Life of AGRICOLA, addresses to his venerable and departed father-in-law. With you we may now congratulate. You are blessed not only because your life was a career of glory, but because you were released when your country was safe, it was happiness to die. We have lost a parent, and in our distress it is now an addition to our heartfelt sorrow that we had it not in our power to commune with you on the bed of languishing and receive your last embrace.

Your dying words would have been ever dear to us. Your commands we should have treasured up, and graven them on our hearts. This sad comfort we have lost, and the wound, for that reason, pierces deeper. From the world of spirits behold your disconsolate family and people. Exalt our mind from fond regret and unavailing grief to the contemplation of your virtues. Those we must not lament. It were impiety to sully them with a tear. To cherish their memory, to embalm them with our praises, and so far as we can to emulate your bright example, will be the truest mark of our respect, the best tribute we can offer.

Your wife will thus preserve the memory, of the best of husbands; and thus your children will prove their filial piety; by dwelling constantly on your works and actions, they will have an illustrious character before their eyes; and not content with the bare image of your, mortal frame, they will have what is more valuable -- the form and features of your mind. Busts and statues, like their originals, are frail and perishable. The soul is formed of finer elements, and its inward form is not to be expressed by the hand of an artist. With unconscious matter our manners and our morals may, in some degree, trace the resemblance. All of you that gained our love and raised our admiration still subsist, and will ever subsist, preserved in the minds of men, the register of ages; and the records of fame of others who figured in the stage of life, and were the worthiest of a former day, will sink for want of a faithful historian into the common lot of oblivion, inglorious and unremembered. But you, our lamented friend and head, delineated with truth and fairly consigned to posterity, will survive yourself and triumph over the injuries of time.

Rev. E.H. GRAY, D.D. pastor of the E-street Baptist Church,[84] closed the solemn services with prayer.

The corpse was then removed to the hearse, which was in front of the door of the Executive Mansion, and at 2 o'clock the procession was formed. It took the line of Pennsylvania-avenue. The streets were kept clear of all incumbrances, but the sidewalks were densely lined with people from the White

---

84   He was also chaplain of the U.S. Senate.

House to the Capitol, a distance of a mile and a half. The roofs, porticos, windows and all elevated points were occupied by interested spectators. As the procession started minute guns were fired near St. John's Church, the City Hall and the Capitol. The bells of all the churches in the city and of the various engine-houses were tolled.

First in the order of procession was a detachment of colored troops, then followed white regiments of infantry and bodies of artillery and cavalry, navy, marine and army officers on foot; the pall-bearers in carriages next; the hearse, drawn by six white horses -- the coffin prominent to every beholder. The floor on which it rested was strewn with evergreens, and the coffin covered with white flowers. Then followed Physicians of the late President, then the grand hearse and the guard of honor and the pall-bearers, Capt. ROBERT LINCOLN[85] and little TAD,[86] the President's favorite son, in a carriage, and TOMMY[87] behind. Mrs. Lincoln was not present at either the ceremony or in the procession, she not having left her bed since Saturday last. The mourners, the delegations from Illinois and Kentucky, came next in order, and then President JOHNSON in a carriage, with Hon. PRESTON KING[88] and the Cabinet Ministers. The carriages on this part of the line were flanked by a strong cavalry guard, with drawn sabres. Then came more carriages with the Diplomatic Corps, Judges, Senators, and others; then members of the House of Representatives, on foot; the officers of the House; the New-York delegations; the Massachusetts delegation, with Gen. BUTLER, in civilian's dress, prominently in the line, delega-

85   Robert Todd Lincoln (1843 - 1926) was Lincoln's oldest son and the only one to survive into adulthood. President Garfield appointed him Secretary of War in 1881. He was present at the assassinations of Garfield and McKinley. A few months before the assassination, Edwin Booth — John's brother — saved Robert's life (without recognizing him) when Robert fell between a train and a station platform in Jersey City, N.J.
86   Thomas Lincoln (1853 - 1871) was nicknamed Tad because as a baby he wiggled like a tadpole. He was watching a play at Grover Theater when his father was shot at Ford's Theater. Robert was his older brother.
87   Apparently an error. Tommy and Tad were the same person.The "Tommy" here was William "Willie" Wallace Lincoln (1850 - 1862), who had died of fever at the age of 11, to the great and lasting grief of his father. He had been buried at Georgetown but was exhumed so his remains could accompany his father's to Springfield.
88   Preston King (1806 - 1865) was a congressman and senator from New York and a founder of the Republican Party. He committed suicide by tying a bag of bullets around his neck and leaping from a ferry into New York Harbor.

tions from other States, Masons, Knight Templars, Perseverance Fire Company of Philadelphia, Catholic clergy, nine delegations, departments clerks two thousand strong, Gen. MEIGS and staff and the Quartermasters department brigade, a regiment of Fenians, the Treasury regiment Gen. MCCALLUM and staff, and a brigade of the employees of the United States military railroads, all wearing an appropriate badge. Next a large delegation from Alexandria, with a car on which was painted, "Alexandria mourns the national loss." Then came one of the saddest scenes in the entire column, a battalion of scarred and maimed veterans, with bandaged limbs and heads, with an arm or leg gone, but hobbling along on crutches, determined that their homage to their great chief should be as sincere as that of their companions. Then more firemen and Sons of Temperance, with a battalion of soldiers, in full regalia of these excellent Sons; then Colored Benevolent Associations, with their banners draped and their walk and mein (sic) the very impersonation of sorrow.

The procession finally ended, but was almost two hours in passing a given point, and the head of it had actually begun to disperse at the Capitol before the rear of the column had passed beyond the Treasury Department.

On the arrival at the eastern gate of the Capitol, the remains were conveyed into the rotunda, where a catafalque like that in the Executive Mansion had been erected to receive them. Here the attendants assembled, and amid profound silence Rev. Dr. GURLEY read the burial service.

The vast assemblage then began to disperse, and the obsequies of the lamented dead were over. During the entire afternoon the bells in the city and in Georgetown and Alexandria were tolled, and minute guns fired from the fortifications. So may we lament with TENNYSON:

Let the bell be toll'd.
And a deeper knell in the heart be knoll'd.
And the sound of the sorrowing anthem roll'd
Through the dome of the golden cross
And the volleying cannon thunder his loss.[89]

---

[89]   From Tennyson's "Ode on the Death of the Duke of Wellington."

The remains lie in state at the capitol until Friday morning, at 8 o'clock, when they will proceed northward. The route has been shortened somewhat from the published programme of this morning at the earnest request of Mrs. LINCOLN, but she has finally consented that they may proceed to Philadelphia and New-York, and they will lie in state at Philadelphia during Sunday, and arrive in New-York on Monday morning, at 7 o'clock, remaining there until Tuesday.

*   *   *   *   *

National Intelligenser[90]
Washington, D.C.
Thursday, April 20, 1865

BOOTH REPORTED IN PENNSYLVANIA.
He Is Seen on the Reading Railroad.

READING, April 19 — Booth, the assassin, it is supposed was on the passenger train that left here at 6 o'clock for Pottsville. A gentleman noticed him on the train, before it reached Pottsville, spoke to him, and shook hands with him. During the conversation Booth colored up several times and appeared annoyed, and desirous of avoiding observation. The gentleman is positive it is Booth, he having known him several years. Why he did not give the alarm at once, as the train left, I do not know, but just as the train left he notified several of the officers of the road, and an extra train was immediately sent in pursuit. Telegrams were sent to all points upon the line of the railroad. The result is unknown as yet.

[Second Despatch.]

---

90   Also in this edition: General John S. Mosby surrenders in Virginia; lynchings "in several places" in the Pacific states for "expressing joy at the assassination"; a classified ad offering $50 reward for a stolen bay mare and buggy; Cincinnati business suspended; Wilberforce University, in Greene County, Ohio, destroyed by fire; two women arrested for a ruckus on the corner of High and State streets.

READING, April 19 — The extra train did not overtake the regular train, but arrived at Pottsville after it.

The conductor informed the party that the suspected man got off at Port Clinton. The train returned, but the man had gone, which way, or how, no appeared to know,

SECRETARY SEWARD MUCH BETTER

Washington, April 18

The following despatch has been received by Col. F. S. Sandford, President of the American Telegraph Company:

F.S. Sandford: Uncle is much better. he sat up for a quarter of an hour this morning, and was bright and cheerful. To-day is a marked improvement upon yesterday.

Frederick is slowly, but surely, regaining his consciousness. He has spoken twice this morning He sleeps much of the time, and breathes regularly and easily His pulse and appetite are good. I think everyone one feels encouraged with regard to both.

The messenger and nurse are doing well.

C.A. Seward

CITY NEWS

THE REMAINS OF LITTLE WILLIE LINCOLN — The Superintendent of Oak Hill Cemetery, in Georgetown, has been ordered to deliver the body of Little Willie Lincoln to Dr. Charles Brown, for the purpose of conveying it to-morrow, to Springfield, Illinois, for reinternment in the ground by the side of his honored and lamented father.

INCEPTION AND CULMINATION OF CRIME

It was four years ago, at the hour in which the procession moved yesterday from the Presidential mansion, since the Massachusetts 6th regiment was assaulted in the streets of Baltimore by an armed rebel mob as the regiment was hastening to the defence of the capital, on the 19th of April 1861.[1] The flag of this State, similar to that borne by the 6th regiment, which was the first actual body of men reaching this city at the opening of the rebellion, was yesterday borne in the procession by Colonel Gardiner Tufts at the head of the Massachusetts delegation.

*   *   *   *   *

---

1   Also known as the Pratt Street Riot and Pratt Street Massacre, the incident occurred just a week after the Ft. Sumter battle. Maryland at the time leaned heavily toward secession, and Baltimore was especially anti-Union. After Lincoln called for volunteers to put down the Southern insurrection, they began moving south, many by train. But there was no connection between the President's station and the Camden St. station. Cars were pulled by horse from one station to the other, passing down Pratt St. When a secessionist mob attacked and blocked the cars carrying the Massachusetts Regiment, the soldiers disembarked and marched down the street. Falling under a barrage of stones and gunfire, the soldiers fired into the crowd, killing 12. Four soldiers died. Unrest continued, and in May Maryland was put under martial law. The Pratt Street incident is considered the first North-South conflict in which Union soldiers died.

April 21. 1865

Friday, April 21, 1865

The Dark Shadow of His Sable Wing

Death has fastened into his frozen face
all the character and idiosyncrasies of life.

He has not changed one line of his grave, grotesque
countenance, nor smoothed out a single feature.

The hue is rather bloodless and leaden;
but he was always sallow.

The dark eyebrows seem abruptly arched;
the beard, which will grow no more,

is shaved close, save the tuft
at the sharp, small, chin.

The mouth is shut,
like that of one who had put the foot down firm,

and so are the eyes,
which look as calm as slumber.

The collar is short and awkward,
turned up over the stiff elastic cravat,

and whatever energy or humor or tender gravity
marked the living face
is hardened into its pulseless outline.

The Ohio Statesman
Columbus, Ohio
Friday morning, April 21, 1865

Charming Consistency

The [Ohio State] Journal of this city is remarkable for its logic, its morality, its truthfulness, candor and consistency. A brilliant specimen of its undoubted possession of these high qualities is afforded in its reply, in its issue of Thursday morning, to our comments on its charges against the Democratic party in its article on the "Rule of Secession."

The Journal says THE STATESMAN "uttered the following abominable, but transparent and characteristic misinterpretation of our [its] language and sentiments."

"Here are two distinct and explicit charges brought against the Democratic party, as a class of citizens, and against every man belonging to it."

Having made this quotation from THE STATESMAN, The Journal proceeds to say:

"If the antidote had not preceded the bane — if our language did not give the lie to the statement — it might possibly have been deemed worthy of contradiction."

After some foolish and absurd remarks about THE STATESMAN individually, The Journal denies that the charges it brings are against the Democratic party as a class of citizens, and immediately adds:

"Our charges as stated by The Statesman, are these:

"1. That the Democrats are inclined to apologize for those engaged in rebellion, and palliate their offense.

"2. That the assassination of the President is DISTINCTLY traceable to the teachings of the Democratic party."

Right underneath this quotation from The Statesman, The Journal says:

"This is the nearest approach to truth The Statesman has made for a month past. We accept it as a reasonably fair statement. We believe each of these statements to be substantially and literally true."

Now, reader, mark the beautiful consistency of our truth-loving contemporary. It says we uttered an 'abominable, but characteristic misrepresentation of its language, and sentiments," and that its "language gave the LIE" to our statement, that its charges were brought "against the Democratic party as a class of citizens," and immediately, in the teeth of these contradictions and denials, returns, like a dog to its vomit, and declares that its statement that "the Democrats are inclined to apologize for those engaged in rebellion and palliate their offense," and that "the assassination of the President is DISTINCTLY traceable to the teachings of the Democratic party" — that each of these statements is "SUBSTANTIALLY AND LITERALLY TRUE."

Thus, out of its own mouth, is the author of that foul slander and base libel upon Democrats "as a class of citizens," condemned. He, like a coward and sneak, first denies that his charges were made against the Democratic party as "a class of citizens," and, then, almost in the same breath, like a mad fanatic who would "scatter firebrands and death," he proclaims that it is SUBSTANTIALLY AND LITERALLY TRUE that Democrats who are "a class of citizens," are inclined to apologize for, and palliate the offense of the rebels; and that the Democratic party, which includes a very large "class of citizens," teaches things, to which the assassination of the President is DISTINCTLY traceable. Out upon the self-stultified liar and miscreant. He is a specimen of a genuine JOHN BROWNITE[1] — a worthy disciple of a murderer and a traitor, whose crime, like that of CAIN'S, bears "the primal elder curse upon it."

The Ohio State Journal Gave Currency to a Suggestion that President Lincoln Should Be Assassinated!

Without a word of disapproval The Ohio State Journal published a letter on the 9th of August, 1864, the writer of which stated that there were 192 men in a certain regiment ready to march to Washington to assassinate President Lincoln, if he undertook to conclude a Peace with the Rebels that was not satisfactory to them. This is the scoundrelly sheet that now charges that the

---

1   A John Brownite would be an abolitionist willing to use violence to do away with slavery.

assassination of President Lincoln is the offspring of the teachings of the Democratic press.

* * * * *

The Jamestown Journal[2]
Jamestown, Chautauqua Co., N.Y.
Friday, April 21, 1865

OUR GREAT GRIEF.

In the experience of nearly every individual there comes a time of all times. Some great, overwhelming grief comes crushing through the cords and nerves of his consciousness, sweeping away the petty cares, the anxious concerns of life, swallowing up all the past, and changing forever the aspect of all the future, making him what he was not. Everything in after years takes color from it, and the man is, thenceforward, as much another man as a change of nature could possibly make him.

So sometimes with Nations. So now with us. The Past seems all a dream. We remember a people united, happy, prosperous, free; we have painful impressions of discord, strife and bloody civil war; remembrances of triumphs and glorious successes to our arms, still are in our minds. But, standing between all these events, that in their day filled our hearts so full, is now a great, black cloud. We know only that he whom we loved and trusted — on whom we leaned as a guide through the wilderness of civil war, and who had led us on until we stood in full view of the promised land of peace and harmony — he, our Nation's father, lies DEAD in our capital by the hands of a cowardly assassin, a martyr to the noble cause in which our hopes and the hopes of humanity are bound up. Death has cast the dark shadow of his sable wing over a nation's hopes. What can we do but sit in darkness and weep?

We weep for the loss of a friend such as the common people never had

---

2   The *Jamestown Journal* was founded in 1826 by Adolphus Fletcher. In 1941, it merged with the *Morning Post* to become the *Post-Journal*, which is still in print. It supported the Whig Party and later the Republican Party and the election of Lincoln, strongly advocating harsh treatment of the treason committed by the South. Its original building is now a church.

before. In a sublimity of reliance on them that nothing ever shook in the darkest, most perilous hour, he rested his hopes and the destiny of a mighty nation. And well did we repay that confidence with love. The people in their devotion said, "he is ours and we are his" all we have shall be at his command until we come out of our thick-set troubles." They gave him their lives and fortunes. Although the work delayed; the war with all its bitter woes was prolonged; the promised peace seemed never to come, yet with a faith and devotion equal only to his, they decided that he should stay at their head until the hoped for day of peace dawned. He promised them nothing, but his honest best efforts. They trusted him in everything. Is there anything in history equal to this supreme confidence of a people in a plain, unassuming man raised up from their midst?

And, now, as he lies in death's cold obstruction at our capital we can smile through our tears with the consoling thought that in life we never doubted, never failed him. It was not in admiration of a mighty genius that the people laid their highest honors at this man's feet. It was not in gratitude for great good and grand successes achieved for us by him. Ours was the "love that casteth out all fear," and leaned on him in the hour of sorest trial with a faith that was so unprecedented that history will attribute it either to the instinct of self-preservation, or to the inspiration of that Great Ruler who holds nations as he does seas in the "hollow of His hand."[3]

While we may recall the consolations that "undying love" affords, we cannot repress the bitter thoughts that come crowding thickly up for utterance: How that poor old man, who died for us, has seen only the dark and gloomy and woeful part of our great national regeneration. How it was granted to him only to catch the first dawnings of that glorious light that began to illuminate from center to circumference the land he had saved. How, standing on his Mount Pisgah,[4] he looked away to the inspiring sight of a people re-united in heart and hand, peaceful, happy, prosperous, confessing at last his agency in

---

3   Isaiah 40:12: "Who hath measured the waters in the hollow of his hand, and meted out heaven with the span, and comprehended the dust of the earth in a measure, and weighed the mountains in scales, and the hills in a balance?"

4   The place from which Moses saw the promised land, a.k.a. Mt.. Nebo (Deuteronomy 34:1)

212

the great work. We know not the feelings that stirred that faithful heart at the sight. The dying Colonel of the 112th, when it was told him that Fort Fisher[5] was ours, exclaimed, "Oh, howI do want to live, now!" Such must have been the prayer of the President for himself, and all the people for him had it been known to them last Friday that "this day thy head shall be taken from thee." We remember him a few days ago down at the front witnessing the dying gasps of the rebellion and sending to his people the greeting, "All is well with us." How he came back to the jubilant nation to prepare a proclamation of thanksgiving and to mature a plan of re-union, full of mercy, kindness and generosity to the unfaithful South. In the very midst of his work which might well have employed an angel's heart and hand, he is shot down like a dog, from behind, by one of those he sought to forgive and bless!

Does not the mind go back eighteen hundred and sixty-five years to recall the scene when he "who spoke as never man spake,"[6] prayed for his murderers: "Lord, forgive them?"

What doom is dark enough, what punishment lasting enough for the actors of his bloody tragedy? What execration is bitter enough, what damnation deep enough for the institution that could father such a monstrous crime?

And, yet, we know that with our martyred President now, as when at the front, "All is well!" His earthly fame is secure; his memory fresh as long as liberty and gratitude live in the heart of man; his reward in another world assured.

But for us — the people — the nation — the loss is sore, the grief bitter. At the time when the most difficult part of the political problem was to be solved and we seem to most need his patience, courage, moderation, good-sense, and good-heart, he is taken away. The deprivation of such a man in the President's chair at this time is the great national loss. We know that by the virtues of our matchless form of government its wheels move on uninterrupted by this event, and we hope for the best — indeed, believing that the hand of the All-Wise is in the blow. Still, the loss, the humiliation, the grief, the wrong, are ours — ours to remember, ours to mourn, ours to avenge. Yes,

5   The fort at the port of Wilmington, N.C., taken by Union troops in January, 1865.
6   John 7:46

— "The first mourner to-day

is the nation, whose father is taken away!

Wife, children and neighbors may mourn at his knell;

He was "lover and friend" to his country as well.

For the stars on our banner grow suddenly dim,

Let us weep, in our darkness — But weep not for him!

Not for him — who departing leaves millions in tears;

Not for him — who had died full of honors and years;

Not for him — who ascended fame's ladder so high

From the round at the top he has stepped to the sky!

It is blessed to go when so ready to die!"

INCIDENTS

The Marching Song of Uncle Sam's Black Boys.

The following song is the ditty sung by Uncle Sam's Colored Infantry on their march into and through Petersburg and Richmond early last Monday morning. Though not exactly classic in diction, it is quite expressive:

Say, darkies, hab you seen de massa,

    wid de muffstach on his face

Go 'long de road some time dis mornin',

    Like he's goin' to leave de place?

He seen de smoke way up de ribber,

    Where de Linkum gunboats lay;

He took his hat and left berry sudden,

    And, I 'spose he's runned away.

        De massa run, ha! ha!

            De darkey stay, ho! ho!

It must be now de kingdom comin',

        An' de yar ob Jubilo.

He's six foot one way and four foot todder,
    An' he weighs six hundred poun',
His coat's so big he could pay de tailor,
    An' it won't reach half way roun';
He drills so much dey call's him cap'n,
    An' he gits might tann'd,
I spec he'll try to fool dem Yankees
    For to tink he's contraband,
        De massa run, ha! ha!
    De darkey stay, ho! ho!
It must be now de kingdom comin'
    An' de yar ob Jubilo.

*   *   *   *   *

The National Intelligenser[7]
Washington, D.C.
Friday, April 21, 1865

The sober second thought of our people is distinguished by common sense; and the popular decision is always just, when the evidence is full and true on which the masses are called to pronounce a verdict. And such will be the case, notwithstanding the exciting circumstances which now influence and distress the nation, when the American judgment shall be called to act "on all the issues" affected by the assassination of the late President. The first demand will be for God-inspired retribution; for a full and adequate punishment of the conspirators, the murderers, and would-be murderers; and then will come a more calm consideration of the political facts and exigencies in the case. This

---

7   Also in this issue: Andrew Jackson, Jr., son of General Jackson, dead of lockjaw (tetanus) after shooting himself in the hand while climbing over a fence. A house in Evansville, Ind. was coated in tar because the owner refused to drape it in mourning; a man and wife are accused of assaulting a child; a 13-year-old girl in Elk Grove, Wisc. weighs 170 lbs.; Montreal is reported to have a place called "the Rink," adopted from Scotch curlers, a covered place to skate on ice, described as "Anything but a Methodist looking place inside."

branch of the question involves much thought and requires clear evidence. If the conspiracy shall be traced directly to the leaders in the rebellion, there will be presented a matter about which it is now unnecessary to say more than this, viz.: that appropriate punishment will follow the crime. It is needless to anticipate here; to write inflammatory language or speak it. Justice will be done, and let that suffice.

But there is a general view of this subject at which it may be timely to glance. If there is treason in the North, it should be promptly ferreted out if possible, and if convicted, ignominious punishment, such as the law affixes, must be summarily inflicted. But it does not, therefore, follow, either as a wise or logical deduction, that we shall be unjust to the loyal sentiment of the South, much of which has been maintained under the crushing weight of the rebellion, and which is daily growing into a prevailing feeling. To protect and to restore this loyalty has been the object of all our sacrifices, and to achieve this glorious result will be to attain our proudest hopes and our ultimate ambition. A great crisis like this cannot be managed to passion in the Government or the governed. The Administration, to be wise and prudent, must move solidly on the path of such statesmanship as we shall gather and garner the harvest of the war, which, we repeat, is peace and restoration; and this kind of husbandry the nation will insist upon.

The terrible assassination of the late President (as it now appears from facts and circumstances) has been the adventure, at most, of a few wicked, perverted, and desperate spirits, not uncommon to such times as these. The letter of Booth, which is before our readers, goes a great way to establish this theory. We cannot see how any doubt can reasonably arise about the genuineness of that letter, since it has been disclosed by members of his family as evidence of his guilt. There is not the suspicion, in reasonable minds, that this letter is put forth to establish the insanity of the criminal; nor is it likely that anybody is in danger in his loyalty either from the secession logic or rhetoric which the document contains. But be this how it may, the assassination and conspiracy, viewed in their most extended light, are false issues, where interpolated into the main features of the national case.

Germaine (sic) to the above reflections we commend the following from the New York Tribune of yesterday:

"On a single point we insist on being better understood. Several have written us, protesting against "sentimentality," "tenderness to criminals," &ct. They entirely mistake our position. It is in the interest, not of the criminal, but of the yet undepraved, that we resist penal inflictions that tend to barbarize the community. It is in the interest of human liberty that we resist all that tends to invest the defeated champions of slavery with the honors of martyrdom. We cannot well agree with those who hold that a great criminal escapes punishment unless the law takes his life or inflicts on him some kind of physical torture; for our respective standpoints are not within hail of each other; but we can possibly make students of history and of human nature comprehend that no party triumphant in a great civil war ever yet suffered from treating its vanquished opponents with too much lenity. The danger is all the other way; for there will always be a hundred voices crying, 'smite!' for every one who pleads 'spare!' In fact, they who would silence the one only evince an uneasy consciousness that their side of the question cannot abide discussion. Better let all be fairly heard, and believe that they who "bear the sword" in such a crisis are most unlikely, even if unprompted to rigor, to "bear it in vain.""

It is very natural that a flood of leading men should act toward the capital at this moment of solemn interest. There is much to attract them; respect for the late President of course inspires all, while solicitude and zeal for the welfare of his successor has naturally taken fresh root in the hearts of the politicians of the nation.

But this solemn moment, as we think, is not the time to persecute the President, either by well-meant speeches about his policy, to which he is forced to reply without special premeditation, or by patriotic appeals on the grave question of his patronage. Weeks hence might answer for these things. Excited and bowed down by the sudden dispensation of Heaven which has devolved on him such responsibilities, the immense pressure upon the President, which we have deprecated, may prove too much (if not checked) even for his vigorous health. We hope that reflections like these may tend to moderate the fervor of the patriotic friends of the Executive and of the country.

———————

Referring to the matter of raising a monument to the memory of the late President, we have to state that an esteemed correspondent has suggested that the site of the murder shall, with adjoining property, be used for the erection of an altar to "liberty," upon which shall stand the statue of her greatest votary and martyr. We subjoin the closing portion of the communication as follows:

"Let the nation adopt his children, and so provide for his family, bereaved for our sakes, that no proud scoffer at republicanism shall repeat that 'Republics are ungrateful.'

"Even 'soulless corporations' show proper regard for those whose fidelity and experience in their employment lead to loss of life, by granting testimonials to their widows and orphans. Shall our nation be less considerate and generous?

"To generals and admirals have been given rich tokens of appreciation and esteem for public services. Now let the Great Nation show its love and gratitude to the greatest and best of all its servants, in that way which would have been more grateful to his loving heart, by bestowing a testimonial upon those dearer to him than life, and who so suddenly have been deprived of husband, father, supporter, protector, and friend.

"Congress should give the acts national character, but societies and individuals should subscribe and raise funds to carry them into effect."

———————

The assassinations of Friday night begin to be developed in the proportions of quite a conspiracy, which had for its object, in common with the rebellion itself, the destruction of the national life. The conspirators must have had some powerful motive of action, and no other can be imagined than the belief that the murder of the President and members of the cabinet would overthrow the Government, and permit rebellion and treason to flourish over it. It was, no doubt, thought by the traitors, as it was formerly by the rebel leaders, that this Government could be destroyed by Northern faction, sympathizing with the Southern arms. The hope might also have arisen in their minds, that the sudden blow whereby the personnel of the Executive Administration would be destroyed, would reunite the expiring elements of the rebellion in the South. No aim of less importance than this could be adequate to so great a crime. The fact exhibits a remarkable degree of ignorance of American character and institutions on the part of all who have been concerned in the rebellion. Treason has drawn its conclusions from a very erroneous estimate of the character of free society, upon which our Government is based. Upon any other basis they might have shaken by treason and rebellion, arising in the slave States.

There are few monarchies and no absolute governments that could have withstood the shock of such a war as the rebels have waged against the Union. There are few governments that would not have been shaken, even by the treasonable murder of its Chief Executive. How common it has been for European politicians and presses to auger revolutions, in the strongest governments of the old world, even from an accidental and untimely death, if it should occur, of some reigning potentate. Often it has been predicted that, if by any mischance the present emperor of the French should be cut off by sudden death, not only France, but all Europe would be convulsed. Let rebellion and treason know, let the world know, the great truth, that this Government depends for its existence upon the broad and firm basis of the Constitution and its laws. As Mr. Beecher eloquently exclaimed, in the Fort Sumter oration, "There is the Constitution, there are the laws, there is the Government. They rise up like mountains of strength that shall not be moved."

The Common Feeling Among Rebel Prisoners

When Confederate Gen. Ewell[8], prisoner on parole, and one of the most earnest of the armed opponents of the Federal Government, heard the tidings of Mr. Lincoln's assassination, he wept, and exclaimed, "That is the greatest misfortune that has happened to the South." There is no doubt this is the general feeling among nineteen-twentieths of the prisoners of war. In Gen. Ewell's

---

8   Richard Stoddert Ewell (1817 - 1872), Confederate general, was pro-Union until his native Virginia seceded.

case, says the News:

That veteran soldier, mutilated in the service of the Confederate cause, and identified with the most unyielding spirit of Southern resistance, has expressed a sentiment that we have heard echos by many Southern people. The fatal bullet that deprived the Republic of its lamented chief was moulded in an unhappy hour for the Confederacy, and the hand that sent it on its murderous errand was inspired by the evil genius in the South. The assassin is guilty of a double murder; for which Abraham Lincoln will be buried the first hope of peace that, through four long, weary, terrible years of havoc and desolation, has revealed itself to an afflicted people.

While Gen. Ewell was at the Provost Marshal's office, in this city, he conversed with several official and private individuals. He took this occasion utterly to deny the allegation that he had ordered the burning of Richmond, or that the fire which occurred upon his evacuation of the city was caused either by his order or that of any Confederate authority. He said the fire was the work of the Richmond mob.

He stated also that he would not have fought the last battles, in which he commanded the rear guard, had he known how large a force was opposed to him. As it was the fight was very severe, as our officers testify. On the field, during a momentary pause in the conflict, he wrote the following despatch to Gen. Lee:

Gen. Lee: For God's sake, and humanity's sake, surrender your army. You are outnumbered and beaten. To continue the contest longer is to court nothing but slaughter in vain.

EWELL

General Ewell made an important suggestion to one of our officers in this city, in reference to the restoration of peace. He said that the paroled or exchanged soldiers of the Confederate armies ought to return to the counties or districts where they belonged, and be there employed in cultivating the soil. It was too late for them to commence the culture of the corn crop. Under the advice of their officers they would do that, and thus their minds would be diverted from war.

Nothing could be more ridiculous than the story of Booth being en route over the Reading (Pa.) railroad. There is a telegraph line on that road, and the railroad company, of course, has wires from station to station. Once on the train, Booth would be sure to be taken.

From the Washington Correspondence of the N.Y. World.

Appearance of the Corpse.

Death has fastened into his frozen face all the character and idiosyncrasies of life. He has not changed one line of his grave, grotesque countenance, nor smoothed out a single feature. The hue is rather bloodless and leaden; but he was always sallow. The dark eyebrows seem abruptly arched; the beard, which will grow no more, is shaved close, save the tuft at the sharp, small, chin. The mouth is shut, like that of one who had put the foot down firm, and so are the eyes, which look as calm as slumber. The collar is short and awkward, turned up over the stiff elastic cravat, and whatever energy or humor or tender gravity marked the living face is hardened into its pulseless outline. No corpse in the world is better prepared according to appearances. The white satin around it reflects sufficient light upon the face to show us that death is really there; but there are sweet roses and early magnolias, and the balmiest of lilies strewn around, as if the flowers had begun to bloom even upon his coffin. We look on uninterruptedly, for there is no pressure; but henceforward the place will be thronged with gazers who will take from the sign its suggestiveness and respect. Three years ago, when little Willie Lincoln died, Doctors Brown and Alexander, the embalmers or injectors, prepared his body so handsomely that the President had it twice disinterred to look upon it. The same men, in the same way, have made perpetual those beloved lineaments. There is no more blood in the body. It was drained by the jugular vein and sacredly preserved and through a cutting on the inside of the thigh the empty blood vessels were charged with a chemical preparation, which soon hardened to the consistence of stone. The long and busy body is now hard and stiff, so that beyond its present position it cannot be moved any more than the arms or legs of a statue. It has undergone many changes. The scalp has been removed, the brain scooped out, the chest opened, and the blood emptied. All this we see of Abraham Lincoln, so cunningly contemplated in this splendid coffin, is a mere shade, an effigy, a sculpture. He lies in sleep, but it is the sleep of marble. All that made this flesh vital, sentient, and affectionate is gone forever.

[Official]

ONE HUNDRED THOUSAND DOLLARS REWARD

WAR DEPARTMENT

Washington City, April 20, 1865

The murderer of our late beloved President is still at large!

FIFTY THOUSAND DOLLARS REWARD will be paid by this Department for his apprehension, in addition to any reward offered by municipal authorities or State Executives.

TWENTY-FIVE THOUSAND DOLLARS REWARD will be paid for the apprehension of G.A. ATZEROT, sometimes called "Port Tobacco," one of Booth's accomplices.

TWENTY-FIVE THOUSAND DOLLARS REWARD will be paid for the apprehension of DAVID C. HEROLD, another of Booth's accomplices.

LIBERAL AWARDS will be paid for any information that shall conduce to the arrest of either of the above-named criminals or their accomplices.

All persons harboring or secreting the said persons, or either of them, or abiding or assisting their concealment or escape, will be treated as ACCOMPLICES in the murder of the President and the attempted assassination of the Secretary of State, and shall be subject to trial before a military commission and the punishment of DEATH!

Let the stain of innocent blood be removed from the land by the arrest and punishment of these murderers!

All good citizens are exhorted to aid public justice on this occasion. Every man should consider his own conscience charged with this solemn duty, and rest neither night nor day until it be accomplished.

EDWIN M. STANTON,

Secretary of War

THE SUSPECTED CRIMINAL IN PENNSYLVANIA

Philadelphia, April 20. — The following despatch was received this evening from a lawyer at Reading:

The despatch of yesterday was somewhat erroneous. The statement given by the citizen of Reading referred to is, that he has no acquaintance with Booth, having seen him but once in seven years, in a theatre in Baltimore, and not being able to identify him now.

He saw the suspected man in a saloon on Tuesday night, in company with another man, drinking freely. Learning that he intended leaving town for Pottsville at six P.M. yesterday, he got upon the train after it had started and recognized the individual, who appeared very much confused at meeting him. He asked the citizen whether he was going up on the train. Upon his answering that he was not, the man said he would be back in Reading in a day or two. The citizen then left the train and communicated these facts to a detective, by whose agency he has been arrested, and is now awaiting recognition at Tamaqua.

[Second Despatch]

Reading, April 20 — to S. Bradford: On my return from Pottsville, representations made to me last evening there were such that I sent a special engine to Pottsville, after the up evening passenger train, but the man had left the train at Auburn before the telegram could reach there. The man walked back to Port Clinton after dark, and stole his passage to Tamaqua on one of our coal trains last night. He is now caught at Tamaqua, where we telegraphed to look out for him, and will be held until identified. There has been some ground for suspicion that it is Booth.

G.A. Nichols,

Superintendent Phila. and Reading R.R.

[Third Despatch]

READING, April 20 — The citizen who recognized Booth was taken before a justice of the peace this afternoon and made an affidavit of his knowledge.

He swears now that he saw Booth some seven years ago, and also that he does not believe the person pursued was Booth. Heretofore he stated positively that it was Booth, and that he knew him intimately.

It is reported here that the suspected party has been arrested at Tamaqua. No particulars received.

*   *   *   *   *

Louisville Daily Journal
Friday, April 21, 1865

J. Wilkes Booth — The Booth Family.

As everything pertaining to J. Wilkes Booth, the assassin of President Lincoln, is of interest to the public, we take the following history of the Booth family from the Cincinnati Commercial:

John Wilkes Booth is a son of Junius Brutus Booth, Sr., by his second wife, who survives him, and now resides with her stepson, Edwin Forrest Booth,[9] in New York City. The elder Booth, the father of the imputed assassin, was an English tragedian, born in London in the year 1796. During his minority he played in several provincial English theatres, with moderate success, and, in 1814, made his debut at Covent Garden Theatre, in his native city, as Richard III. His personal resemblance to "that hunch-backed toad" conformed so well to the stage traditions, and his personification of the character was, in other respects, so striking, that he at once took a prominent rank in his profession, and successfully competed with Edmund Kean,[10] then the rising

---

9   An error. This was Edwin Thomas Booth, who was named after Edwin Forrest and Thomas Flynn, both of whom had worked with Edwin's father, Junius Sr.

10   Edmund Kean (1789 - 1833), highly acclaimed English Shakespearean actor,

star of the English stage, at Drury Lane Theatre. He shortly after placed with Kean at Drury, and was subsequently announced to reappear at Covent Garden. Meantime an affair occurred which rendered him very unpopular with the public, and his reappearance was the signal for a serious theatre riot, which resulted in driving him temporarily from the London stage. We do not distinctly recollect the particulars. Jealousy, professional or otherwise, stirred up the fiery nature of Booth, and he attempted the life of the obnoxious person, but failed to take it. The man survived the assault, and is now, we believe, a resident of St. Louis. Booth remained in England till about the year 1820, when he crossed the Atlantic, and made his first professional appearance in this country at Petersburg, Virginia, and the year following at the Park Theatre, New York, on both of which occasions he assumed his favorite role of Richard III. From that time to the close of his life, he fulfilled engagements in nearly, if not every theatre in the United States, and was accounted one of the greatest actors of his time, though the range of characters which he assumed was limited, and was confined to almost exclusively those which he had studied in the beginning of his career. Having secured a moderate competence, Booth purchased a property near Baltimore, known as "The Farm," where, during his latter years, he resided, making occasional professional visits to other cities. He made an excursion to California somewhere about the year 1850, where he fulfilled a very lucrative engagement, and on his way home stopped in New Orleans, where he made his last appearance at the St. Charles as Sir Giles Overreach in "a New Way to Pay Old Debts." It was while on his passage from that city to Cincinnati that he died. His remains were taken to "The Farm" for burial.[11]

Booth's habits were exceedingly irregular, and so interfered with his performances at times that an actor less gifted would have forfeited his popularity beyond redemption. It was rarely that he appeared sober on the stage, and toward the close of his life, it required all the vigilance and art of managers to keep him in a condition to appear on the stage at all. The stories told of him

---

starting when he played a cherub at the age of four, ending when charges of adultery turned his popularity negative. His final words are said to be "Dying is easy...comedy is hard."

11   He died on November 30, 1852, after drinking river water on a steamboat trip bound for Cincinnati out of New Orleans.

in this connection were innumerable, and some of them extremely ludicrous. His appetite for liquor was absolutely voracious. Being without money at one time when in New York, he went to a pawn-broker's shop, literally pawned himself for money to purchase liquor, was regularly ticketed and exhibited in a window, where he stay till "redeemed" by a friend. On another occasion, being announced to appear in Philadelphia — at the Walnut street, we believe — the manager, on the day for the performance, had Booth locked up, but was outwitted by the actor, who bribed the servant to bring a bottle of brandy, a saucer, and a clay pipe. Inserting the pipe through the key-hole, with the bowl inverted, the brandy was poured into the saucer, and sucked up through the pipe by the thirsty tragedian, and the fact was disclosed when in the twilight the manager proceeded there to conduct him to the dressing-room and found him in an insensible condition. It was considered somewhat perilous to play Richmond to Booth's Richard III., particularly if the actor was in liquor. During the combat on Bosworth Field he was apt, in his excitement, to consider himself in reality the King, and cut and thrust with the fierceness and ferocity of a man engaged in an earnest and life-depending trial of arms. At such times it was necessary to disable him, and it was in one of those "crazy spells" that his face was disfigured for life by an imperiled actor, the bridge of his nose being broken by the blow delivered through sheer defence. The very ludicrous scene which occurred at a New York Theatre between Booth and the celebrated "fat girl" of Barnum's Museum is probably familiar to most of our readers, and is, perhaps, one of the most amusing incidents in the annals of the stage.[12] It is very doubtful whether Booth was insane at any time when not under the influence of strong drink. He was, however, of a very fiery quality, and in his peculiar sphere — the sudden and nervous expression of concentrated passion, as also in the more quiet and subtle passages of his delineations — he was, perhaps, unsurpassed by any actor of his time, and would have passed for crazy if it were supposed he was guided in his dramatic outbursts by feeling rather than consummate artistic skill. Off the stage, the elder Booth was convivial, genial, warm-hearted, and as much loved as in his profession he was admired.

---

12   She was Anna Crouse.

The family of Booth consisted of the following: Junius Brutus Booth, Jr., and a daughter, who, if living, is still unmarried — children by his first wife, an English lady; and Edwin Forrest, John Wilkes, Joseph, and a daughter, now wife of John S. Clarke, the comedian — children of his second wife, an American lady, still surviving, and who must be, at this time, past fifty years of age.

The eldest of the boys, Junius Brutus, was born in Charleston, South Carolina, in 1821. He made his first appearance on the stage in 1834, at Pittsburgh, Pennsylvania, as Tyrrel in Richard III, and appeared first in New York, at the Bowry, in 1851. The same year he went to California, and, if we mistake not, he spent most of his time on the Pacific coast. He was married twice, first to Miss Clementina DeBar, an Irish actress, from Dublin, and reputed to have been one of the most beautiful women of her day. They subsequently separated, and Mr. Booth married Miss Harriet Mace, who died in San Francisco in 1859, after a lingering illness. This member of the family would have completed a two weeks' engagement at Pike's Opera-house, on Saturday night, but for the terrible news which associated the family name inseparably with the cruel assassination at Washington. Mr. Booth, who had been up late the previous night, left his room and went direct to Pike's Opera-house on Saturday morning to attend rehearsal, totally unaware of what had transpired. An excited crowd had already clamored at the door for him, torn down the bill in which he was announced, and had only left on assurance that he would not play, and that no performance would be had that evening. When he appeared on the stage, Mr. Simmonds, acting manager, drew him to one side, and cautioned him against too much publicity. He inquired why, and, on being told the news, exclaimed, "My God! can (sic) it be possible!" swooned away, and was conveyed from the stage in an insensible condition. He is reported to have since left the city. He is said, by those who claim to know him, and speak advisedly, to be a Union man, without a tinge of secession poison or sympathy; but of his political notions we know nothing. He resembles his father, personally, more than any other of the family, having his antique type of face, and features capable of wonderful expression under the influence of excitement.

Edwin Forrest Booth, the eldest son by the second wife, has attained a greater eminence in his profession than any member of the family. A more versatile and finished actor than his father, he has surpassed him in the reputation he has gained on the American stage, and stands confessed, to-day, the most distinguished star in the profession, excepting, perhaps, Edwin Forrest, after whom he was named. He has undoubted genius and great scholarly attainments. During the present season he played Hamlet over one hundred consecutive nights at the Winter Garden, of which he was one of the [illegible]. He cannot be over thirty-two or three years of age. His residence is in New York city, and his engagements have of late been exclusively in the East. He has, in company with his brother-in-law, Mr. Clark, purchased the Walnut-street Theatre, which it was their intention to open and manage during the coming season. Mr. Booth's wife, Mary, a most estimable woman, greatly loved and deeply mourned in Boston, died some two years ago, leaving one child, a daughter. The poetic tributes to her memory by Emerson, Stoddart, and other poets, would of themselves make a small volume. Her loss greatly affected Mr. Booth, and gave to his pale intellectual face, a tinge of sadness, which some of his friends attributed, in part, to his concentrated study and personification of Hamlet, a very probable effect. He is regarded as needy and eccentric, frequently shutting himself in his study, and refusing admittance to his most familiar friend, for days together. The telegraph announces his intention to withdraw from the stage altogether. His assassin brother will have added to other stings of remorse, the reflection that he has blighted the fair prospects of Edwin, and driving from the stage one of the brightest ornaments in the heyday of his renown.

Of Joseph Booth, the youngest of the brothers, we know very little, other than that he tried the stage only long enough to satisfy himself and friends that his vocation was not in that direction. When the rebellion broke out he was studying medicine in Charleston, but, not satisfied with the cause of the South, escaped to Philadelphia, where he has since resided.

John Wilkes Booth — the infamous — was born on "the Farm," near Baltimore, Maryland, in 1838, and is consequently but twenty-seven years old. He made his first stage appearance in 1855, at Richmond in Richard III, at the

St. Charles theatre in Baltimore, and, in the fall of 1857, appeared under the name of Wilkes, at the Arch-street theatre in Philadelphia, where he played stock parts during the entire season. The name of Wilkes was given him by his father, in honor of an old Baltimore friend, Jim Wilkes, a successful merchant and great wit. Young Booth next became a member of the Richmond, Virginia, theatre, improved rapidly in his profession, and became a great favorite there. During the season of 1860-'61 we find him still engaged at Montgomery and Columbus, GA. Probably not fancying conscription into the Southern army, however much he favored the cause, he escaped North, and in 1861-'62 played in St. Louis, Louisville, and other Western cities. It was during the season following, we believe, that he first appeared in Cincinnati, at Wood's Theatre, and left the impression that, though rather an unequal actor, as might be expected of one of his limited experience, he gave unmistakeable evidence of genuine dramatic talent. He had, added to his native genius, the advantage of a voice musically full and rich; a face almost classic in outline; features highly intellectual; a piercing black eye, capable of expressing the fiercest and the tenderest passion and emotion, and a commanding figure and impressive stage address. In his transitions from the quiet and reflective passages of a part to fierce and violent outbreaks of passion, his sudden and impetuous manner had in it something of that electrical force and power which made the elder Booth so celebrated, and called up afresh to the memory of men of the last generation the presence, voice, and manner of his father. Convivial in his habits, sprightly and genial in conversation, John Wilkes made many acquaintances and friends among the young men of his own age in the city – an acquaintance that was renewed during two subsequent engagements.

Our recollection of Booth is somewhat indistinct, but, we remember, his features in repose had rather a sombre and melancholy cast; yet, under agreeable influences or emotions, the expression was very animated and glowing. His hair, jet black and glossy, curled slightly, and set off in fine relief a high, intellectual forehead, and a face full of intelligence. Both chin and nose were markedly prominent, and the firm-set lips, and lines about the mouth, indicated firmness of will, decision, and resolution. He was scrupulously neat in his dress, and selected his habit with a rare perception of what was becoming to his figure and complexion. He would pass anywhere for a neatly and not over-ly-dressed man of fashion.

Of his political views very little was known. He kept a still tongue on the subject, so far as we have heard. Being of Southern birth and education, it was presumed his sympathies tended in that direction; but he exhibited no particular warmth or zeal for the rebellion, and nothing to indicate the remotest desire to further the cause by so much as giving it pecuniary aid, much less personal assistance. It is reported by a gentleman who heard the conversation, that, during his engagement in Louisville in 1862, Booth fell into a controversy with the treasurer of the theatre — a rabid secessionist — while standing one morning in the box-office. He remarked, in effect, that he was a Southern man, and liked the people of the South, who had been kind to him, but he could not, for all that, admit that they had any right or occasion to secede; that they had it all their own way in Congress, and that if they insisted on fighting, they should have taken the American flag and fought under that. There is another story to the effect that Booth, while playing an engagement in Cleveland, a year or more ago, asserted in a public bar-room that the man who would kill Abraham Lincoln wold gain a more enviable notoriety than Washington himself. It is, of course, impossible to say whether these reported sayings are apocryphal or not.

The last appearance of Booth on the stage (except for one or two benefits in Washington) was at the Winter Garden, New York, and in conjunction with his brothers, Edwin and Junius Brutus, in the play of "Julius Caesar," for the benefit of the Shakespeare Monument Fund. He was, we believe, to have played with them again at the same theatre on the 22nd of this month, for the benefit of the same fund. The play selected was "Romeo and Juliet," the cast of the Booths being — John Wilkes as Romeo, Edwin as Mercutio, and Junius as Friar Lawrence. As we have said, he has played no engagement the present season. He left the stage to engage in oil speculations, in which he was quite fortunate, having netted within six months between $50,000 and $75,000. Nor had he any intention of resuming the stage, and declined all managerial ap-plications, petroleum, as he wrote, being more profitable than the profession.

The President After Death.

Maunsel B. Field, Esq., who was present at the death-bed of the President writes:

The President's eyes, after death, were not, particularly the right one, entirely closed. I closed them myself, with my fingers, and one of the surgeons brought pennies and placed them on the eyes, and subsequently substituted for them silver half dollars. In a very short time, the jaw commenced slightly falling, although the body was still warm. I called attention to this, and had it immediately tied up with a pocket-handkerchief. The expression immediately after death was purely negative, but in fifteen minutes there came over the mouth the nostrils,and the chin, a smile that seemed almost an effort of life. The body grew cold very gradually, and I left the room before it had entirely stiffened. Curtains had been previously drawn down by the Secretary of War.

Barber Shot on Saturday Evening. — About half past ten o'clock on Saturday evening, several white barbers from J.H. Gerhard's bathing and shaving saloon, visited a beer-saloon to take a glass of beer. While they were drinking, a quarrel arose in the the back part of the saloon between several men in regard to the assassination of President Lincoln. Someone having expressed his pleasure at the report, the provost guard took up the quarrel, and as the crowd rushed out of the saloon the guard fired some eighteen shots at them. One shot struck one of the unoffending barbers under the left shoulder, and glancing off, but the wounded man, Fred Young, is confined to his bed. Another shot struck Murice Elbert, who died instantly.

Frank Bache, of Jeffersonville, Ind., had the misfortune to be arrested last Friday night, in the bar-room of the United States Hotel, for being in the company with disloyal parties, and was reported in the Journal as using disloyal language. He was honorably discharged from custody, as he proved beyond a doubt to be innocent of the charge. He is, and always has been, a loyal man.

April 21, 1865

Two of the ladies that were arrested a few days ago for disloyalty, Miss Mary Sweeny and Susan Kerrick, were released yesterday, on taking the oath.

* * * * *

**Daily State Gazette
Trenton, N.J.
April 21, 1865**

Moseby. — A private letter from an officer on board the U.S. steamer Tiger, dated at Point Lookout, Chesapeake Bay, April 18, says that all gunboats are under orders to patrol the bay and river, stop all vessels, seize all small boats, and prevent anyone from crossing the river. The writer says that it is reported that Moseby, with a thousand desperadoes, is in the lower counties of Maryland. On the 17th a regiment was sent from Point Lookout to find and capture the scoundrels.

There appears to be no doubt of the fact that there is an organized gang of ruffians in that part of Maryland — probably accomplices of the assassin Booth — but it's hardly probable that Moseby or any of his men are with them. Advices from the Valley of the Shenandoah state that Moseby surrendered to Gen. Chapman on Monday last.

* * * * *

**Xenia Sentinel
Xenia, Ohio
Friday, April 21, 1865**

Abraham Lincoln

We know not what will be recorded in the page of impartial history. We are in the shadow of great events. We are liable to arrive at wrong conclusions. Much that appears false to us now, will be the stern truth of history; and much that appears true to us now, will be false in the searching eye of future ages.

We are at the focus, the culminating point, of a conflict that originated previous to the beginning of this century. Private individuals and presidents; armies and states are tossing in the wild whirlpool, some going up, some going down. The storm rages; clouds lower; darkness closes in around; and in the heat, passion, and confusion of the period, we may seek, but vainly, for the truth of all things. But truth will ultimately vindicate itself, and history will not be false. We know not what place on the historic page will be occupied by the name of Abraham Lincoln; because all now is dark. We know not how events now transpiring will finally shape themselves. We know not what the mystic future will unfold. And thus while our intelligence enables us to know nothing in the future, our faith, strong and unshaken, teaches us to believe that the name Abraham Lincoln will be an illustrious one through time.

We cannot but suppose that two names will go down to posterity quite inseparably connected — the names of Washington and Lincoln. They each lived in a crisis; and each was the hero of his time. The former, not alone in poetry, but in reality, was the Father of his Country. Others labored, fought and died, to bring about the great result; but Washington was the master. In his hands were the materials. He was the originating, governing, shaping spirit. He held over this people the line of right. When the public enthusiasm ran too low, he inspired it; when it ran too high, he moderated it. He held the army to-gether for seven years, and the Continental Congress merely put his wisdom in the shape of legislative enactments. He won independence, and for eight years held the helm of the Ship he launched. He stamped his genius indelibly upon the young Republic. He started the youthful Nation in the right direction; but with strange, prophetic eye, he saw a coming crisis — a crisis of Disunion. It came, and but for a hero, all would have been lost. But a hero was not lacking. Heaven provided. Abraham Lincoln was given to be the genius of the conflict. The brunt of the conflict is passed, and the hero genius of it is no more.

But some will say that herein is too much belief in the interference of Providence in the affairs of men; to which we only answer, that to believe that this people stumbled by accident upon Abraham Lincoln for President, is to believe also that nations are guided more by the uncertainties of chance than

233

by an All-ruling God.

And others will say that herein is too much more man-worship. As to this let us see.

* * * * *

New York Daily Tribune[13]
Friday, April 21, 1865

The Assassin Seen

Sergt. J.M. Dye, Battery C., Pa. Ind. Artillery, stationed at Camp Berry, Washington City, in a private letter of the 15th inst. to his father, J.S. Dye, No. 100 Broadway, gives the following account of the conduct of Booth immediately before the assassination, which proves that he had a confederate on the ground, actively cooperating in his preparations for the bloody work. It seems that they expected the President to leave the house at the close of the second act, and meant to have assassinated him between the door and his carriage:

"Washington, D.C., April 15, 1865.

"Dear Father: With sorrow I pen these lines. The death of President Lincoln has deeply affected me. And why shouldn't it, when I might have saved his precious life?

"I was standing in front of the theater when the two assassins were conversing. I heard part of their conversation. It was not sufficiently plain for an outsider to understand the true meaning of it; yet it apprised Sergt. Cooper and myself that they were anxious that the President should come out to his carriage, which was standing just behind us. The second act would soon end, and

---

13   The *New York Tribune* founded in 1841 by Horace Greeley, offered solid journalism in a city with little alternative to the sensationalism of other newspapers. The *Tribune* supported the Republican party from its formation in 1854 and later held a radical Republican position, that is, opposing slavery well before the war, insisting on subjugation of the South rather than a negotiated compromise, and favored kind treatment of the South after the war. Karl Marx was the paper's European correspondent from 1851 - 1861. Having a wide and influential readership, the paper was able to affect federal policy, including war strategy. The paper merged with the *New York Herald* in 1924. The *Herald-Tribune* ceased publication in 1966. Greeley was considered the preeminent editor of his time. Objecting to the corruption of the Grant administration, he founded the Liberal Republican party and ran for president in 1872.

they expected he would come out then. I stood awhile between them and the carriage, with my revolver ready, for I began to suspect that the act ended, but the President did not appear; so Booth went into a restaurant and took a drink; then came out and went into the alley where his horse was then standing, though I did not know that any horse was there. He came back and whispered to the other rascal, then stepped into the theater. There were at this time two police officers standing by them. I was invited by my friend C. to have some oysters, and we went into a saloon around the corner, and had just got seated when a man came running in and said, the President was shot! This so startled us that we could hardly realize it, but we stepped out and were convinced.

"Yours,   J.M. Dye."

*   *   *   *   *

FREEDOM'S IMMORTAL TRIUMPH!

FINALE of the "JEFF DAVIS DIRNASTY."
"Last Scene of all, that ends this strange eventful History."

Saturday, April 22, 1865

Honor to Whom Honor is Due

Is justice revenge?
Is the punishment of crime
essential, or obligatory?

Has law any attribute of permanence,
of sanctity, of supremacy
over generations and rulers?

Or is it but the sliding-scale
of the impulse of the hour?

Is impartial equity
the essential element
of preventive as well as retributive justice?

Or is that majesty which men tremble at
as a viceregent of Deity in the soul,
to wilt, like the effrontery of a bully,
before gigantic crime?

In short, is the law of crime ours, or God's?
By what authority dare we take,
by what authority dare we forbear to take,
life for life?

The Daily National Intelligencer[14]
Washington, D.C.
Saturday, April 22

POPULAR PASSION

From the New York Tribune

The tidings from California of lawless assaults on the offices of certain Democratic and French journals, incited, (at least, precipitated) by the news of the double assassination at Washington, afford fresh proof of the truth we have already recognized and acted on — that the general and just indignation needs to be moderated and controlled, not inflamed and aggravated. Here is a specimen of many letters received by this among other journals:

To the Editor of the N.Y. Tribune:

Sir: The bells are tolling for our dead President — the bravest, truest heart in all the land is still.

If you don't hang 500 of your Northern pro-slavery traitors within a month, I hope my soul they'll have you within two. They show little vim in the devil's service. I am a born and bred

SOUTHERN WOMAN.

Baltimore, April 15, 1865

We shall certainly hang nobody, nor incite others to hand political opponents, no matter what they may do, two months hence. We believe in freedom of opinion and (within limits prescribed by law) action as well. We were too many years under the ban of mob sentiment, and have recorded too many acts of wicked violence to which men — and women, too — were subjected because they were alleged to be "Abolitionists" — as they had a legal and moral right to be. Our country has nobly passed through the initial ordeal imposed on her by abhorred assassins — let us all do our utmost to keep her calm and

---

14   Also in the news: Earthquake in southern California; Confederate Major Taylor given 10 days to leave the country for refusal to take oath of loyalty.

law-abiding to the end. Every act of mob violence is a national calamity and shame.

———

Mental Character of Abraham Lincoln

———

Extract from a Speech by Gov. Andrew[15]

During the more than four years since his first inauguration as President, it has been my duty and my great honor to participate in bringing to the support and defence of the National Government, under his Presidential administration, the powerful resources of patriotic will, of loyal hearts, of means, of arms and of men, contributed by Massachusetts to the establishment of the rights of the nation and the liberties of the people. Brought by these means into relations with President Lincoln, personal not less than official, which could not fail to disclose the character and reveal the man, I desire on this grave occasion to record my sincere testimony to the unaffected simplicity of his manly purpose, to the constancy with which he devoted himself to his duty, to the grand fidelity with which he subordinated himself to his country, the clearness, robustness, and sagacity of his understanding, to his sincere love of truth, his undeviating progress in its faithful pursuit, and to the confidence which he could not fail to inspire, in the singular integrity of his virtues and the conspicuously judicial quality of his intellect. He had the rare gift of discerning and setting aside whatever is extraneous and accidental, and of simplifying an inquiry or an argument by just discriminations. The purpose of his mind waited for the instruction of his deliberate judgment, and he was never ashamed to hesitate until he was sure it was intelligently formed.

Not greatly gifted in what is called the intuition of reason, he was nevertheless of so honest an intellect that, by the processes of methodical reasoning, he was often led so directly to his result that he occasionally seemed to rise into that peculiar sphere which we assign to those who, by original constitution are natural leaders among men. Not by nature a leader, neither was he

---

15   This extract was published as a single paragraph.

by nature a follower and by a force of his rare union and balance of certain qualities, both intellectual and moral, he was enabled to rise to the dignity of master of his own position, in a place exacting and difficult almost beyond the precedents of history. Educated wholly as a civilian, his fame will be forever associated with his administration of public affairs in a civil war unexampled in its proportions, and conducted on his own side with such success as to command his own re-election by the free will of a free people.

Perhaps little that he wrote or spoke will pass into literature; yet few men have ever written or spoken with greater effect or to better purpose in appealing over the passions of the hour, to the sober judgment of men, face to face with their combined duties and interests; and very few there have been who knew so well as he how to reach the understanding of plain and honest men who compose the intelligent classes of the American people.

Possessed of a will of unusual firmness and tenacity, his heart was placable, humane, and tender. He exerted powers the most extensive and various, stretching into that undefined and dangerous regime of administrative jurisprudence where the rights and duties of the military commander-in-chief limit and merge into themselves the functions of the civil magistrate, and even of the judicial tribunal. And yet, if we should concede to his enemies all that disappointed animosity and defeated disloyalty have been able to allege against him, we should be enabled to challenge all human history to produce the name of a ruler more just, unselfish, or unresentful. Cheerful, patient, and without egotism, he regarded and treated himself as the servant of the people, using his powers only for their cause, using no more than the cause seemed clearly to demand, and using them alike without passion and without perturbation.

It were premature for us to assess how, or how far, during the four years of his administration, he led this American people. The unfolding of events in the history we are yet to enact, will alone determine the limits of such influence. It is enough for his important glory that he faithfully represented this people, their confidence in democratic government, their constancy in the hour of adversity, and their magnanimity in the hour of triumph.

Of that narrow and bigoted conceit of intelligence which affects to measure truth by the standard of its own conceptions, he had none. Nor did the argument of apparent and superficial constancy, so often the bugbear of meaner minds, weigh down for an instant, in the scales of this serene and conscientious adjudications of duty and verify the impressive demands of any doctrine or any method, however newly discovered. Coming to the Presidency, preoccupied by the traditional theories and opinions of the political school in which he was educated, he devoted himself with a purpose, single and exclusive, to the practical interpretations of events, to the study of those lessons taught by the experience through which the country was called to pass; and learning, in common with a majority of his countrymen, in the strife and agonies of the rebellion, by the lurid glare of the fire of treason and of civil war, how to accommodate opinion to the altered relations of States, interests, and sections of the people, he marched side by side with the advancing hosts of the best and most discerning, in the direction where Divine Providence pointed the way.

* * * * *

The Sun
Baltimore
Saturday, April 22, 1865

PRESIDENT LINCOLN'S REMAINS.[16]

———

MOURNFUL OVATIONS THROUGH THE COUNTRY

———

Arrival of the Funeral Cortege in Baltimore — GREAT DEMONSTRA-TION — Procession of the Military and Civic organizations. — The Body in State at the Exchange — Scenes and Incidents, etc. — Departure for the West

The remains of the late President Lincoln were borne to this city yesterday [April 21] from Washington, after having lain in state in the rotunda

---

16   A few sections have been deleted from this report. They are indicated by ellipses (...).

of the National Capitol since Wednesday afternoon, and were received with imposing honors. The morning opened rather unpropitiously, with rain, and a somber aspect of the heavens continued afterwards to hang over the scene, but notwithstanding this drawback, the citizens were astir at an early hour, and by eight o'clock A.M. it was apparent that a great movement was afoot. At dawn of day guns were fired from prominent positions, which was continued until after the remains had been taken from the city in the afternoon. The streets through which the procession passed were filled with eager spectators, whilst the sombre emblems of mourning on every side gave such impressive aspects to the scene as is not often observed during a lifetime. The windows along Eutaw, Baltimore, and other streets through which the procession passed, were crowded with ladies, children, and others, all evincing sorrowing and sympathetic interest.

During the hours that the remains were in the city all business was suspended, the city passenger railway cars ceased running, the public and private schools suspended, and the entire populace appeared to be on the streets.

According to the programme, the remains were removed from the Capitol at Washington about 7 1/2 A.M., and escorted to the depot by the Congressional Committee of one from each State, the Illinois delegation and other officials, and the funeral train left that city about 8 'clock.

The Funeral Train

The train consisted of engine No. 138, six first-class passenger cars and a United States government car. This car was appropriately decorated, and in one portion of it the coffin containing the remains was placed. In the passengers were the distinguished gentlemen accompanying the remains to Springfield. The train was in charge of Captain Dukehart, conductor of the Baltimore and Ohio Railroad Company.

The Route from Washington to Baltimore

All along the route between Baltimore and Washington the different stations were appropriately decked with mourning, the national flag was displayed, and every manifestation of the respect paid the deceased. Large crowds were congregated at all points, but the funeral cortege made but one stoppage, at the Annapolis Junction, where a delay of only a few minutes was had. The train was joined at Annapolis Junction by Governor Bradford[17] and staff, who went from Baltimore for the purpose, in a special train. General Tyler and staff, with other officers, also joined the train at the Junction. Preceding the train was a pilot engine, which reached the Camden street depot 10 minutes before ten o'clock, giving notice that the train was close at hand.

The Arrival of the Funeral Train

On exact time, at ten o'clock, the train entered the Camden street depot, on the east side track of the platform. The rear car of the train reached back between Barre and Lee streets. The car containing the remains was the third from the rear car, and was stopped under the depot shed, near Lee st. (sic)

The Camden Street Depot

The Camden street depot and the depot sheds were appropriately festooned with drapery, and the sable trappings in and around the large structures were quite imposing. A number of engines were placed in various parts of the depot yards and their bells kept continually tolling.

Major Wiegel, assistant provost marshal, and aide to Colonel Woolley, grand marshal of the procession, had in charge the depot and depot buildings. He placed a company of the 97th Pennsylvania volunteers and a company of the 91st New York volunteers, (both of which comprise the provost guard,) in and around the depot and depot yards, giving the command to Captain W. Jones, of the 97th Pennsylvania and Lieut. Vanatun, of the 91st New York. No one was allowed to enter the depot or depot sheds, except officers of the army and navy, and the State and city authorities.

The Railroad Arrangements

---

17   Augustus Williamson Bradford (1806 -1881) served as governor form 1862 to 1866. He supported the Union but vehemently opposed Federal intrusion on state issues.

The remarkable elegance of the funeral train from Washington to Baltimore, and the perfection of the whole arrangements of the Baltimore and Ohio Company, attracted much favorable comment from the distinguished gentlemen embraced in the official cortege, as well as from the public at large, who witnessed them. But it was at Camden Station, Baltimore, where the greatest display and completeness were shown. All the cars were cleared from the east side of the main depot building, and the platform freed from all obstruction and nicely cleansed and draped. The chief building on Camden street, occupied by the officers of the Company, was very elaborately and tastefully prepared.

The whole funeral train, engine and cars, were handsomely decorated with the national ensign and insignia of woe — and for elegance, comfort, unit and completeness, was pronounced by the railroad men from other lines who observed it to be the most perfect perhaps that has yet been made up in the railway history of the country.

The president of the company, Mr. Garrett, was one of the special committee, appointed by the Secretary of War, to arrange the schedule from Washington to Springfield for the funeral party, and he came from Washington to Baltimore with the remains. At Camden stations the other principal officers of the company were ready to receive the train on behalf of the road, and were gathered in the main hall of the station building, which was brilliantly lighted with gas.

Reception of the Remains and the Funeral Cortege

On getting out of the train, the special guard of honor appointed by the War Department, with the various representatives of the State of Illinois and other sections and communities, were formed in line of procession upon the spacious platforms, with General McCallum, chief superintendent of military railroads, in the lead, flanked by Mr. Garrett, the president, and W.P. Smith, master of transportation, and marched to the upper hall of the station where the military authorities, the Mayor and City Council and other distinguished parties, were in readiness to receive them. Assembled in the hall were also officers of the army and navy, headed by Com. Dornin, Maj. Gen. Wallace, Bdg.

243

Gen. Kenly, and the judges and officers of the courts. They were here joined by Gov. Bradford, Lieut. Gov. Cox, Hon Wm. B. Hill, Robert Fowler, State Treasurer, and others.

The special delegation of distinguished citizens of Illinois, and the committee of the United States Senators and Representatives, Gen. Townsend, Gen. McCallum, and other officers, military and naval, and representatives from the various departments, also formed on the third platform, and marched in procession through the depot sheds. Two companies of the Second United States Regulars, assigned by General Wallace as the Grand Guard to the remains, formed two full platoons, and marched in front and rear of the remains and those accompanying them. Gov. Oglesby, of the State of Illinois, with the Illinois delegations, and Governor Brough, of Ohio, with John W. Garrett, Esq., and many other distinguished personages, were in the procession through the depot buildings. The band of the Second United States Regulars performed a solemn dirge as the cortege passed out to Camden street. Minute guns were fired, and as the coffin was being placed in the hearse, all the bands stationed either on Camden, Eutaw, Howard, or Pratt streets, played solemn music.

...

The Hearse

Here followed the hearse containing the remains. The coffin, which has been already described, was in full view, the American flag falling loosely about it and the floor of the hearse. The hearse is one of the latest style, oval form with large French glass side plates, the wood dark, with all the empannelling beautifully gilded. Six black side plumes with a large centre plume, was the top decoration. The hearse itself is made of pure rosewood, and its polish and embellishment are such as to claim the attention of any beholder. It is understood that there is but one like it in the United States, and that is in California. The coffin of the President was as clearly distinguishable in it, although enclosed in glass, as if it had been on the sidewalk, open to every observer. — On either side of the driver's seat is placed silver-plated lamps. The hearse and its accompaniments were particular objects of remark by all who witnessed them, and reflected much credit upon the owner, Mr. Elisha Cox, of

East Baltimore, the well known proprietor of the East Baltimore livery stable, on Bank street, between Broadway and Bond street. The hearse was drawn by four jet black horses, well matched, most beautifully and appropriately caparisoned and were driven by Mr. Elisha Cox. It is understood that the cost of the hearse was $3,500.

On each side of the hearse and in front and rear, were platoons of the Second United States Artillery, as also the twenty-one Sergeants of the Veteran Reserve Corps, who are the guard accompanying the remains to Springfield.

...

The City Police
The entire force of the city police, four hundred in number, were on duty, under Marshal Carmichael and Deputy Marshal Manly, assisted by the captains and lieutenants of the various police stations. In front of the procession two platoons of police marched, keeping back the crowd, and at the rear of the procession two platoons marched, while all along the line, on either side of the street policemen were stationed, keeping the crowds upon the sidewalks. This made up the funeral cortege, and they passed along (in the order given above) Baltimore street to Gay, Gay to Chew, to Caroline, to Baltimore, to Gay to Lombard, and thence to the south door of the Merchant's Exchange.[18] As they passed along these various streets, they were witnessed by thousands of spectators, men, women and children. All along the line, the houses, public and private, were appropriately decorated in mourning. At the intersection of Baltimore and Holliday streets the apparatus of the Fire Department, consisting of seven engines and several hook and ladder trucks, were arranged, and there kept until after the funeral ceremonies were over.

...

The Catafalque
The catafalque alluded to above, on which the magnificent coffin, containing the remains of the late President was placed, was eleven feet high, eight feet long, and about five feet wide, the surface resting on a frame about three

18   Built in 1815-1820, the building was at the southwest corner of Gay and Water streets. It had a Greco-Roman design with a dome and catwalk promenades outside. It was demolished in 1901-02.

feet from the floor, surrounded with evergreens and japonicas. — four posts, six feet in height, rose from the corners of the surface; these were surmounted by a square canopy, extending one foot on either end. The top was covered with the finest quality of black cloth, and gracefully festooned with silver bullion and tassels, which heavy curtains of black cloth were looped back to the posts. The surface of the dais or platform was covered with black broadcloth, and was bordered with a heavy silver fringe and festoons of black cloth.

The Scene Outside the Exchange

As before stated, the crowd on the streets on both fronts of the Exchange building was immense, and the scene very exciting. Women and children were jammed in, unable to get from the crowd, and several persons were more or less injured in this way, but happily none were seriously hurt. At one time, as the crowd surged to and fro, the scene was almost indescribable. Women fainted, and were borne from the crowd; children were crying, and everything tended to cause alarm, but the military guard and the police succeeded in preserving order, although in doing so there were several instances of slight injury from the bayonets of the soldiers.

...

Willie Lincoln

The remains of little Willie Lincoln, who died in February, 1862, and were placed in a vault at Oak Hill Cemetery, Georgetown, were brought on in the same car with the remains of his lamented father. The body was embalmed at the time and placed in a metallic burial case; but yesterday the case was in a handsome black walnut coffin, silver mounted. The silver plate on the bust of the burial case is inscribed —

"William Wallace Lincoln
Born December 21st, 1850;
Died February 20th, 1862."

The remains of the child were not taken from the car, but were conveyed from depot to depot under proper guard.

...

Departure of the Train

Precisely at 3 o'clock the engine gave a shrill whistle, and the train slowly passed from the depot, preceded by the pilot engine, thus closing the last sad rites that the city of Baltimore can pay to the memory of the beloved ruler of the country.

THE LATE ASSASSINATION

The Arrest of Atzerott and Richter[19] — Suicide of Supposed Accomplice.

The Washington Star of last evening has some particulars of the arrest of Atzerott and his cousin, and their arrival in that city, which we annex:

George A. Atzerott, sometimes known as "Port Tobacco," and one of Booth's accomplices, who was arrested yesterday morning at Germantown, Montgomery county, Md., by Capt. Townsend's company of the 1st Delaware cavalry, arrived here last night in a special car attached to the regular 10 o'clock train.

The authorities here have been informed by telegraph of the arrest of Atzerott. Col. Ingraham, Col. Luddington, and Marshal Murray, of New York, with a strong military force, were in attendance at the railroad station, and immediately upon the arrival of the train a guard was placed at every door of the passenger cars to prevent the passengers from leaving the cars until the prisoner had been removed to a place of safety. This precaution was taken to avoid any tumult by the fact of his arrival being divulged.

Atzerott was then taken quietly from the train and placed in an omnibus, which had been seized by the military authorities, for the purpose, and rapidly driven to a same place of confinement.

As soon as the passengers were allowed to leave the train, and it became known that the prisoner had arrived here, the news spread rapidly, and in a very short time an immense crowd of persons had assembled at Col. Ingraham's office, in anticipation that he would be brought there, but in this they

---

19   Ernest Hartman Richter (1834 - 1920), Atzerodt's cousin. He lived on a farm Atzerodt's father had sold to Richter's father. Richter would be arrested and held only briefly.

were disappointed.

While on the way, Atzerott maintained a sullen silence, and endeavored to assume an air of indifference. He was well dressed, and appears to have made no efforts to conceal his identity. He has a thoroughly bad face and repulsive manner.

The Star adds that he was taken at the house of his cousin, Ernest Hartman Richter, who was also brought to Washington. The latter stated that Atzerott slept, on the 14th instant. at the Pennsylvania House, formerly the Kimmel House, in O Street; that he left Washington on Saturday and went to Rockville by stage, there hired a buggy, drove to Gettysburg, and then rode on a farmer's wagon to Kloppersville, where he arrived late at night, and remained till next morning; thence he walked to Richter's farm. Atzerott is twenty-eight years old, five feet five inches in height, has a swarthy complexion, and dark hair, moustache, and imperial. He seems to be shrewd, and was very reserved in his answers. Richter said that he had not seen him for about three months until he came to his farm on Sunday last.

The Star also has the following:

On Wednesday night a man who made several attempts at different points to pass the outer line of pickets around the city, was placed in the guard room at Fort Thayer for examination, and there deliberately committed suicide by cutting the jugular vein on each side of his neck with a penknife. He was about 5 feet 10 inches high, light curly hair and beard, small feet and delicate hands, was evidently educated, had on a new fine officers fatigue coat, gray pants and a vest, new underclothing, in double, and fine calf boots. On him was (sic) found three hundred and twenty dollars, a penknife, two conflicting army discharges of the same date for George B. Love, a receipt from H. Stockbridge, of Baltimore, for two hundred and fifty dollars from George B. Love for legal services, and a watch and chain.

The evidence seems to indicate that he was concerned in the assassination plot.

The Prediction of Nostradamus. — Most of our readers will recollect that at the commencement of the present civil war the following prediction of Nostradamus, which, it is said, can be found in the second volume of his "Centuries," was generally published in the papers:

"About that time (1861) a great quarrel and controversy will arise in a country beyond the seas (America,) and many poor devils will be hung, and many poor wretches will be killed by a punishment other than a cord. Upon my faith you may believe me, the war will not cease for four years, at which none should be surprised or astonished, for there will be no want of hatred and obstinacy in it. At the end of that time, prostrate and almost ruined, the people will re-embrace each other in great joy and love."

Nostradamus was a French physician, philosopher and prophet, born in1533, who, after meeting with great success in the first named capacity, turned his attention to astrology, and in 1555 published his "Centuries," a work of predictions. In 1558 he foretold the remarkable death of Henry I, which took place at a tournament in the spring of 1559, and is said also to have predicted the death of Charles I, of England, Louis XVI, and the elevation of Napoleon to the empire of France.

We are not among those who are disposed to place such reliance upon the soothsaying of pretended prophets, but as this ancient divinator seems to have been right so far in his prognostications as regards our civil war, we hope his reputation will not be damaged by any failure in the fulfillment of the latter portion of his prophecy. We regret to say, however, that our credulity does not keep pace with our wishes in this respect.

* * * * *

The New York Times
April 22, 1865

The Logic of Booth's Letter.

To the Editor of the New-York Times:
BOOTH's letter is not that of an illiterate man, and its tone of feeling may

beguile the unthinking. To this end it will, no doubt, be paraded in sympathizing papers. I will, therefore, reduce its verbiage to logical propositions, that your readers may see to what it really amounts.

Its foremost thought is: JOHN WILKES BOOTH is a sincere Secessionist and advocate of Southern slavery. Here he agrees with many who profess to love the Union, as he says he has done, but who hold secession to be lawful, and bondage a blessing to the black man. This point will be the text on which apologists of the assassin will prefer to dwell.

Its second thought is, that JOHN WILKES BOOTH, being a sincere Secessionist, may do anything whatever to promote secession -- any evil, that the great good may come. Here he agrees with Confederates only, who justify lying, theft, robbery, repudiation, breach of trust, conspiracy, arson, assassination, on the same ground. On this point apologists will say as little as possible, or will try to prove that FLOYD was an honest man, that BEAUREGARD did not lie when he said beauty and booty was the Union watchword at Bull Run, that BRECKINRIDGE is no Catiline, that KENNEDAY was a martyr, and that the persons who set a price on BUTLER's head were no assassins.[20] Its third thoughtamounts to this, that as war kills and wounds men, devastates fields, destroys towns, makes homes uncomfortable, and, in the nature of things, is attended by occasional outrages, therefore, those States which voluntarily gave themselves to be battle-fields, suffered an intolerable wrong. Of course BEAUREGARD should have challenged ANDERSON, and LEE, GRANT, to fight with pop-guns on top of a pine table. Virginia invited desolation -- the

---

20   John Buchanan Floyd (1806 - 1863) was U.S. Secretary of War under James Buchanan but was indicted for (and exonerated from) financial malfeasance. Though ostensibly against the secession, he sent federal materiel to Southern federal military posts in anticipation of the war. He later served as a Confederate brigadier general. Pierre Gustave Toutant Beauregard (1818 - 1893), a French-Spanish creole from Louisiana and one of the Confederacy's most important generals, led the South to victory at Bull Run. John Cabell Breckinridge (1821 - 1875) was Lincoln's first vice president and later a general in the Confederate army and then the South's Secretary of War. To avoid charges of treason after the war, he fled to Cuba in a small boat. Upon returning to his native Kentucky in 1869, he vehemently opposed the Ku Klux Klan. Lucius Sergus Catilina (108 BC - 62 BC) orchestrated a conspiracy to murder several senators of the Roman senate and then lead a small army to overthrow the government, ostensibly to relieve the poor from debt. Benjamin Franklin Butler, who served as a U.S. Representative from Massachusetts and governor of that state, was a Union general known to Southerners as "Beast Butler" for various offenses and "Spoons Butler" for his tendency to steal silverware from Southern houses where he was a guest.

"last ditch," nonsense dared it.

Its fourth and fifth thoughts I take together. They are these: J.W.B., is proud of the part he took against JOHN BROWN, and is a Secessionist "on his own account." JOHN BROWN was also a secessionist on his own account, and paid the penalty of his treason. So BOOTH owes the penalty of his. But here all likeness ends. BROWN took up arms like a soldier. BOOTH carried pistol and dagger like an assassin; BROWN aimed his blow at slavery, BOOTH at ABRAHAM Lincoln; BROWN called slavery a monster, BOOTH called Lincoln a tyrant; BROWN lost his all in Kansas. BOOTH made $20,000 a year in the North; BROWN fought like a true man. BOOTH skulked like a stage-villain; BROWN died like a hero, BOOTH will probably die like a play-actor: BROWN, as BOOTH hints, will hereafter be extolled as an imprudent demi-god -- a Prometheus, BOOTH will be execrated as a BRUTUS, who, unlike the first BRUTUS, was a fool in fact, and, longo intervallo, like the

John Brown

second -- a vain man encouraged by conspirators -- yet these as different from the Roman patriots as JEFFERSON DAVIS is from CATO.

Your obedient servant.

A BRITISHER.

The Vindication of Justice.

Is justice revenge? Is the punishment of crime essential, or obligatory? Has law any attribute of permanence, of sanctity, of supremacy over generations and rulers? Or is it but the sliding-scale of the impulse of the hour? Is impartial equity the essential element of preventive as well as retributive justice? Or is that majesty which men tremble at as a vicegerent of Deity in the soul, to wilt, like the effrontery of a bully, before gigantic crime? In short, is the law of crime ours, or God's? By what authority dare we take, by what authority dare we forbear to take, life for life?

Questions like these press upon the mind, when false conscienceless philanthropy sets up the catch-word "no more bloodshed," as murderers soaked to the marrow with innocent blood are falling within the reach of tardy justice. They are questions which are to have an answer from the men of this nation now.

The plea of "no more bloodshed" is touching and potent, yet who thinks of appealing to it when we see the murderer on the drop, overwhelmed with the anguish of his fate? No one wishes to see his execution. Few like to witness his end. Every right-hearted man would fain see justice reconciled with mercy to him here, if possible, and gladly finds the least ground for hope in sovereign mercy for him hereafter. But we are made the sad submissive ministers of a certain measure of justice here, with a fatal penalty upon ourselves if we neglect it. There are high reasons for this, but highest of all is the necessity of keeping the soul of society alive to the sense of justice, without which disorganization is sure.

JEFF. DAVIS and the other original conspirators have committed the most monstrous crime, and, in its consequences, the most terrible ever witnessed. If justice ever made a claim on earth, it claims these men for punishment. Of course the blow would be terrible, and no humane man could help a degree of commiseration. What then? Shall we therefore spare ourselves? Which is the nobler, the necessary sacrifice -- justice to feeling, or feeling to justice? This question is of supreme moment. Its due discussion should, in accordance with the decision reached, either revolutionize criminal law to the bottom, or settle its principles, if they are right, more firmly than ever, by the most solemn and instructive vindication they have ever known. It should be decided by the reason and conscience, with passion closely barred out on the one side, and sympathy just as closely barred out on the other.

The principle of human justice has been considered settled. It has been established that it has two essentials -- first, strict equity to guide it impartially, inflicting due degrees of punishment for every kind of offence; and second, an object to attain in the protection of rights, and the sustenance of a public moral sense. No human society has a right to do wrong, whether to harm the innocent or to punish disproportionately the guilty, for any ends of expediency, however plausible. The argument that punishment may prevent crime and protect society is insufficient of itself to justify any penalty that is not intrinsically and relatively just. Upon the divine equity and impartiality of punishment depend all its moral power, all its claim to submission and veneration, and all its worth for any purpose. "He that justifieth the guilty, and he that condemneth the just, even they both are abomination to the Lord."[21] After the immense guilt of this rebellion, comprehending, in incalculable quantity, every crime man can commit, shall have been condoned and covered up, what poor single-handed murderer may not call his gallows to witness the meanness and injustice of the pseudo law by which he dies?

Turning from the inflexible law of impartiality which alone can make our justice aught but a hypocritical mockery, we see in the prudential ends of justice a still further necessity for its sternest vindication in the case of the rebel conspirators. When formidable armies were in the field against us, and when thousands of innocent and heroic lives might have to be sacrificed to overcome the rebel chiefs and bring them to justice, there was some argument for the offer of amnesty, on the maxim that it is better for ten guilty men to escape than for one innocent man to suffer. Now that these criminals are disarmed, there is no shadow of excuse for compounding or condoning their crimes. Impunity to the guilty is cruelty to the innocent. It is virtually throwing the weight and patronage of the law on the side of the lawless, and against the cause of the loyal. The failure to punish treason is in itself treason to all law and order for all time.

Look to the example. All agree that our first duty is to deal with this rebellion in such a manner that the least possible temptation and the greatest possible terror shall be presented to the rebellious in the future. The punishment which has fallen upon the rebels as a people is, doubtless, already ample for their purpose. But, unfortunately, it is not for these alone or chiefly that the chastening and the warning are needed. No people are in danger of rushing

21   Proverbs 17:15

spontaneously into causeless revolt. No people ever concocted and committed treason against a just government at their own instance. The perilous stuff by which nations are convulsed lies in the breasts of ambitious and unprincipled individuals. To them the terrible example must be brought home. What care they for the blood and tears of our nation, if they see a chance of empire for themselves, and, at the worst, a worldwide notoriety without personal danger. To let JEFF. DAVIS and his confederates go unpunished, would be not so much an amnesty for the past as a plenary indulgence for future treason; for a precedent so mighty as this once set, must stand forever.

Let the old terms of amnesty offered by President Lincoln remain. So far as reason allows, and expediency prescribes, let them be enlarged, so as to grant life, liberty, and even property, without political rights, to a higher grade of offenders -- always reserving for justice every man found responsible for torturing prisoners or murdering unarmed Union men. Then let the law against treason take its course. Let every unamnestied traitor be fairly tried, and lawfully sentenced. Afterwards, if any real ground for mercy exists, let him be spared. But whenever guilt is found unmitigated, let punishment, too, be without mitigation.

THE FUNERAL TRAIN

Affecting Scenes and Incidents — Exhibitions of Veneration and Sorrow.

Harrisburg, April 21

At Baltimore at 3:30 a bell was tolled as the train passed on. All the citizens of the neighborhood made their appearance, and so it was at other points. At Sutherville, (3:40 P.M.) the scholars of the Female Seminary formed in a line and displayed the American flag draped with mourning, while the gentlemen in the company stood with uncovered heads. It was an humble but silent and impressive scene. Cockneysville was approached at 4 o'clock.

The entire neighborhood, old and young, men and women with infants in arms, and youths, occupied the most desirable positions, and earnestly watched the going train. Phoenix, a factory village about twenty miles from Baltimore, was reached at 4:12, where the bells were tolled. At Monktown a sign was displayed, (white letters on a black ground) bearing the words, "Honor to whom honor is due." The crowd which gathered around it had thus appropriately expressed their feelings of sorrow and respect. Some of the most notable and affecting scenes were of exceedingly plain and poorly dressed men and women at different places on the route, with handkerchiefs at their eyes, and having the appearance of weeping. Clusters of men at various points raised their hats as the funeral car glided before them. The deepest sorrow was expressed in every countenance.

Upon reaching the State line at 5:30, it was found that Gov. Curtin[22] had arrived from Harrisburg in a special train accompanied by his staff, consisting of Adj.-Gen. Russell, Quartermaster Gen. Reynolds, Inspector-General Lemuel Todd, Surgeon-General James A. Phillips, and cols. R.B. Roberts, S.B. Thomas, Frank Jordan and John A. Wright.

Gov. Curtin joined Gov. Bradford, who was in the front car with his staff, consisting of Adj.-Gen. Berry, Gen. Edward Shriver, and Lieut.-Cols. Thos. J. Morris, Henry Tyson and A.J. Ridgeley. Gen. Cadwallader, commanding the Department of Pennsylvania, accompanied Gov. Curtin. The General's staff consisted of Maj. W. McMichael, A.D.C., and Capt. L. Howard.

The greeting of the Governors of Pennsylvania and Maryland, adjoining States, was exceedingly cordial.

Shrewsbury was reached at 6 o'clock. The common-dressed laborer stood beside the well-dressed citizen, and black and white formed an interesting group. The gloom produced by the death for the time leveled all distinctions.

At various other places the national banner was displayed, either festooned with crape or bearing a black border. The same solemnity of countenance was everywhere seen, and all seemed to be profoundly silent spectators of the funeral cortege.

At York, the sidewalks, as well as the doors and windows swarmed with people. Badges of mourning and draped flags were everywhere seen. The train

---

22   Andrew Gregg Curtin (1817 - 1894) served as Republican governor from 1861 to 1867. He inspired the National Cemetery at Gettysburg. After his second term he became a Democrat. U.S, Grant made him Ambassador to Russia. He later served three terms in the House of Representatives.

was tastefully festooned with black cloth, both inside and out. Here occurred a scene of unsurpassed interest, and the ladies of York asked permission to lay on the coffin a wreath of flowers. Gen. Townsend, Assistant-Adjutant-General of the United States Army, granted the request with a modification, that six of them might perform the service. During the performance of a dirge by an instrumental band, the flowers were brought forth and carried in procession to the funeral car, while the bells tolled, and all the men stood uncovered. The ladies, names: Mrs. Samuel Smalley, Mrs. Harry E. Miles, Mrs. David E. Smalley, Miss Plover, Miss Louisa Docka, Miss Susan Smalley and Miss Jane Latimore entered the car, three on each side of the coffin, and the wreath having been handed to them they placed it on the centre of the coffin, and then returned — those who witnessed the scene bitterly weeping. The bells continued to toll, and the band to sound its mournful strains. The wreath was very large, about three feet in circumference. The outer circle was of roses, and alternate parallel lines were composed of white and red flowers of the choicest description. The band of affection could not have contributed a more choice and delicate tribute to departed worth.

This scene occurred near night fall, and at 6:50 the trains moved onward to Harrisburg, at which city it arrived at 8:30. It was heavily raining; but not withstanding this the streets were densely thronged. A large military escort accompanied the remains of President Lincoln to the State House, amid the sound of minute guns, where the corpse was exposed to the view of the public until a late hour to-night.

The burial cortege will leave Harrisburg for Philadelphia to-morrow at 11 o'clock A.M.

The reporters for the press return their thanks to Conductor Hambright for courteous attendance.

* * * * *

Monday, April 24, 1865

As the Train Rumbled Onward

While his wise and noble acts
are duly honored,
let not his equally beneficent
hesitations and reticences
be forgotten.

April 24, 1865

Daily State Gazette
Trenton, N.J.
Monday, April 24, 1865

WHO ARE RESPONSIBLE?

John Wilkes Booth was the murderer who took the life of President Lincoln, and as such his life is justly forfeit. But he is not alone responsible. He would never have been guilty of such a crime, if he had not been encouraged and educated to the point of assassination by some of the leaders and instructors of the opposition party, who for four years past, have denounced President Lincoln as a despot, tyrant, and usurper, and the war for the suppression of the rebellion, as a war against liberty and the rights of the people. In every political canvass (sic) since 1860, almost every Democratic meeting has heard these charges, and they have been re-echoed by a large part of the Democratic press. Such teachings have, at last, had their legitimate result in a foul assassination.

Candidate Lincoln, 1860

Take the following, one of the most atrocious from the La Crosse (Wisconsin) Democrat.

"The man who votes for Lincoln now, is a traitor. Lincoln is a traitor and a murderer. He who pretending to war for, wars against the Constitution of our country is a traitor, and Lincoln is one of these men. He who calls and allures men to certain butchery is a murderer, and Lincoln has done all this. Had any former Democrat President warred upon the Constitution or trifled with the destinies of the Nation as Lincoln has, he would have been hurled to perdition long since. And if he is elected to misgovern for another four years, we trust some bold hand will pierce his heart with dagger point for the public good."

This is the conclusion of a long article breathing the same spirit throughout. No excitement of a party canvass can excuse or palliate the avowal of such sentiments as these; they are a direct incitement to murder, and the man who penned them, should in justice, forfeit his life. But though more direct and pointed, this paragraph is not more atrocious than some of the utterances of the extreme copperhead press of this State. In July last, the Newark Journal, a leading Democratic organ published the following in relation to the call for men by the President:

It will be seen that Mr. Lincoln has called for another half million of men. Those who desire to be butchered will please step forward at once. All others will stay at home and defy Old Abe and his minions to drag them from their families. We hope that the people of New Jersey will at once put their feet down and insist that not a man shall be forced out of the State to engage in the abolition butchery, and swear to die at their own doors rather than march one step to fulfill the dictates of that mad revolutionary fanaticism, which has destroyed the best government the world ever saw, and would butcher its remaining inhabitants to carry out a mere fanatical sentiment — This has gone far enough and must be stopped, let the people rise as one man and demand that this wholesale murder shall cease."

Is it wonderful that after such counsel as this had been repeated week after week, and day after day, for years, that some traitor more desperate than his associates, should act on the advice thus constantly tendered? The very men who have been loudest in their denunciations of Mr. Lincoln, as a tyrant, usurper, despot, and traitor, are now professing to shed tears over his dead body, dead by the hand of the assassin who acted upon their counsel.

We willingly admit that the great mass of the opposition party sincerely condemn the atrocious crime of the assassination of the head of the government, and mourn the national loss, but we charge that this crime is the direct and inevitable result of the teachings of such papers as the New York Daily News, the Philadelphia Age, the La Cross Democrat, the Newark Journal and their allies. If they believed the charges they made against Mr. Lincoln, then their pretended regret over his assassination is the baldest hypocrisy and pretence. If they did not believe them, then their crime is equally infamous with that of the wretched instrument whose hand they armed with the fatal weapon, and whose heart they steeled to the commission of the fearful crime.

It is these men, who have labored to pervert and corrupt the popular mind, and to lead the people into acts of violence and treason, who are morally responsible for the assassination of Mr. Lincoln and all its consequences, and such will be the verdict of impartial history.

COPPERHEADISM RUN MAD. — The following extraordinary statement is copied from a Western paper: — "About eight miles from Shelbyville, Indiana, is the little town of Marietta, a place noted for nothing in particular, save the virulent type of copperheadism prevailing there. The reception of the dreadful news from Washington set the honest Democrats thereabouts crazy with joy. In the absence of a cannon they loaded and fired an anvil repeatedly, shouted, danced, sang, and in every possible manner gave expression to their demoniac joy, after which they constructed an effigy of President Lincoln, with a rude representation of the bullet-hole in his head, which they carried about the streets, a big ruffian following, and ringing a bell. The effigy was afterward burnt."

This is disgraceful enough, but who are to be properly held responsible for such a display? Not the ignorant and brutal wretches who took part in it; but those orators and newspaper editors who, for four years past, have denounced Mr. Lincoln as "a tyrant," "an usurper," and a despot unfit to live. It is such teachings that have led to murder, and is it not wonderful that it should be followed by open rejoicing over the assassination of the man so denounced.

SERVED THEM RIGHT

We copy two paragraphs below from an exchange. There have been many other instances in which the bad men have allowed their party passions to lead them into open avowals of their sympathy with treason and assassination. It is to be regretted that all could not be choked, and if the process was continued a little longer than in the cases mentioned, very little harm would be done:

"A notorious copperhead living in the vicinity of Waterbury, on hearing of the President's death displayed a flag with the words, "The Devil is dead," upon it. A party of young men proceeded to the residence of the scoundrel, and made a demand for the flag. The man denied having exhibited any; whereupon a rope was fastened about his neck and he was threatened with hanging unless he 'showed his colors.' He still stuck to his denial, but as he felt the halter drawn tighter about his neck he confessed his infamy and brought out the flag. After giving him a thrashing his visitors withdrew."

"At Camp Burnside, Indianapolis, on Wednesday, a soldier of the Fifty-third remarked that he would 'have a hoe-down' over the news of President Lincoln's assassination, and began frisking around and indulging in extravagant demonstrations of joy. His comrades swung him up by the neck, so that his toes just touched the ground, and kept him there until he was black in the face, and his spirit was just fluttering on the borders of eternity. Others who expressed their gratification at the news were served likewise. Five, in all, were elevated."

The Montreal Witness says, "But our danger will be imminent if any of the scoundrels implicated in this assassination (of President Lincoln) make their escape to Lower Canada. They would undoubtedly meet here plenty of influential friends. — There would be found here Judges and juries to decide that they had used only a belligerent right. Indeed it will argue a strange inconsistency if those papers which have been foremost in screening the raiders, and have excused as a belligerent right the assassination of an innocent civilian at St. Albans, find fault now with those concerned in the murder of the Commander-in-Chief of the Federal armies."

The Witness does not speak without reason. If the assassins should reach Canada, there can be little doubt that convenient judges would be found to secure them from punishment, by refusing to deliver them up to the justice of the country whose laws they have offended. In such a case no power on earth could save Canada from swift and terrible retribution. The assassins, if remaining there would be seized if it required half a million of armed men to accomplish it, and nothing could save Canada from a war that would lay her cities in ashes, and turn her fields to deserts.

————

This morning, at half-past five o'clock, the remains of Abraham Lincoln, late president of the United States, will reach the Clinton street Station (sic) . it is expected that the funeral train will halt at that point for some time, in order to give our citizens an opportunity to pay to the memory of the deceased the mournful tribute of their respect.

The Mayor has issued a proclamation, directing a proper observation of the occasion, and we trust that notwithstanding the early hour at which the train will arrive, there will be a large attendance of citizens. A full band will be present at the Station, and perform funeral dirges during the time that the train halts. A detachment from the military post at Camp Perrine will be present. The bells will be tolled, and minute guns will be fired.

A special train left the Clinton street Station at 8 o'clock yesterday morning, with a number of our citizens, who desired to participate in the ceremonies at Philadelphia. The train returned in the evening.

————

Booth Reported in Jersey City. — A strange and improbable report obtained currency in Jersey City, on Saturday, that Booth had arrived there the night before on the train from Philadelphia. The Times says: — "Somebody started the story this (Saturday) morning, that the murderer Booth, was seen in a horse car in this city last evening, and that being accosted by a gentleman who called him by name, he drew a pistol upon the interrogator, and jumped out of the car. It is about as possible that Booth is gallivanting around in these parts, as that the virulent rebels, and unrepentant copperheads, are sincerely sorry that Abraham Lincoln is dead. People will do wisely not to put forth in any unauthorized rumors, or wild stories will be flying about.

* * * * *

New York Daily Tribune[23]
April 24, 1865

What He Did Not Say

The earthly remains of our late President will this morning reach our City on their way to their final rest, and will remain with us till tomorrow afternoon. It seems, then, a fit moment for recalling attention to the wisdom and patriotism evinced by our loved and lost leader in his reserve and silence — in what he took care not to say or do during his occupancy of the Presidential chair. For many a fool has the credit of clever or smart sayings — perhaps justly; but to refrain from follies that are current and popular, steadfastly refusing to lend them any countenance whatever, evinces a profound and invincible sagacity rare among even the ablest of public men.

I. Mr. Lincoln, throughout his arduous term of service of President — in fact, throughout his entire public career — utterly, stubbornly refused to utter a work calculated to embroil us in a contest with any foreign power. "ONE WAR AT A TIME" — the words with which he decided the Trent case[24] — were the key-note of his entire official career. He never proposed the idea, once so popular, of getting out of our domestic struggle by plunging into one with a European power. None of the bogus "Monroe Doctrine" bravado, which so tickles the ears of most groundlings, ever escaped his lips. He was of course annoyed and embarassed by the French invasion of Mexico, and he never concealed his dislike to that Napoleonic blunder; but he felt that it ill became a chief of a great nation to indulge in warnings and menaces which he was noto-

---

23   Also in the news: Brazil, unsatisfied with the treaty ending the civil war in Uruguay, has recalled its foreign minister from Montevideo. In almost every town in Canada, businesses closed, churches were thronged, and public buildings and private homes are draped with mourning. The entire population of Memphis turned out to testify their respect for the late president. Booth is reported to have fled into rebel territory in Maryland. Snow in Cincinnati.

24   On November 18, 1861, a Union ship intercepted a British mail packet, the RMS Trent, and arrested two Confederate envoys, James Mason and John Slidell, who were on their way to Europe, hoping to persuade England and France to recognize the Confederacy. They also hoped to ignite a war between the North and England. Their arrest succeeded in inspiring talk of war in both countries, but to secure international peace during the national crisis, Lincoln released the prisoners. Mason and Slidell then proceded to Europe but failed to secure recognition of the Confederacy.

riously unable, during our Civil War, to back by material persuasions. It would have been easy and popular to plunge the country into a great foreign war; but that would have been to ensure its permanent disruption and overthrow. Mr. Lincoln saw that right from the outset, and had the courage and patriotism to pursue it.

II. He never talked vindictively, nor threatened to hang or shoot men who were not in his power. He probably had as clear and keen a perception of the wickedness of the Slaverholders' Rebellion as any other man could have; but he said little about it, and never barked at those who were not within reach of his bite. Mrs. Glass's initial direction for hare-cooking — "First, catch your hare" — he was never tempted to violate. And if wrath and bitterness, with a fearful looking-for of judgment, now pervade the Rebel breast, it was not incited by anything ever uttered by President Lincoln.

III. He always kept us clear as might be of the tangle of premature "Reconstruction." He instinctively saw from the start, in this as in other respects, the folly of quarreling over the disposition of the fox's skin while the fox was still uncaught. First, break the back of the Rebellion before you undertake to pass sentence on the Rebel chiefs; vanquish and disperse the Rebel armies before you quarrel about the terms of readmitting to our counsels States not yet ready to come back on any terms. To settle questions as they severally arise, and not to divide the loyal strength on topics not yet in order, were among the maxims by which President Lincoln's course was steadily guided. When "Reconstruction" became practical, he was ready to act on it, and not before. His refusal to approve the Wade-Davis bill of last year was based avowedly on this principle.[25] And his successor will find his task lighter in consequence.

Our country has had greater statesmen, abler speakers or writers, more efficient administrators, than Abraham Lincoln; but which of them ever evinced

---

25   The Wade-Davis Bill of 1864, sponsored by Sen. Benjamin Wade, of Ohio, and Henry Davis, of Md. (both Radical Republicans) proposed readmitting Confederate states to the Union only if a majority in each state took an "Ironclad Oath" that they had never supported the Confederacy. Both houses of Cognress passed it, but Lincoln let it die with a pocket veto. He preferred his "Ten Percent Plan," which would allow readmittance if only 10 percent took an oath of allegiance and swore to respect emancipation. He reasoned that this would end the war sooner and more quickly resolve differences.

such a talent for silence where speech was perilous and the events of tomorrow very likely to overset the wisest judgment of to-day? While his wise and noble acts are duly honored, let not his equally beneficent hesitations and reticences be forgotten.

* * * * *

North American News and United States Gazette[26]
Philadelphia
April 24, 1865

Progress of the President's Funeral

———

From Harrisburg to Philadelphia.

HARRISBURG, Pa., April 22, 11.15 A.M. — The train is now leaving this city. Thousands of persons are sad witnesses of its departure. Our company was increased at the State capital by the addition of the Hon. Simon Cameron, Hon. Joseph Bailey, Hon. Jos. K. Moorehead and Mr. Hall Stanton. The duty assigned to these gentlemen is to extend the hospitalities of this city to those who have been especially invited to accompany the remains to Springfield. The rain has ceased and the sun shines from an unclouded sky. Governor Bradford, of Maryland, and staff, took leave of the party at Harrisburg.

Acting High Constable Clarke, of Philadelphia, is on board the train, and will meet a police force of 600 men on his arrival in that city.

At one point a few miles from Harrisburg a national flag, with mourning appendages, was spread upon the green, and crowds stood uncovered on side of it. In quick succession we pass country houses and workshops, and small settlements, every resident appearing to witness the passing of the train.

Middletown, 11.45. — The people here assembled in full numbers. Passing a few miles beyond we reach a partially cleared wood. Fronting the

<hr/>

26   Also in the news: Generals Sherman and Johnston agree to suspend hostilities; more bone fragments are being removed from Secretary Seward's wounds, and he is improving and "cheerful"; rebels fleeing Richmond are gathering in Atlanta to flee to the "trans-Mississippi"; Philadelphia a "carnival of grief."

road are immense rocks on which laborers and humble farmers and their families are silently standing.

Elizabethtown, 12.15. — We stop here for a few moments. There is a rush over wood piles by men, women and children to see the funeral car. This scene is more animated than mournful. There were, however, large groups of other parties who are evidently solemnly impressed. One man slowly waves a black flag.

12.30. — We are making rapid time. Many persons are scattered along the road, not a few of them taking off their hats and bonnets as we pass on to Mount Joy, and thens to Landisville and Dillerville.

1 P.M. — We are now near Wheatland, and the attention of the passengers is directed towards the residence of James Buchanan, about two miles from the road. The house was imperfectly seen, but the locality was designated. Five minutes pass and we are at Lancaster.

The vicinity of the railroad station is crowded with people, and further on the streets were densely filled. Thirty or forty thousand persons are here as spectators. Over a door is seen the American flag, festooned with black, and crowned with its folds is a likeness of the honored dead. On a white cloth ground, in black letters, are the words "Abraham Lincoln, the illustrious martyr. The nation mourns his loss." The car house was densely packed with human beings, the track, however, being kept clear, people are surging in every direction. The funeral car attracts impatient attention, and crowds press towards it. A voice is heard that a lady has fainted, but this does not keep back the impetuous crowd.

Then the words "Grant is on board" electrify the crowd. "Where is he?" is shouted in thousands of voices. Many rushed into the last car and others to the front, showing that they had no definite idea as to his locality. A gentleman of the funeral party approaching the platform makes a request that the people remain in their places, where they can have a good opportunity of seeing the funeral car. This had a partially good effect. At this point a small party of ladies are seen with a large and magnificent bouquet — a gentleman in their front endeavoring to clear a path that they may reach the funeral car. The ladies struggle to that direction and are soon lost in the crowd. They succeed in their effort, and deposit on the coffin their floral tribute of honor and affection.

The train moves on, and in a few moments we are at the Lancaster Locomotive Works. Probably five hundred or six hundred workmen and their families are either on cars, tenders or on the ground. They, like many others, wear mourning badges. Lancaster is soon lost to sight, and country wagons with occupants and pedestrians are met at every wayside. They have but a few seconds of time to gratify their curiosity for the train moves rapidly.

2.05 P.M. — We are now at Penningtonville, where the people turn out in large numbers.

2.15 P.M. — Parkesburg. — Here at least a thousand people were collected on the steps of the houses.

At the windows on the lawns were spectators. Small groups are elsewhere seen on the way, and now and then a solitary man or woman is seen looking from a hillside or from the door of a lowly cabin.

At Coatesville, a beautifully situated manufacturing village, the country is remarkably picturesque; the various groups of spectators in different localities give increased interest to the scene. Heads are bowed and hats raised as the train rumbled onward.

At ten minutes of three o'clock we are at Downingtown. Quite a crowd of men, women and children hung to the rear car to see the funeral car Further on there is a large collection of people in front of a public house, which is suitably festooned, with a portrait of President Lincoln prominently exhibited.

At West Chester intersection, groups of the inhabitants line the sideway. All the men lifted their hats in respectful homage to the memory of the deceased.

We next come to Paoli, where a similar mark of respect is shown. Emblems of mourning are displayed, and the citizens appear all along the route.

At Eagle Station amid a group, a woman held in her arms a child, probably not over three years of age, who wore a dark sack, with a mourning scarf across its shoulders, waving a flag which was trimmed with crape. This incident found ready appreciation in all who witnessed it from the cars.

267

From the time of leaving Harrisburg until we reached Philadelphia, we saw no person whatever engaged at labor. The day seemed to be appropriately observed by the tens of thousands of person residing in this largely populated, prosperous and industrious part of the State. Plows were left in the furrows, shops were closed and a Sabbath quiet prevailed. Respect was shown the deceased all along the way, affording another evidence, if any were needed, of the deep feeling of affection associated with the memory of the distinguished dead.

So far the party accompanying the President's remains have been free from any oratorical displays. It is presumed that none will have the bad taste to mar the solemnity of the occasion by unnecessary speech making.

———

Jeff. Davis Fleeing to Texas

New York, April 23, — The Suffolk, Va., correspondence of the Herald states that revel officers who had arrived there report that the news of Lee's surrender reached Jeff. Davis at Danville three days after his proclamation, and Jeff. left at daylight next morning for Greensboro, N.C. He stated that if hard pushed he should go to Texas, where he was sure he could rally an army around him and make another stand, and that he would never leave the limits of the confederacy. He issued orders for the cavalry to join him and to burn the bridges over the Meherrin and Roanoke rivers, which is reported to have been done, and also, for the evacuation of Weldon.

* * * * *

Lincoln with sonTad

Daily Constitution Union[27]
Washington, D.C.
Monday Afternoon, April 24, 1865

The Escape of Booth

We are still inclined to believe that this assassin and a companion in crime escaped over the Navy Yard bridge, in a few minutes after he left the scene of his great crime, and at once made his way into Prince George's county (sic), Md., and crossed the Potomac into Prince William county, Va., and then into Farquier county, and from thence to the Blue Ridge in Rappabannock county. Reaching this range of mountains, he could pass down to the western part of the Carolinas, and might, with assistance, reach Mexico. Our gunboats patrol the Mississippi, but a dark night and a canoe could evade these. A single individual might steal across, where an army would be cut to pieces by the gunboats. This is our theory of his escape, but if there is the slightest doubt of his escape from this city, every building should be thoroughly searched, and no loyal person would object to this procedure on the part of the government.

———

Pickpockets — At Philadelphia there were at least 300 pickpockets mixed up with the spectators. The police arrested a large number, and we saw detective officers Henderson and Lemon arrest nine New York thieves while "working the crowd." These vagabonds will follow the funeral cortege all the way to Springfield.

———

Snow. — There was quite a sprinkling of snow in Philadelphia, yesterday, and this morning, between here and Baltimore, the frost was quite heavy.

———

A Strange Story About the Booth Family.

---

27   Also in the news: A plague advances into eastern Europe from Russia; a Washington man is fined for selling liquor to a minor; a man is arrested for attempting to steal cash from a cigar store; someone piled up books in a public school and torched them; Jefferson Davis reported to have crossed the Mississippi; 8,000 prisoners at Andersonville are ready to return home.

From the Cincinnati Commercial

We have been placed in possession of some facts relative to the Booth Family, which are, at this time, exceedingly interesting. It has been generally understood that Junius Brutus Booth Sr., was legitimately married to the lady who passed in this country as his second wife. Indeed, when some seven years ago, the announcement of the death of the first wife, Mrs. Mary Booth, in Baltimore, was made in the New York Clipper, the statement that she had been divorced being added, the sons united in a card, which was published in that journal, setting forth that their father had but one wife, and that one their mother then and now living — the putative Mrs. Rosalie Booth, from whom he had never been divorced. Mrs. Ward, however, stated to our informant that this was incorrect. The elder Booth was a married man at the time he last appeared at Covent Garden Theatre. While there, he chanced to meet in the Covent Garden market (then as well known as Haymarket) a flower girl named Rosalie, who regularly sold flowers to market customers in that quarter of London. She possessed rare personal attractions, and was, in fact, exceedingly beautiful. Booth cultivated an acquaintance with her, which ripened into intimacy, and resulted in an elopement, Booth at once taking passage to America, where the fair Rosalie was presented as, and passed for, his wife. By his first wife Booth had one child, at the time of his desertion of her — an infant. When she ascertained where Booth had gone, she also followed, bringing the child with her, and subsequently took up her residence in Baltimore. This child, when arrived at man's estate, adopted the profession of the law, and Richard Booth, Esq., was afterwards known as a prominent and influential member of the Boston Bar. He never so much as recognized the other children of Booth, and for years did not speak to his father. It was probably out of consideration for this child, that the elder booth did not sue for a writ of divorce from his wife Mary, if, indeed, there were any grounds upon which he could hope to obtain the legal severance, without which, it seems, a second marriage was out of the question. Her troubles and trials led her gradually into the habits of dissipation. She became almost as intemperate as Booth himself, and it was a custom with her, when in liquor, to haunt the Baltimore markets for a chance meeting with the woman who had usurped her place in the heart and home of her husband. These encounters were as much avoided by the one, as sought for by the other. Mrs. Booth assailed Rosalie with violent and often coarse language, and opprobrious epithets, which the other never resented, but cut short by the speediest exit. The fact growing out of this condition of affairs is, that the children — Junius Brutus, Edwin Forrest, John Wilkes, Joseph, and the sisters — are of illegitimate birth; and it is a fact which would probably have died out with the few who were privy to it, but for the great crime which has quickened public curiosity, and unlocked the secrets of the family charnel house, whose gates had been so securely closed and guarded by the children, in their struggle for professional rank and social position, that even a legal inquisition would hardly have forced them ajar.

* * * * *

Mrs. Lincoln

Tuesday, April 25, 1865

Evidences of the Burden

The flowers filled with dust,
and their white and crimson mouths,
instead of being filled with soft silver dew,
were dry and parched and arid,
sprinkled over with dust, as though
it had been distributed by a sifter.

The wax tapers were discolored with it,
and it seemed even to make the flames
of the candles sputter.

It had settled in thick layers
upon the portion of the coffin lid
which had not been removed, and,
above all, on the features of the dead.

This it was, the dusty accumulation
of a whole day, which lent so leaden
a cast to the face,
and covered with an unruffled
and unnatural veil the really
genial and kind expression.

But the undertaker's skillful brush,
long, thick, light, and flossy,
removed, with a few artistic touches,
the unseemly discoloration,
and a white cambric handkerchief,
delicately applied, transformed to itself
the last molecule lingerings.

The Age [28]
Philadelphia
Tuesday, April 25

The President's Quarters

President Johnson has removed his quarters from his hotel to the residence of Hon. Samuel Hooper, on H street. Mr. Hooper is away with the funeral cortege of the late President.

Mrs. Lincoln.

Mrs. Lincoln has not sufficiently recovered to remove from the White House. She is more composed, and is undecided whether to remove to Illinois.

The Rebel Government at Augusta

The Richmond Whig, of yesterday, says: for some days it has been reported here that the so-called Confederate Government, consisting of Jeff. Davis and a handful of office-holders, had reached Augusta, and made a show of establishing itself there, preparatory to a flight to trans-Mississippi.

A Letter from J.B. Booth to J.W. Booth.

A letter received at Ford's Theatre, directed to J. Wilkes Booth, has been handed to the police. It is in the handwriting of Junius Brutus Booth, and is simply signed, "Jun." The writer speaks significantly of the oil business, and advises young Booth to abandon it now that Richmond has been given up and Lee has surrendered, and his friends believe that it will not be profitable. A postscript signed "Alice" is appended, giving Booth similar advice.

It is stated that J. Wilkes Booth studied law in the office of the late Judge Buel, Troy, about ten years ago. He remained there but a short time.

---

28   Also in *The Age* this day: Major General Canby reports on materiel and prisoners captured at Mobile. Macon has been captured. Jefferson Davis said to have crossed the Mississippi. In Stockholm, Count O. Cronjelm has shot and killed his grandmother for refusing to give him money. A plot to introduce yellow fever in New York via infected clothing was discovered.

Secretary Seward

War Department, Washington, April 22, 10:30 P.M. — Hon E. M. Stanton, Secretary of War: I have the honor to report that the Secretary of State is stronger and more comfortable tonight.

Mr. Seward's condition justifying and requiring it, a further removal of fragments of bone was made this evening. The operation was borne well, and has been productive of partial relief.

> Very respectfully,
> Young obedient servant,
> J.K. Barnes,
> Surgeon General.

Arrival and Departure of the Remains of President Lincoln. — The body of President Lincoln arrived in Philadelphia at 4:30 on Saturday afternoon, and was received by the escort of military and civic bodies, as already published in the Age. It was nearly dark before the procession commenced to move, owing to some difficulty in the formation of the various divisions. In consequence of this people along the route had but a poor opportunity of witnessing the attractiveness of the display. At 8 o'clock the body was deposited in the hall,[29] and between the hours of 10 and 12 in the evening a private exhibit of the body was granted to about 3,000 persons, tickets for that purpose having been issued by the committee of arrangements of City Councils. On Sunday morning at 6 o'clock the hall was opened to the public. The scene was most imposing. The coffin lay in the middle of the apartment, with the face of the deceased exposed. Grouped about the room was the guard of honor, while members of the First City Troop, with drawn sabres, stood guard upon either side of the coffin. Wax candles were kept burning all day in silver candlebras (sic). Exquisite flowers in beautiful vases filled the room with beauty and perfume, and gave a grace to the grand and solemn scene. The crowds filing through and casting a last look at the features of the murdered President made up a constant shifting panorama.

---

29   Independence Hall

The scene witnessed on Sunday around and about the hall is indescribable. Steps were arranged to the two front windows, for the admission of the throng, and corresponding steps at the windows on the square afforded egress for the crowd. Before daylight in the morning crowds began to gather, and at five o'clock, when the windows were thrown open, there were thousands of people in the line.

These lines were formed of persons two abreast, closely packed in solid column, and they reached from the Schuylkill to the Delaware, and around on Delaware avenue during the greater part of the day.

In front of the State house the rush and crush were frightful, crowds of people bursting through the lines and causing infinite disorder. There was a perfect tempest of screams and outcries. Women fainted and were only saved from being trampled to death by the strong arms of those who were about them. The scene viewed from a point above the crowds was terrific at times.

General Cadwalader,[30] with the 187th regiment, came upon the ground. During the entire day and evening the entire police force of the city were on duty, under the immediate eye of Mayor Henry[31] and Chief of Police Ruggles. They had an arduous time of it. A large number of persons were badly hurt by being crushed in the jam, and the faintings among females were innumerable. At about quarter past one o'clock yesterday morning the entrance windows of Independence Hall were closed, and the public denied further admission. The stream of visitors had lasted from 5 o'clock Sunday morning, without the intermission of a second. Within those twenty hours a ceaseless throng, in two distinct files, had poured through the sanctuary. Allowing one visitor in each of the two separate files for every second of time included within those hours, only one hundred and forty-four thousand people could by any possibility have viewed the remains. But the average number was not equal to this.

Long after the windows were closed, the crowd lingered around them, pressing against the panes at the imminent danger of breakage, and peering

---

30   George Cadwalader (1806 - 1879)

31   Alexander Henry (1823 - 1883), a Republican, helped move public opinion from anti-abolitionist to anti-secessionist.

wistfully through the slats of the Venetian blinds. Standing within the hall, it was curious to gaze towards the windows at the north end, and view them tessellated with human faces, and remember that the large and disappointed crowd was but the remnant of the immense populace that had besieged the building all day. A view from the outside, too, through the slats of the blinds, gave a fair idea of the interior of the hall, but was at the same time attended to with so much detriment to the window panes, that at the signal of cracking of one of these the slats were summarily reversed, so as to bar the vision and to withdraw from the imagination any facts for it to feed upon. This done, the hall was entirely cleared of all lingerers, save the Guard of Honor, a few military officials, a few Councilmen, a few policemen, and the undertaker and his assistants.

The apartment having been freed from the presence of the public, the undertaker and his assistants began their cleansing preparations of the corpse.

Every article in the room bore evidences of the burden and heat of the day, and shared in the purifying attentions. The flowers filled with dust, and their white and crimson mouths, instead of being filled with soft silver dew, were dry and parched and arid. These were completely sprinkled over with dust, as though it had been distributed from a dredger box. The wax tapers were discolored with it, and it seemed even to make the flames of the candles sputter. It had settled in thick layers upon the portion of the coffin lid which had not been removed, and, above all, on the features of the dead. This it was, the dusty accumulation of a whole day, which lent so leaden a cast to the face, and covered with an unruffled and unnatural veil the really genial and kind expression which was preserved there. But the undertaker's skilful brush, long, thick, light, and flossy, removed, with a few artistic touches, the unseemly discoloration, and a white cambric handkerchief, delicately applied, transformed to itself the last molecule lingerings.

About two o'clock the magnificent hearse was brought into Chestnut street, and placed in front of the hall for the purpose of conveying the body to the depot.

Previously the City Troops mounted, and several civic bodies with torches had arrived upon the ground. There were but few people about. The procession was formed in line near three o'clock in the following order:

187th Regiment P.V. — First City Troop. — Perseverance Hose Company. — Hearse. — Carriages containing the Funeral party. — Beck's Band. — National Union Club. — Republican Invincibles. — Good Intent Engine Company. — Fairmount Engine Company. — Good Intent Hose Company. — Southwark Hose Company.

The cortege moved up Fifth street to Oxford and thence to the Kensington depot, but owing to the lateness of the hour but few people witnessed the solemn procession. The train left for New York at 4:30 A.M., where, our telegraphic despatches inform us, it arrived safely at a reasonable hour. The reception of the remains in New York took place in the afternoon, and, of course more satisfaction was afforded than in Philadelphia, where, as we have stated, the procession did not begin to move till after dark, and consequently an imperfect view was afforded to the many thousands of spectators who were assembled along the line of the route.

Sneak Thieving. — During yesterday about fifty complaints were made at the detective office by parties whose houses had been entered and robbed on Saturday night during the passage of the procession. In all of these cases the houses had been locked up and no one left in charge. Our citizens should remember that thieves are always on the lookout for such occasions. It is unsafe to go away from the home without leaving some responsible person on the premises.

———

Reports in Relation to Booth

New York, April 23. — Circumstances which have come to the attention of the Government render it nearly certain that Booth's horse fell with him on Friday night, the 19th inst., and it is believed caused a fracture of one of his legs; it is also reported that he has divested himself of his moustache. The likeness of Booth published in Harper's Weekly is said to be correct. The attention of surgeons and of the public is called to these circumstances. If Booth is lying concealed and wounded, the rewards offered and the detestation of his crime by all loyal citizens, will soon bring him to light.

———

Tragic Effect of the Assassination in New York
A Boy Cuts his Throat with a Razor
[From the New York Herald of Friday]

The influence which the present national calamity exercises over persons of a morbid temperament has been fearfully exemplified within the last few days. A youth names Charles Johnson, residing with his father, at 187 East Fourteenth street [in New York City], who had been for some time subject to fits, during dinner on Tuesday last said, "I am going to follow Abraham Lincoln, and I will die under this roof before to-morrow night." He then rose from the table and proceeded up stairs, stating that he was going to bed. His family thought no more of the matter till his mother, on going down to the front basement, saw him in the back room in the act of brandishing a razor. He looked very excited and exclaimed, in a loud voice, "This is the razor." His mother immediately screamed for help, but before any could respond the unhappy boy had succeeded in putting an end to his existence.

* * * * *

**Evening Bulletin
San Francisco
Evening, April 24, 1865**

Mysterious Affair in the County Jail at Redwood City. — The San Mateo Gazette of 22nd April says:

Three Chinamen were arrested at Halfmoon Bay about a month ago on the charge of burglary, and lodged in the County Jail to await their trial. On last Monday the attention of some passers-by were attracted by the calls of one of the Chinamen for assistance. When the Sheriff was summoned it was found that one of the Chinamen was stretched out upon the floor of the jail, and upon a physician being summoned he was pronounced dead. It appears that the dead Chinaman was to be the principal witness against the remaining two at their trial, which is to come off at the next term of the Court. The body was much bruised, and bore unmistakable marks of violence.

* * * * *

Evening Bulletin
San Francisco
Evening, April 25, 1865

Local Religious Items

Allusions to the death of President Lincoln and its influence upon the country were again made in several of the pulpits yesterday, the Rev. Messrs. Bissell, Stebina, Strong and Williams making it the exclusive theme of their discourses during a portion of the day. Mr. Bissell thought that President Lincoln had been taken away because he would have been too lenient with the rebels in bringing to a close the scenes of this terrible rebellion. A more rigid man was needed at the helm to bring the good Ship of State safely across the breakers into the secure and peaceful haven of the permanent rest and prosperity. He hoped that such a man had succeeded the lamented dead. Mr. Stebbins paid a glowing tribute to the late President, and the great and glorious work he had accomplished for the country. His loss was seemingly irreparable, but God would take care of the Union and perpetuate its existence. Mr. Strong saw the hand of Providence in the event which had clothed a nation in mourning and saddened the hearts of its millions of loyal inhabitants. The assassination of Abraham Lincoln was not accidental. God had a purpose to perform toward this nation in permitting that dark deed to be consummated. Mr. Williams was not so conservative that he could not keep pace with all true progress. The events of the past four years are full of meaning in their influence upon the country and upon the cause of God among the children of men. It was well to study these things, and to shape one's course in accordance with the spirit of the times. All these discourses were listened to by large and appreciative congregations.

———

Treasonable Demonstrations in Solane County — The Military Called Out
Four Men Wounded — The Traitors Captured

Green Valley, in Solane county, is infested with some of the boldest secessionists on this coast. Ever since the war commenced, they have been open and loud-mouthed in their abuse of the Government, and have made it a custom to shout for Jeff. Davis and his tribe on every occasion. Upon receipt of the news of the dastardly assassination of Lincoln, these men, true to their instincts, collected together and rejoiced over the fiendish act. The military authorities at Benicia were notified of what was going on by some Union citizens, and a company was sent to the spot. Upon the arrival of the troops, the ringleaders fortified themselves in the house of David James, in the upper part of the valley. As the troops approached the premises they were fired upon, and two of the soldiers wounded. The fire was returned, and two of the traitors were wounded, when the whole secesh party surrendered, and were brought to Benicia yesterday morning. The prisoners are David James and two sons, William P. Durbin and son, Charles Ramsey and son, A.O, Laramee and son, and Stiltz. They will be tried for treason, the penalty for which is death. Ramsey has a son in the rebel army, who shot a man in Green Valley during a squatter difficulty. It is said that he shot his opponent through the head killing him instantly, and the father stood by and applauded the act.

Some hard stories are told of the locality where these men lived. The precinct always had a Copperhead majority, and the people boasted that no other ticket could be carried. In 1861, it is said, a camp meeting, under the auspices of the Methodist Church South, was held, when the very parties now under arrest, who were then the most active at the meeting, threatened to raise a secesh flag, and boasted of having on the camp grounds. On the 4th of July, 1862, they attempted to break up the procession of the Union people to pull down the Stars and Stripes and raise the flag of Secession in its stead; but the Union men rallied, and they abandoned the project. Capt. Richardson, of the California Volunteers, visited the valley for the purpose of recruiting for his Cavalry company in 1861, when Durbin threatened to shoot him through the head with a shot gun if he came about there recruiting men "to fight against the south." Charles Ramsey is the most intelligent of the party, and has at times counselled moderation, and succeeded to some extent in keeping the others in check, more particularly in the case of Capt. Richardson, when he showed them how utterly useless it would be for them to oppose the enlisting of men,

as the Captain was acting under orders from the Government. He still entertained the same feelings as the others, but had sense enough to keep quiet
at the proper times. James lives at the upper part of the valley, where he has
a ranch, with elegant and commodious dwellings and outbuildings. Durbin
lives lower down the valley, and Laramee still in Benicia, but the parties have
actual control of the whole valley and precinct, and a Union man's life has not
been safe there at any time during the way. All these men declared when the
act of secession was passed, that we had no government, and have continued
their declarations to that effect ever since. Still, while they were denying the

supremacy of our government, they were regis-
tering their lands at $1.85 per acre and taking
out warrants therefor (sic). All of this party came
here in the early days of California, bringing their
live stock with them, and squatted down in the
Green Valley. They have held possession of the
lands by force, and often by bloodshed, and not
until after the commencement of this war did they
acquire a shadow of other than a possessor's title.
They have improved their property, having built
elegant houses, planted the hillsides with vine-
yards and made one of the most attractive spots in

Francis Bicknell Carpenter

California out of the locality. But their secession sentiments, and their loud
traitorous talk have disgusted Union men, and prevented them from settling
in the valley, and so they have had things all their own way. J. Milton Jones,
one of the Chapman pirates, belonged to this clique and lives in Fairfield,
Solane county, adjoining. It will be remembered that Jones wrote a letter to
Greathouse recommending one Perry Williams as a proper person to join the
piratical expedition, and as a man who could be trusted in the premises. This
Perry Williams has also been a sympathizer and cooperator with the party
arrested. It is a relief to know that the ringleaders of the gang are at last likely
to receive their just deserts. Their secesh proclivities and traitorous language
had not heretofore been resented, but when they commit so outrageous an act,

insulting to every loyal man in the land and traitorous to the Government, they have overshot the mark and made patience no longer a virtue.

* * * * *

Daily State Gazette
Trenton, N.J.
Tuesday, April 25, 1865

Reception of the Remains of President Lincoln in Trenton. — At 5 o'clock yesterday (Monday) morning, the City Hall bell commenced tolling. Soon after the bell of the First Presbyterian Church, and in the course of a few minutes all the bells in the city were also solemnly tolled, in honor of the memory of our murdered President. Even before that hour, the citizens — ladies as well as gentlemen — were assembling at the Clinton street station, in order to, at least, gaze on the funeral train that was bearing all that was mortal of Abraham Lincoln to its last resting place. By half-past five o'clock, the platforms, the bridge, and every [illegible] of 'vantage' that afforded an opportunity to see the train was occupied by an anxious, but orderly, quiet and serious throng of citizens.

The Trenton band was stationed on the platform, and the soldiers of the U.S. Reserve Corps stationed in this city, were present as a guard and as a mark of honor and respect to the memory of the late commander-in-chief.

About half-past five, the funeral train, consisting of nine cars, entered the station. The field pieces stationed near by fired minute guns during the halt — about half an hour — and the band performed solemn funeral dirges.

The cars of the train were all heavily draped in mourning, and the hearse car, containing the body and the car for the committee of escort were elaborately decorated with the solemn emblems of woe.

The train halted for about half an hour while the crowd of interested citizens had an opportunity to view the cars — very few being permitted to enter the car containing the remains. It is estimated by cautious men that, notwithstanding the early hour, not less than five thousand of our citizens attended at the station to pay their last tribute of love and respect to his memory of our venerated and beloved Chief Magistrate — Abraham Lincoln.

A large number of our citizens visited New York yesterday, in order to take part in the funeral ceremonies in that city.

* * * * *

Albany Journal [32]
Albany, N.Y.
Tuesday Evening, April 25, 2010

The Late President
Interesting Reminiscences of His Life
President Lincoln's Favorite Poem

Mr. F.B. Carpenter,[33] the well-known painter of "The Emancipation Proclamation before the Cabinet," has written a note in reference to a poem much admired by Mr. Lincoln. He says:—

I have been urged by several friends to send you the enclosed poem, written down by myself from Mr. Lincoln's lips, and although it may not be new to all of your readers, the events of the last week give it now a peculiar interest.

The circumstances under which this copy was written are these: I was with the President alone one evening in his room, during the time I was painting my large picture at the White house, last year. He presently threw aside his pen and papers, and began to talk to me of Shakespeare. He sent little "Tad," his son, to the library to bring a copy of the plays, and then read to me several of his favorite passages, showing genuine appreciation of the great poet. Relapsing into a sadder strain, he laid the book aside, and leaning back

---

32   Originally an organ of the Anti-Masonic Party, the Albany Journal was edited by Thurlow Weed, who later became a Republican Party boss who pushed to have William Seward nominated over Lincoln in 1860. Weed subsequently supported Lincoln in the election.

33   Francis Bicknell Carpenter (1830 - 1900) lived in the White House for four months while working on "The First Reading of the Emancipation Proclamation of President Lincoln," using the State Dining Room as his studio. He continued to paint pictures of Lincon and his family after the assassination. His many previous paintings included portraits of presidents Fillmore, Pierce, and Tyler.

in his chair, said:—

"There is a poem which has been a great favorite with me for years, which was first shown to me when a young man by a friend and which I afterwards saw and cut from a newspaper and learned by heart. I would," he continued, "give a great deal to know who wrote it, but I have never been able to ascertain."

Then half closing his eyes, he repeated to me the lines which I enclose to you. Greatly pleased and interested, I told him I would like if ever an opportunity occurred, to write them down from his lips. A few days afterward he asked me to accompany him to the temporary studio of Mr. Swayne, the sculptor, who was making a bust of him at the Treasury Department. While he was sitting for the bust, I was suddenly reminded of the poem, and said to him that then would be a good time to dictate it to me. He complied, and sitting upon some books at his feet, as nearly as I can remember, I wrote the lines down one by one from his lips.

With great regards, very truly yours,

    F.B. Carpenter.

Oh! Why Should the Spirit of Mortal be Proud?

Oh, why should the spirit of mortal be proud?
Like a swift, fleeting meteor, a fast-flying cloud,
A flash of lightning, a break of wave,
He passeth from life to rest in the grave.

The leaves of the oak and the willow shall fade,
Be scattered about and together be laid;
And the young men and the old, and the low and the high
Shall moulder to dust and together shall lie.

The infant and mother attended and loved;
The mother that the infant's affection who proved;
The husband that mother and infant who blessed,

April 25, 1865

Each, all, are away to their dwellings of Rest.

The hand of the king that the sceptre hath borne;
The brow of the priest that the mitre hath worn;
The eye of the sage and the heart of the brave,
Are hidden and lost in the depths of the grave.

The peasant, whose lot was to sow and to reap;
The herdsman, who climbed with his goats up the steep;
The beggar, who wandered in search of his bread;
Have faded away like the grass that we tread.

So the multitude goes, like the flower or the weed
That withers away to let others succeed:
So the multitude comes, even those we behold,
To repeat every tale that has often been told.

For we are the same our fathers have been;
We see the same sights our fathers have seen;
We drink the same stream and view the same sun,
And run the same course our fathers have run.

The thoughts we are thinking our fathers would think;
From the death we are shrinking our fathers would shrink;
To the life we are clinging they also would cling;
But speeds for us all, like a bird on the wing.

They loved, but the story we cannot unfold;
They scorned, but the heart of the haughty is cold;
They grieved, but no wail from their slumber will come;
They joyed, but the tongue of their gladness is dumb.

They died, aye! they died; we things that are now,
That walk on the turf that lies over their brow,
And make in their dwellings a transient abode,
Meet the things that they met on the pilgrimage road.

Yes! hope and despondency, pleasure and pain;
We might gather in sunshine and rain;
And the smile and the tear, and the song and the dirge,
Still follow each other, like surge upon surge.

'Tis the wink of an eye, 'tis the draught of a breath,
From the blossom of health to the paleness of death.
From the gilded saloon to the bier and the shroud.
Oh why should the spirit of mortal be proud?

* * * * *

Daily Constitutional Union
Washington, D.C.
Tuesday Afternoon, April 25, 1865

By the President of the United States of America.

A PROCLAMATION

Whereas, by my direction, the Acting Secretary of State, [34] in a notice to the public of the seventeenth, requested the various religious denominations to assemble on the nineteenth instant, on the occasion of the obsequies of Abraham Lincoln, late President of the United States, and to observe the same with appropriate ceremonies; but whereas our country has become one great house of mourning, where the head of the family has been taken away; and believing that a special period should be assigned for again humiliating ourselves before Almighty God, in order that the bereavement may be sanctified to the nation:

Now, therefore, in order to mitigate that grief on earth which can only be

---

34   William Hunter, Jr. served as Acting Secretary of State until August, 1865.

assuaged by communion with the Father in heaven, and in compliance with the wishes of Senators and Representatives in Congress, communicated to me by resolutions adopted at the national Capitol, I, Andrew Johnson, President of the United States, do hereby appoint Thursday, the twenty-fifth of May next, to be observed, where in the United States the flag of country may be respected, as a day of humiliation and mourning; and I recommend my fellow-citizens then to assemble in their respective places of worship, there to unite in solemn service to Almighty God, in memory of the good man who has been removed, so that all shall be occupied at the same time, in contemplation of his virtues, and in sorrow for his sudden and violent end.

In witness thereof, I have hereunto set my hand and caused the seal of the United States to be affixed.

Done at the City of Washington the twenty-fifth day of April in the year of our Lord one thousand eight hundred and sixty-five, and the Independence of the United States of America the eighty-ninth.

Andrew Johnson.

By the President:

W. Hunter

Acting Secretary of State.

———

LOCAL INTELLIGENCE
Assault and Robbery

The moral status of Paddy Welch and Billy Harris has gone downward in an enormous degree. Paddy, who is a gentleman of Irish extraction, persuaded Billy that it would be eminently proper to go to the house of Charles and Margaret Johnson and relieve them of their surplus greenbacks. Billy coincided with Paddy, and they immediately moved their forces forward and charged upon the said Charles and Margaret. Charles was knocked down and Margaret upset, being thus placed hors du combat, Paddy moved himself forward toward the enemy's rear and succeeded in capturing fifteen dollars — no arms or ammunition were discovered. William remained on the field to look after the prisoners, and while "picking up little old articles lying about loose," the attacking column was surprised and captured to a man, by Officers Lappell, Walling, Groves and Hill. They were committed to jail for Court by Justice Giberson.

*   *   *   *   *

Columbia Phoenix
Columbia, S.C.
Tuesday, April 25, 1865

The Latest Tidings

News or rumor? Fact or fable? Which? We know not exactly. Everything is in the clouds. Events, now-a-days, tread so rapidly on each other's hells, that one has need of a fast courser, a very Pegasus, to keep pace with them. It seems to be a confirmed thing that Lincoln has been assassinated, and Seward nearly so — whether by a Virginian, revenging his country's wrongs — a patriot after the type of Brutus — or whether the deed be done, as is somewhere conjectured, by creatures of a Northern faction, with whom Lincoln had survived his uses, and who were anxious for a new change of dynasty — Grant or Sherman being the coming man — must be mere matters of conjecture, and it matters not much to us in what way we resolve our doubts and settle our conjectures. But, on the heels of this pretty catastrophe, we learn that the fleet of the French — *on dit* — have been battling that of the Yankees off New Orleans into fragmentary considerations. This comes to us by way of Greensboro. *Pari passu,* the Northern papers renew the story of French intervention, and with additional plausibilities. We are told by a Paris correspondent of the New York *Times,* dates February 28, that the relations of France with the United States are those of increased uneasiness; and the New York correspondent of the Savannah *Herald* gives us the following *morceau:*

"Foreign intervention is again talked of — this time the interfering gent being the fellow who once occupied a cell in our tombs as a drunken midnight brawler, but now the Emperor of France. He has appointed M. Montholon as French Minister to Washington, who is known to have been, when French Consul at this port, a sympathizer with the abettor of rebels. it is argued that this obnoxious personage is thus sent to this country to pave the way for an imbroglio, the upsot of which shall be the claiming of Texas as part of the old French domain on this continent, fortified by the special plea that the cession to Louisiana did not carry Texas with it, the latter having been originally colonized by Frenchmen. As at present planned, the programme is that Magruder[35] shall declare Texas an independent republic, and asking, shall receive the protection of France. Many profess to see in this a well-concocted plan to carry out the favorite idea of European monarchs to divide the Union into little principalities, and thus break the strength of that unity in which lies our power."

Couriers and soldiers arrived in this city report President Davis as in Charlotte; and, in a speech to the people, holding forth encouraging assurances of our future, with a special reference to the certainty of French and armed intervention. He denied that the army of Northern Virginia had made any surrender, and as fully equal in numbers to that of Sherman, and is in most excellent spirits for a fight. It does not appear that President Davis or his Cabinet are at all downcast. They express themselves hopefully, and, we may add, as the most significant of all signs to some minds, that gold has declined, and Confederate money is once more looking up. We give these details without any assurances of the vital facts in any instance. People must take them at their due worth, as the currency of loose report and rumor. Another day may enable us to be more precise. All we would add, briefly, is that we are not subdued — not likely to be subdued; that we have only to hold on tenaciously for a few months, perhaps weeks, and we may see a bright cure to an otherwise dismal day. It is very sure that the Yankees are exceedingly anxious. Just now, to hurry up to a conclusion of the game. But we must not suffer ourselves to be hurried. A little more endurance in the trough of the sea, and we shall weather the gale and make our port. Despondency does not become us. A long pull, a strong pull and a pull altogether, and the haven of independence will be reached, as surely as our

---

35   John Bankhead Magruder (1807 - 1871) was a U.S. lieutenant colonel in the Mexican-American War, a Confederate general in the Civil War, and then a general in the Imperial Mexican Army.

cause is just. We shall try to give copious details from other papers in our next, tending to the fuller information of our readers.

Counter Revolution

If Lincoln be really slain, as we believe, and Seward *hors du combat*, then the probability is that the North is now agitated with the progress of a counter revolution, which will overthrow the present Abolition faction, in power, and whihc has so long brutally controlled the country. What shape this revolution will take, is only of moment to us as it shall affect the prospects of the party at the North which urges peace unreservedly. Whatever party shall aim, at power, it will seek to fortify itself by putting at its head the most conspicuous military chieftain. It is highly probable — nay, we should say almost certain — that Grant and Sherman are both in Washington at this moment. What Grant may think, in political matters, cannot well be said — that Sherman is insanely sworn to maintain the old Union, without regard to the feeling or opinion of the people of the seceding States, is sufficiently well known. Perhaps we shall have nothing to hope for, of justice, from either of these unless controlled by personal ambition, or under the exacting requistions of the party by which they may be lifted to power. Under all aspects of the case, it is our policy to be wary of any concessions, to be reserved in all communications, to keep aloof from all hasty alliances, and be prepared to struggle on, arms in hand, for six months more.

Senator Lincoln, 1858

Wednesday, April 26, 1865

Mourning Deep and Universal

God buries
his workmen,

but the work
goes on.

Daily State Gazette
Trenton N.J.
Wednesday, April 26, 1865

A Disloyal Editor Killed by Citizens.

Joseph Shaw, editor of the Westminster (Carrol county) Democrat, whose paper was mobbed and material destroyed the night after the murder of the President, on account of disloyal sentiments expressed by the editor, and who was also warned away by the people, returned yesterday to Westminster. Last night he was waited upon by a delegation of citizens, who knocked at his door. He appeared and fired into the crowd, wounding a young man named Henry Bell. Upon this the enraged citizens killed Shaw on the spot.

*   *   *   *   *

The New-York Times
Wednesday, April 26, 1865

THE GREAT TRAGEDY

———

OUR WASHINGTON CORRESPONDENCE

The Search for Booth - The Detectives Surely on his Trail - Startling Facts to be Revealed. — From Our Own Correspondent.

Washington, Saturday, April 22, 1865

The authorities deem it essential to the ends of justice that there should not be the slightest mention of the investigations and arrests connected with the assassination. As usual, this was thought of too late, and when the order was issued it was only partially enforced. The prohibition was put on the telegraph, but the columns of Washington, even those papers were left open. To-day, however, even those papers are silent, and perhaps they have also been convinced of the good policy to say nothing. There are too many rumors and not a few reliable facts in circulation, but I conform cheerfully to the requirements of the War Department and say nothing but this: that the trail of Booth yesterday was so positive that the detectives expressed the greatest confidence of speedily unearthing the place of his concealment, which is on the north side of the Potomac, and outside of Berkes County, Pennsylvania, where they chased a poor traveler three days on suspicion. Atzerot and Paine, two of Booth's accomplices, are closely confined in irons, awaiting the swift vengeance of the law. It is understood that these villains will all be tried by military commission, the offence having been committed upon the person of the Commander-in-Chief, and within the military lines. Atzerot was captured by a scouting party of five of a cavalry regiment, who will be entitled to the reward of twenty-five thousand dollars offered by the Secretary of War.

There is an immense force at work on the conspiracy and the track of the conspirators. When the time comes for revelations, such startling facts will be revealed as will make people shudder. It will then be seen that all the talk about "Knights of the Golden Circle," "Sons of Liberty," "American Knights," &c., was not without foundation; that though much of the action of such bands was either futile or betrayed, yet from the seed thus implanted, fostered by inspiration drawn from the enemy's coffers, sprang the hellish idea of assassination, and the tools by which it was successfully executed were only a tithe of the class who would have done the same thing had they possessed sufficient nerve.

The people of the South will suffer the consequences of this great crime, though they may have never connived at it. But it will be known in the end that the chief instigators of the crime were Northern men, who, under the cloak of "free speech," "liberty of person," &c, denounced Abraham Lincoln as a merciless tyrant, and conceived the plot to take his life. The country will yet have cause to thank Gens. Burnside, Burbridge, Wallace, Hooker and others, who have come in contact with this internal element, that they treated it as sternly as they did, and to regret that they did not use hemp on the spot. I should regret to stir up the passions and resentments of people, but let them think this over thoroughly, and perhaps they will be cooler when the developments of the evidence now accumulating are made public.

* * * * *

Albany Journal
Albany, N.Y.
Wednesday Evening, April 26, 1865

The Obsequies

Those who witnessed the scene of last night will never forget them. Every feature of the mournful pageant will be stamped upon the memory, where it will remain forever. The procession of firemen, with torches filling the air with lurid light — the military escort — the veterans who accompanied the remains from Washington — the line of carriages containing the official directors of the obsequies and others — the sable hearse drawn by four white horses —

The engine Nashville, of the Cleveland, Columbus & Cincinnati Railroad, was one of several that took turns pulling the funeral train.

the vast crowd that lined the sidewalks, watching the progress of the procession with anguished hearts and bated breath — the cannon uttering its hoarse salute and announcing the arrival of the cortege in the city — the bells shivering the midnight air with their mournful peal; — what a picture for the pencil of the artist! We have seen larger demonstrations; the funeral procession of Henry Clay was more imposing and struck the eye with a grander emphasis; — but never has our city witnessed a funeral spectacle that had such a mournful significance or touched the general heart with so profound a grief. Strong men wept like children as they witnessed the solemn train and listened to the wailing notes of the death-dirge. Even the most indifferent felt that it was not merely a ruler but a Friend whom the people had lost.

April 26, 1865

The spectacle presented in our city to-day beggars descriptions. Our streets thronged with strangers from an early hour. Thousands from the surrounding cities and villages — from distant portions of the State — from Vermont and Massachusetts — came in to pay the last tribute of respect to the revered dead. Every train and boat and omnibus was crowded — every avenue leading to the city, was thronged with vehicles. Thousands viewed the remains during the latter part of the night and the earlier hours of the morning; while before the nine o'clock in the forenoon State street, from its foot to the Capitol, was a solid mass of humanity. The arrangements for seeing the remains were admirable; so that most of those who had the patience to keep their places in the procession had their desire to look upon all that is mortal of Abraham Lincoln gratified.

The mournful scenes of the day will make a profound and abiding impression upon our people. They will end to chasten and sanctify the public grief, increase the popular reverence for the murdered President and enshrine his memory more deeply and sacredly in the popular affections. They will breathe into our spirits something of that earnest yet magnanimous spirit that made Mr. Lincoln's last moments so glorious.

God grant that our country may never again be called upon to mourn a murdered President.

The Work Goes On. — Martin Luther once said, in his terse way, "God buries his workmen, but the work goes on." With mourning deep and universal, this nation follows its honored Chief to the grave; but the work goes on. The heavy hand of war crushes out the last traces of Rebellion. The battled traitors are flying before an avenging Nemesis. The freed people of the South are rising to new life and exalted destiny. Government, hardly jarred by the commotion which in any other land would have wrecked a throne, proceeds steadily to the accomplishment of its majestic task. Barbarism is disappearing before the advance of enlightenment. The slaves are to be emancipated. The States will all be returned to their allegiance. The glorified banner of the Republic will float over a restored Union, consecrated by the illustrious valor and noble self-sacrifice of its people. And amid the splendid results toward which we hasten, the world will recognize the patent influence of the martyr-leader who, "Being dead, yet speaketh."[36]

What To Do With The Drapery. — It is suggested that the drapery with which our city is clothed, might be appropriately distributed among the several Relief Associations, the Sanitary and Christian Commission, and the Freedmen's Association. We hope our citizens will think of this suggestion.

Governor Seward's Assassin.

He Attempts to Beat Out His Brains.

The Times' Washington special says: —

Some days ago we gave the announcement of the arrest of Paine, who it is alleged attempted the assassination of Secretary Seward. Yesterday it was discovered that this prisoner had attempted to take his own life by butting his head against the iron walls of his prison. It was found that he had beaten his head almost into a jelly, and was bleeding profusely.

A cap was prepared for him padded all over and fastened securely to his head, and his hands secured so that he can do himself no further injury.

Departure of the Train

In accordance with the timetable, the train left the Crossing at 4 P.M. The following are the points of arrival and departure: —

Leave Albany at 4 P.M. of Wednesday, the 26th, and arrive Buffalo at 7 A.M. of Thursday, the 27th.

Leave Buffalo at 10:10 A.M. same day, and arrive at Cleveland at 7 A.M. of Friday, the 28th.

Leave Cleveland at midnight the same day and arrive at Columbus at 7:30 A.M. of Saturday, the 29th.

---

36   Hebrews 11:4

Leave Columbus at 8 P.M. same day, via Columbus and Indianapolis Central Railroad, and arrive at Indianapolis at 7 A.M. on Sunday, the 30th.

Leave Indianapolis at midnight of the same day, via Lafayette and Michigan City Railroad, and arrive at Chicago at 11 A.M. on Monday, May 1.

Leave Chicago at 9:30 P.M. of May 2, and arrive Springfield at 8 A.M. of Monday, May 3.

The railroads over which the remains will pass are declared military roads, subject to the order of the War Department, and the railroads, locomotives, cars and engined engaged will be subject to the military control of the Brigadier General McCallum.

The speed of all trains is reduced to twenty miles per hour. The time of departure and arrival is ordered by the military authorities to be closely observed. A pilot engine is to be kept ten minutes in advance of the train and the special train is in all cases to have the right of the road.

*　*　*　*　*

Daily National Intelligencer
Washington, D.C.
Wednesday, April 26, 1865

A Remarkable Observation By The President — About four years ago Abraham Lincoln raised with his own hand the national flag over Independence Hall, Philadelphia. On that occasion he said:

I have often inquired of myself what great principle or idea it was that kept this Confederacy so long together. It was something in the Declaration of Independence giving liberty, not only to the people of this country, but hope to the world for all future time. It was that which gave promise that in due time the weights should be lifted from the shoulders of all men, and that all should have an equal chance. * * * Now, my friends, can the country be saved upon that basis? If it can, I will consider myself one of the happiest men in the world if I can help save it, but if this country cannot be saved without giving up that principle — was about to say I would rather be assassinated upon this spot than to surrender it.[37]

The Booths

"Erasmus" offers his profound sympathy to young Edwin Booth, the hope and bright particular star of our stage, and through him to every loyal member of his family. May God comfort and sustain them, one and all. Rest upon Him, trust in Him, and fear not that a just public will turn to you and yours with generous confidence, patronage, and respect.

We knew the elder Booth intimately well. He was the dramatic sun, in mid-day splendor, when we were a youth. We knew him in his familiar hours. We admired him, and were attached to him. Whatever his eccentricities, they were those of genius; certainly inexcusable, but unpremeditated. No kinder heart ever beat. He was a true friend, an accomplished gentleman, a benevolent nature, and his mind was keen and bright as a polished sword; and within it were galleries adorned with all that art and literature have made highest, dearest, and most enduring. His temperament was deeply poetic; he was a genuine classic, and a vein ran through and through him of religious sentiment, which purified and elevated points of his character; but about this the cold and

---

37   Prior to these quoted lines, Mr. Lincoln said, "I am filled with deep emotion at finding myself standing here, in this place, where were collected together the wisdom, the patriotism, the devotion to principle, from which sprang the institutions under which we live. You have kindly suggested to me that in my hands is the task of restoring peace to the present distracted condition of the country. I can say in return, Sir, that all the political sentiments I entertain have been drawn, so far as I have been able to draw them, from the sentiments which originated and were given to the world from this hall. I have never had a feeling politically that did not spring from the sentiments embodied in the Declaration of Independence. I have often pondered over the dangers which were incurred by the men who assembled here, and framed and adopted that Declaration of Independence. I have pondered over the toils that were endured by the officers and soldiers of the army who achieved that Independence."

And following the quoted lines, he said, "Now, in my view of the present aspect of affairs, there need be no bloodshed and war. There is no necessity for it. I am not in favor of such a course, and I may say, in advance, that there will be no bloodshed unless it be forced upon the Government, and then it will be compelled to act in self-defence.

"My friends, this is wholly an unexpected speech, and I did not expect to be called upon to say a word when I came here. I supposed it was merely to do something toward raising the flag. I may, therefore, have said something indiscreet. (Cries of "No, no") I have said nothing but what I am willing to live by and, if it be the pleasure of Almighty God, die by."

careless world knew but little. How often he has made us sad by a revelation of the presentiments which sometimes seems to link him with the Far Beyond!

If there was a madness in the elder Booth, it was no vulgar fire, but the genuine Promethean heat. It was no swaggering affectation, no stupid wooing of coarse notoriety, that swayed him to and fro, and now and then dashed him, all wild and reckless, hither and yon, at the mercy of his resistless passions and impulses. This we know, and we know it so well that our heart sickens at the vulgar anecdotes which some people are producing and publishing about him, one-half of which are mere and wanton inventions, got up to gratify the public curiosity. Had we been but a cold observer of the freaks of the elder Booth, ourself a man destitute of impulses, perhaps we might afford to gratify the millions by columns of true incidents about him. But we were, as fast as it was possible to be, his friend, and we knew the man, and we testify that he had a lofty and aspiring soul, and an intense enthusiasm, which only found full sympathy with the master works of such master minds as "wreaked" the noblest and strongest "thoughts" upon "expression." How calmly he was at home in the classics! With what delight, power, and dramatic fervor he could read and recite the "Ancient Mariner," of the Greek and Latin dramatists and orators, and the finest productions of the French theological and dramatic writers! It is somewhere on record that his rendition of the Lord's Prayer (we never heard him attempt it) before a party of clergymen was an effort whose effect, in humility, fervor, devotion, penitential expression, deep trust, and awful reverence, cannot be conveyed in words. We can easily comprehend this, for the man's soul was full of the sentiment of that prayer, strange being though he was. He flashed through life, but he was not of it. He was no sensualist, he was no sybarite; he was simply an ill-starred, ill-omened genius.

We knew him and pitied him of later years, and we marked his decline with deep sorrow. Among our private papers are many letters from him, all impulse, all affection, all sentiment, all true and wise advice and philosophy. The last time that we remember him was in Chicago, where, in the office of a mutual friend, (an eminent advocate and politician, now no more,) he delighted and awed us by turn with his powerful recitations, from early candlelight until sunrise. Then we lost sight of him; for we would not see what remained of him on the stage. Presently we heard that he was dead. We were not sorry for it; for we had an humble hope that he was pardoned and saved. His impulses were kindly; he designed wrong to no man, and his life was tempest-tossed. He was a great actor: one who never was surpassed in electrical power. He was essentially a wonderful orator, whose influence over men was irresistible, when he was in full possession of his powers. We have said this much to offset coarse narratives which are put afloat now about this eminent actor. His memory brings to our heart sentiments which are not ashamed to acknowledge, because we think that the better part of him was so little understood. His was truly "a voiceless thought," forever sheathed, as the scabbard sheathes the sword.

And Edwin inherits much of his father's genius, but his nature is better tempered. And as did this dreadful assassin, (whom God forgive, since man may not!) who has brought this shock upon his family, this disgrace upon his race, and who now wanders about hunted by tens of thousands of indignant men; but no bloodhound can so steadily and closely pursue him as does that unrelaxing, unrelenting REMORSE which trails him night and day, sleeping and waking! The monster wretch, compared with whose foul deed (the time, the place, the man murdered considered) the records of all other assassins pale; a deed without a single manly motive, engendered of cowardice, cruelty, and loathsome egotism — else the execrable offspring of hire and pay.

We sympathize with the profession which this villain has degraded; and we enter our indignant protest at the thoughtlessness which, at this moment of general excitement, publishes actors to the world as disloyal. Why is this? Why should this inoffensive class of men and women be thus assailed? It is a downright cruelty, if not a wanton falsehood, thus indiscriminately to strike at people who instincts are generally patriotic. it is a small business, and the public will so pronounce it.

Erasmus.

The Remains at Poughkeepsie.[38]

------

38   Poughkeepsie is on the east bank of the Hudson, about halfway between New York and Albany.

Poughkeepsie, April 25, — 7:25 P.M. — The body of our lamented President has just passed through this place. All along the way the outpouring of the people was immense.

* * * * *

Louisville Daily Journal
Wednesday, April 26, 1865

Police Proceedings —Tuesday, Aril 25.—

P.J. Taylor, Geo. Pettitt, alias Jim Taylor, suspected felon. Each fined $5 for disorderly conduct.

Jennie (she refused to give any other name) was found asleep on the Court-house steps. Discharged.

Henry Johnson was arrested for walking the streets with his arm around a negro woman's waist. He says he is from Philadelphia, and didn't think it was improper at all. Fined $5 for disorderly conduct.

William, slave of S.P. Thomas, stealing harness from Hamilton Zane. Committed to the Work-house until his master gives bonds that his slave will not be permitted to run at large or hire his own time.

Joe Carroll, common gambler. Continued and peremptory attachments ordered for the Commonwealth's witnesses.

Walter Harris, stabbing and shooting with intent to kill, but without wounding, Jon Hernon, of Cubas Saloon. Security in $200 to answer an indictment.

Daniel Carroll, arrested on a warrant for stealing $226 from Michael Keeler. Continued till to-morrow.

A peace warrant was then disposed of.

* * * * *

Philadelphia Inquirer
Wednesday, April 26, 1865

An Incident in Booth's Life

Pittsburg (sic), April 25. — Mr. Duncan, a reliable citizen of Pittsburg, has just returned from Meadeville, and mentions a singular circumstance in connection with the assassin Booth. While stopping at the McHenry House, in Meadeville, on the fourth of June last, Booth wrote on a pane of glass with his diamond ring the following words: "Abe. Lincoln departed this life August 13th, 1864 by the effects of poison."

Booth's name was written on the hotel register in the same handwriting. Several of his friends, at different times, occupied the same room. A complete register has been kept of all the names of the occupants of that room since June last.

* * * * *

JEFF D. HUNG ON A 'SOUR APPLE TREE' OR TREASON MADE ODIOUS.

Thursday, April 27, 1865

The Drapery of Woe

It has insanely sought to overthrow
the best structure of government

which mankind ever erected;
it has deluged this continent

with the blood of our noblest and best;
it has piled on us mountains of debt,
and thrown civil discord into a happy people.

In its mad efforts, it has ruined the hopes
and desolated the country of its supporters;

and now, when just dying under the executioner's stroke,
with garments stained with the best blood of the nation,

it turns to strike with assassin's blow
at the head of the republic, and culminates

its long course of iniquities by a crime which,
in dishonor, cowardice and atrocity,
is almost without a parallel in history.

It was not enough that it should die
amid the flames of burning cities

and with the wails of thousands of widows and orphans
whom its crimes had desolated;

it adds to all its guilt
the stain of private murder and base assassination
of the purest public man of the day.

Philadelphia Inquirer
Thursday, April 27, 1865

THE LINCOLN TRAGEDY

————

Arrest of Junius Brutus Booth in This City.

Junius Brutus Booth, a brother of the infamous murderer of President Lincoln, has been arrested, and is now an inmate of the Old Capitol Prison at Washington. It is stated that Booth was arrested at his residing place in this city, on Tuesday night, and conveyed at once to Washington. The arrest was made very quietly, and the fact was not generally known in this city until some hours after the arrested party was safely lodged in the above mentioned prison.

It is understood that the arrest was caused by the peculiar wording of a letter written by Junius Brutus Booth to his brother, the assassin. The said letter alluded to the evacuation of Richmond, and contains advice to the assassin to give up the oil business. A strong suspicion exists the allusion to the oil business is intended as a cypher, and the real meaning of it has some reference to the, at the time, contemplated assassination of the President.

The subject will receive a full and searching investigation at the hands of the authorities at Washington, and it is hinted that some startling developments will be brought to light. It was not known except to a very few persons that the arrest of Junius Brutus Booth was made in this city until a late hour last night. The arrest was made by order of the War Department.

—————

Arrival at Syracuse[1]

SYRACUSE, April 26, 11:10 P.M. — The funeral train has just arrived.

————

1   Located 145 miles west of Albany, Syracuse was a key junction of the railway and the Erie Canal. With strong Unitarian and Quaker churches, the city was actively abolitionist well before the war. It saw a lot of traffic from the underground railroad. When a fugitive slave was arrested in 1851 under the Fugitive Slave Law, several hundred citizens stormed the jail and released him.

Rain has set in and the night is very dark, but the demonstrations of the people are not diminished. Every house is illuminated and draped in mourning. There are tens of thousands of people along the railroad, a dozen bells are tolling and the band is playing dirges at the depot. Such a display of universal grief and respect, has never been witnessed in this or any other country. At every station since we left Utica, bonfires and torches and illuminations have lit out entire route.

SUMMARY OF THE NEWS

— It is said that Mr. Seward has remarked since the tragedy: "This is only history repeating itself — all great revolutions have their assassins as well as their heroes."

— A movement has been started in Boston to raise one hundred thousand dollars, by one dollar subscriptions, to be presented to Mrs. Lincoln.

— A guard has been placed around the residence of Senator Sumner at Washington, evidence having been adduced to show that he was one of the parties intended to be assassinated.

Junius Brutus Booth, Jr.

— Despatches are received almost hourly from all parts of the country, giving details of the obsequies of President Lincoln. They are all of the same character, bitter tears and intensified hate of the leaders of this infamous Rebellion.

— W.C. Rose, of New Albany, Indiana, who said he "would like to dance on Lincoln's coffin," has been sentenced by the Provost Marshal of Louisville to sixty days' hard work on the fortifications.

— Harvey Ford, an old man in New Haven, was very much affected by the news of President Lincoln's decease, and after appearing much depressed all day, he dropped down dead in the evening.

— James L. Chapman, son of Sheriff Chapman, of Pittsfield, bears so strong a resemblance to the assassin, Booth, that he was stopped three times while traveling on Wednesday, and made to establish his identity. — The body of a Frenchman was recently found in the Ramble of the New York Central Park, with a neat placard upon the breast stating that he and misfortune were brothers. This unfortunate relationship undoubtedly accounted for his untimely demise.

— Ex-President Millard Filmore has refused to put out a flag since the outbreak of the Rebellion, and declining to inaugurate the precedent at the demonstration in Buffalo, a few days since, in memory of Abraham Lincoln, has his house smeared with ink by the excited populace.

— Mrs. Lincoln seems quite feeble. She has been confined to her bed ever since Saturday morning, the shock having completely prostrated her. President Johnson has kindly requested that she will remain at the White House until she has sufficiently recovered to decide as to her future movements.

— The Washington correspondent of the New York Evening Post says there are many intelligent persons who believe that Booth still lurks in some hiding place in the Capital. The detectives generally believe that the horsemen who rode in haste over the Navy Yard Bridge on the fatal Friday night were decoys, and that Booth was not one of them.

— General Garfield[2] says: — A year ago, when there were reports of a conspiracy in Richmond to murder President Lincoln, he said to a friend, "Well, even if true, I do not see what the Rebels would gain by either killing or getting possession of me. I am but a single individual and it would not help their cause or make the least difference in the progress of the war. Everything would go right on, just the same."

— The Lacrosse (Wis.) Democrat, in its issue of August 29th, 1864, closed a fierce political leader against Mr. Lincoln's re-election with the following words: — "If he is elected to misgovern for another four years, we trust

---

2   James Abram Garfield (1831 - 1811) grew up poor on a farm in Ohio, became a state senator, then a major general in the Union army, then served nine terms in the House before being elected 20th president of the United States. He was assassinated 200 days into his term.

some bold hand will pierce his heart with a dagger point for the public good."
Is not the man who wrote the above a proper subject for arrest as an "accessory" to Booth "before the act?"

— In Sheldon, Vermont, on the 15th instant, the pastor naturally preached on the death of President Lincoln, and an aged Secessionist, after listening as long as he could to the scathing denunciation of traitors and assassins, got up and left the church. Just as he got to the door the minister called out to him, "Don't stop, brother, till you get to Canada," which was responded to by a hearty amen from the whole congregation.

Funeral Incidents in New York

The population in the neighborhood of Canal and Hudson streets is of a hybrid character — Irish, Dutch and African blending together in charming confusion. Yet upon all of the tenement houses were exhibited the drapery of woe. Incidents of the sentiment of the people were very numerous.

As the great procession turned up Debrosses street, an uncouth Irish woman observed, from the balcony of a tenement house, as the hearse was passing — "Well, is that all that's left of Owld Abe?" "It's more than you'll ever be," was the response of another Milesian near by. "Oh, I have nothing against him," was the reply. "I never knew nor cared much for him when living, but, he died like a saint."

Another Incident

A great, brawny six-footer, who looked as if he might be able to cut six cords of wood a day, and paint a picture afterward, pressed forward very earnestly to see the hearse as it was passing. There was a strange eagerness on his hard bronzed face. "Don't walk over me," said an irate individual whom he was pressing rather sharply. "Excuse me sire," said the backwoodsman, "but I must see the coffin." "Why must you see it?" "Because I love the man — he's one of my craft," was the reply. "All right" was the answer, still petulant. "I must get through," persisted the backwoodsman, "two of my brothers have died in the same cause as old Abe. I'll never go back to the prairies till I see and bless his coffin. And he pushed his way through with his brawny shoulders, and that was the last we saw of him."

Still Another.

As the solemn procession swept past the Alhambra Palace, a saloon of pleasure on Canal street, the windows were crowded with the sad faces of negroes and mulattoes, most of whom were ladies, and all of whom were bathed in tears. To illustrate the depravity of a certain class, as we perceived one colored lady, who was weeping copiously and at the same time partaking of some refreshment, which resembled a piece of pancake, we heard a bystander remark in the words of an antiquated strain: —

"The buckwheat cake was in her mouth,

The tear was in her eye."We did not stop to hear him repeat the remainder of the ballad, but pushed onward for more meaning (sic) demonstrations. We found one at the corner of West Broadway and Canal street, where an old negress was weeping very violently, exclaiming: — "He died for me! He died for me! God bless him!" Indeed he did die for her and her down-trodden race.

A gentleman who knows the assassin Booth, said that he (Booth) was a great admirer of Orsini,[3] and when that Italian attempted the life of Napoleon, Booth expressed great admiration for the act, saying that had he (Booth) undertaken the business it would have been successful, and then said he, "I should have lived forever."

* * * * *

---

3   Felice Orsini (1819 - 1838) was an Italian revolutionary who believed that by assassinating Napoleon he might free Italy from Austrian rule and inspire a liberal uprising throughout Europe. He hurled three bombs at Napoleon's carriage, killing eight, and wounding 142, including himself. He was executed by guillotine in 1858.

The Highland News
Hillsborough, Ohio
Thursday, Aril 27, 1865

Opposition Press on the Presidents Murder

It is gratifying to notice, that without an exception, as far as we have heard, the opposition papers all speak of the President's death in the strongest terms of regret for the great calamity to the nation, and denounce the assassin and his acomplices with unmeasured severity. Even the Dayton Empire declares that any one who rejoices over the event is no better than the murderer. It is greatly to be regretted, however, that these papers could not see any good qualities in Mr. Lincoln until after his death, and if they are sincere in their sorrow it must be a painful reflection to their editors, that had they not denounced him so bitterly and unjustly during his life time, perhaps the assassin's hand would never have been lifted against him. It should teach all partisan writers and speakers the duty of weighing their words more carefully, and refraining from the common practice of violent and unmerited abuse of their political opponents.

*   *   *   *   *

New York Times[4]
Thursday, April 27, 1865

Slavery has written its guilt and its folly on the record of history, as no other human crime has ever done. It has insanely sought to overthrow the best structure of government which mankind ever erected; it has deluged this continent with the blood of our noblest and best; it has piled on us mountains

---

4   Also in *The Times* this day: In Mexico, General Juan Cortina and a force of Mexicans and Texans declares against the Mexican empire and lays siege to Matamoros. In England, the London Times expresses dismay over Australians sympathizing with the pirate ship Shenandoah. Controvesy in France over the unification of Italy. Two blockade-running steamers out of Texas arrived in Havana with loads of cotton bound for Spain. From Canada, rumors of rebel assassins in Montreal. Charles Steinway, of the 14th street piano making firm, died of typhoid while visiting his native Germany.

of debt, and thrown civil discord into a happy people. In its mad efforts, it has ruined the hopes and desolated the country of its supporters; and now, when just dying under the executioner's stroke, with garments stained with the best blood of the nation, it turns to strike with assassin's blow at the head of the republic, and culminates its long course of iniquities by a crime which, in dishonor, cowardice and atrocity, is almost without a parallel in history. It was not enough that it should die amid the flames of burning cities and with the wails of thousands of widows and orphans whom its crimes had desolated; it adds to all its guilt the stain of private murder and base assassination of the purest public man of the day.

And yet in its dying crime the finger of the dread Nemesis -- the retribution of Providence -- is still plainly visible. To us, who once bore something of the responsibility of its accursed guilt, it strikes down the one best beloved, most honored, who had been identified with the great struggle of the nation, and was now just leading its triumph. We could have received no keener blow.

And yet, like the crimes of the guilty, this sin will bring no advantage to its perpetrators or approvers. It exposes to the world and all history the fearful character of that crime, against which the nation has been struggling; for all men will see that from no society under the blue sky, except a slaveholding society, could a deed so revengeful, so mean, have arisen. It evidently belongs to the same category with the selling of human beings, the burning alive of unfortunate and helpless slaves, and the starving and insulting of prisoners.

But here too, the folly and the retribution of slavery are seen. The secession assassin, in his blind frenzy, strikes down the kindest friend of the South in all the North, one just planning measures of good-will toward the rebels, and in a moment when the people of the Free States were inclined to fall into almost an excess of leniency, and to forgive every one. In place of compassion the murderer now kindles up a fire of inextinguishable hate and wrath in the hearts of the Northern people. All thoughts of clemency to the leaders have been swept away by the storm of indignation which is now aroused. And in place of the mild and forgiving President, they have put into power over the South a man who has felt the iron of oppression in his soul, who knows the crushing weight of the slaveholding aristocracy on the masses, and has himself experienced the diabolical spirit of the rebellion; a man of generous nature, but whose feeling and whose principle will be to crush to atoms the proud, re-bellious class of the South and to exterminate the rebellion. Slavery has elect-ed her own judge from the very class she has most wronged; she has chosen her executioner. Let her abide the result!

In these grand events we may all, without hypocrisy, attempt to read Heaven's purpose; and if anything now is clear to the people, it is that that institution and those men which have begotten the rebellion, and now, having failed on the battle-field, are madly trying the assassin's weapons, should be utterly extirpated from the land, and the South itself be thoroughly and forever revolutionized.

* * * * *

Hartford Courant
Thursday Morning, April 27. 1865

Slaveholders in the United States

From the eighth census report of the United States relating to agriculture, made by Mr. Kennedy, is gleaned that the number of persons in the United States owning:

1 slave, is 77,333;
2 slaves, 46,155;
do. 3, 34,850[5]
do. 4, 28,979;
do. 5, 24,279;
do. 6, 20,632;
do. 7, 17,280;
do. 8, 14,864;
do. 9, 12,511;

---

5   "do." meaning ditto.

10 and under 15, 40,367;

15 do. 20, 21,315;

20 do. 30, 20,796;

30 do. 40, 9,648;

40 do. 50, 5,179;

50 do. 70, 5218;

70 do. 100, 3,149;

100 do. 200; 1,980;

200 do. 300, 244;

300 do. 500, 74;

500 do. 1000, 13;

1000 and over, 1;

whole number of slaveholders, 384,884;

whole number of slaves; 3,953,742.

Twenty per cent of all slaves are children under ten years of age. The average age of these children is something less than five years. The number of persons owning from one to nine slaves each is 276,881. Only 108,003 persons own from ten to several hundred.

* * * * *

Friday, April 28, 1865

Them's the Gentlemen

He made an effort
to lift his hands up
before his eyes.

In this he was assisted,
and upon seeing them
he exclaimed somewhat incoherently,

"Useless! - useless! -
blood! blood!"
and swooned away.

**The Liberator
Boston
Friday, April 28, 1865**

Assassination of President Lincoln

The Slaveholder's Dagger Has Reached the Nation's Heart

Gloucester, April 15, 1865

Dear Garrison — The assassination of President Lincoln is accomplished. Slaveholders and their allies have done the deed. Slavery, that instigated the rebellion, that began and for four years has carried on this civil war, has done it. The spirit that has assassinated and mutilated five hundred thousand of our sons and brothers and fathers and husbands on the battlefield, and one hundred thousand in rebel prisons, and carried desolation and anguish to the homes and hearts of the whole land, has done it. It is the sprit of slaveholders and their apologists and allies in the North and in Europe. The man who can buy and sell men and women, and hold and use them as chattels, is an assassin at heart. So are those who plead or apologize for slavery. There is no conceivable crime which they will not commit, if an opportunity offers.

And this spirit has ruled the national legislation, courts and Presidents for fifty years previous to 1861. The spirit of slaveholding assassins has ruled the pulpit, the press, the commerce, the politics, the literature, and the social and family relations of the North.

While the slaveholder's dagger was aimed at the heart of the despised negro, Curch and State, priest and politician, acquiesced, openly or silently, and hugged the assassin to their bosoms. When it was aimed at the life of the republic, even then the North could hardly be aroused. In the great Convention of the Northern wing of the Rebellion at Chicago, one of the leaders exclaimed, "We'll cut the throat of every Lincoln we meet. Will you help us?" Yes, yes," was the response of thousands.

April 28, 1865

At length, the assassin that struck down Lovejoy in Alton,[6] Sumner in the Senate, and five hundred thousand other defenders and friends of freedom, has pierced the heart of President Lincoln, Secretary Seward and his son. The blow was struck by slaveholders and their allies. *Slavery is the assassin.* Shall that assassin ever again be admitted to place and power in the nation? Will this deed find apologists in the North? Stern and terrible will be the spirit it will awaken throughout the land.

President Lincoln is a martyr to free labor. Hundreds of thousands have been sacrificed to slavery as *soldiers,* in prisons and battles. Now the slaveholder's dagger has pierced the heart of the representative man of the nation. Will this open the eyes of the North to see slavery as it is? Could nothing less atone for wrongs done to the slave than the blood of our twice-chosen and most esteemed President? God save the people from the spirit of revenge!

I have been through the streets and public places of resort in the town of Gloucester, and have just come in, have met many citizens and returned soldiers. The business and amusements of the town seem almost entirely suspended. Flags are flying at half mast in the harbor, on the forts, and all over the city. The bells are tolled. Deep anguish is in all hearts, and a stern sorrow clouds every brow. A terrible and determined purpose is expressed in the faces and tread of the soldiers. The men are huddled together, and speaking in emphatic tones, to one another, the thoughts and emotions that well up within them. The wives, mothers, daughters and sisters of the town are gathered in groups in parlors and kitchens, to whisper to one another the terrible news, and give vent to the thoughts that oppress them. Even the children suspend their sports of merriment to listen to the deep, stern, sorrowing utterances of their elders. The atmosphere overhanging Gloucester seems surcharged with grief. Though always before Democratic, and the stronghold of Democracy is in the State, out of 1300 votes at the last Presidential election, it gave 1100 for

---

6   Elijah Parish Lovejoy (1802 - 1837) was a Presbyterian minister who was ardently and insistently abolitionist. He had a church and published a newspaper in St. Louis, Mo. It criticized not only slavery but churches that failed to resist it. After mobs destroyed his printing operation three times, he moved to Alton, Ill. and began publishing there. Even though the state was "free," an irate pro-slavery mob attacked his press. He and supporters resisted gunfire with gunfire, and Lovejoy was killed.

Abraham Lincoln.

Now, to feel that he is immolated on the altar of that piratical power that has cost their country so much blood and treasure, is more than they can bear. Lincoln would not think his life itself of more value than that of any of our sons and brothers that the dagger of the assassin (slavery) has stricken down. But he was the President of a republic regenerated and redeemed from slavery; of a republic which he has done much to save to the cause of impartial justice and equal rights. As *such*, the dagger of the slaveholder has pierced his heart, and, through him, the heart of the nation, whose politial head he was. Millions of slaves has this nation victimized on the bloody altar of slavery. The same spirit has now immolated its President on the same altar. The nation will miss and mourn its genial, honest hearted and noble President.

He was the people's President. No head of any nation ever got nearer to the hearts of the people. The very elements of his nature, which many in this and in foreign lands deemed so undigified in a President, and which all that is slaveholding, murderous and unprincipled in the nation has tried to turn against him, have only made him nearer and dearer to the great popular heart. His warm, hearty, genial and *truly* democratic nature, that found expression in spicy, telling anecdotes, stories, and jokes, broiught him close to the sympathies, thoughts, affections and every day (sic) life of the people in every cabin. They made him the bosom friend of the fathers and mothers and little ones of the country, in their kitchens, parlors, nurseries and bed-rooms. No one ever dreamed that his warm, social nature, that thus found expression, was unbecoming the *man*. I have yet to learn that what becomes a *man*, can ill become a *President*. What does not disgrace a man, cannot disgrace a President. Most every family feels that one of the family circle is gone, and that a vacancy is there which none but their kindly and great-hearted President could fill. He is identified with the domestic and social thoughts, feelings and life of the people as no man before him, in a position so exulted, ever was. At the same time, no ruler nor statesman was every more pleasantly, gratefully and honorably associated with the life and history of any nation, than will President Lincoln be with the life and glory of the American Republic. What will the emancipated negro, the continent of Africa, and the toiling millions of the world think and say of him in all coming time? While *in the body,* no man was ever more thoroughly cursed by slavemongers and their allies, and by tyrants and oppressors generally, than President Lincoln, *and out of it* no man will be more heartily and gratefully admired and blessed by the world's true democracy.

SLAVERY IS THE ASSASSIN! The ball that pierced the brain of our kind-hearted and noble President was aimed by slaveholding rebels and their sympathizing allies. The man who apologizes for slavery, apologizes for the assassin, and makes himself an accessory to the murderous deed. This assassin, (slavery) is the monster that has been held up by AMERICAN THEOLOGY as approvingly ordained of God, and the Heaven-sent missionary to carry salvation, through the loving, gentle martyr of Calvary, to Africa! President Lincoln, as the people's right hand, gave this assassin of the negro, of freedom, justice and free institutions, the death-blow. Now the surviving tools and minions of that assassin, instigated by the same spirit of murderous "hatred to free labor, free schools, free press, free society, free thought and speech and a free Republic," have slain the *political* embodiment of freedom to labor and the laborers of the nation, the continent and the world. In so doing they have given to President Lincoln a name and place in the history of nations, and in the great human heart, never before given to man.

God save the people from the spirit of revenge! God save the loyal masses from retaliation! from "blood for blood!" from "evil for evil!" Also, from that mawkish sentimentalism, that more unwise, most thoughtless and hurtful sympathy with the conquered rebels and slavemongers which shall make earth's most colossal criminals feel that, in involving the nation in the horrors of war to enslave its laborers, they have done no wrong! Like Burr, Arnold, and Cain, let them be made to feel that they are "fugitives and vagabonds on the earth," till they cry out — "My punishment is greater than I can bear."

GOD SAVE THE AMERICAN REPUBLIC!

Henry C. Wright.[7]

---

7   Henry Clarke Wright (1797 - 1870) was an outspoken abolitionis and columnist for The Liberator. He was a radical pacifist but spoke up for John Brown for his resistance to slavery.

* * * * *

Philadelphia Inquirer
Friday, April 28, 1865

Arrest of Mr. Edward Ingersoll. — An exciting scene took place yesterday morning, in the cars belonging to the Germantown Railroad. It appears
that Mr. Edward Ingersoll, who resides at Germantown, left that place at nine
o'clock yesterday morning for the purpose of coming to the city, and that soon
after getting on the cars, at Tioga Station, a number of persons commenced
taunting him with the cry of "Traitor." Having taken shelter in the smoking car,
a number of passengers left it after expressing themselves as being unwilling
to stay where there was treason.

On the arrival of the train at Ninth and Green streets a number of gentlemen took their position about the door of the car, with the view, it is said,
of greeting Mr. Ingersoll as he left, but he passed out of the back door. The
crowd followed him, however, and when at Eighth street it is alleged Mr. Ingersoll turned about and faced them. Captain J.H. Wythington, (sic) Jr., One-
hundred-and-ninety-eighth Regiment Pennsylvania Volunteers, then stepped
forward and said: — "Ingersoll, I'm a soldier, and have risked my life for my
country. I think you owe an apology to the country for your speech which you
delivered in New York, and particularly to the soldiers."

Mr. Ingersoll replied to these observations in a manner that gave offense
to Captain Withington (sic), who it is alleged raised his cane to strike Mr.
Ingersoll. The blow was warded off by Mr. Ingersoll with the cane which he
carried, but he received a wound in the face, while his cane was broke (sic) in
striking at Captain Withington.

It is alleged that Mr. Ingersoll then drew a revolver on the Captain, when
he was seized by Officer Jones, of the Eighth Police District.

Soon after, Mr. Ingersoll was handed over to the police, who took him to
the station at Spring Garden hall. The crowd by this time had been augmented

considerably and were much excited.

The defendant had a hearing before Alderman Massey. The testimony of the captain was then given; the evidence was in accordance with the previous statement of this gentleman.

Officer Jones having been sworn, stated that he made the arrest, and that the defendant at the time had a revolver in his hand, which was cocked. The evidence of guilt having been substantiated, Mr. Ingersoll was required to enter bail in $2000 to answer the charge of assault and battery with intent to kill, and carrying a concealed deadly weapon. Bail not being ready, the defendant was detained until he should answer the requirements of the law in this respect.

*　*　*　*　*

New York Times
Friday, April 28, 1865

Full Account of the Pursuit and its Result. — He is Traced to St. Mary's County, Maryland. — Harrold[8] and Booth Discovered in a Barn. — Booth Declares he will not be Taken Alive. — The Barn Set on Fire to Force Them Out. — Sergt. Boston Corbett Fires at Booth — He is Shot Through the Neck and Dies in Three Hours. — His Body and Harrold Brought to Washington.

War Department,
Washington, April 27, 1865 - 9:20 A.M.

Maj.-Gen. John A. Dix, New-York:

J. Wilkes Booth and Harrold were chased from the swamp in St. Mary's County, Maryland, to Garrett's farm, near Port Royal, on the Rappahannock, by Col. Baker's force.

The barn in which they took refuge was fired.

8　　David Edgar Herold (1842 - 1865) had known Booth since 1863. He conspired with Booth, Atzerodt, and Powell and led Powell to Seward's house. He then fled and met up with Booth outside of Washington.

Booth, in making his escape, was shot through the head and killed, lingering about three hours, and Harrold was captured. Booth's body and Harrold are now here.

EDWIN M. STANTON,

Secretary of War.

DETAILS OF THE CAPTURE OF BOOTH.

Special Dispatch to the New-York Times.

Washington, Thursday, April 27.

About 8 o'clock last evening we received the intelligence of the capture of J. Wilkes Booth, the assassin of Abraham Lincoln, and one of his accomplices in the murder, David C. Harrold. The following are such of the particulars as we were enabled to gather, which, with the exception of the precise locality where the occurrence took place, we give as being reliable and correct. It having been pretty clearly ascertained that Booth and his accomplice had crossed the Potomac River at or near Aqula Creek, our cavalry scouts in that vicinity have been in consequence unusually active in their endeavors to get on their trail. Early yesterday morning a squad of about twelve men, belonging to the Sixteenth New-York Cavalry, under command of a Lieutenant, whose name we did not learn, succeeded in discovering the fugitives in a barn on the road leading from Port Royal to Bowling Green in Caroline County, Va. As soon as they were discovered, the place was surrounded and the assassins ordered to surrender. This they both refused to do, Booth declaring that he would not be taken alive, and offering to fight the whole squad if he would be permitted to place himself twenty yards distant from them. His proposition was not, however, acceded to, and as they persisted in their refusal to surrender, the Lieutenant determined to burn them out, and accordingly set fire to the barn, shortly after which Harrold came out and gave himself up. Booth remained in the burning building for some time, and until driven out by the fire, when he rushed out and was immediately shot through the neck by the sergeant of the squad.

Since the above we have had an interview with two of the cavalrymen engaged in the capture of the assassins. From them we learn that the whole party consisted of twenty-eight, including two detectives. The first information respecting Booth's crossing the river, and his probable whereabouts, were obtained from disbanded rebel soldiers who were met with in all directions in that part of the country. From one and another of these the clue to Booth's movements was gathered and held until just at daybreak they came upon the barn, where he and Harrold were secreted. A parley was held, and Booth manifested the most desperate determination not to be taken alive, and to take as many of the lives of the party as possible. Lieut. Edward P. Dougherty, who commanded the scouting party, determined to make short work of him. When Harrold saw the preparations for firing the barn, he declared his willingness to surrender, and said he would not fight if they would let him out. Booth, on the contrary, was impudently defiant, offering at first to fight the whole squad at one hundred yards, and subsequently at fifty yards. He was hobbling on crutches, apparently very lame. He swore he would die like a man, etc. Harrold having been secured, as soon as the burning hay lighted the interior of the barn sufficiently to render the scowling face of Booth, the assassin, visible, Sergeant Boston Corbett fired upon him and he fell. The ball passed through his neck. He was pulled out of the barn, and one of his crutches, and carbine and revolvers secured; the wretch lived about two hours, whispering blasphemes against the government, and messages to his mother, desired her to be informed that he died for his country. At the time Booth was shot he was leaning upon one crutch and preparing to shoot his captors. Only one shot was fired in the entire affair -- that which killed the assassin.

Lieut. Doughtery is one of the bravest fellows in the cavalry service, having distinguished himself in a sharp affair at Culpepper Court-house and on other occasions. The Sixteenth New-York Cavalry is commanded by Col. Nelson Sweitzer, and has been doing duty in Fairfax County. This regiment formed part of the cavalry escort on the day of the President's obsequies in Washington. The body of Booth and the assassin's accomplice, Harrold, were placed on board the [steamer] Ide and sent to Washington, arriving here about 6 o'clock this morning.

ACCURATE ACCOUNT OF THE PURSUIT AND CAPTURE OF BOOTH.

Special Dispatch to the New-York Times.

Washington, Thursday, April 27.

Without recursing to the circumstances that brought together and put to work a large body of detectives in pursuit of the assassin Booth and his accessories in crime, I propose to state briefly and consecutively the incidents in the pursuits from the time the detachment started from that city until their arrival here this morning with the corpse of Booth and the body of Harrold. The following facts I obtained from Col. Baker and the other persons engaged with him.

From the time the Secretary of War telegraphed Col. L.C.Baker at New-York, twelve days ago, to come here immediately and take charge of the matter of ferretting (sic) out the facts, and arresting the criminals in the assassination, up to last Sunday, but little progress was made in the right direction. All the lower counties of Maryland were secured by a large force consisting of 1,600 cavalry and 500 detectives and citizens. On Sunday last Col. Baker learned of a little boy in Maryland some facts which satisfied him that Booth and Harrold had crossed the river about 11 o'clock A.M. and had gone into Virginia. A telegraph operator with a small body of soldiers was sent down the river to tap the wires at a given place and make certain inquiries. This party returned on Monday morning last, bringing with them a negro man whom they picked up at Swan Point, who on being closely interrogated, disclosed that he had seen parties cross in a boat, and the description of these parties assured Col. Baker that Booth and Harrold were the men. No examination or search had yet been made by official authority in Virginia. Demand was made upon Gen. Hancock for a detachment of cavalry, and twenty-eight of the Sixteenth New-York were immediately sent to Col. Baker, under command of Lieut. Dougherty, one of this detachment being Boston Corbett. The whole party were put in charge of Lieut. L.B. Baker and Lieut.Col. E.J. Conger. They were instructed to go immediately to Port Royal; that Booth had crossed the river, and had had about time to reach that point; that he could not ride on horseback, and must therefore have traveled slowly.

At twenty-five minutes past four o'clock on Monday afternoon, this force left the Sixth-street wharf in the steamer Ida. They were directed that when they arrived at the landing place - Belle Plain - they should shove or swim their horses to the shore, if they could not make a landing, for they must have the horses on land. That night the party went down the river four miles, but heard nothing satisfactory. They finally, at daylight, brought up below Port Royal some miles. They returned, finding no trace of the criminals till they got to Port Royal Ferry. Lieut. Baker rode up, found the ferryman, and made inquiries. The ferryman stoutly denied having seen any such persons as those described. Lieut. Baker throttled him and threatened him, yet he denied any knowledge of the persons sought. By the side of the ferryman a negro was sitting. Lieut. Baker presented a likeness of Booth and Harrold. The negro upon looking at these exclaimed, "Why Masse, them's the gentlemen we brought cross the river yesterday." The ferryman then admitted that he had brought Booth and Harrold over the river in his boat. The cavalry was started off and went fourteen

The killing of John Wilkes Booth

miles beyond Garrett's place. There they met a negro who said he saw two men sitting on Garrett's porch that afternoon. The description of one accorded with that of Booth. Lieut. Baker and his party returned to Garrett's house. Garrett denied that the two men had been there. Baker threatened to shoot him if he did not tell the truth. Garrett's son thereupon came out of the house and said the two men were in the barn. The barn was at once surrounded. This was about 2 A.M. Baker went up and rapped at the door. Booth asked "Who are you, friends or foes? Are you Confederates? I have got five men in here, and we can protect ourselves." Col. Baker replied, "I have fifty men out here; you are surrounded, and you may as well come out and surrender." Booth answered, "I shall never give up; I'll not be taken alive." The instructions were that every means possible must be taken to arrest Booth alive, and Baker, Conger and

Sgt. Boston Corbett

Dougherty held a consultation a few feet from the barn. In the meantime Booth was cursing Harrold for his cowardice, charging him with a desire to meanly surrender, etc.

Col. Baker and his party returned and held a parley with Booth, thus consuming about an hour and a quarter. Another consultation of officers was held, and it was determined that, in view of the probability of an attack from a tolerably large force of rebel cavalry, which they had learned were in the neighborhood, the barn should be fired, and Booth thus forced to come out.

Conger garnered a lot of brush, and placed it against and under the barn, and pulled some hay out of the cracks, in the mean time holding a lighted candle in his hand. Booth could now see through the openings of the barn all their movements. The lighted candle was applied to the hay and brush, and directly the flames caught the hay inside the barn. Booth rushed towards the burning hay and tried to put out the fire. Failing in this, he ran back to the middle of the floor, gathered up his arms and stood still pondering for a moment. Whilst Booth was standing in this position Sergt. Boston Corbett ran up to the barn door and fired. Col. Baker, not perceiving where the shot came from, exclaimed "he has shot himself," and rushed into the barn and found Booth yet standing with a carbine in hand. Baker clasped Booth around the arms and breast; the balance of the party had also, in the mean time, got inside. Corbett then exclaimed "I shot him." Booth fell upon the floor apparently paralyzed. Water was sent for and the wound bathed. It was now just 3:15 o'clock. The ball had apparently passed through the neck and the spine. In a few moments Booth revived. He made an effort to lift his hands up before his eyes. In this he was assisted, and upon seeing them he exclaimed somewhat incoherently, "Useless! - useless! - blood! blood!! and swooned away. He revived from time to time, and expressed himself entirely satisfied with what he had done. He expired at 7.10 yesterday morning.[9]

The body was placed in a cart and conveyed to the steamer Ide, and brought upon that vessel to the navy-yard, where the boat arrived at 5:20 o'clock this morning.

While the barn was burning, Harrold rushed out and was grappled by Lieut. Baker, thrown to the ground and secured.

Corbett says he fired with the intention of wounding Booth in the shoulder, and did not intend to kill him.

Booth had in his possession a diary, in which he had noted events of each day since the assassination of Mr. Lincoln. This diary is in the possession of the War Department. He had also a Spencer carbine, a seven-shooter, a revolver, a pocket pistol and a knife. The latter is supposed to be the one with which he stabbed Major Rathbone. His clothing was of dark blue, not Confederate gray, as has been stated.

Corbett, who shot Booth, was born in England, and is about 33 years old. He came to this country some years since, and resided for several years in Troy, N.Y. He resided for a time in Boston, where he became a member of a

---

9   The *Philadelphia Inquirer,* April 28, reports the death at 7:03.

Methodist Church, and took in baptism the name of "Boston." He is a man of small stature, slight form, mild countenance and quiet deportment.

Surgeon-Gen. Barnes says the ball did not enter the brain. The body, when he examined it this afternoon, was not in a rapid state of decomposition, but was considerably bruised by jolting about in the cart. It is placed in charge of Col. Baker, in the attire in which he died, with instructions not to allow any one to approach it, nor to take from it any part of apparel, or thing for exhibition hereafter; in brief, it is necessary for the satisfaction of the people that two points shall be positively ascertained: first, that the person killed in Garret's barn, and whose body was brought to this city, was J. Wilkes Booth; secondly, that the said J. Wilkes Booth was positively killed. The first point was to-day confirmed by overwhelming testimony, such as no jury would hesitate to accept. The substantial one of the second point is shown in the report of Surgeon-General Barnes, which will be officially announced.

Booth's leg was not broken by falling from his horse, but the bone was injured by the fall upon the stage at the theatre.

Besides the articles heretofore mentioned, Booth had on his person a draft for sixty pounds drawn by the Ontario Bank of Canada on a London banker. The draft was dated in October last.

* * * * *

The Philadelphia Inquirer
Friday, April 28, 1865

[from an article on the killing of Booth]

Appearance of the Body

Booth's moustache had been cut off apparently with scissors, and his beard allowed to grow, changing his appearance considerably. His hair had been cut somewhat shorter than he usually wore it.

Booth's body, which we have described, was at once laid out on a bench and a guard placed over it. The lips of the corpse are tightly compressed, and the blood has settled in the lower part of the face and neck. Otherwise the face is pale and wears a wild, haggard look, indicating exposure to the elements and a rough time generally in his skulking flight. His hair is disarranged and dirty, and apparently had not been combed since he took his flight. The head and breast is alone exposed to view, the lower portion of his body, including the hands and feet, being covered with a tarpaulin thrown over it. The shot which terminated his accursed life entered on the left side at the back of the neck, a point, curiously enough, not far distant from that in which his victim, our lamented President, was shot.

Bowling Green

Bowling Green, near which place Booth was killed, is a post village, the capital of Caroline county, Virginia, on the road from Richmond to Fredericksburg, forty-five miles north of the former, and is situated in a fertile and healthy region. It contains two churches, three stores, two mills and about three hundred inhabitants.

The Presidential Obsequies
The Remains at Buffalo

BUFFALO, N.Y.,[10] April 27. — The train has met at the depot in this city by a large concourse of people, and the funeral party were entertained at Bloomer's dining rooms by the city authorities.

The procession formed between seven and eight o'clock, and marched to St. James Hall, the coffin being prominently in view on the funeral car. The body was taken from the car and deposited on a dais at the hall.

In the gallery, outside the canopy, was the St. Cecilia society, an amateur musical association, who, as the remains were brought in, sang with deep

---

10   Buffalo is on the eastern shore of Lake Erie where the famous canal meets the lake. Lincoln had been in Buffalo before, in 1861 on his trip from Illinois to Washington after being elected president. Grover Cleveland was mayor of Buffalo before becoming governor of New York and then president. President William McKinley was assassinated in Buffalo. Theodore Roosevelt subsequently took the oath of office in that same city.

pathos, "Rest, spirit, rest."

The society then placed a heart composed of white flowers at the head of the coffin, and the public were then admitted.

BUFFALO, April 27. — As erroneous statements have been made in the press, it is necessary to say, on the authority of the embalmer and undertaker, that no perceptible change has taken place in the body of the late President since we left Washington. In that city the physicians removed part of the brain only for the autopsy, but this was replaced so that no part of the body whatever is now deficient.

The remains were visited throughout the day, from 9:30 A.M. until 8 P.M., by an immense number of persons. The arrangements generally are pronounced better than elsewhere on the route. During the morning an anchor, made of camelias, was presented by a party of ladies from the Unitarian Church of Buffalo, and was laid on the coffin.

A cross of white flowers was also laid upon his coffin at the request of Major-General Dix. The procession, with the remains, left St. James' Hall at 8:45 P.M., escorted to the depot by military, followed by a large crowd. The depot was surrounded by persons anxious to get a last view of the coffin as the train left about 11 P.M. for Cleveland.

* * * * *

Daily Ohio State Journal
Columbus, Ohio
Friday Morning, April 28, 1865

Items of General Interest

A Boston paper pronounces false the report that Booth, the assassin, was engaged to a daughter of Senator Hale.

At a meeting of prominent citizens held in Brooklyn on Saturday evening, it was determined to raise a monument to the late President in that city, single subscriptions to be limited to one dollar.

Dr. W.P. Parr, recently a surgeon in charge of Camp Butler, Ohio has six thousand acres of land in Tensas Parish, La. willed to him by Thomas J. Buck, a rebel prisoner of war, upon whom he had attended for about a year, and who died recently at Camp Butler.

Mr. Ford,[11] manager of the theatre where the President was murdered, has published a card in which he defends his loyalty; protests against being implicated in the conspiracy, and expresses his poignant sorrow that the event occurred in a building which was under his control.

In the garden of the Military Hospital at Chattanooga, there were grown one thousand and eighty-eight varieties of flowers last year, and from these floral beauties, nearly six thousand papers of seeds were put and given to soldiers to send home.

The pastor of the Second Presbyterian Church, Rev. Moses D. Hoge, D.D. was the only minister that left the city upon the evacuation of Richmond by Gen. Lee. His peculiar relations to the Confederate Government, and a few that perhaps he would be arrested and thrown into prison, no doubt influenced him in his course.

[...]

John Wilkes Booth, the assassin of President Lincoln, was a firm believer in spiritualism, and during his engagement in Louisville the last time, became very much attached to the Davenport brothers,[12] who were exhibiting in the

---

11   James Reed Ford (1840 - 1916) was the business manager of the theatre. His brother, John Thompson (1829 - 1894) was the owner. Harry Clay Ford (1844 - 1915) was the treasurer. The latter supervised preparation of the presidential box on the night of the assassination. He and James were arrested after the assassination but soon released, John was in Richmond that night.

12   Ira Erastus and William Henry Davenport were a traveling magic act that purported to enlist the aid of the dead in their performances of amazing, inexplicable feats. They were exposed by various magicians and by P.T. Barnum.

city at the time. He attended most of the private seances of the brothers, and appeared very enthusiastic at their success. He was a man of bitter prejudices, and has evinced them on many occasions.

*   *   *   *   *

Ohio Statesman [13]
Columbus, Ohio
Friday, April 28, 1865

The Proper View

To our mind that clergyman does no reverence to the Almighty by saying that it was to further some purpose of His that he allowed an assassin to terminate the earthly existence of Abraham Lincoln, and we think it atrocious in an Administration journal to intimate that President Lincoln's "most partial friends" "could scarce have selected an hour more auspicious for his fame than that in which he so unexpectedly met his fate," as The Ohio State Journal has declared. With great satisfaction, therefore, have we read the following sentence in The New York Tribune's editorial on the obsequies of President Lincoln in New York city (sic)f. It is the language of a sincere friend:

"In every good fortune which hereafter attends us, we shall mourn that he did not share it, and in each calamity that the future brings we shall fondly believe that had he lived it might have been averted."

*   *   *   *   *

---

13   Also in the news: Reports of Booth's death; preparations for the funeral train; soldiers organizing opposition to Governor Brough because of inadequate concern for veterans; Booth had performed in Columbus five years earlier; criticism of competitor The *Ohio State Journal* for writing "Lincoln's most partial friends could scarce have selected an hour more suspicious for his fame than that in which he so unexpectedly met his fate"; in a brief filler, this item: A man was disparaging Grant in Sherman's presence, when the latter broke out with: "It won't do, sir, it won't do, sir! Grant is a great General! He stood by me when I was crazy, and I stood by him when he was drunk, and now, sir, we stand by each other."

The National Intelligencer
Washington, D.C.
Friday, April 28, 1865

The drama of J. Wilkes Booth's life, on this stage, is over. The curtain has fallen on his mortal career. An escaped assassin, he fell by the hands of justice, and by a bullet. His last words were a message to his mother.[14] Alas, how the extremes of life meet! That mother whom he has cursed; the brother whom he has nearly driven to madness, and whose career he has blighted; the sisters who were so proud of the professional reputation of the family, all blasted by his deed of the foul fiend, who remembers them and sends words to them as his felon-life is dribbling away and ebbing out!

He murdered the great and good Lincoln; he escaped to live a week in torture and vagrancy, hearing his name on all hands branded, feeling that the mark of Cain was on his forehead, that a price was on his head, that the avenger of blood was near, and now nearer, knowing that neither earth, nor sea, nor air had a place where he could bestow his guilty secret, and feel that it was safe. And this was the fame after which he panted; for which he, as it now appears, had been known to sigh, when he foolishly expressed himself, by a hackneyed quotation, as desiring to emulate the "aspiring youth that fired the Ephesian dome."[15] What a lesson to all the world, and especially to the youth of the country, is taught in the contrast between him who had filled the measure of a useful and honored life, and who fell lamented by the civilized world, and the young man of good opportunities and the handsome talents and acquirements, who sought notoriety in the character of an assassin, and died accursed, and embalmed in infamy! The contrast thus presented is that of Heaven and of Hell; it is that of the celestial choir of glorified and sainted spirits, and the scowling ranks of the grim-visaged fiends of eternal night.

But the curtain is yet to rise upon this felon-actor. He is to meet his Eternal Judge. He is to abide His justice who has written VENGEANCE IS

---

14   "Tell my mother I died for my country...useless, useless."

15   From Colley Cibber's *Richard III*, Act I, Scene 4.. Cibber(1671 - 1757) was an English poet actor and playwright.

MINE AND I WILL REPAY. He has yet to pass the melancholy flood with that grim ferryman that poets write of, unto the kingdom of perpetual night. And it is reserved for him to realize the fearful vision, as told by him who wrote as no uninspired mortal else has written —

O, no, my dream was lengthen'd after life;
O, then began the tempest to my soul;
I passed, methought, the melancholy flood
With that grim ferryman that poets write of,
Unto the kingdom of perpetual night;
The first that there did greet my strange soul
Was my great father-in-law, renowned Warwick,
Who cry'd aloud, What scourge for perjury
Can this dark monarchy afford false Clarence?
And so he vanished: Then came wand'ring by
A shadow like an angel, with bright hair
Dabbled in blood; and she shrieked aloud,
Clarence is come — false, fleeting, perjured Clarence, —
That stabbed me in the field of Tewksbury;
Seize on him, Furies, take him to your torments!"[16]

Is there hope for the final salvation of such a wretch, "cut off even in the blossom" of his sin, "unhousel'd unanel'd, no reckoning made,"[17] but sent to his account with all his load of unatoned-for guilt upon his head? The answer to question lies beyond our ken; but the dreadful certain seems to be that even as he fell so he lies, and that so he will remain forever, accursed of men and doomed of God, the very arch-fiend's mock! For let the youth of the land remember well that this Booth was no cavalier, no romantic knight, seized with the monomania that it was his duty and his destiny to rid the world of a tyrant and an oppressor. On the contrary, he was a cold, cautious, cowardly,

---

16   Shakespeare's The Life and Death of Richard the Third, Act I, Scene 4.

17   Hamlet, Act I, scene 5, in which Prince Hamlet is visited by the spirit of his father, who was murdered without receiving the eucharist (unhousel'd) and without last rites (unanel'd, or "unannointed") and thus sent into death with unatoned-for guilt.

planning knave, who knew well the good and gentle and lovely character of his victim; one who dogged the unsuspicious steps of the great deceased for months, with poison, dagger, and bullet; who contrived his crime with mechanical deliberation and wit; who lay in wait a mere murderer; a dastard who approached his unsuspecting object from behind, when in the midst of his family and friends; who ran away on the track of a line of escape which he had long planned, and which he believed to be secure; and who carried on his person the evidence, in the shape of blood money, that he was the hired tool of conspiracy. Then he was neither the excuse of the madman nor of the frenzied devotee; of one who marched upright, in front, and boldly, and did his bloody work with manly eye; and who consummated it by desperate suicide, or voluntary surrender. He was a mean, cowardly, sneaking murderer; in other words, J. Wilkes Booth was an assassin. Is there any sympathy for him? Will any grieve for him? Will not all good and noble young men turn away with a shudder from his example? Will such not thrill with detestation of his memory whenever they hear his infamous name? Such will be the estimation in which this mortal rascal and poltroon will be held through all time.

Over the fallen braves, officers and men, who had expired in this war, on the field, in prison, or elsewhere in the line of duty, or of mistaken duty, there will be true mourners; the memory of these will be honored and loved as soldiers by their families and friends, and even the tear of the stranger will fall upon such graves; nor are we without reasonable hope that such are forgiven and accepted. But take heed how any confound with noble spirits this crawling serpent Booth, who dragged his reptile length into an opening paradise, and darted his venom when the roar of the cannon was hushed, when the sword was well-nigh restored to its scabbard, when hostile banners were furling, when bonfires and illuminations blazed in token that the deluge of blood had subsided, when mothers, and wives, and fathers, and neighbors were waiting with beating hearts to hear the bells of peace that should herald a restored country, and, with its honored flag, the return of their jewels, their sons and husbands, whom they had offered up on the altar of patriotism. It was such a paradise that this fiend entered. And how changed seems the scene from that of the prospect which he has blighted! Hearts then all flesh are now nearly stone! Whatever the end — and we hope and expect the best and the happiest — this infamous reptile forever and forever will remain the same. His memory is a monument of guilt, reared to such a height that all men's eyes must see it, and shudder when they behold it, until time shall be no more. While, side by side with this record of infamy, the fame of the good and great Lincoln, made all the brighter by the assassin, shall—

"with increase of ages grow
As streams roll down, enlarging as they go."[18]

* * * * *

Lincoln with wife and sons Thomas and Robert Todd

---

18   From Alexander Pope's *Essay on Criticism*.

Saturday, April 29, 1865

To His Cause Triumphant

He knows this base and treasonable class;

these men who,

having spent their lives

in robbing the hireling of his wages,

and having of necessity become hardened

to every species of cruelty and brutality and dishonor,

looking down on the honest and self-supporting poor,

find it most natural to rob their country,

to betray her honor,

to torture and murder prisoners,

to fire peaceful cities by stealth,

to despise and oppress the laborers,

to carry desolation over a nation

for the sake of their mad ambition,

and, finally,

to murder by assassination

where they could not overcome in battle.

The Daily Age[19]
Philadelphia
Saturday, April 29, 1865

Additional Facts Respecting Booth's Capture
A Maryland Surgeon Arrested

A letter received in this city yesterday says, "Booth's leg having been broken, he went to the house of Dr. Mudd,[20] in Charles county, and had it set at 8 o'clock in the morning of Sunday, April 16 the second day after the murder of the President.

"Dr. Mudd split Booth's boot open to get it off, and when he left, the Doctor gave him a pair of crutches, and it is supposed that he left in an easterly direction from the neighborhood of Bryantown.

"Harrold was with Booth at that time.

"Dr. Mudd was arrested by the military with one of Booth's boots in his possession, which had Booth's name in it. The Doctor was immediately taken to Washington."

Harrold is a young man — less than twenty-five years of age — a native of Washington, formerly a druggist's clerk in that city, but for some months without the visible means of support, though during that time apparently well supplied with money. He has frequently been in St. Mary's county, Md., always taking his gun with him. The night of the assassination he was seen, it will be remembered, at the livery stable with Booth. — New York Tribune.

---

19   Also in the news: Attitudes among women in Raleigh; Mexico's General Ortega in Washington to request aid in rebellion against Maximilian; President Johnson postpones Fast Day until June 1; the steamboat Sultana explodes seven miles north of Memphis, killing or injuring all but 200-300 of 2,100 passengers; abolitionist Wendell Phillips opposes hanging of rebels photos of LIncoln's corpse in New York City have been seized; quicksilver discovered in Nevada; a rebel attack from Canada is feared in Vermont.

20   Dr. Samuel Alexander Mudd (1833 - 1883) treated Booth's broken leg when he and Herold arrived at his house five hours after the shooting. The two left 15 hours later. Mudd reported them to the military authorities but upon subsequent questioning, he denied knowing their identifies. he was found guilty of conspiring with Booth and was given a life sentence under hard labor. Pres. Johnson pardoned him in 1869.

*   *   *   *   *

The New York Tribune
Saturday, April 29, 1865

Appalling News from Washington
Reception of the Intelligence of the Murder of the President
and Attempted Assassination of the Secretary and the Younger Seward

From Our Special Correspondent

Raleigh, N.C., April 17, 1865

Gen. Sherman and staff left the Central Depot at 8 o'clock this morning, with an engine and two cars, for Durham Station, to meet Gen. Johnston. None but his staff accompanied him.

The train which bore Gen. Sherman to the front to receive the surrender of Johnston's army had been gone less than an hour, when the telegraph flashed to Gen. Howard's[21] headquarters the horrible and astounding news of the assassination of the President of the United States, and the fatal wounding of Mr. Seward and his son. For the greater part of the forenoon, the dreadful tidings were suppressed, and only known to a few persons immediately about headquarters; but by degree it began to circulate in whispers through the town, and though generally disbelieved, created a profound feeling of horror and alarm. A courier was immediately dispatched with the news to Gen. Sherman,

---

21   General Oliver Otis Howard (1830 - 1909), known as "the Christian General" for basing policies on scripture, he is remembered more for his defeats than his victories. He received Medal of Honor after continuing to lead a charge in which he was wounded so severely that he had an arm amputated. In good Christian spirit, he advocated and worked for the rights and equal opportunity for freed blacks. After the war, he directed the Freedmen's Bureau, which attempted to integrate blacks into white society. He founded and served as president of Howard University, then returned to military service to wage war against various Indian tribes.

who had already arrived at Durham Station, and was in conference with Johnston when the messenger arrived. Officers hurried into town from the camps to learn the facts, or to verify the report. It was too dreadful to be believed. Crowds of officers and soldiers met and discussed in suppressed breath the probabilities of its truth, and it was not until noon that the report could be traced to a trustworthy source — the telegraph operator and officers at Gen. Howard's headquarters, fearing the effect of the news upon the soldiers, kept it quiet. A feeling of awful suspense, of horrible foreboding, spread over the city and camps. Officers met and passed in silence, scarcely daring to break the dreadful secret to each other. universal gloom settled like a pall over the place. Sad faces were everywhere, all hearts were heavy, all minds appalled by the dreadful news of this triple murder. At Gen. Schofield's[22] headquarters and other places I have seen officers and men in tears, as if mourning for the loss of a father or a beloved friend, a sorrow like that which fell upon Egypt when the angel of death smote the first born broods over all minds.[23] Others with clenched fists and firm-set teeth were calling for vengeance upon the whole race of traitors, from Jeff. Davis down. A people who could conceive of such transcendent wickedness, and every one who can apologise for or excuse it, say they, ought to be blotted from the face of the earth.

The whole current of feeling in the army has been changed by this crowning act of villainy — this final fiendish stab at the nation's life. Brave and noble men who but yesterday were reading the God-like plea of Mr. Beecher[24] for pardon and conciliation for the Rebels, and were half consenting to a general amnesty to the bad men who have bathed the land in blood, and brought so much woe upon us, to-day cry with trumpet tongues for justice. Gen. Johnston on hearing the news declared it was the heaviest blow which has ever fallen

---

22   General John McAllister Schofield (September 29, 1831 - March 4, 1906), served under various generals, later appointed military governor of Virginia, then Secretary of War. He recommended that the U.S. Navy establish a base at Pearl Harbor, HI.

23   The tenth of the Ten Plagues of Egypt, Exodus 11:1- 12:36.

24   Henry Ward Beecher, (1813 - 1887), Congregational minister and abolitionist, advocate of women's suffrage, defender of Darwin's theory of evolution. In a widely followed trial for adultery, he was exonerated of charges that he had had a sexual relationship with Elizabeth Tilton, the wife of a friend.

upon the Confederacy. He appeared much troubled by the intelligence.

Among intelligent officers this is regarded as only the beginning of a reign of terror which has been long maturing — the opening of a bloody drama to be enacted by hired assassins, in obedience to a deeply-laid conspiracy. That now, beaten in the open field, honorably defeated in war, they intend to adopt the assassins's last resort; and that our chief public men, and even our generals, are marked as victims of the bullet or the knife. This is the natural fruit of rebellion — the appendix to the May mob and the firing of New-York hotels.

The officers and soldiers everywhere speak in terms of the highest admiration of the great and good man who has fallen. He seems to have been spared by a kind Providence to witness the fruit of his long and wearisome labors for the salvation of his country, and then, has mingled his blood with the thousands who have fallen in the struggle, in a manner to show to the world as no other even could teach, the fiendish spirit which has animated these enemies of liberty of the country, and of mankind. I hear nothing but words of the most affectionate eulogy of the departed President, and earnest prayers ascend from many hearts that God would disappoint the assassins, and yet spare the precious lives of Mr. Seward and his son.

THE ASSASSINATION

Our Special Account

Special Dispatch to the N.Y. Tribune

WASHINGTON, April 29, 1865

Edwin Booth is here for the purpose, it is stated, of procuring the body of his brother. His desire cannot be granted, as the grave of the assassin will never be known.

The surgeons who held the autopsy upon Booth assert that he must have endured untold anguish of body, as well as of mind, from the nature of the fracture of his leg, the small bone having cut its way through the flesh, and protruded.

Mortification of the flesh had also commenced, and it was the opinion of the Surgeon-General that he could not have lived many days more in any event. This may account in part for the horrid expression of countenance and the general repulsiveness of the corpse.

Associated Press Dispatch

WASHINGTON, Friday, April 28, 1865

The excitement which prevailed in this city yesterday has considerably subsided. While all regret that the assassination, owing to its rashness among the soldiers engaged in the capture, was not taken alive, they at the same time felt grateful that the murderer had paid the penalty for his crime. Had he been brought to the Washington Navy-Yard alive, nothing could have withstood the fury of the excited congregated thousands.

What disposition was made of Booth's body after the autopsy upon it, is impossible to ascertain, but that a fitting disposal, in keeping with his ignominious career was made, is certain.

The public breathe more freely, as the great burden which has been on their minds for two weeks has been removed.

Harrold, who has been exhibiting great stoicism since his capture, now appears to seem to realize the awful position in which he is placed, and through the day has given way to frequent fits of weeping. He is quite young, and his appearance would indicate him to be not over 20. Some time ago he was an applicant for the position of the surgeon's steward on the Potomac flotilla, but was unsuccessful.

Very great curiosity prevails as to the disposition to be made of the remains of Booth; but it seems the authorities are not inclined to give the wretched carcass the honor of meeting the public gaze, and it will probably be deposited in whatever place promises the most utter obscurity for them. Yesterday a photographic view of the body was taken before it was removed from the monitor. It was then placed in an ordinary gray army blanket, in which it was sewed up. A plain casket-shaped box, measuring six feet by two, had been previously made in the joiners shop for the remains, but it was not used.

Suicide in Baltimore

BALTIMORE, Friday, April 28, 1865

A well-known citizen of Baltimore committed suicide last Monday, a short distance from this city, by shooting himself with a pistol. No cause could be assigned for the rash act except that he had recently seemed depressed and melancholy.

Subsequent events have induced suspicion that he was in some way implicated in the conspiracy, and last night the body was exhumed, embalmed, and sent to Washington by orders of the Government.

The affair causes much speculation, and there are many reports in connection with it as well as some facts, which it is deemed imprudent to publish at this time.

The Body of Booth

CINCINNATI, Friday, April 28, 1865

At a public meeting at Dayton yesterday it was resolved that the body of Booth be taken to mid-ocean and there buried.

* * * * *

The Sudbury American
Sudbury, Pa.
Saturday, April 29, 1865

[Extract from a private letter of our Correspondent H.d.W.]
Camp Near Washington, D.C.
April 24, 1865

Dear Wilvert:

It is true we have sustained a great loss in the death of our much beloved President, but as it has pleased Divine Power to remove him from our midst, we should be thankful that He has given us such a great and determind man

342

in his stead (Andrew Johnson) to drive on the machinery of the Government. It was a wise thing in the framers of the Constitution when they put in that clause, where if we lose our President the wheels of the Government can never be stopped. This is done by the Vice President, a plain unpretending citizen, on the death of the Chief Magistrate, stepping forward to take the oath administered by the Chief Justice, and at once takes the responsibility of the office. No flourish of trumpets, nor convulsion of nations, but by the simple power vested in a Judge, a fellow citizen assumes power. This little fact proves that our Republic can never die.

I cannot describe to you the feeling of the army when the news reached us that Abraham Lincoln had been murdered by the assassin. I will not attempt it, for in doing so, I would work myself into a state to make me miserable. One thing — if the boys had gone into a fight that morning no prisoners would have been taken — no quarters given.

In coming from the Shenandoah Valley to Washington, the train containing the remains of our late President, passed us near the Annapolis Junction. There was [sic] nine cars heavily draped in mourning. Our train stopped on a siding. It was solemn time. The men all uncovered in respect, and stout men wept as the last of him they loved, passed them, to be conveyed to its resting place. Along the whole route, houses were draped in mourning. This showed the deep hold Mr. Lincoln had in the hearts of our people.

*   *   *   *   *

The Times of London
April 29, 1865

FOREIGN INTELLIGENCE

France.

(From Our Own Correspondent.)

PARIS, Friday, April 28, 7 A.M.

The murder of Mr. Lincoln is regarded with horror by the Paris journals of every denomination. The Moniteur expressed itself thus:—

"There can be but one feeling of horror, in Europe as well as in America, at the miscreants who place assassination at the service of political parties."

The Constitutionnel says: —

"Such crimes cannot but wound the feeling of the whole world, and provoke universal indignation."

The Siècle, after expressing its detestation of such a crime, adds:—

"One more victim falls for the cause of liberty and humanity."

The Temps expresses itself in these terms:—

"We are unwilling to express any hasty judgment. For the honour of humanity it is to be hoped that this atrocious crime has only been the act of some isolated fanatics. It could be too painful to see a defeated cause respond by assassination to the magnanimity of its conquerors. We may safely affirm, however, that this crime is not only odious but useless. Mr. Lincoln dies by the purest glory that has ever crowned a statesman, but his work will survive him, and the greatest victory of liberty will not have been won in vain. The providential mission of the United States does not depend on the life of one man, and the liberty which Mr. Lincoln has extended and served will not fail to raise up worthy successors."

The Union employs the subjoined language:—

"We are as yet without details which can give us the slightest idea of the cause or character of so grave an event. However, it seems difficult to suppose that a crime committed on the two principal personages of the American Union had not been dictated by a political motive; but on whom, or on what party, or what fraction of a party, does the responsibility lie? We must wait for more complete information."

The following is from the Avenir:—

"The great citizen has fallen a martyr to his cause, but to his cause triumphant. The loss of a citizen, however great and illustrious he may be, can in no way compromise the destinies of a people which possesses free and democratic institutions. But if with certainty it may be said that the triumph of the United States will not be imperilled by the death of Abraham Lincoln, no one can avoid feeling a certain apprehension in seeing removed from the

344

political scene the man who, with the prestige and authority of a spotless patriotism, could serve as a moderator to his fellow-citizens, when carried away by the excitement of victory."

* * * * *

The National Intelligencer
Washington, D.C.
Saturday, April 29, 1865

Mrs. Lincoln

In conversation with a person who has been constantly near Mrs. Lincoln since the death of her husband, we learn that her nervous system recovers but slowly from the severe and terrible blow. We hope the measure proposed so generously by Mr. Roberts[25] will be pressed forward to early and complete success. Let Mrs. Lincoln have the assurance that the heart of a great nation beats with sympathy and kindness in this hour of her sore bereavement — no truer testimonial of love for the departed than generosity to those he loved.

* * * * *

Louisville Daily Journal
Saturday, April 29, 1865

TELEGRAPHIC NEWS.
Some Additional Interesting Details. — Account of the Affair by Harrold.
Booth's Conversation with Lt. Baker. — Proposal to Bury him in Mid-Ocean.—Statement of Sergt. Boston Corbett—Account of Wilson's Great Raid.

---

25   Marshal O. Roberts, of New York, who offered $10,000 for the benefit of the Lincoln family. Mrs. Lincoln is believed to have suffered severe depression accompanied by headaches and occasional irrational outbreaks, caused or aggravated by the death of Willie Lincoln in 1862 and the deaths of her siblings in the war.

To The Associated Press

NEW YORK, April 28.

It appears by Harrold's account, that Colonel Baker sent Lieutenant Colonel Conger and Lieutenant Baker, of his detectives, with Lieutenant Dougherty and his cavalry. On reaching Garrett's farm, they were told by a son of Barrett that there were two men in their barn. This was at 2 A.M. on Wednesday, and, proceeding to the barn, Baker was sent forward, and called upon Booth to come out and give up his arms and surrender, and that young Garrett would go into the barn to receive the arms.

Upon his entering the barn, Booth exclaimed, "Get out of here, you have betrayed me."

A colloquy then ensued, of which the following is a substance:

Lieut. Baker. — "You must give up your arms, and surrender. We have come to take you a prisoner, and will treat you as a prisoner. We will give you five minutes to surrender or burn the barn."

Booth— "Who are you, and what do you want?"

[Instructions had been given to Lieutenant Baker not to disclose the character of those who were in pursuit.]

Lieut. Baker— "We want you; we intend to take you prisoner."

Booth— "This is a hard case; it may be that I am to be taken by my friends." After some further colloquy of this sort, Booth, seemingly convinced that he was in the toils of Federal soldiers, said: "Give me a chance for my life. I am a cripple, with one leg. Withdraw with your men one hundred yards from the barn, and I will come out and fight you."

Lieut. Baker.— "We did not come here to fight, but to take you prisoner. You must give yourself and your arms up and surrender."

Booth— "Let me have time to consider." A conversation in the barn between Booth and Harrold then took place which was not overheard by the party outside. In about 15 or 20 minutes Booth called out, "Who are you? I could have picked off half a dozen of your men while we were talking; I could have shot two or three times, but I don't want to kill anybody."

Lieut. Baker— "Then give up your arms and surrender. We have come here to take you."

Booth— "I will never surrender. I will never be taken alive."

Lieut. Baker— "If you don't do so immediately we will set fire to the barn."

Booth— "Well, my brave boys, prepare a stretcher for me."

After this conversation took place between Booth and Harrold, during which Booth was heard to say, "You d—d coward, will you leave me now, but George (sic) go, I don't want you to stay with me." He then addressed the party outside, and said, "There is a man here who wants to come out."

Lieut. Baker— "Then let him hand out his arms and come out."

Another talk here occurred between Booth and Harrold, in which it appeared that the latter was begging to be allowed to take out some arms with him, and Booth was heard to say, "Go away from me, I don't want anything more to do with you."

Harrold then came to the door, and asked to be let out.

Liet. Baker said, "Hand out your arms."

Harrold replied, "I have none."

Lieut. B — "Yes, you have; you carried a carbine when you came here. You must hand it out."

Booth— "He has no arms, they are all mine' upon my word as a gentleman he has no arms. All that are here belong to me."

Lieut. Baker then approached the door. Harrold thrust out his hands and was pulled from the door, tied, and placed in the charge of a guard. Col. Conger was then satisfied further parley with Booth was in vain, and proceeding to the other side of the barn he pulled out a wisp of hay and lighted it. Within a few moments the blazing hay lighted up the inside of the barn.

Booth was discovered leaning on a crutch, which he threw aside, and with a carbine in his hands came towards the side where the fire had been kindled, paused, looked at the fire a moment, and then started toward the door. When he reached about the middle of the barn he was shot. Col. Conger and Lieut. Baker at once entered the barn and brought Booth out. After identification, by order of the War Department, the body was there privately interred in the clothing that was upon it.

The Herald's correspondent says the parley with Booth lasted a long while. Booth told Lieutenant Dougherty that he had a bead drawn on him, and could shoot him if he chose. Booth could see them outside plainly, which could not see him inside.

When the fire was lighted Booth could be seen, and then Lieut. Dougherty ordered Sergeant Corbett (sic) to fire, which he did, through one of the crevices. Booth was armed with two six barrelled and one seven barrelled revolver.

When the party started to return with the body Harrold refused to walk, when a rope was fastened to his neck and the other end of it to a saddle of one of the cavalrymen. As soon as a horse could be procured, he was mounted.

From the World's correspondent it is learned that Harrold joined Booth just after the assassination, and it is believed he brought the horse to the alley.

Cleveland, April 28

All along the route from Buffalo to this city, which was reached this morning, the usual demonstrations of sorrow were witnessed. The remains were escorted by a large military and civic procession to the beautifully constructed temple prepared to receive them, and soon thereafter the face of the honored dead was opened to the thousands who, in admirable order, entered and retired from the enclosure.

The entire population of this city are abroad, all seemingly impressed with the solemnity of the occasion.

Springfield, Ill. April 28.

The time of the funeral of the late President has been changed from Saturday, the 6th, to Thursday, May 4th.

Cincinnati, April 28.

The river has fallen 13 inches. Light rain all night. Weather cloudy. Thermometer 60. Barometer 29.38 and falling.

348

* * * * *

New York Times
Saturday, April 29, 1865

A Class Revolution

Our readers will bear in mind that we have from the beginning of the war urged that this struggle was essentially a struggle between a class -- the slave aristocracy and the people. We have always maintained that only as this feature is considered both in legislation and executive action, can we hope for a permanently successful issue. It is a matter of hope and congratulation to us, and to all who take the deeper views of the contest, that President JOHNSON has from the beginning felt and acted on this idea. If his course be examined while he was upholding the government against tremendous odds in Tennessee, and his speeches at the time of his nomination as Vice-President, it will be seen that the prominent thought in his mind was that a base aristocracy, founded on slavery, who had long weighed on the poor and middle classes of the South, were now striving to overthrow all the franchises of the people on this continent, and were striking a blow at universal democracy.

In his speeches in Tennessee he appealed to the honest poor and laboring class against the traitorous rich. With the eye of a statesman, he saw then that the chief hope of our final victory in the rebel States lay in destroying the aristocracy and raising up the masses.

He himself, by a remarkable circumstance, represents at this time the position, and struggles, and capacity of the great Democratic classes of the South. He has felt "the cold shade" and heavy hand of a barbaric but able and desperate aristocracy; he has suffered untold wrongs from them; he has been the object of their boundless scorn and contempt; they have murdered his friends and children and destroyed his property; they hunted him from home and kindred; and though they offered him place and power to take part with them in their treason, they could never tempt or bribe him a hair's breadth

349

from his loyalty and duty. He knows this base and treasonable class; these men who, having spent their lives in robbing the hireling of his wages, and having of necessity become hardened to every species of cruelty and brutality and dishonor, looking down on the honest and self-supporting poor, find it most natural to rob their country, to betray her honor, to torture and murder prisoners, to fire peaceful cities by stealth, to despise and oppress the laborers, to carry desolation over a nation for the sake of their mad ambition, and, finally, to murder by assassination where they could not overcome in battle. Mr. JOHNSON fully understands the cruelty, the dishonor, the boundless ambition, the unquenchable hate and the utter desperation of the Southern slave aristocracy. In his brief but trenchant speeches since his inauguration, he always distinguishes between the deluded and poor of the rebel States and the rich and powerful leaders.

The sketch of President JOHNSON's policy, which SHERMAN's extraordinary negotiations have called out, shows how clearly the dangers from this class stand before his mind. He is determined that the old treasonable and powerful class of slaveholders shall no longer control the South. They are to be rooted out to their lowest fibres. Their treasonable State Governments, forced and sprung upon the people, are not to be recognized. They are, of course, to be stripped of the iniquitous source of their power -- their slaves; they are to be exposed to the pains, penalties and shame of treason, which means, to large numbers of them, poverty or banishment or death. Their public debts, whether of States or Confederacy, are to be wiped out, and a new class of loyal men -- however small their number -- is to form the nucleus of the future loyal State, and no others, unless repentant and loyal, are to have part in it. The President means to build up a new and loyal class from the poor whites and others who have been faithful, and to trust to immigration and a gradual change of the middle class to form a new community.

But the old are to pass away. An aristocracy without means is only contemptible. As a class they will lose their influence; some will emigrate, and in proud poverty abroad curse the Yankees and democracy; many have died already, and others will pay the penalty of their crimes on the scaffold.

The bona fide slaveholding class probably did not, in the rebel States, number 300,000 in the beginning of the war; and of these only a portion were wealthy enough to be leaders -- a small but able and courageous body. This class the revolution must grind to powder; and to this result the policy of the President will evidently lead.

* * * * *

The Ohio Statesman
Columbus, Ohio
Saturday, April 29, 1865

THE CITY.

The Impressive Multitude of People in the City.

Columbus is full of people this morning. It has never contained so many — and each train that arrives brings its hundreds to thousands already here. By the middle of the afternoon yesterday, the hotels and boarding houses were all crowded, and those who had not previously secured quarters were compelled to seek them elsewhere. Private houses were thrown open yesterday and last night with a liberality and a hospitality never before known in this city. Notwithstanding the tremendous rain storms last night, the streets were running over with a constant stream of humanity. People crowded the sidewalks everywhere to view the public buildings, the private residences, and the business houses, all of which are clothed in the habiliments of mourning. There has never before been witnessed here such a sight. Sadness is depicted on every countenance, grief pervades all hearts, and a sombre hue overspreads and envelops the whole city.

The trains this morning will bring many more thousands of people to the Capital of Ohio, to join the unnumbered multitudes already here who will take part in the funeral solemnities of the Martyr President.

* * * * *

Monday, May 1, 1865

The Genius of Liberty Weeping

Poetry swarms up like the frogs of Egypt,
overruns our tables, floors and exchange basket.

It salutes us in every letter,
drops from every visitor,
crawls into our drawers,
and bites at our files.

It appeals to our hardened conscience,
pleads with our lukewarm patriotism,
explains with the blushing modesty
of conscious genius its merits,
and demands like a duelist
"the apology due between gentlemen,"
for the insult of neglect.

An accurate inventory of
the "windfalls" of the past three days
discloses forty-five poems
which open with a particular request to
"Toll, toll, ye mournful bells —
With cadent sadness toll."

The Chicago Tribune
Monday, May 1, 1865

The Funeral Cortege.

———

The Route from Columbus to Indianapolis

———

The Whole State of Indiana in Mourning

[...]

[Special Dispatch to the Chicago Tribune.]

Columbus, O., April 29.

We depart from Columbus as dated. The vast concourse of citizens who escorted the remains to the depot speaks well for the people of Columbus and the adjacent country. The procession which accompanied the remains to the State House this morning conducted it to the starting point this evening. B. Smith, President, and J. M. Taunt, Superintendent of the Columbus and Indianapolis Railway, are on board giving personal attention to the wants and wishes of passengers. S.W. Hughes, conductor, and Mr. James Gormly, engineer, are in charge of the train.

[Special Dispatch[es] to the Chicago Tribune]

Pleasant Valley, April 29 - 9 P.M.

Here a great bonfire lit up the country for miles. A large concourse of citizens assembled around the depot. Two fine American flags, draped in mourning, held in hand by two ladies. Depot decorated with evergreens.

Unionville, O., April 29 - 9 P.M.

There are only a dozen people here and yet there were about 200 persons present, most of them sitting in wagons, the people having come in from the country.

353

Milford, O., April 29 - 9:19 P.M.

Bonfire here, around which are assembled some 400 or 500 people present. The ladies presented bouquets. One by Miss Willard, Miss Lucy Kimball and Miss Mary Ormanston, on the part of the ladies of Woodstock; another by Miss Ann M. Curbier, and another by Mrs. G. Martin and Miss Dilleah. These ladies were permitted to enter the President's car and strew flowers on the coffin. The Woodstock cornet band played a dirge. The village bells slowly rang, and men stood silent with uncovered heads. The scene was as affecting as it was beautiful.

Cavalo, April 29 - 10 P.M.

The gentlemen on the train asked the Superintendent where all the people came from who had assembled at this place. It was amazing. There were large bonfires. A soldier stood in the center of the assemblage holding a flag. All the men stood uncovered.

Urbana, O., April 29 - 10:30 P.M.

Some three thousand people present. A large cross on the platform, entwined with the wreaths of evergreens which was worked under the direction of Mrs. M.G. Williams, President of the ladies' Soldiers' Aid Society. From the top of the cross and the short arms were hung illuminated colored transparencies. On the opposite side of the track was an elevated platform, on which were forty gentlemen and ladies who sung with pathetic sweetness the hymn entitled "Go To Thy Rest." The singers represented the Methodist, Baptist, Episcopal and Presbyterian churches. Large bonfires made the night light as day. Minute guns were fired. Ten young ladies entered the cars and strewed flowers on the bier. One of the ladies was so affected that she wept in great anguish.

Gettesburg, O., April 30 (sic) - 11:20

A large number of people congregated around. Huge bonfires, drooping flags and other evidences of mourning are seen. There were like scenes at

354

Richmond Junction and Corrington, just passed.

St. Paris, O., April 29 - 11:24

An illumination by which may be seen a large assemblage present, who stand in silence as they look on the moving train. A beautiful boquet (sic) was presented and placed on the coffin. The boquet (sic) was most artistic. At Westville Station crowds were gathered to pay their respects to the dead.

Conover, O., April 29 - 11:39

A long line of people and two lines of soldiers standing in file. On the right little boys and girls, then young men and women, people in the center supporting a large American flag. Three young ladies sang a patriotic song to a solemn and mournful air and was chaunted (sic) by the flag bearers.

Greenville, O., April 29 - 12 P.M.

Thirty-six young ladies in white, and slowly waving the Star Spangled Banner, greeted the train. A requiem was sung with thrilling effect by a number of ladies and gentlemen. About 800 people were congregated on the platform. The depot was tastefully decorated. On either side of the depot were two bonfires, which shed a most brilliant light all around the train and depot.

Piqua, O. April 30 - 12:30

Not less than ten thousand people are around the train. A great desire is manifested to see the President. The Troy band and the Piqua band played appropriate music after which a delegation from the Methodist Churches and Rev. Granville Moody sang a hymn. As you may imagine, it was a scene which is seldom witnessed.

New Paris, April 29 (sic) 2:41.

Great bonfires light up the skies. A crowd is gathered about who stand with uncovered heads. A beautiful arch of evergreens was formed above the track under which the train passed. The arch was twenty feet high and thirty feet in circumference. At Wiley's, New Madison and Weaver's Stations, mourners were congregated to pay their respects to the passing dead.

Richmond, Ind., April 30 - 3:10 a.m.

The scene here was not only imposing, but magnificently solemn. From twelve to fifteen thousand people were assembled. As we approached the city the bells of the engines on a line of railroad, lit with revolving lamps, &c. tastefully decorated in mourning. A gorgeous arch was constructed, under which the train passed. On both sides of the structure were American flags, wrought into triangles, down the sides of which were suspended, at equal distances, transparencies of red, white and blue alternately. Chaplets of evergreens clambered up the sides of the triangles, centered at the summit in velvet rosette. Across the structure, at about eighteen feet from the base was a platform carpeted with black velvet. On the ends of this tasselated platform were two flags, which reared themselves up in drooping folds. In the center of this upper work was a young lady in sitting posture, representing the genius of Liberty weeping. On one side was a boy soldier, and on the other a boy sailor, both acting as mourners. Above this groupe (sic) was reared another triangle, which was covered with roses and rosettes, and linked wreathes of green, again clasped about the flag-staff and folding themselves gracefully around the already wreathed triangle. In the center of this net-work of nature's embroidery, was Miss Mary McCloud, as the Genius of Liberty, Henry Cole, as the soldier, and Charles Bemmerman, as the sailor.

Centreville, 3:41 a.m.

Depot splendidly robed in mourning. At each end of the platform were two chandeliers brilliantly lighted. The people seemed anxious that the cortege should stay, but of course their wishes could not be complied with.

Germantown, Ind. — 3:45 a.m.

A number of splendid bonfires were blazing, flags draped, and the usual evidences of grief exhibited.

Dublin, Ind. — 4:00 a.m.

Platform and side tracks lined with people whose look and actions bespoke that deep grief was theirs. Their floral offerings to the dead were an evidence of the finer sensibilities. A neat and handsome arch of entwined evergreens was erected for the funeral to pass under. On the right was a large draped flag. The depot was artistically draped. On the outer walls was a fine steel portrait of our murdered President shrouded in evergreens.

Lewisville, Ind. 4:38 a.m.

Fine engravings of the President are suspended on the walls of the depot surrounded by decorations. Links of evergreen are joined and form a continuous line, circling all around the front of the depot. The following are the inscriptions at this place. "We mingle our tears with yours." "Lincoln, the savior of his country, emancipator of a race and friend of all mankind, triumphs over death and mounts victorious upward."

Charlottsville, Ind. , April 29 - 5:27 a.m.

The sight here was really beautiful. Mourning couches around whose entrance evergreens were erected and in front of which were young ladies each clasping each others hand. Our country's flag was drooped in its bereavement. At Kingston, Raysville, Ogden and [illegible] the people turned out to pay their respects to the great and good dead.

Philadelphia, Ind. April 30, 5:57 a.m.

Again we chronicle reverence and devotion of the people to the fallen leader. At Greenfield and Cleveland, as here, the multitudes are sorrowing. The grief of some can only find relief in tears.

Cumberland, Ind. April 30 - 6:30 a.m.

The depot draped in mourning. People stand uncovered as the cortege

357

May 1, 1865

flies by rapidly.

Indianapolis, Ind. April 30 - 7 a.m.

Again we are safely landed at another haven. The remains were met by theMayor, Common Council and other delegations, and escorted to the State house, followed by an imposing procession. The remains of the President have been lying in the State House from nine o'clock this morning to six this evening. They have been visited by vast numbers, although it is the most disagreeable of days. It has rained constantly since eight a.m., and the roads are in a frightful condition. Still, the people thronged to see the illustrious dead up to the hour of closing the doors. The interior of the State House are of the most simple and imposing character. Over the door, as you enter, in large letters is the following: "I shall not return to slavery any person who is free by the terms of this proclamation."

As you pass out is the motto, "Sic gloria transit mundi." Along the walls hang pictures of Washington, Lincoln, Seward, Sheridan,[26] Hovey,[27] Morton,[28] Douglas, Sherman, Grant, col. Dick O'Neil, and Edward Everett.[29] Busts of Washington, Lincoln, Jackson, Webster, Clay and Douglas, are placed at intervals, their brows crowned with the ever living laurels. The solemn sombre looking hall is curtained with black and brilliantly lighted with numerous

---

26   Philip Henry ("Little Phil") Sheridan (1831 - 1888), though graduating from West Point near the bottom of his class, rose quickly in the Union army to become a general, and he later served in the Indian Wars in the west. He defended — militarily and politically — the preservation of Yellowstone National Park as soon as it was established.

H27   Alvin Peterson Hovey (1821 - 1891), Union general, Indiana Supreme Court Justice, U.S. Representative, and governor of Indiana, Minister to Peru. When Indiana wrote a new constitution in 1850, he opposed suffrage for blacks and women and even proposed banning blacks from the state. However, he uncovered a plot by the Knights of the Golden Circle and the Sons of LIberty to overthrow the government of Indiana.

28   Oliver Hazard Perry Throck Morton (1823 - 1877) was elected a Republican governor of Indiana as the war was beginning. He supported Lincoln and the war effort and bitterly opposed the Copperheads (Peace Democrats). Elected to the senate in 1867, he led the movement to pass the 14th amendment, providing suffrage for blacks.

29   Edward Everett (1794 - 1865) served as U.S. representative and senator from and governor of Massachusetts, secretary of state, and president of Harvard. At the 1863 dedication of the National Cemetery at Gettysburg he gave a two-hour speech that was followed by Lincoln's famous two-minute address.

chandeliers. The catafalque on which the coffin rests is covered with fine black velvet trimmed with silver fringe. But the crowning glory of the interior decoration is the canopy overhanging and surrounding the catafalque. It is constructed of black material, in pagoda shape, with white cords and tassels. The roof, if such a term may be properly used, is studded with golden stars. This gorgeous room is by far the most faultless in elegance that has yet contained the remains. Owing to the heavy rain and inclemency of the weather, the procession which was to have taken place at 11:00 a.m., was abandoned. The funeral cortege leaves to-night at 12 o'clock, and will arrive at Chicago at 11 a.m. to-morrow, bringing with them all that is mortal of Abraham Lincoln.

* * * * *

The New-York Daily Tribune[30]
Monday, May 1, 1865

The Assassination

———

Harrold Confesses.

Special Dispatch to the N.Y. Tribune.
Washington, April 30, 1865
The young man, Harrold, has made a voluminous confession. Whether he overcame his innate habit of lying is not known to the public.

———

John Wilkes Booth's Last Letter to His Mother.

A letter written by John Wilkes Booth to his mother, dated on the morning of the 14th of April, the day of assassination, has fallen into the hands of the government authorities. It is directed to "Mrs. M. A. Booth, No. 28 East Nineteenth-st., New York, N.Y.," and bears a Washington, D.C., Post-office

---

30   Also in the news: Rebel governor of Florida commits suicide; General Washburn, in Memphis, declares that after April 25, all rebels in his district will be considered felons, not prisoners of war; President Johnson lifts restrictions on commerce in the South, in Russia, the Czarewich is dangerously ill, and the Czar has left for Nice.

stamp, dated April 14. It bears the appearance of having been written in considerable haste, and is all contained on one side of half a sheet of notepaper:

April 14 — 2 a.m.

Dearest Mother — I know you expect a letter from me, and am sure you will hardly forgive me. But indeed I have had nothing to write about. Everything is dull; that is, has been till last night. (The illumination) Everything was bright and splendid. More so in my eyes if it had been a display in a nobler cause. But so goes the world. Might makes right. I only drop you these few lines to let you know I am well, and to say I have not heard from you. Excuse brevity; am in haste. Had one from the Rose. With best love to you all, I am your affectionate son ever,

John.

Circumstances of the Arrest of Junius Brutus Booth.

From the Philadelphia Ledger, April 29.

There were peculiar circumstances connected with the arrest of Junius Brutus Booth in this city. After his arrest by Detective Krapp, he was taken to the Provost-Marshal's office, to await the departure of the train for Washington. While in the office, he was in charge of two men as a guard. He engaged in very little conversation, but was smoking a cigar, and during this time he frequently took from his pocket what appeared to be scraps of paper with which to light his cigar. The guard did not attach an importance to the act, but it afterward transpired that these were letters and envelopes which were thus destroyed. After he had been sent away, the attention of Capt. Lane and Commissioner Barret was called to the fact; they gathered together the fragments, but the letters were so effectively destroyed that nothing can now be gained from them. The corner of an envelop showed the printed inscription, "British Province," and a small remnant of the letter inside of this envelope contains only the words "your brother."

While in the office Junius Booth was engaged in looking over a Bible on the table. When he had finished this he took a narrow slip of paper. It was written on both sides; but as soon as finished he tore them into small pieces and threw them into the spit-box or on the floor. After he was gone an attempt was made to collect the fragments of the letter, but without success. Enough was found to show that the letter was intended for his sister, and referred to the fact that he was waiting in the Marshal's office for the cars. He bade her be of good cheer. There is also reference to "grandma," but the rest of the sentence is gone. Attention is called to two psalms, one can be made out — the forty-ninth;[31] the other is not decipherable, as part of the numbers are torn off and lost.

Arrest of John S. Clarke, the Actor, a Brother-in-Law of the Assassin.

From the Philadelphia Ledger, April 29

Since the arrest of Junius Brutus Booth, Mr. John S. Clarke has been taken into custody, by whom or on what charge is not known. His wife only knows that he was taken away by three men two days ago, and has not returned since. The last letter written by J. Wilkes Booth is now in the city. It is dated April 14, two a.m. at Washington, and is addressed to his mother in New York. There is nothing in it, except a reference to the illumination of the previous night, coupled with the statement that it would have been better if done for a better cause. "But," he adds, "might makes right." This, no doubt, is the letter written in the hotel at Washington when he inquired of the book-keeper the year. (sic)

* * * * *

The Chicago Tribune
Monday, May 1, 1865

Our Poets and Poetry

We have suffered for several weeks past under a severe attack of Poetry. It broke out simultaneously with the capture of Richmond, increased alarmingly with the surrender of Lee, and has ever since completely overwhelmed one

---

31   The 49th Psalm warns people about loving wealth more than God and about using wealth and power to abuse those less well endowed.

of our most athletic editors, who is seriously considering the expediency of resigning his chair, and accepting a situation as a coal-heaver or in some other light occupation involving less physical and more intellectual labor than is required in reading five pecks of manuscript "pomes" per diem. Poetry swarms up like the frogs of Egypt, overruns our tables, floors and exchange basket. It salutes us in every letter, drops from every visitor, crawls into our drawers, and bites at our files. It appeals to our hardened conscience, pleads with out lukewarm patriotism, explains with the blushing modesty of conscious genius its merits, and demands like a duelist "the apology due between gentlemen," for the insult of neglect. An accurate inventory of the "windfalls" of the past three days discloses forty-five poems which open with a particular request to

"Toll, toll, ye mournful bells —

With cadent sadness toll."

One hundred and fifteen writers give the corresponding direction,

"Mourn, mourn, ye tolling bells.

With cadent sadness morn."

Far be it from us to intimate that any of these poems are written by persons who have not already advanced, in literary style an capacity, far beyond the plain prose of Irving, Presscott and Bancroft. We assure them that in all instances the versification is more delicate than Tennyson, more simple than Goldsmith, more careful than Longfellow, and more studied than Bryant. None of these poems, if we should print them just as they are written and spelled, would lay us open to an action for libel in favor of their authors for holding them up to public ridicule and contempt. No such thing! We are compelled to say that, while in our judgment but half a dozen persons in the land are capable of writing a good poem on the subjects we have named, those persons are not Holmes, Longfellow, Bryant, Stoddard, Stedman, and Read, but they are our said correspondents, and each and every one of them. There is not one among them who belongs to the same "school of poets" which produced the following irregular outbreak of genius:

"When you see their eyes glisten,

362

Then, my men, Fire!

These were the last words of A. Jackson, Esquire."

Yet though they are all written in the most exquisite style of poetic art, we beg their authors not to take it to heart if we find ourselves compelled to part with poems we think exceedingly smart, when we've more than enough to fill the cart. Let the Federal Government open a mart for the vending of peanuts and "pomes" by the quart, or the "piece," as we now sell a fritter or tart, so that the poetic genius can have a fair start, without riding on to its throne mid the mart, o'er the pulsating road of an editor's heart, so that every step inflicts its smart.

"It is not every man can be a poet,

No more than every sheep can be a go-at."

* * * * *

The National Republican
Washington, D.C.
Monday, May 1, 1865

Punishment of a Traitor at Harrisburg

Harrisburg, April 27 — On last Saturday week, when the news reached here of the assassination of the President, a man on the street gloried in the fact, and made a most obscene remark in regard to the corpse. The people desired to treat the man in a summary manner, but a guard of soldiers took possession of him. This afternoon he was marched through the principal streets to the tune of the Rogue's March, holding in his hand a board with the inscription, "William Young, a traitor too cowardly to fight for the Rebels, ejects his vulgar venom by insulting the remains of our dead President."

The soldiers desired to ride him on a rail, but the officers would not allow it.

On being released he was followed by a large crowd yelling and hooting at him, treating him rather roughly.

A notorious copperhead living in the vicinity of Waterbury, Conn., on hearing of the President's death, displayed a flag with the words, "The devil is dead," upon it. A party of young men proceeded to the residence of the scoundrel and made a demand for the flag. The man denied having exhibited any, whereupon a rope was fastened about his neck and he was threatened with hanging unless he "showed his colors." He still stuck to his denial, but as he felt the halter drawn righter about his neck, he confessed his infamy and brought out the flag. After giving him a threshing, his visitors withdrew.

* * * * *

Freedmen and families arriving in Baltimore

Tuesday, May 2, 1865

A Quarrel in Embryo

Dey part us all.
Dey send us away from our family.
Dey send us jus whar dey please.

Dey han-cuff us.
Dey put us in jail.
Dey give us thirty-nine lashes.
Dey starve us.

Dey do ebery ting to us.

The Columbia Phoenix
Columbia, S.C.
Tuesday, May 2, 1865

Ranaway

From the subscriber, a NEGRO MAN, his WIFE, with two CHILDREN. The man is about five feet high — the woman about six; the latter may be known by a scald or baked place on the head. Of the children, the oldest is a boy of little more than two years, the other a girl, a little more than one. The complexion of the man and woman is inclined to yellow; that of the youngest child very light. ONE HUNDRED DOLLARS reward is offered for their apprehension. Address

Rev. T. Hendrix

Columbia, S.C.

April 29

* * * * *

The Chicago Tribune
Tuesday, May 2, 1865

From Springfield

———

Change of Burial Place — Preparations for the Funeral — Military Matters

[Special Dispatch to the Chicago Tribune]

Springfield, May 1.

The remains of Mr. Lincoln will be deposited at Oak Ridge Cemetery[32] instead of the Mather Place,[33] which has been purchased for that purpose. This

---

32   Oak Ridge Cemetery was founded in 1855. At the time it was about two miles outside of Springfield. It is the second-most visited cemetery in America (after Arlington). Mary Todd Lincoln (1818 - 1882) and sons Edward Baker Lincoln (1846 - 1850), William Wallace Lincoln (1850 - 1862), and Thomas Lincoln (1853 - 1871) are in crypts near Lincoln's tomb. (Robert is buried at Arlington.) The cemetery has memorials for World War II, the Korean War, and the Vietnam War.

33   The Mather Place was an eight-acre plot inside Springfield on one of the highest

change has been made at the urgent and peremptory request of Mrs. Lincoln and Captain Robert Lincoln. The vault at the Mather Place was almost finished, but the work has been suspended and preparations to receive the body made at Oak Ridge Cemetery.

The committee of gentlemen appointed to receive the remains of the noble dead will leave here on special cars provided through the kindness of Virgil Hickox, Esq., who gives free transportation to Chicago and return.

The decoration of the State House is nearly completed, and will, when finished, present a fine appearance.

A gentleman who has just returned from Washington says that the catafalco and its surroundings will exceed anything he has seen on the route for beauty of design.

About one hundred men, non-veterans, belonging to the 62nd regiment, were paid off and mustered out to-day.

The public schools of our city will be given a recess during Wednesday, Thursday, Friday and Saturday, out of respect for the lamented dead.

Our hotels are rapidly filling up with strangers, who come to witness the final obsequies of President Lincoln.

* * * * *

Hartford Courant
Tuesday, May 2, 1865

Richmond Negroes — Richmond darkies are on all sides, telling of their joy at the capture of their city. "I was jus so happy when I knowed dat I couldn't do nuffin but ju lay right down and larf, and larf," said one. "I could jus roll up and larf. I declar I jus feel as happy as a man's got religion in his

---

points in town, not far from the train station. It had been bought from Mrs. H.G. Mather by the Lincoln Monument Association for the dear price of $53,400. Work on a stone tomb was underway before Lincoln's funeral train arrived, and donations were already being taken in for a memorial on the site. Mather Place was planted with trees, but Mrs. Lincoln claimed her husband had requested a bucolic scene, so she insisted on Oak Ridge. Her demands arrived by telegraph before the train.

soul." "Some folks says a man carn't tote a bar'l flour," chimed in another, 'but I could tote a bar'l flour *dat* day, or a bar' sugar." "I see'd a rebel gwine down the street dat mornin," said a third, with evident appreciation of the privileges of a freedman, "wid a big ham, and I just tuck dat ham from him and run'd right down da street. An he holler to me to stop; but I jus keep that ham." "We hab more liberty in one hour after you Yankees come dan in all our lives," was the comment of yet another. Then followed a touching recital of the sufferings of a slave: "Dey part us all. Dey send us away from our family. Dey send us jus whar dey please. Dey han-cuff us. Dey put us in jail. Dey give us thirty-nine lashes. Dey starve us. Dey do ebery ting to us." Poor fellows! The end of all this has come, and they know it. — *Cor. Springfield Republican.*

* * * * *

The New York Times
Tuesday, May 2, 1865

THE ASSASSINATION
Large Number of Arrests of Persons Supposed to be Implicated
Their Trial to Commence Immediately — Great Magnitude of the Plot.

———

Special Dispatch to the New-York Times
WASHINGTON, Monday, May 1

In the further progress of the preliminary examinations as to the assassination conspiracy arrests are continually being made, and thus far the whole number taken into custody will reach nearly three hundred. The trial of these conspirators will be commenced, however, before a military commission, and if upon this hearing the same facts are brought out that have been disclosed in the preliminary examinations, the magnitude of the plot will astonish the whole country. It is not true as reported, that Harrold has been tried — his trial is set for to-morrow.

There is a small bit of a quarrel in here among the detectives and others, about the division of the reward for the capture of Booth. Several of them

368

who were actively engaged in the capture say there is an attempt on the part of others to crowd them out and claim the lion's share. Lieut. Doherty, who commanded the detachment of the Sixteenth New-York Cavalry that assisted the capture of Booth, has been promoted to a Captaincy, by a commission of the Governor of New-York.

––––––

Arrest of Suspected Characters

SHEFFIELD, MASS. Monday, May 1.

The town is under considerable excitement from the arrest of a person connected with a traveling exhibition, supposed to be an accomplice of Booth, who appears to answer the advertisement exactly. He has a prominent chin, a full moustache, and a large scar under the left ear. Detectives from towns on the line of the Housatonic Railroad have been secreted in the village part of the day, awaiting his appearance in the evening. His identity is not yet fully determined.

––––––

A Plea for the Assassin. — The organ of the rebels in Canada desires that the murderer of the late President shall be thoroughly identified with the cause of the "confederacy." It is not content, apparently with having offered a justification of the assassin's act; it seems to consider it due to his memory to protest against the cold-blooded manner in which his death was compassed by those sent in pursuit of him. We do not know that there is anything in the whole range of modern journalism to equal the following. It appeared in the Toronto Leader of Saturday:

"The shooting of Booth was a cold-blooded murder — nothing more or less. Granted that he was a criminal of the deepest dye — that was no reason why he should have been shot down the way he was. He was a foolish man, but a brave one. He died like one who loved his country dearly, according to his idea of what a noble death was. It was very obvious that the detective gang were a lot of cowards, or they would never have had recourse in the means they adopted to finish up the 'brief eventful history' of a man who was already half disabled."

369

It is a fitting sequel to this eulogy of the murderer that the same print ridicules the indictment of the leading rebels in Canada for a breach of the neutrality laws. On this point it says:

"The absurdity of finding true bills against Messrs. Thompson, Clay and Cleary will be evident to every one, when they come to know that one of these gentlemen was in Richmond when last heard of; the other is on the Atlantic, on his way to Europe; and the third is — well, we shall let the Federal spies find that out, if they can."

*   *   *   *   *

The Shreveport Weekly News
Shreveport, Louisiana
Tuesday, May 2, 1865

The News

The news for the last week or so has not been well calculated to encourage the timid, nor to inspirit even the more hopeful. It would be unwise, however, as our noble Chief Magistrate has said, to become dispirited or think of giving up the contest.

The fall of Richmond will have the effect to demoralize our people to some extent, and even to lessen our resources, but some advantages will grow out of it that will more than compensate for all the evils. Our whole army being now mobilized, we can strike here or there, as our President has said, cutting them up and destroying them in details. The advantage of that mode of fighting must be apparent to all who have given any attention to the past history of the war. In one more instance, thirty men — picked men — under a bold and skillful leader — Captain Shannon — killed, wounded and captured about 700 of the enemy in the course of two months, and that without the loss of a man. Forrest and Morgan have on several occasions killed, wounded and captured twice their own numbers in the course of a single campaign. The surrender of Gen. Lee with a portion of his army is nothing like as bad as we at first heard it was. His whole loss will not exceed 6 or 7000 men, the balance having previously gone to Johnston and swelled his numbers to the dimensions of a powerful army, capable of protecting itself against any force of the enemy.

370

Johnston, whose army was reported to be in great danger, or actually taken was at last accounts perfectly safe, with the way southward fairly open. Johnston has a powerful and effective army, and operating as it will hereafter in the interior — advancing or retreating at leisure, it will be able to strike telling blows.

The evacuation of Mobile, which occurred on the 12th, did not result in any serious loss.

The garrison made its escape, taking away everything valuable that could be hauled.

All these acquisitions will tend to divide and weaken the enemy, and strengthen the effective strength of our forces in the field the exact number of the garrisons.

Upon the whole the people must not be discouraged. Many a people have seen a much darker day than we have. Our dark day would have been a glorious sunshine to the immortal Washington in the dark days of the revolution.

Says he, "The highest qualification of a people who are capable of conducting a revolution to a successful issue is fortitude under reverses. Not all men can stand the intoxicating effects of property, and fewer can resist the enervating and dispiriting tendency of adversity. The great heart and large soul will rebound from the shock of misfortune with renewed vigor, and the spirit that is determined to succeed recognizes no obstacle in the way of success, but perseveringly and surely mounts to the goal of its ambition, deluded by no false promises of success, and deterred by no frowns of inauspicious fate." This is true and noble. Are we equal to the occasion?

The assassination of Lincoln and Seward by some unknown person is an event in this country. Its tendency at first will be to enrage the people of the North against the South, but this will subside in a short time, as all reasonable people will see that our authorities had nothing to do with it. What effect it will have upon the great struggle it is difficult to say at present. Certainly Lincoln and Seward were the main pillars of the Republican party, and their death must tend to the disorganization of that party.

* * * * *

Wednesday, May 3, 1865

Delicate Evidences

The sweet, sad sounds
of musical dirges,
the occasional mutterings
of muffled drums,

the human figures,
passing and passing,
look like spectres
as the glare of lamps and torchlights

send their shadows across the pale faces.

Chicago Tribune
Wednesday, May 3, 1865

HONORS TO THE GREAT DEAD
The Martyr Dust Consecrated in the Hearts of the People.

———

Imposing Reception of the Remains in Indianapolis.

———

Women Wave Chaplets of Flowers and Strew them on the Sacred Bier.

———

The Progress of the Funeral Train. — Arrival of the Remains in Chicago

[Special Correspondence of the Chicago Tribune.]

INDIANAPOLIS, May 1, 1865

I have given your readers very accurate and as voluminous dispatches as possible up to date, concerning obsequies of the assassinated President Abraham Lincoln — obsequies the grandest, most magnificent and most solemn ever witnessed on this earth. I will now continue this memorable record;

Indianapolis, May 1 — 12:20 a.m.

The funeral train is slowly moving out from the depot, watched by several thousands of anxious hearts. The sweet, sad sounds of musical dirges, the occasional mutterings of muffled drums, the human figures, passing and passing, look like spectres as the glare of lamps and torchlights send their shadows across the pale faces. As the moments fly by we are hastily glancing over the honors that Indianapolis and her people paid to the great dead. We have seen how, through torrents of rain, the mourners all day thronged about the State house, where lay the remains, eagerly waiting and watching for an opportunity to gaze on the features of the great martyr. See, too, how all the public buildings and private residences are robed in the weeds of bereavement. Look at the arches of roses and evergreens spanning the streets, and observe the delicate evidences of a people's devotion to a fallen chief in the artistic manner in which his portrait is shrouded and interwoven with chaplets of flowers. But above all places, except the hearts of the people, go to the State Chambers where lies in state the illustrious dead. It excels everything we have yet seen in the extent, variety, and beauty of its arrangement. Its interior is covered entire with black mourning velvet and crape, and on the sides hang chaplets of evergreens and circular boquets, surrounding the likenesses of many of the heroes of modern and ancient times. The dome is studded with stars, and as I stood gazing at the dark, solemn mysterious cavern-like chamber, I was forcibly reminded of the grand and awful sublimity which one feels while gazing at the star chamber in the Mammoth Cave. Then there is the gorgeous catafalque, and the costly coffin, with its gold and silver lining; then are the mourners, silent and thoughtful, passing in and out as quietly as if there were walking with death. In the center of these weird pictures is the mighty dead, upon whose features men, angels and stars gaze with equal wonder and admiration.

The Funeral Route Today

The route today lies over the Lafayette and Indianapolis Railroad to Lafayette, a distance of sixty-four miles, at which place we take the new Albany, Louisville and Chicago Railroad to Michigan City, a distance of ninety-two miles, where we take the Michigan Central to Chicago, a distance of fifty-seven miles.

We are now under special care of J.M. Kerper, Esq., Conductor and Assistant Superintendent of the Lafayette and Indianapolis Railroad, Charles Lamb, Engineer of the Stockwell, and Thomas Cullen, Engineer of the pilot engine Boon.

Precautionary Measures

The utmost precautionary measures have been taken for our safe and speedy transit. The train will not run faster than twenty miles an hour, and only at the rate of five miles an hour while passing through stations, towns, and cities. Telegraph offices will be open during the entire route, and the progress of the train from depot to depot will be instantly telegraphed. Pilot engines will be invariably ten minutes in advance of train engine, and will pass no station without giving information that the Funeral Train has passed last preceding station. Signal lights and special guards are along the entire way. On the pilot engine are telegraph operators and skilled railroad mechanics, with their implements, to be made available in case of an accident occurring.

[...]

Zionsville, Ind., 12:47 a.m.

A crowd of people with lighted lamps and torches were assembled, and upon hearing in which car was the President's remains, they flocked about it with the greatest anxiety, eagerly endeavoring to get a look at the remains.

Whitestown, Ind. 1:07 a.m.

Around a huge bonfire are congregated about one hundred people, the men remaining with uncovered heads while the train passed.

Lebanon, Ind., 1:30 a.m.

This is the county seat of Boon county, and it seems as both the town and county were gathered together to honor the dead. Lamps, torches and bonfires send their brilliant light about the assemblage. Suspended from wires are transparent lamps, behind which are drooped flags dressed in mourning. A beautiful arch of evergreens and roses was erected, under which passed the cars. This handsome structure was festooned with velvet rosettes, miniature banners and other decorations. Colored transparencies lent their attractions to make the embellishments more fairy-like than real.

Thorntown, Ind. 2:10 a.m.

A large number of people were standing at the depot and on the side-tracks, the men standing with uncovered heads as the funeral cortege passed. Bonfires were lighted. The community in and about Thorntown is composed principally of Quakers, and certainly their assembling thus to honor the dead is but additional testimony to their well-known devotional life.

Clark's Hill, Ind., 2:40 a.m.

Congregation assembled at the depot with lighted lamps. The people stood uncovered while in presence of the remains.

Stockwell, Ind., 2:50 a.m.

A very fine display presented itself. Crowds of people surrounded the depot looking solemn and thoughtful. Many bonfires were burning, and lighted lamps were suspended by the wayside. On a transparency was the following:

"Down with treason; death to traitors."

Lafayette, Ind., 3:35 a.m.

As we enter the city private residences are brilliantly illuminated, contrasting strangely with the black drapery which shrouds the windows and door frames. The assemblage present was very large and orderly. A band of music discoursed appropriate airs. Departing, bonfires light up our way, habitations are illuminated, and flags, dressed in mourning, droop.

At this point we take the Louisville, New Albany and Chicago Railroad, a distance of ninety-two miles from Michigan City. The steam engine Persian, handsomely decorated, now bears us on, under the charge of a cautious and experienced engineer, Mr. A. Ruperts. Harry Mershon, Esq., is conductor. Mr. Rhodes is engineer in charge of the pilot engine Rocket.

Battle Ground, Ind. 3:55 a.m.

Bonfires are blazing, around which some three hundred people are congregated. They slowly wave flags and stand uncovered as the cortege passes.

Reynolds, Ind. 5:55 a.m.

A great many farmers and their families have come to town, some of them a distance of twenty miles, to pay their respects to the dead. The village people have been anxiously awaiting to get a sign of the funeral train.

Francisville, Ind., 5:45 a.m.

The crowd of people assembled here flock about the car containing the President's remains, and stand on tip-toe to get a look at the coffin. Numbers of country people are here likewise.

Singing Old Hundred.

A few moments previous to the cars departing, the young ladies who presented the cross commenced singing that ever appreciative hymn which heads this paragraph, and while the cars were in motion we fancied we could hear the sweet and mellow voices of the chorists ascending to Heaven, in praise of the great departed, and there re-echoed by the angel hosts gathered about God's throne. But we must leave this world of the beautiful — this living with roses and flowers — and continue to chronicle the walks of the living as they tread in the walks of the dead.

Crossing of Michigan Southern R.R.

At the intersection of the Michigan Southern with the Michigan Central, a few miles this side of Michigan City, over a hundred people had assembled on either side of the track, and stood with their uncovered heads as the remains passed them by.

San Pierre, Ind. — 6:25 a.m.

The usual signs of bereavement are seen; people wearing mourning badges, and flags drooping. Here, as at Medaryville, there was a large number of people in waiting, to satisfy their uppermost wish of getting a look at the funeral cortege.

Westville, Ind., — 7:40 a.m.

Two thousand people are here assembled, and a more serious, thoughtful congregation has not been seen. The men stand with uncovered heads, and women look on in silence. A number of little children were in groups together, holding in their hands white flags with mourning fringes. At another place was a number of very intelligent young women, holding miniature flags of the Republic bordered with rosettes, which they waved gently, in token of their love. The some

A tasteful and pretty arch was constructed, under which the train passed. It was the handiwork of the ladies of the village, and most artistically interwoven with wreaths of evergreen and roses. On the top was a beautiful flag waving, the support of which was trimmed with green and black drapery, its base nesting in a boquet and surrounded by rosettes. On each side of the arch of the base of the curvature were portraits of the martyred President, which were shrouded with black and white trimmings. The inscription, "Though dead he yet speaketh," was printed in large letters on white cloth, reaching across the arch, where commenced the formation of the semi-circle. As the funeral train slowly moved out, a choir of ladies and gentlemen, under leadership of Mr. Wilkins, a prominent citizen, sang with a sweet mournfulness the peculiarly appropriate hymn, entitled, "The Departed."

May 3, 1865

La Croix, Ind. — 7:50 a.m.

Quite a nice demonstration was made here by the people of the village and those from the surrounding country, who received the cortege in the most sacred manner.

Michigan City, Ind. May 1 — 8:35 a.m.

Another change at this place. We are now in the care of the Michigan Central Railroad. R.N. Rice, Esq., General Superintendent, and C. Knowlton, Esq., Assistant Superintendent, accompanied the remains from Indianapolis, and will continue until the cortege arrives in Chicago. They are unremitting in their care and attention. The engine "Ranger," Major George Harper conductor, and the pilot engine "Rambler," in charge of Frank Van Valkenberg, are ready for our accommodation. These engines are very handsomely decorated.

Delegations from Chicago and elsewhere came in on the train at this point to assist in the funeral rites.[34]

An Hour of Sunshine

God's bright universe which has been shrouded in gloom and darkness for the past twenty-four hours, is lit up this morning with a light and glorious sun, whose refulgent rays lend to Nature a touch of exquisite beauty; — the rains which have beaten with such violence have ceased, and the air is once more sweet and balmy, as if the fragrance of the Orient were suddenly wafted thither. Thanks to the merciful Father for this long-wished for change; and methinks it must have come to be in harmony with the warm hearts and fervent patriotism of the men and women of Michigan, whose

Lincoln as State Representative 1846 or '47

34   Not everyone was on board. On May 4, the Chicago Tribune reported the following: "...At [Michigan City], at which the funeral train arrived at 8:25 yesterday morning, Gen. Hooker stepped off to get breakfast, and while he was eating, the train left. Major Jas. S. Hopper, grain dispatcher of the Michigan Central at Michigan city, went to the Company's shop, and took out a locomotive, which, with the General on board, overtook the train at Lake Station. The distance between Porter and Lake Station, eight miles, was run in the unprecedented time of nine minutes."

touching, sublime memory of the great dead — our own,— the world-beloved Abraham Lincoln, I am about to hand down to history, to future ages, for surely such divine devotion of the noble living to the reverend dead can never die.

Let us now see how this devotion was manifested, this devotion so touchingly beautiful, so harmoniously blended with the creations of nature and art, so artistically wrought and interwoven by the gentle hand of woman and the strong arm of man.

An Arch Magnificent of Wreaths and Roses Wrought.

As the funeral train entered the depot it passed beneath a magnificent arch of roses and evergreens twenty-five feet wide and thirty feet in height, and resting on nine arches [It was designed by Dan Kennedy, Esq.] At a point twenty-three feet from the case upward commences a dome which rises proportionately to a height of twelve feet, thus making the entire height thirty-five feet. The dome is surmounted by a circular woodwork some twelve inches through and five feet high, wreathed in serpentine form by links of evergreen, and from the top float small flags, draped in mourning, surrounded by a network of floral beauty. Through the center of the main arch and dome a Liberty tree stretches its tall form, and from the top floats free to the four winds of heaven the old flag of our fathers, the glorious stars and stripes. On each side of the arch, directly beneath the dome is an inscription:

On the East Side.

"The principles of the Almighty are perfect and must prevail" — A. Lincoln.

The letters in the above were wrought of arbor vitae of medium size, and perfect in their harmony of their outline.

On the West Side.

"Abraham Lincoln! Noblest Martyr to Freedom! Sacred thy dust! Hallowed thy resting place!"

The letters were wrought of the same material as describe above.

On the North Side.

"With tears we resign thee to God and history."

379

Construction of the letter and material were as those of the easterly side. On the South Side.

"Abraham Lincoln! Our guiding star has fallen! The nation mourns!"

The letters in the above were counterparts of those already described, and the handiwork of the ladies of Michigan City. They are most remarkably beautiful in execution and design. Mrs. Ann C. Heartwell was the only lady whose name I had time to receive as being one of the noble women who were specially instrumental in thus strewing flowers in the path of the dead. The pillars supporting the arch were alternately woven with black and white stripes of cloth, and a third was a continued circling of evergreens. Approaching the upper part of the pillars splendid flags flowed gracefully and then linked about the entire arch, emblematic of those folds being so closely interwoven in the hearts of the people, that to tear down one is to tear down all. The wealth of flowers, chaplets, boquets and evergreens in the interior of the arch, and the harmony displayed in their arrangement, were as profuse as they were excellent. At an equal distance from the base, on the four corners supporting the dome, were portraits of the great dead, looking calmly down, as now we trust he is looking from the great arch of God's universe. In the brief moment we have to describe this wonderful place of beautiful mechanism it is impossible for us to do it justice. We have only to say that the women of Michigan City have reared a monument to the moral worth of Abraham Lincoln, most lasting and enduring, more solid and substantial than the laurels of the warrior or the crown of kings.

A Cross of Solid Flowers.

A delegation of ladies, sixteen in number, through Miss Hattie Colfax, (cousin of Schuyler Colfax,) on the part of the ladies of the city, presented a beautiful cross made of solid flowers, which they asked permission to place upon the coffin. The request being granted, the fair women entered the car containing the remains, Miss Colfax placing the cross on the coffin, the other ladies following till they passed out through the opposite end of the car. These angels of mercy, for such they may be termed, were dressed in white, and wore black sashes. The names of the ladies accompanying Miss Colfax were: Mrs. Colfax, Mrs. Hoyt, Mrs. Peck, Miss Woodward, Miss Mary Goodhue, Miss Minnie Sherman, Miss Mary Sammons, Miss Mary White, Miss Kate Palmer, Miss Kate Higgins, Miss Nellie Jernegen, Miss Mary McAdoo, Miss Mary Sperry, and Miss Mary Potter.

Thirty-Six Little Girls Representing the States in the Union.

In a group stood thirty-six little girls representing the entire number of States in the Republic. They looked young and beautiful, even like the virgin soil they represented. These little ones were dressed in white, with black sashes and rosettes of trailing arbutus on right shoulder. In their middle was a young lady representing the Goddess of Liberty, in whose left hand was the Constitution of the United States of America. The genii was robed in spotless white, and the features were poetically enshrined in majestic folds of the finest black veiling. Miss Hattie Gustine is the name of the young woman who personated the worshipped goddess.

Lake, Ind. — 9:30 a.m.

The depot was handsomely draped about the entrance to the main door. A number of people were assembled who gazed upon the funeral train with reverential looks.

Gilson's, Ind. — 10.05 a.m.

This, like every other station along the route, had its mourners, those who watched with anxious heart the solemn cortege as it passed by.

Calumet, Ill. — 10:30 a.m.

A group of people are standing on the platform, and while the train is stopping for a few moments, they gather about the President's car, vainly endeavoring to get a glimpse of the urn containing the ashes of the mourned.

Chicago, Ill., May 1, 1865 — 12 n.

The funeral cortege has arrived, and the great heart of the city of Chicago is throbbing as her people bear the sacred dust of the murdered martyr, to the silent chambers where will lie in state the remains of the great and good man, the wise and the merciful ruler, Abraham Lincoln.

Thursday, May 4, 1865

Sorely Tried and Never Found Wanting

He was thoroughly American,
had never crossed the sea,
had never been spoiled
by English insularity or French dissipation;

a quite native, aboriginal man,
as an acorn from the oak;
no aping of foreigners,
no frivolous accomplishments,

Kentuckian born, working on a farm,
a flatboatman, a captain in the Black Hawk War,
a country lawyer, a representative
in the rural legislature of Illinois —

on such modest foundations
the broad structure of his fame was laid.
How slowly, and yet by happily prepared steps,
he came to his place.

The Daily National Intelligencer
Thursday, May 4, 1865

CHARACTER OF PRESIDENT LINCOLN
Address by Ralph W. Emerson.

The following address was delivered by Ralph Waldo Emerson, Esq.,[35] in Concord, Massachusetts, on the occasion of the funeral services in honor of Mr. Lincoln[36]:

The President stood before us as a man of the people. He was thoroughly American, had never crossed the sea, had never been spoiled by English insularity or French dissipation; a quite native, aboriginal man, as an acorn from the oak; no aping of foreigners, no frivolous accomplishments, Kentuckian born, working on a farm, a flatboatman, a captain in the Black Hawk War, a country lawyer, a representative in the rural legislature of Illinois — on such modest foundations the broad structure of his fame was laid. How slowly, and yet by happily prepared steps, he came to his place!

All of us remember — it is only a history of five or six years — the surprise and the disappointment of the country at his first nomination by the

---

35   Ralph Waldo Emerson (1803 - 1882) was a renowned essayist, poet, and lecturer most famous as a transcendentalist thinker, defender of individualism and freedom.

36   The actual address, delivered at the Unitarian Church in Concord on April 19, began with the following two paragraphs:

"We meet under the gloom of a calamity which darkens down over the minds of good men in all civil society, as the fearful tidings travel over sea, over land, from country to country, like the shadow of an uncalculated eclipse over the planet. Old as history is, and manifold as are its tragedies, I doubt If any death has caused so much pain to mankind as this has caused, or will cause, on its announcement; and this, not so much because nations are by modern arts brought so closely together, as because of the mysterious hopes and fears which, in the present day, are connected with the name and institutions of America.

"In this country, on Saturday, every one was struck dumb, and saw at first only deep below deep, as he meditated on the ghastly blow. And perhaps, at this hour, when the coffin which contains the dust of the President sets forward on its long march through mourning states, on its way to his home in Illinois, we might well be silent, and suffer the awful voices of the time to thunder to us. Yes, but that first despair was brief: the man was not so to be mourned. He was the most active and hopeful of men; and his work had not perished: but acclamations of praise for the task he had accomplished burst out into a song of triumph, which even tears for his death cannot keep down."

convention at Chicago. Mr. Seward, then in the culmination of his good fame, was the favorite of the Eastern States. And when the new and comparatively unknown name of Lincoln was announced (notwithstanding the report of the acclamations of that convention), we heard the result coldly and sadly.

It seemed too rash, on a purely local reputation, to build so grave a trust in such anxious times; and men naturally talked of the chances in politics as incalculable. But it turned out not to be chance. The profound good opinion which the people of Illinois and of the West had conceived of him, and which they had imparted to their colleagues, that they also might justify themselves to their constituents at home, was not rash, though they did not begin to know the riches of his worth.

A plain man of the people, an extraordinary fortune attended him. He offered no shining qualities at the first encounter; he did not offend by superiority. He had a face and manner which disarmed suspicion, which inspired confidence, which confirmed good will. He was a man without vices. He had a strong sense of duty, which it was very easy for him to obey. Then, he had what farmers call a long head; was excellent in working out the sum for himself; in arguing his case and convincing you fairly and firmly.

Ralph Waldo Emerson

Then it turned out that he was a great worker; had prodigious faculty of performance; worked easily. A good worker is so rare; everybody has some disabling quality. In a host of young men that start together and promise so many brilliant leaders for the next age, each fails on trial; one by bad health, one by conceit, or by love of pleasure, or lethargy, or an ugly temper, -- each has some disqualifying fault that throws him out of the career. But this man was sound to the core, cheerful, persistent, all right for labor, and liked nothing so well.

Then he had a vast good nature, which made him tolerant and accessible to all; fair-minded, leaning to the claim of the petitioner; affable, and not sensible to the affliction which the innumerable visits paid to him when President would have brought to any one else. And how this good nature became a noble humanity, in many a tragic case which the events of the war brought to him, everyone will remember; and with what increasing tenderness he dealt when a whole race was thrown on his compassion. The poor negro said of him, on an impressive occasion, "Massa Linkum am eberywhere."

Then his broad good humor, running easily into jocular talk, in which he delighted and in which he excelled, was a rich gift to this wise man. It enabled him to keep his secret; to meet every kind of man and every rank in society; to take off the edge of the severest decisions; to mask his own purpose and sound his companion; and to catch with true instinct the temper of every company he addressed. And, more than all, it is to a man of severe labor, in anxious and exhausting crises, the natural restorative, good as sleep, and is the protection of the overdriven brain against rancor and insanity.

He is the author of a multitude of good sayings, so disguised as pleasantries that it is certain they had no reputation at first but as jests; and only later, by the very acceptance and adoption they find in the mouths of millions, turn out to be the wisdom of the hour. I am sure if this man had ruled in a period of less facility of printing, he would have become mythological in a very few years, like Aesop or Pilpay,[37] or one of the Seven Wise Masters,[38] by his fables and proverbs.

But the weight and penetration of many passages in his letters, messages and speeches, hidden now by the very closeness of their application to the moment, are destined hereafter to wide fame. What pregnant definitions; what

---

37   Pilpay is held to be the name of the author of a series of Buddhistic fables written in Sanskrit in India, perhaps as early as 300 BC, perhaps as late as 500 AD. Pilpay is also known as Bidpai. The set of fables is known as the Panchatantra, Sanskrit for "Five Principles."

38   The Seven Wise Masters is a cycle of stories of uncertain Indian, Persian, or Hebrew origin. In the stories, the Seven Wise Masters, led by Sindbad, confuse devious stories told by an evil empress.

unerring common sense; what foresight; and, on great occasion, what lofty, and more than national, what humane tone! His brief speech at Gettysburg will not easily be surpassed by words on any recorded occasion. This, and one other American speech, that of John Brown[39] to the court that tried him, and a part of Kossuth's speech[40] at Birmingham, can only be compared with each other, and with no fourth.

His occupying the chair of state was a triumph of the good sense of mankind, and of the public conscience. This middle-class country had got a middle-class president, at last. Yes, in manners and sympathies, but not in powers, for his powers were superior. This man grew according to the need. His mind mastered the problem of the day; and as the problem grew, so did his comprehension of it. Rarely was man so fitted to the event. In the midst of fears and jealousies, in the Babel of counsels and parties, this man wrought incessantly with all his might and all his honesty, laboring to find what the people wanted, and how to obtain that.

It cannot be said there is any exaggeration of his worth. If ever a man was fairly tested, he was. There was no lack of resistance, nor of slander, nor of ridicule. The times have allowed no state secrets; the nation has been in such ferment, such multitudes had to be trusted, that no secret could be kept. Every door was ajar, and we know all that befell.

Then, what an occasion was the whirlwind of the war. Here was place for no holiday magistrate, no fair-weather sailor; the new pilot was hurried to the helm in a tornado. In four years, — four years of battle-days — his endurance, his fertility of resources, his magnanimity, were sorely tried and never found wanting.

There, by his courage, his justice, his even temper, his fertile counsel, his humanity, he stood a heroic figure in the centre of a heroic epoch. He is

39   After being convicted of treason and murder, Brown gave a brief speech in which he admitted that he had led the attack at Harpers Ferry in hopes of inspiring an insurrection among slaves and reiterated that he believed it the moral thing to do.

40   Lajos (Louis) Kossuth (1802 - 1894) was a Hungarian political leader who eventually fled to England and the U.S. The Birmingham mentioned here was in England. In the U.S. he was welcomed as the George Washington of Hungary. Though he advocated democracy, he never condemned slavery.

386

the true history of the American people in his time. Step by step he walked before them; slow with their slowness, quickening his march by theirs, the true representative of this continent; an entirely public man; father of his country, the pulse of twenty millions throbbing in his heart, the thought of their minds articulated by his tongue.

Adam Smith remarks that the axe, which in Houbraken's[41] portraits of British kings and worthies is engraved under those who have suffered at the block, adds a certain lofty charm to the picture. And who does not see, even in this tragedy so recent, how fast the terror and ruin of the massacre are already burning into glory around the victim? Far happier this fate than to have lived to be wished away; to have watched the decay of his own faculties; to have seen — perhaps even he — the proverbial ingratitude of statesmen; to have seen mean men preferred.

Had he not lived long enough to keep the greatest promise that ever man made to his fellow-men — the practical abolition of slavery? He had seen Tennessee, Missouri and Maryland emancipate their slaves. He had seen Savannah, Charleston and Richmond surrendered; had seen the main army of the rebellion lay down its arms. He had conquered the public opinion of Canada, England and France. Only Washington can compare with him in fortune.

And what if it should turn out, in the unfolding of the web, that he had reached the term; that this heroic deliverer could no longer serve us; that the rebellion had touched its natural conclusion, and what remained to be done required new and uncommitted hands — a new spirit born out of the ashes of the war; and that Heaven, wishing to show the world a completed benefactor, shall make him serve his country even more by his death than by his life? Nations, like kings, are not good by facility and complaisance. "The kindness of kings consists in justice and strength." Easy good nature has been the dangerous foible of the Republic, and it was necessary that its enemies should outrage it, and drive us to unwonted firmness, to secure the salvation of this

---

41 Jacobus Houbraken (1698 - 1780), Dutch engraver of over 400 portraits of European historical figures.

country in the next ages.

The ancients believed in a serene and beautiful Genius which ruled in the affairs of nations; which, with a slow but stern justice, carried forward the fortunes of certain chosen houses, weeding out single offenders or offending families, and securing at last the firm prosperity of the favorites of Heaven. It was too narrow a view of the Eternal Nemesis. There is a serene Providence which rules the fate of nations, which makes little account of time, little of one generation or race, makes no account of disasters, conquers alike by what is called defeat or by what is called victory, thrusts aside enemy and obstruction, crushes everything immoral as inhuman, and obtains the ultimate triumph of the best race by the sacrifice of everything which resists the moral laws of the world. It makes its own instruments, creates the man for the time, trains him in poverty, inspires his genius, and arms him for his task. It has given every race its own talent, and ordains that only that race which combines perfectly with the virtues of all shall endure.

* * * * *

The disposal of Booth

Chicago Tribune
Thursday, May 4, 1865

Assassination as an Institution.

It was hoped by abolishing slavery in the District of Columbia to change the political atmosphere of the nation's capitol from barbarism to civilization. This has been but half accomplished. It has been changed from slavery to copperheadism — which, in many respects, is a change from bad to worse. The copperhead is meaner than the slaveholder. Owning no slaves but loving slavery, saturated with its depravity without any share in its prerogatives, the copperhead is the eunuch in the harem of which the slaveholder is lord. He has all his master's passions without his satiety, and all his hates without his indolence. His master rebels, but the copperhead assassinates. His master makes war, but the assassin waylays and commits a fire in the rear. The master we have fought and crushed, but his unpaid minion at the North, who commits treason in the dark, and stabs the nation without risking his person, must be hanged.

Washington is full of this class. By the hand of two of them — Booth and Harrold — Abraham Lincoln fell. By the hand of another, the Secretary of State, nearly slain. — Probably those who lay in wait for Stanton and Johnson, but were foiled in their purpose. — And now we learn that Senator Sumner, who, prior to the war, nearly fell victim to an open rebel assassin, has again barely escaped death at the hands of a secret assassin, whose cowardly stealth brands him as a copperhead in good standing.

The Union residents of Washington are mainly confined to the members of the republican (sic) party. The "democratic party" (so self-styled) there consists of returned rebels and whipped secesh. They are so numerous that out of over two hundred marshals appointed to conduct the funeral of the late President in Washington, only sixteen had voted the Republican ticket. This indignity has been suitably atoned for, by the resignation of the deputy marshal, who made the appointments. This is well so far as it goes. But the question still remains whether assassination is to become one of the "institutions" of the capital, the legitimate successor of slavery. If not, slavery's bastard child, copperheadism, the offspring of southern slavery and northern depravity, must be driven from the capital at once and forever, with a whip of scorpions. Better than a thousand bodyguards would it be to purge the capital of copperheads. We are not sure that the arrest of some three hundred of their number of whom eighty are about to be put on trial for complicity in the assassination plot may not have a healthy effect. But let the capital be so purged of copperheadism, by hanging, shooting and drowning if necessary, that Presidents and Chief Justices may at least look out of their front windows without being fired at, as if they were prisoners in a rebel slaughter-pen. A little judicious hanging is now in order.

The Body of the Assassin.

The disposition made of the body of the Assassin is a subject which now excites much interest. The journals each have a theory of their own. The New York Times declares that, after the autopsy by the Surgeon General, "the body was dissected, and, in separate pieces, sewed into cloths with heavy weights, and placed in a small vessel, which made a short, circuitous trip upon the Potomac, and, without landing, returned to the navy yard minus the body."

The New York World is even more dramatic that this. The writer says:

"Yesterday the Secretary of War, without instruction of any kind, committed to Colonel Lafayette C. Baker,[42] of the secret service, the stark corpse of The Assassin." The secret service never fulfilled its volition more secretively. 'What have you done with the body?' said I to Baker. 'That is known,' he answered, 'to only one man living besides myself. It is gone. I will not tell you where. The only man who knows is sworn to silence. Never till the great trumpeter comes shall the grave of The Assassin be discovered.' And this is true. Last night, the 27th of April, a small row boat received the carcass of the murderer; two men were in it; they carried the body off into the darkness,

---

42   Lafayette C. Baker (1826 - 1868) was head of the National Detective Police during the war.

and out of the darkness it will never return. In the darkness, like his great crime, may it remain forever, impalpable, invisible, nondescript, condemned to that worse than damnation, annihilation. The river-bottom may ooze about it, laden with great shot and drowning manacles. The earth may have opened to give it that silence and forgiveness which man will never give its memory. The fishes may swim about it, or the daisies grow white above it — but we shall never know."

The Herald says that "the authorities are not inclined to give the wretched carcass the honor of meeting the public gaze, and it will probably be deposited in whatever place promises the most obscurity for them. Yesterday a photographic view of the body was taken before it was removed from the monitor. It was placed in an ordinary gray army blanket, in which it was sewed up. A plain, cask-shaped box, measuring six feet by two, had been previously made in the joiner's shop for the remains, but it was not used."

The News says, in its special dispatch, that "the body has been disposed of in some manner unknown to the public. Current reports concerning it remind us of the manner in which young Dahlgren's body was said to have been treated."

Other persons think that the remains have been given to the doctors. The probability is, however, that they have been interred by the authorities in some obscure spot, of which the public will never be informed.

Debate in the French Chamber on the Address
The Amendment Expressing Sympathy with the United States
[from the Moniteur's (official) report.]
M. Eugene Pelletan — In the present stage of the debate, I should be very cruel to the assembly, and still more cruel to myself, if I were to make a speech in extremis on the death-bed (as I fear it will be) of our last amendment. (Laughter.) I had but a word to say to repair the omission. The speech from the throne passed over America in silence; your draft address maintains the

same reserve; the yellow book itself contains on this subject nothing but a pure white page. — Now it seemed to us that the American question was one of sufficient importance to be treated of otherwise than by reticence. However there is now no occasion for discussion, because while I am speaking to you the news arrives that the victorious swords of Grant and Sherman have settled the question. — Richmond is taken. (Interruption.)

A Voice — So much the worse.

M. Pelletan — The pro-slavery rebellion is crushed and the American Republic is restored in all its majestic unity. [Further interruption.]

President Schneider — Gentlemen, by your interruption you only lengthen the speech.

M. Pelletan — Do not murmur so loud, I conjure you; they may hear us on the other side of the Atlantic. [Exclamations and noise.]

Several voices — Make an end of it.

M. Pelletan — For the last four years North America has borne the burden of the most terrible civil war that ever ravaged a nation, and during the course of this cruel trial she never for a single instant entertained the idea of suspending liberty. [Ah, ah.] She never dreamed of invoking the principle of public safety or opening that door through which all political crimes make their way. But more; it has renewed its executive power under — we may almost say — the very fire of the enemy, and that without violence and without disturbance — [interruption] — and it has done this so orderly and calmly that this page of American history is the page of honor of the 19th century. [Confused and increasing noise.]

M. Pelletan — President Lincoln — (Cries of "Divide, divide.")

Other voices — Hear the speaker.

Mr. Pelletan — President Lincoln felt that he held the fate of the New World in his hands, and he lifted up his heart to the height of his destiny; he has abolished slavery — ("redoubled cries of "Divide") — and he has restored the glorious American republic. ("Divide, divide.") Confused and tumultuous noise.)

A member — Enforce silence, Mr. President.

President Schneider — Let the speaker try to get a hearing.

M. Garnier Pages — If people would only listen, the speech would have been done by this time.

Several voices — "Divide."

M. Schneider — I cannot deprive M. Pelletan of his right to go on. It is for the chamber to — (exclamations); but, at the same time, it for him to speak in such a way as to induce his auditors to hear him.

M. Pelletan — The President asks a miracle of me which I am not able to work. It did appear to me that whenever in the world anything great and noble was done, France was present and an approving party, and I would that my voice this day could be heard on the other side of the Atlantic with an address of congratulations to the President of the United States. (Tumultuous exclamations of dissent.) I cannot struggle against your determination not to hear me, and I shall sit down.

* * * **

The funeral arch at Chicago.

Friday and Saturday, May 5 - 6, 1865

Why This Wonderful Mourning

The horse is a dark bay
and is a fine looking animal.
It appeared on the square to-day
shrouded in elegant trappings of woe.

A rich cover of sable hue,
its plainness relieved by festoons
of white and black crape,
draped the neck and body of the animal.
A gorgeous plume of
white and black feathers
nodded with the head.

A negro man,
with hat in one hand
and bridle reins in the other,
stood in front of the horse,
while another black servant,
in an attitude of respect,
rested his hand upon the hip of the noble animal.

The faithful animal, in his mournful trappings,
will follow, on Thursday next,
the body of his late master
to the darkness and the silence of the tomb.

Louisville Daily Journal
Friday, May 5, 1865

OUR SPRINGFIELD CORRESPONDENCE

St. Nicholas Hotel, Springfield, Ill.

Monday Evening, May 1, 1865

The clouds have parted and the sun has shone brightly to-day. The streets are still muddy, but are drying fast. Springfield is built on a level prairie, where the outlines of timber can only faintly be discerned in the distance. The roads are graded but not bowldered or gravelled. When it rains a large portion of the water remains where it falls; consequently mud is king. But with the passing clouds the sun streams brightly forth, and the winds which constantly sweep over the bosom of the prairie soon render the soil dry again.

Oak Ridge, the cemetery where the remains of Abraham Lincoln are to be deposited, in accordance with a request from Mrs. Lincoln, is about a mile and a half from the State-house, and to get to it you have to travel over one of the worst roads leading from the city. As it is proposed for the procession to proceed there on foot on Thursday, it is earnestly hoped that no more rain may fall. The road is barely passable now, yet it is thought that two days of wind and sun will render it comparatively dry.

The work on the ground purchased by the city for the burial place of Mr. Lincoln is still pushed vigorously forward. The vault will be completed by to-morrow night. It is hoped that Mrs. Lincoln may be prevailed upon to change her mind, and that the body of her husband will be laid away in the tomb prepared by the city of Springfield, and that the proposed monument, the grandest on the American continent, will be erected there.

Mr. Lincoln's Horse

A large crowd was collected on the State-house square, this afternoon, to witness the taking of a photograph of the favorite horse owned by Mr. Lincoln in this city. A mournful interest is attached to everything connected with the life of the lamented President, and the horse, which, four years ago, claimed scarcely a passing notice, to-day is the idol of an admiring throng, and is watched even more tenderly than an infant sleeping on its mother's breast.

The horse is a dark bay and is a fine looking animal.[43] It appeared on the square to-day shrouded in elegant trappings of woe. A rich cover of sable hue, its plainness relieved by festoons of white and black crape, draped the neck and body of the animal. A gorgeous plume of white and black feathers nodded with the head. A negro man, with hat in one hand and bridle reins in the other, stood in front of the horse, while another black servant, in an attitude of respect, rested his hand upon the hip of the noble animal. A file of six soldiers, with bayonets fixed and muskets at a shoulder arms, formed the back ground (sic) of the picture. An excellent negative was obtained, and no doubt the photographs will be extensively sold throughout the country. Almost every day, previous to the removal of Mr. Lincoln to Washington, he could be seen, seated in his carriage, leisurely driving his dark bay through the streets of this city. Since the tragic death of the President, his horse has increased in value at an enormous rate. He is now regarded as worth his weight in silver. The faithful animal, in his mournful trappings, will follow, on Thursday next, the body of his late master to the darkness and the silence of the tomb.

Mr. Lincoln's House

A plain two-story structure — a frame house painted brown, with green window blinds, standing on the corner of Jackson and Eighth streets in a suburban part of the city, now attracts unusual attention. The stranger inquiring for the former residence of Mr. Lincoln, is directed to this spot, and, if not particular, he will pass the unassuming front many times before finding the object of his search. A low white railing fence, resting on a brown

Lincoln at home with Tad.

---

43   The horse's name was named Robin, but everyone called him Old Bob. Lincoln left him in Springfield wen he moved to Washington, where he rode a horse named Old Abe.

stone wall, incloses the little yard in front; vines and rose-bushes clamber here and there up the sides of the building. A narrow yard extended back leading to the low carriage-house and other outbuildings. In its plain simplicity the house wears a rustic appearance. Save the few creeping vines and green window shutters, there is nothing to contrast with the brown and relieve the sternness of the front. Yet here was where Mr. Lincoln spent the most peaceful years of his life, and the spot will ever be held sacred by the American people. To-day the house wears no sign of meaning. Not even the fluttering of a black ribbon, or the tie of a single yard of crape, indicates an expression of grief. We understand, however, that by Thursday it will be arrayed in the sable weeds of woe.

Mr. Lincoln's Remains

will arrive in this city from Chicago at six o'clock on Wednesday morning. They will be taken to the Great Western Railroad Depot, the place where the distinguished patriot delivered his farewell speech to the citizens of Springfield before taking the cars on his road to Washington, to assume the robes of his official office — President of the United States. A little more than four years ago, full of life and vigor, and flushed with high hope, he spoke a sad farewell to the friends of his home, and closed his eyes, as it has proved, forever upon Springfield, the birth-place of his children. He returns to his old home now with the seal of death upon his brow and with his lips firmly closed for aye.[44] He returns, a marble form, stretched upon the bier over which a great nation has bowed in reverence, and wept bitter tears of sorrow. The light has faded from his eyes, the color from the cheek, and the lips are mute. They can speak no words of gratitude now for an earnest welcome home. The city is draped in mourning and sorrow reigns on every side. Alas! how little did the people of Springfield think when Abraham Lincoln said farewell, four years ago, that it was forever. They little dreamed then that with bowed heads and tearful eyes they would welcome him back to his old home.

---

44   "for aye" is an archaic Scottish expression meaning "for ever."

May 5-6, 1865

*   *   *   *   *

The Manchester Guardian
Manchester, England
Saturday, May 5, 1865

ENGLISH SYMPATHY WITH AMERICA
Town's Meeting in Manchester

A meeting, convened by the Mayor, in compliance with a numerously signed requisition, was held at the Town Hall, yesterday morning, for the purpose of considering the most appropriate mode of conveying to the authorities of the United States the deep sympathies of the citizens with them on the diabolical assassination of their late President, and also to express their respectful condolence with Mrs. Lincoln. — The Mayor (J.M. Bennet, Esq.) took the chair. The room was crowded, and on the platform were several members of the City Council and many influential citizens. — The Mayor said he could not hesitate to comply with a requisition, so numerously and respectably signed, to call that meeting. Whatever might have been the feelings and sympathies of the citizens of Manchester with respect to the great struggle that had been going on in the States during the last four years, he was sure that they would be unanimous in passing a resolution of sympathy with the United States on the great loss that had recently sustained. He hoped that the gentlemen who would speak to the resolutions would not enter into those debateable subjects, which agitated the community at the present time — (Hear, hear.) That [it] was a meeting of the citizens of Manchester, not a meeting of one particular party, not a meeting of those who sympathised with the South, not yet of those who had strong opinions with respect to the conduct of the North.

Mr. W.R. Wood, in moving the first resolution, said they were assembled to express their grief and indignation of the great crime which had been committed on the othe side of the Atlantic — the greatest crime in its nature and extent that had been committed, he believed, since the assassination of Julius Ceasar, and the greatest crime which had been committed since the time

398

when Christ appeared in the world as the messenger of peace and goodwill to men — (hear, hear); — and they wished to express their sympathy with their friends on the other side of the Atlantic in great national misfortune which has befallen them. — (Hear, hear.) He thought they might draw from what had occurred the great moral lesson that in disputes, whether between two nations, between parts of the same nation, or between individuals, great value should be placed on the practice of moderation, conciliation, and courtesy. — (Hear, hear.) That great crime was a striking instance of the evils of civil war, and the result of the violent passions which had unhappily existed in a small section of the community. The effects produced by the commission of the crime might, and probably would, be serious and lasting, and the prospect of re-union in America might be seriously damaged thereby; but most of all that crime was likely to damage those on whose side it might be said to have been committed. He did not mean for a moment to say that the leaders of the Southern party had had any hand in the crime, but they might suffer from the exasperated feelings of the North. He sincerely hoped it would not be so; and it would be creditable to the American people as a body if they looked upon it as the desperate act of a few desperate men, and not visit the crime upon the general body of citizens of the South. One of the most important conclusions to be drawn from the whole matter was that those who suffer the more from crimes of that serious nature were not those who were the objects, but those who were the authors. He moved the following resolution:

"That the citizens of Manchester now assembled desire to express their horror and detestation of the deplorable event which has resulted in the violent death of the Chief Magistrate of the American republic, Abraham Lincoln, and of the attempt to murder Mr. Seward and some members of his family; and they desire more earnestly and respectfully to convey to the authorities of the United States their deep sympathy with the American people in the heavy loss they have sustained."

Mr. Alderman Curtis, in seconding the resolution, said if there was any crime which was more than another alien and detestable to the feelings of Englishmen, it was that of assassination. Other countries had not the same horror of giving vent to their feelings of revenge by assassination that Englishmen had, and he trusted that the English feeling on that subject would ever continue. He was glad that the Confederates and the Confederate prisoners were repudiating complicity in Mr. Lincoln's assassination; and he thought that, when we remembered the spirit in which they had conducted themselves during the war, it could not be supposed that they would sanction such a horrible crime. — (Hear, hear.) — The resolution was adopted.

Mr. O. Heywood said he shared with all present the just anger, indignation, sorrow, and sympathy which had called them together that day. It would therefore be impossible for him to refuse to propose the second resolution, which was to this effect: —

"That this meeting desires most respectfully to present to Mrs. Lincoln its sincere sympathy and condolence on the melancholy loss she has sustained in the death of her husband."

The last time the Mayor called them together in public meeting in that room, it was that the citizens of Manchester might express their deep sorrow and regret at the loss of a great and distinguished statesman of their own; a distinguished man who had peacefully and quietly passed to his rest after a life spent promoting the arts and blessings of peace.[45] Almost precisely at the same moment that we received from the other side of the Atlantic tidings of the terrible event which had there taken place, and were lamenting it, the Ameican people were beginning to sympathise with us on the great sorrow which we, too, had suffered; and it seemed as if the two events and the coincidence might somewhat draw the people of the two countries more closely to one another. ("Hear, hear," and applause.) Almost precisely as our own distinguished man of peace had passed away, another had been removed by a coward and a cruel crime from a scene on which during the midst of warfare, struggle, difficulty, and contest, he had had to do his life's duty and his work. He believed that in many respects Mr. Lincoln was not less of a man of peace than the man who had also been taken from the midst of us — (applause); — and, taken as Mr.

---

45   Richard Cobden, the manufacfturer and politician, died of illness 12 days before Lincoln.

Lincoln was in a critical moment, might he not almost say that he was taken in the crowning moment of his life? — (Hear, hear.) Without presuming to dwell upon the events that had taken place, he might recall what came to his own mind at the moment, and what perchance would be on the minds of many who heard him, a few lines written ten or eleven years ago, and placed in the mouth of one who had witnessed, and perhaps taken part in, the great struggle of the battle of the Alma during our first essay in the Crimean war. Those lines opened with these words —

"What will they say in England?"

They went on to describe the struggle which had taken place, the gallantry which had been displayed, the lives which had been lost, and those lines concluded with these words, — "They'll say in Christian England

'God's holy will be done.'"

(Applause.) — This terrible calamity had fallen so suddenly upon the Americans that they had had no time to ask, "What will they say in England." All the more beautiful would it be thought that before they had had time to ask that question there would go back to them what England had to say. — (Cheers and applause.) What the people of England had to say in very few words was this: First, they had to express their sincere sympathy with the great loss of the American people. They had to say how tenderly and affectionately, — because as was justly said by Mr. Disraeli in the House of Commons, this was a matter which appealed to their domestic feelings, — the people sympathised with Mrs. Lincoln in her great and terrible loss. They had also to say of this great calamity there should come forth the universal good that out of it should ere long come peace throughout the great empire of America; that out of it might come freedom for those who had hitherto been in bondage — (cheers); — and that out of it might also come that which they all earnestly desired, that those perpetual bickerings and unkindnesses which from time to time passed between America and England might cease — (hear, hear); — that both America and England might understand that their interests and sympathies, their hopes and purposes, should be and would be the same. — (Cheers.) — Mr. W. M'Clure, in seconding the motion, said that he thought their sympathies on behalf of

Mrs. Lincoln should be called forth doubly, owing to the trying circumstances under which the foul deed was committed. — the motion was adopted.

The Mayor of Salford (Wright Turner, Esq.) proposed a resolution asking the Mayor of Manchester to transmit the resolutions adopted at that meeting to Mr. Adams, the American Minister in London. He said he was glad the people of Manchester had requested their Mayor to call a meeting to express their sympathy with the American people, and their indignation at the crime that had been perpetrated in Washington. The crime was one which we could hardly contemplate; but it would no doubt be an unmitigated evil, inasmuch as there would no doubt arise from it a better understanding between England and America. — (Hear, hear.) he was sure that the spontaneous expression of sympathy that was being made by all classes would convince the Americans that the people of England were as friendly towards them as any nation could possibly be, and would tend to allay that irritation that had existed on the other side of the Atlantic during the past four years. — Mr. M. Ross seconded the resolution. He said he had never seen in that room a more unanimous answer to the resolutions proposed, nor a greater demonstration of the respectful sympathy. He trusted that it was no sham motion that was guiding them, but a real feeling of regret at the loss of an amiable man in the very usefulness of his career. — The resolution was adopted.

The Mayor of Salord then took the chair, and Mr. Alderman Heywood proposed a vote of thanks to the Mayor of Manchester for calling the meeting, and for presiding. He said he did not agree that it was advisable not to express heartily their feelings in relation to that matter, for he thought the movers of resolutions should speak out with the voice of honesty, so that the people might clearly understand their views. — (Hear, hear.) Civilization shuddered at the act that had been committed in America. — Mr. W. R. Wood rose to order, and said he thought it irregular that Mr. Heywood should go into into a discussion of the question before the meeting in moving a vote of thanks to the Mayor, but his remarks were received with loud cries of "No," and for a time caused some interruption. — Mr. Heywood said that great honour was due to the Mayor for calling that meeting; and why had it been called but to let the people of Manchester express indignation at the detestable act that had been committed, their sympathy with the American nation — (cheers) — and their hope that what had taken place would be the means of uniting more strongly the people of England and the people of America. — (Hear, hear.) He was sure that the people who had presented the requisition to the Mayor expected that such a declaration of opinion would be given by the people that the inhabitants of America should not mistake them. — Mr. James Bannerman seconded the resolution. — Mr. W. Pickstone said that, as a citizen of Manchester, who had spent six months travelling in America, and who was in that country when the assassination of President Lincoln took place, he could not allow that that, the first meeting he had had the opportunity of attending since his return, pass without repeating what he told the people of America would be said by his country when the news arrived of Mr. Lincoln's assassination. He told them that all feeling against them on the part of Great Britain would pass away — (applause); that they did not understand the people of England; that the people of England did not understand them; and that to have more knowledge of each other there should be more intercourse between them. — (Hear, hear.) He believed that the people of American would be as deeply moved by the expression of opinion that seemed to be so general in this country as they were by the death of the President. Their wish was to be friendly with England. — (applause.) They had had war, and now they desired peace. Only two days before his death Mr. Lincoln said to one of his ministers, "Of all things, I desire that Mr. Davis may escape the boundary of the United States, (applause); — I do not wish that my hands may be imbued with blood." — (Applause.) What greater clemency could be desired than that, and was there ever a general who behaved more handsomely than General Grant had done? – (Hear, hear.) He (Mr. Pickstone) told the people of America that there would be a letter from the Queen to Mrs. Lincoln (cheers), and he was glad to find that that would be the fact. He also wished to say, if he was not breaking the rules of debate, that the new President (Mr. Johnson) was not a drunkard. — (applause, "Question," and "Go on.") The people of England needed only to have the same confidence in him that it took them four years to feel in Mr. Lincoln, then would they act justly toward the United States. — (applause.) — The resolution was passed with enthusiasm.

In returning thanks, the Mayor said that however gratifying to the Americans would be the expressions of sympathy from London, Liverpool, Birmingham, and other towns, they would be still more gratified with the feelings that were expressed by the people of Manchester. The proceedings then terminated.

* * * * *

New York Times
Friday, May 5, 1865

THE BURIAL.
President Lincoln Again at His Western Home.
The Mortal, Four Years Absent, Returns Immortal.
Close of the Grandest Funeral Procession in History.
Two Weeks' Solemn March Among Millions of Mourners.
The Place of Sepulture and the Last Ceremonies.
Eloquent Funeral Oration by Bishop Simpson.
Touching Manifestations by Mr. Lincoln's Neighbors.

BISHOP SIMPSON'S ADDRESS[46]
SPRINGFIELD, Ill., Thursday, May 4.

The already large number of visitors who have been called here to view the remains of the late President LINCOLN, was increased last night and this morning by numerous arrivals from all quarters.

The remains will be accompanied to the vault by a military and civic procession.

The ground selected for the burial is exceedingly beautiful.

The weather is clear and calm.

---

46   Matthew Simpson (1811 - 1884), bishop of the Methodist Episcopal Church and close friend of and advisor to Abraham Lincoln.

SPRINGFIELD, Ill., Thursday, May 4.

Large numbers have continued to visit the former residence of the late President, on the corner of Eighth and Jefferson streets. It is hung with mourning without, and tastefully decorated within.

Large delegations from the adjoining States and neighboring settlements arrived through the night, and this morning the hotels are overflowing. Some of the visitors are being entertained by the citizens, while thousands of others are unable to find accommodations.

The weather is warm and the sun unclouded. Everybody in Springfield are (sic) on the streets. The State House continued to be visited. At 11 o'clock last night, the ladies of the Soldiers' Aid Society laid upon the coffin a beautiful cross of evergreens, studded with rare flowers. Other similar tokens have been contributed to-day.

At noon, twenty-one guns were fired, and afterward, single guns at intervals of ten minutes. About noon, the remains were brought from the State House and placed in the hearse, which was from St. Louis, and was used at the funerals of Hon. Thomas H. Benton, Gen. Lyon and Gov. Gamble. The hearse was surmounted by a magnificent crown of flowers. Meanwhile, a chorus of hundreds of voices, accompanied by a brass band, sang the hymn,

Illinois State House as Licoln lies in state.

"Children of the heavenly King,

Let us journey as we sing,"

The funeral procession was under the immediate direction of Major-Gen. Hooker, Marshal-in-Chief; Brig.-Gen. Cook and staff, and Brevet Brig.-Gen. Oakes and staff. The military and the firemen made a fine appearance. The guard of honor consisted of Gen. Barnard, Rear-Admiral Davis, and Gens. McCallum, Ramsay, Caldwell, Thomas, Howe, Townsend and Eakin, and Capt. Field, of the Marine Corps. The relations and family friends of the deceased were in carriages. Among them were Judge Davis, of the Supreme Court; the officiating

The hearse at Springfield

clergyman, Bishop Simpson; Dr. Gurley and others. In the procession were the Governors of six or seven States, members of Congress with their officers, the State and municipal authorities, and delegations from adjoining States. The long line of civilians was closed by the Free Masons, Odd Fellows and citizens at large, including colored persons. The hearse was immediately followed by the horse formerly belonging to Mr. Lincoln. Its body was covered with black cloth trimmed with silver fringe.

Never before was there so large a military and civic display in Springfield. There were immense crowds of people in the immediate vicinity of the Capitol to see the procession as it passed, and the people for several miles occupied the sidewalks.

The procession arrived at Oakwood Cemetery at 1 o'clock. On the left of the vault in which the remains of the President and his son were deposited immediately on their arrival, was a platform, on which singers and an instrumental band were in place, and these united in the chanting and singing of appropriate music, including a burial hymn

The catafalque at Springfield

by the deceased President's Pastor, Rev. Dr. Gurley. On the right was the speaker's stand, appropriately draped with mourning.

A short time ago, a piece of property containing eight acres, and located in the heart of the city, was purchased by the citizens for $53,400. The ground is improved with several substantial houses, and trees and shrubbery. It was designed to render the site additionally beautiful and attractive, and to erect thereon a monument to the illustrious dead. A vault has been completed for the reception of the remains, but owing to the wishes of Robert Lincoln, the remains were deposited in Oak Ridge Cemetery nearly two miles from the city.[47] The vault at this place is erected at the foot of a knoll in a beautiful part of the grounds, which contains forest trees of all varieties. It has a doric gable resting on pilasters, the main wall being rustic. The vault is fifteen feet high and about the same in width, with semi-circular wings of bricks projecting from the hillsides. The material is limestone, procured at Joliet, Illinois. Directly inside of the ponderous doors is an iron grating. The interior walls are covered with black velvet, dotted with evergreens. In the centre of the velvet is a foundation of brick, capped with a marble slab, on which the coffin rests. The front of the vault is trimmed with evergreens. The "Dead March" in Saul was sung, accompanied by the band, as the remains were deposited.[48]

Thousands of persons were assembled at the cemetery before the arrival of the procession, occupying the succession of green hills. The scene was one of solemnly intense interest. The landscape was beautiful in the light of an unclouded sun.

The religious exercises were commenced by the singing of a dirge. Then followed the reading of appropriate portions of the Scriptures and a prayer. After a hymn by the choir, Rev. Mr. Hubard read the last inaugural of President Lincoln. Next a dirge was sung by the choir, when Bishop Simpson delivered the funeral oration. It was in the highest degree eloquent, and the patriotic portions of it were applauded. Then followed another hymn, when benediction was pronounced by Rev. Dr. Gurley. The procession then returned to the city.

---

47   As noted above, it was Mrs. Lincoln's insistence.

48   *Saul* was an oratorio by George Frideric Handel. It tells the story of the first king of Israel, Saul, and his deteriorating relationship with the next king, David. "The Dead March" is a requiem for Saul and his son.

We have followed the remains of President Lincoln from Washington, the scene of his assassination, to Springfield, his former home, and now to be his final resting-place. He had been absent from this city ever since he left it in February, 1861, for the national Capital, to be inaugurated as President of the United States. We have seen him lying in state in the executive mansion, where the obsequies were attended by numerous mourners, some of them clothed with the highest public honors and responsibilities which our republican institutions can bestow, and by the diplomatic representatives of foreign governments. We have followed the remains from Washington through Baltimore, Harrisburgh, Philadelphia, New-York, Albany, Buffalo, Cleveland, Columbus, Indianapolis and Chicago to Springfield, a distance in circuit of 1,500 or 1,800 miles. On the route millions of people have appeared to manifest by every means of which they are capable,

Bishop Matthew Simpson

their deep sense of the public loss, and their appreciation of the many virtues which adorned the life of Abraham Lincoln. All classes, without distinction of politics or creeds, spontaneously united in the posthumous honors. All hearts seemed to beat as one at the bereavement, and, now funeral processions are ended, our mournful duty of escorting the mortal remains of Abraham Lincoln hither is performed. We have seen them deposited in the tomb. The bereaved friends, with subdued and grief-stricken hearts, have taken their adieu and turn their faces homeward, ever to remember the affecting and impressive scenes which they have witnessed. The injunction, so often repeated on the way, "Bear him gently to his rest," has been obeyed, and the great heart of the nation throbs heavily at the portals of the tomb.

FELLOW-CITIZENS OF ILLINOIS AND OF MANY PARTS OF OUR

ENTIRE UNION:[49] Near the capital of this large and growing State of Illinois, in the midst of this beautiful grove and at the open mouth of the vault which has just received the remains of our fallen Chieftain, we gather to pay a tribute of respect and drop the tears of sorrow around the ashes of the mighty dead.

A little more than four years ago, from his plain and quiet home in yonder

FREEDOM TO THE SLAVES

city, he started, receiving the parting words of the concourse of friends who gathered around him and in the middle of the dropping of the gentle shower he told of the pains of parting from the place where his children had been born and his home had been made so pleasant by early recollections. And as he left he made an earnest request in the hearing of some who are present, that as he was about to enter upon responsibilities which he believed to be greater than any which had fallen upon any man since the days of Washington, the people would offer up their prayers that God would aid and sustain him in the work they had given him to do.

His company left your quiet city. But as it went, snares were in waiting for the Chief Magistrate. Scarcely did he escape the dangers of the way or the hands of the assassin as he neared Washington;[50] and I believe he escaped only through the vigilance of the officers and the prayers of the people; so that the blow was suspended for more than four years, which was at last permitted, through the providence of God, to fall. How different the occasion which

49   Matthew Simpson (1811 - 1884) was a friend and spiritual advisor of Lincoln and a Bishop of the Methodist Episcopal Church. His funeral address begins here. The *Times* printed it as a single paragraph. It is broken into several here for ease of reading.

50   Warned by Allan Pinkerton that there was a plot to stab him as he came through Baltimore on his way to his first inauguration in 1861, Lincoln sneaked through the city by night in a horse-drawn railroad car. He was ridiculed as a coward for many years. The existence of a real conspiracy has never been proven.

witnessed his departure and that which witnessed his return! Doubtless you expected to take him by the hand, to feel the warm grasp which you felt in other days, and to see the tall form walking among you which you had delighted to honor in years past. But he was never permitted to return until he came with lips mute and silent, his frame encoffined, and a weeping nation following as his mourners.

Such a scene as his return to you was never witnessed among the events of history. There have been great processions of mourners. There was one for the patriarch Jacob, which came up from Egypt, and the Egyptians wondered at the evidences of reverence and filial affection which came from the hearts of the Israelites. There was mourning when Moses fell upon the heights of Pisgah and was hid from human view. There have been mournings in the kingdoms of the earth when kings and warriors have fallen. But never was there in the history of man such mourning as that which has accompanied the funeral procession, and has gathered around the mortal remains of him who was our loved one, and who now sleeps among us.

If we glance at the procession which followed him we see how the nation stood aghast. Tears filled the eyes of many sunburnt faces. Strong men, as they clasped the hands of their friends, were unable to find vent for their grief in words. Women and little children caught up the tidings as they ran through the land and were melted into tears. The nation stood still. Men left their plows in the fields, and asked what the end would be. The hum of manufactures ceased, and the sound of the hammer was not heard. Busy merchants closed their doors, and in the Exchange gold passed no more from hand to hand.

Three weeks have passed. The nation has scarcely breathed easily yet. A mournful silence is abroad upon the land. Nor is this mourning confined to any class or to any district of the country. Men of all political parties and of all religious creeds seem united in paying this mournful tribute. The Archbishop of the Roman Catholic Church in New-York and a Protestant minister walked side by side in the sad procession, and a Jewish Rabbi performed a part of the solemn service. There are gathered around his tomb representatives of the army and navy, Senators, Judges, Governors and officers of all the branches of the government and members of all the civic associations, with men and women from the humblest as well as the highest occupations. Here and there, too, are tears, as sincere and warm as any that drop, which come from the eyes of those whose kindred and whose race have been freed from their chains by him whom they mourn as their deliverer. Far more have gazed on the face of the departed than ever looked upon the face of any other departed man. More eyes have looked upon the procession for sixteen hundred miles or more, by night and by day, by sunlight, dawn, twilight and by torchlight, than ever before watched the progress of a procession.

We ask why this wonderful mourning; this great procession. I answer: First, a part of the interest has arisen from the times in which we live, and in which he that had fallen was a principal actor. It is a principle of our nature that feelings once excluded from the object by which they are excited, turn readily to some other object, which may for the time being take possession of the mind. Another principle is that the deepest affections of our hearts gather around some human form in which are incarnated the loving thoughts and ideas of the passing age. If we look then at the times, we see an age of excitement. For four years the popular heart has been stirred to its utmost depth. War had come upon us, dividing families; separating nearest and dearest friends -- a war, the extent and magnitude of which, no one could estimate -- a war in which the blood of brethren was shed by a brother's hand. A call for soldiers was made by the voice now hushed, and all over this land, from hill to mountain, from plain to valley, they sprang up, hundreds of thousands of bold hearts, ready to go forth and save our national Union.

This feeling of excitement was transferred next into a feeling of deep grief, because of the dangers in which our country was placed. Many said: Is it possible to save our nation? Some in our country, and nearly all the leading men in other countries, declared it to be impossible to maintain the Union, and many an honest heart was deeply pained with apprehensions of common ruin, and many in grief, and almost in despair, anxiously inquired what shall the end of these things be. In addition, the wives had given their husbands, mothers their sons. In the pride and joy of their hearts, they saw them put on the uniform, they saw them take the martial step, and they tried to hide their deep feelings of sadness. Many dear ones slept on the battle-field, never, never, to return again; and there was mourning in every mansion and in every cabin in our broad land. Then came a feeling to deepen sadness, as the story came of prisoners tortured to death or starved through the mandates of those who are called the representatives of the chivalry, or who claim to be the honorable ones of the earth; and as we read the stories of frames attenuated and reduced to mere skeletons, our grief turned partly into honor and partly into a cry for vengeance.

Then the feeling was changed to one of joy. There came signs of the end of this rebellion. We followed the career of our glorious Generals. We saw our army under the command of the brave officer who is guiding this procession, climb up the heights of Lookout Mountain and drive the rebels from their strongholds. Another brave General swept through Georgia, South and North Carolina, and drove the combined armies of the rebels before him; while the honored Lieutenant-General held Lee and his hosts in a death grasp. Then the tidings came that Richmond was evacuated, and that Lee had surrendered. The bells rang merrily all over the land. The booming of cannon was heard. Illuminations and torchlight processions manifested the general joy, and families were looking for the speedy return of their loved ones from the field of battle.

Just in the midst of the wildest joy, in one hour -- nay, in one moment -- the tidings rang throughout the land that Abraham Lincoln, the best of Presidents, had perished by the hand of an assassin. And then all that feeling which had been gathering for four years in forms of excitement, grief, honor and joy, turned into one wail of woe -- a sadness inexpressible; anguish unutterable. But it is not the time, merely, which caused this mourning; the mode of his death must be taken into account. Had he died on a bed of illness with kind friends around him; had the sweat of death been wiped from his brow by gentle hands while he was yet conscious; could he have had the power to speak words of affection to his stricken widow; words of counsel to us like those which we heard in his parting for Washington, in his Inaugural, which shall now be immortal -- how it would have softened or assuaged something of the grief! There might at least have been preparation for the event. But no moment of warning was given to him or to us. He was stricken down when his hopes for the end of the rebellion were bright and the prospects of a joyous life were before him. There was a Cabinet meeting that day, said to have been the most cheerful and happy of any held since the beginning of the rebellion. After this meeting he talked with his friends, and spoke of the four years of tempest, of the storm being over, and of the four years of pleasure and joy now awaiting him, as the weight of care and anguish would be taken from his mind, and he could have happy days with his family again. In the midst of these anticipations, he left his house never to return alive. Though the evening was Good Friday, the saddest day in the calendar for the Christian church -- henceforth in this country to be made sadder if possible by the memory of our nation's loss. And so filled with grief was every Christian's heart that even all the joyous thought of Easter Sunday, failed to remove the crushing sorrow, under which the true worshiper bowed in the house of God.

But the great cause of this mourning is to be found in the man himself. Mr. Lincoln was no ordinary man, and I believe the conviction has been growing on the nation's mind, as it certainly has been on my own, especially in the last years of his administration. By the hand of God, he was especially singled out to guide our government in these troublesome times, and it seems to me that the hand of God may be traced in many of the events connected with his history.

First, then, I recognize this in his physical education which he received, and which prepared him for enduring Herculean labors in the toils of his boyhood and the labors of his manhood. God was giving him an iron form.

Next to this was his identification with the heart of the great people -- understanding their feelings, because he was one of them, and connected with them in their movements and life. His education was simple; a few months spent in the school-house gave him the elements of education. He read few books, but mastered all he read. Bunyan's Progress[51] and the Life of Washington[52] were his favorites. In these we recognize the works which gave the bias to his character, and which partly moulded his style. His early life with its varied struggles joined him indissolubly to the weeping masses, and no elevation in society diminished his respect for the sons of toil. He knew what it was to fell the tall trees of the forest and to stem the current of the hard Mississippi. His home was in the growing West, the heart of the republic, and invigorated by the wind which swept over its groves he learned the lesson of self-reliance which sustained him in seasons of adversity. His genius was soon recognized as true genius always will be. He was placed in the Legislature of a State. Already acquainted with the principles of law, he devoted his thoughts to matters of public interest.

[The report is unfinished in consequence of the bad working of the wires.][53]

* * * * *

The New-York Tribune
Saturday, May 6, 1865

Address of Bishop Simpson

SPRINGFIELD, Ill., Friday, May 5, 1865

The following is the concluding portion of Bishop Simpson's address at the grave of the late President Lincoln:

Already acquainted with the principles of law, he devoted his thoughts to matters of public interest and began to be looked on as the coming statesman.

---

51   John Bunyan's *The Pilgrim's Progress from This World to That Which Is to Come* has been in print since 1678.

52   *The Life of Washington*, a five-volume biography by Chief Justice John Marshall (1755 - 1835).

53   The *Times* did not run the rest of the sermon, but the next day it appeared in the *New-York Tribune,* which had run the first part on May 5, suffering the same problem with the telegraph lines. The *Tribune* version is quite different from later published versions. Many words and phrases are left out, some paragraphs out of order, and the final paragraph did not appear. (That paragraph has been added here for the sake of a satisfying conclusion.)

As early as 1849 he presented resolutions in the Legislature asking for emancipation in the District of Columbia, although, with rare exceptions, the whole popular mind of his State was opposed to the measure.

From that hour he was a steady and uniform friend of humanity and was preparing for the conflict of later years. If you ask on what mental characteristic his greatness rested, I answer on a quick and ready perception of facts and a memory unusually tenacious and retentive, and on a logical turn of mind which followed sterlingly and unwaveringly every link in the chain of thought on any subject which he was called on to investigate.

I think there have been minds more decided in their character, more comprehensive in their scope, but I doubt if there has been a man which could follow step by step with logical power the points which he desired to illustrate. He gained the power by a close study of geometry and by a determination to persevere in the truth. It is said of him that in childhood, when he had any difficulty in listening to a conversation to ascertain what people meant, if he retired to rest he could not sleep till he tried to understand the precise points intended, and when understood to convey it in a clear manner to those who had listened with him.

Who that has read his message fails to perceive the directness and the simplicity of his style and this very trait which was scoffed at and derided by his opposers is now recognized as one of the strong points of that mighty mind which has so powerfully influenced the destiny of this nation, and which shall for ages to come influence the destiny of humanity. It is not, however, chiefly by his mental faculties that he gained such control over mankind. His moral power gave him prominence. The convictions of men that Abraham Lincoln was an honest man led them to yield to his guidance.

As has been said of Cobden, whom he greatly respected, he made all men feel and own the sense of himself, and recognized in him, individually, a self-relying power. They saw in him a man whom they believed would do that which was right, regardless of all consequences. It was this moral feeling which gave him the greatest hold on the people, and made his utterances almost oracular. When the nation was angered by the perfidy of foreign Powers, in allowing privateers to be fitted out, he uttered the significant expression, "One war at a time," and it stilled the national heart. When his own friends were divided as to what steps should be taken as to Slavery, that simple utterance, "I will save the Union if I can with Slavery, but if not, Slavery must perish, for the Union must be preserved," became the rallying word. Men felt that the struggle was for the Union, and all other questions must be subsidiary. But after all the acts of a man, shall his fall be perpetuated? What are his acts? Much praise is due to the men who aided him. He called able counselors around him and the generals into the field — men who have borne the sword as bravely as ever any human arm has borne it. He had the aid of prayerful and thoughtful men everywhere. But under his own guiding hands the movements of our land have been conducted.

Turn toward the different departments. We had an unorganized militia — a mere skeleton army, yet under his care that army has been enlarged into a force which for skill, intelligence, efficiency and bravery surpasses any which the world has ever seen. Before its veterans the renowned veterans of Napoleon shall pale (applause), and the mothers and sisters on these hillsides and all over the land shall take to their arms again braver men than ever fought in European wars.

The reason is obvious: money or a desire for fame collected their armies, or they were rallied to sustain favorite theories or dynasties; but the armies he called into being fought for Liberty, for the Union, and for the right of self-government; and many of them felt that the battles they won were for humanity everywhere, and for all time, for I believe that God has not suffered this terrible Rebellion to come upon our land merely for a chastisement to us or a lesson to our age. There are moments which involve in themselves eternities. There are instants which seem to contain germs which shall develop and bloom forever. Such a moment comes in the tide of time to our land when a question must be settled. The powers of affliction, all the earth, the contest, was for human freedom — not for the Republic merely, not for the Union simply, but to decide whether the people, as a people, in their entire majesty were destined to be the government, or whether they were to be subjects of tyrants, or autocrats, or to class-rule of any kind.

This is the question for which we have been fighting, and its decision is at hand, and the result of the contest will affect the ages to come. If successful, Republics will spread, in spite of monarchism, all over this earth. [Exclamations of "Amen!" "Thank God!"] I turn from the Army to the Navy. What was it when the war commenced? Now we have our ships of war at home and abroad, to guard privateers in foreign sympathizing ports as well as to take care of every part of our own coast. They have taken forts that military men said could not be taken, and a brave Admiral, for the first time in the world's history, lashes himself to the mast, there to remain as long as he had a particle of skill or strength to watch over his ship while it engaged in the perilous contest of taking the strong forts of the enemy.

I turn to the Treasury Department. Where should the money come from? Wise men predicted ruin, but our National credit has been maintained, and our currency is safer today than it ever was before. Not only is this so, but through our National bonds, if properly used, we shall have a permanent basis for our currency; and they are also an investment so desirable for capitalists of other nations, that under the laws of trade, I believe, the centre of exchange will be transferred from England to the United States.

But the great act of the mighty chieftain, on which his fame shall rest long after his frame shall moulder away, is that of giving freedom to a race. We have all been taught to revere the sacred character of Moses, of his power and the prominence he gave to the moral law, how it lasts, and how his name towers among the names in Heaven, and how he delivered three millions of his kindred out of bondage, and yet we may assess that Abraham Lincoln, but his proclamation, liberated more enslaved people than ever Moses set free, and those not of his kindred or his race. Such a power or such an opportunity, God has seldom given to man.

When other events shall have been forgotten, when this world shall have become a net-work of republics, when every throne shall be swept from the face of the earth, when literature shall enlighten all minds, when the claims of humanity shall be recognized everywhere, this act shall still be conspicuous on the pages of history; and we are thankful that God gave Abraham Lincoln the decision, wisdom and grace to issue that Proclamation which stands high above all other papers which have been penned by uninspired men. [Applause.]

Abraham Lincoln was a good man. He was known as an honest, temperate, forgiving man, a just man, a man of noble heart in every way; as to his religious experience I cannot speak definitely, because I was not privileged to know much of his private sentiments.

My acquaintance with him did not give me the opportunity to hear him speak on this topic. I know, however, he read the Bible frequently; loved it for its great truths and for its profound teachings and he tried to be guided by its precepts. He believed in Christ, the Saviour of Sinners, and I think he was sincerely trying to bring life into the principles of revealed religion. Certainly if there ever was a man who illustrated some of the principles of pure religion, that man was our departed President. Look over all his speeches. Listen to his utterances. He never spoke unkindly of any man; even the Rebels received no words of anger from him, and the last day illustrated, in a remarkable manner, his forgiving disposition. A dispatch was received that afternoon that Thompson[54] and Tucker[55] were trying to make their escape through Maine and it was proposed to arrest them. Mr. Lincoln, however, preferred rather to let them quietly escape, and this morning we read the Proclamation offering twenty-thousand dollars each for the arrest of these men, as aiders and abettors of his assassination. So that in his expiring acts he was saying, "Father, forgive them; they know not what they do." As a rule I doubt if any President has ever shown such trust in God or in public documents so frequently referred to Divine aid. Often did he remark to friends and to delegations that his hope for our success rested in his conviction that God would bless our efforts because

---

54   Jacob Thompson (1810 - 1885) was a Congressman and then U.S. Secretary of the Interior but resigned in January, 1861, just before the war broke out. He served as inspector general of the Confederate army. He led a delegation to Canada, from where he devised various plots that never worked out, including the burning of New York. He was reputed to have conspired with Booth, but it was never proven. He fled to England after the war.

55   Nathaniel Beverly Tucker associated with the confederates in Montreal but denied any involvement or knowledge of the conspiracy. He remained in Canada until 1872 and was never put on trial.

we were trying to do right. To the address of a large religious body he replied, "Thanks be unto God, who, in our national trials, giveth us the churches." To a minister who said he hoped the Lord was on our side, he replied that it gave him no concern whether the Lord was on our side or not, for, he added, "I know that the Lord is always on the side of the right," and with a deep feeling, added, "But God is my witness that it is my constant anxiety and prayer, that both myself and this nation should be on the Lord's side." In his domestic life he was exceedingly kind and affectionate. He was a devoted husband and father. During his Presidential term he lost a second son, Willie. To an officer of the army he said, not long since: "Do you ever find yourself talking with the dead?" and added, "Since Willie's death I catch myself every day involuntarily talking with him, as if he were with me." On his widow, who is unable to be here, I need only invoke the blessing of Almighty God that she may be comforted and sustained. For his son, who has witnessed the exercises of this hour, all that I can desire is that the mantle of his father may fall upon him. [Exclamations of "Amen."] Let us pause a moment in the lesson of the hour before we part. This man, though he fell by the hand of an assassin, still he fell under the permissive hand of God. He had some wise purpose in allowing him to fall. What more could he have desired of life for himself? Were not his honors full? There was no office to which he could aspire. The popular heart clung around him as around no other man. The nations of the world have learned to honor him. If rumors of a desired alliance with England be true, Napoleon trembled when he heard of the fall of Richmond, and asked what nation would join him to protect him against our Government. Beside the goodness of such a man, his fame was full, his work was done, and he sealed his glory by becoming the nation's great martyr for liberty. He appears to have had a strange presentiment early in political life, that some day he would be President. You see it, indeed, in 1839. Of the slave power he said: "Broken by it I, too, may be asked to bow to it. I never will. The probability that we may fail in the struggle ought not to deter us from the support of a cause which I deem to be just. It shall not deter me if I ever feel the soul within me elevate and expand to those dimensions not wholly unworthy of its Almighty architect. It is when I contemplate the cause of my country, deserted by all the world besides, and I standing up boldly and alone and hurling defiance at her vicarious oppressors. Here, without contemplating consequences, before high heaven and in the face of the world, I swear eternal fidelity to the just cause, as I deem it, of the land, of my life, my liberty and my love." And yet secretly, he said to more than one, "I never shall live out the four years of my term. When the Rebellion is crushed, my work is done." So it was. He lived to see the last battle fought and to dictate a despatch from the home of Jefferson Davis — lived till the power of the Rebellion was broken, and then, having done the work for which God has sent him, angels, I trust, were sent to shield him from one moment of pain or suffering, and to bear him from this world to that high and glorious realm where the patriot and the good shall live forever. His example teaches young men that every position of eminence is open before the diligent and the worthy, to the active men of the country. His example urges the country to trust in God and do right. Standing as we do to-day by his coffin and his sepulchre, let us resolve to carry forward the policy which he so nobly and wholly began. Let us do right to all men. Let us vow, in the sight of Heaven, to eradicate every vestige of human slavery, to give every human being his true position before God and man, to crush every form of rebellion, and to stand by the flag which God has given us. How joyful we ought to be that it floated over parts of every State before Mr. Lincoln's career was ended! How singular is the fact that the assassin's foot was caught in the folds of the flag, and that for this we are indebted for his capture! The flag and the traitor must ever be enemies. The traitors will probably suffer by the change of rulers, for one of sterner mold, who himself has deeply suffered from the Rebellion, now wields the sword of justice. Our country, too, is stronger for the trial through which it has passed. A republic was declared by monarchies too weak to endure a civil war; yet we have crushed the most gigantic rebellion in history, and have grown in strength and population every year of the struggle. We have passed through the ordeal of a popular election while swords and bayonets were in the field, and have come out unchanged, and now, in an hour of excitement, with a large minority having preferred another man for President, the bullet of the assassin has laid our President prostrate; has there been a mutiny? Has any rival proposed his claims? Out of an army of nearly a million of men, no officer or soldier has uttered one word of dissent, and in an hour or two after Mr. Lincoln's death, another leader, with constitutional powers, occupied his chair, and the Government moved forward without one single jar. The world will learn that republics are the strongest governments on earth. And now, my friends, in the words of the departed, "with malice toward none,"[56] free from all feeling of personal vengeance, yet believing the sword must not be drawn in vain, let us go forward in our painful duty. Let every man who was a Senator or Representative in Congress, and who aided in beginning this Rebellion, and thus led to the slaughter of our sons and daughters, be brought to speedy and certain punishment. Let every officer educated at public expense and who, having been advanced to position, has perjured himself and turned his sword against the vitals of his country be doomed to this. I believe in the will of the American people. Men may attempt to compromise and to restore these traitors and murderers to society again, but the American people will arise in their majesty and sweep all such compromises and compromisors away, and will declare that there shall be no peace to Rebels; but to the deluded masses we shall extend arms of forgiveness. We will take them to our hearts and walk with them side by side, as we go forward to work out a glorious destiny. The time will come when, in the beautiful words of him whose lips are now forever closed: "The mystic cords of memory, which stretch from every battle-field and from every patriot's grave shall yield a sweeter music when touched by the angels of our better nature."[57] To the ambitious there is this fearful lesson of the four candidates for Presidential honors of 1860. Two of them, Douglas and Lincoln, once competitors, but now sleeping patriots, rest from their

---

56   From the end of Lincoln's second inaugural address, "... With malice toward none; with charity for all; with firmness in the right, as God gives us to see the right, let us strive on to finish the work we are in..."

57   From the concluding paragraph of Lincoln's first inaugural address. The previous two sentences were: "We are not enemies, but friends. We must not be enemies. Though passion may have strained, it must not break, our bonds of affection." An earlier draft, nixed by Seward, had ended on a more threatening note that was aimed due south: "Shall it be peace or sword?"

labors. Bell perished in poverty and misery as a traitor might perish. And Breckinridge is a frightened fugitive with the brand of traitor on his brow. That will be vouched by the angels of our better nature. [Cries of "good, good."]

Chieftain, farewell! The nation mourns thee. Mothers shall teach thy name to their lisping children. The youth of our land shall emulate thy virtues. Statesmen shall study thy record and learn lessons of wisdom. Mute though thy lips be, yet they still speak. Hushed is thy voice, but its echoes of liberty are ringing through the world, and the sons of bondage listen with joy. Prisoned thou art in death, and yet thou art marching abroad, and chains and manacles are bursting at thy touch. Thou didst fall not for thyself. The assassin had no hate for thee. Our hearts were aimed at, our national life was sought. We crown thee as our martyr, and humanity enthrones thee as her triumphant son. Hero, Martyr, Friend, FAREWELL!

"The Emancipation Proclamation before the Cabinet," by Francis Bicknell Carpenter

July 8, 1865

Epilogue

Tried,
convicted
and sentenced,
they stood this morning
upon the threshold
of the house of death,

all covered
with the great sin
whose pall
fell darkly
upon the land.

Young and old,
equal in crime,
they spent the night
as is told hereafter,

and when the first grey pencillings
of the early morning
traced the dawning day upon the sky,
the city was all agog for the coming scene
of retribution
and of justice.

New-York Times
Saturday, July 8, 1865

END OF THE ASSASSINS;

Execution of Mrs. Surratt, Payne, Herrold and Atzeroth.

Their Demeanor on Thursday Night and Friday Morning.

Attempt to Release Mrs. Surratt on a Writ of Habeas Corpus.

Argument of Counsel — Order of the President.

SCENES AT THE SCAFFOLD.

The Four Hang Together and Die Simultaneously.

Interesting Incidents--Excitement in Washington--Order and Quiet in the
City.

Special Dispatch to the New-York Times.

WASHINGTON, Friday, July 7, 1865.

The conspirators have gone to their long home (sic), the swift hand of justice has smitten them, and they stand before the judgment seat. Electrified -- saddened as the country was by the terrible calamity brought upon it by the damnable deeds of these deep-dyed villains, astounded as it has been by the daily revelations of the trial of the criminals, it was doubtless unprepared, as were all here, for the quick flash of the sword of power, whose blade to-day fell upon the guilty heads of the assassins of our lamented President.

Tried, convicted and sentenced, they stood this morning upon the threshold of the house of death, all covered with the great sin whose pall fell darkly upon the land. Young and old, equal in crime, they spent the night as is told hereafter, and when the first grey pencillings of the early morning traced the dawning day upon the sky, the city was all agog for the coming scene of retribution and of justice.

Mrs. SURRATT's friends have been constant and faithful. They have manipulated presses and created public sentiment. The papers received here to-day were singularly unanimous in the supposition that the President would

424

commute the sentence of Mrs. SURRATT to imprisonment for life. Such a sentiment found no echo here. It was well known that the counsel, family and friends of the culprit were determined to make every exertion, to strain every nerve in a strong pull and tug at the tender heart of the President in her behalf. She was a woman, and a sick woman at that. Her daughter was with her, and her cowardly son, with secrets in his possession that might mitigate her guilt -- these and like arguments, it was said, would be brought to bear upon the President, backed with certain political strength which could not fail to succeed. But such talk has seemed idle from the first. Woman as she was, she knew her business well; sick as she was, she had strength sufficient for her fearful purpose, and stern as the sentence was, its justice was absolute, its execution certain. We have heard many express the desire that the woman's life might be spared and its weary hours passed in the quiet of the prison, but no one who knew the President and his unmoveable nature supposed for an instant that the sentence would be changed in jot or tittle.

The hotels were thronged on Thursday. The streets were filled with restless, impatient people. The headquarters were surrounded by crowds of anxious men, who desired above all things to witness the execution, and who were willing to spend hundreds of dollars for that poor privilege. All day long the trains came in loaded with people from the North; all night long the country roads were lined with pedestrians, with parties hurrying on to the city, where they might at least participate in the excitements of the occasion.

Officials of every grade and name, with or without influence, were pestered by applications for tickets; the subordinate officers of the department were approached in every conceivable way, and by every possible avenue, by those whose idle or morbid curiosity impelled them to come to this hot and sweltering city in search of food for gossip and remembrance. Of course all endeavor was futile. Major-Gen. HANCOCK, who had charge of everything, had carefully prepared the list of people entitled to admission, and beyond those thereon named, no one was permitted to be present.

The[58]

---

58   This is the way this sentence was presented.

SCENES AT THE OLD CAPITOL

Prison[59] on Thursday night were by no means so harrowing in intensity as the public doubtless imagine. So far as the authorities were concerned, there was possibly an increased vigilance, and extra precautions were taken with Mrs. SURRATT; but beyond that, matters went along quite in accordance with the general custom.

MRS. SURRATT

about whose fearful participation in the murder of the President there has been thrown so much mystery, was a very remarkable woman, and, like most remarkable women, had an undertone of superstition which served her in place of true religion, and enabled her to sleep peacefully even while cognizant of such a crime as that for which she has now suffered. She was fifty years of age, but, although since her illness of the past two weeks she has grown old and looked pale and thin, she would be called rather forty-two or three. Firmness and decision were part and parcel of her nature. A cold eye, that would quail at no scene of torture; a close, shut mouth, whence no word of sympathy with suffering would pass; a firm chin, indicative of fixedness of resolve; a square, solid figure, whose proportions were never disfigured by remorse or marred by loss of sleep -- these have ever marked the personnel of MARY SURRATT -- these, her neighbors say, were correct indices of her every-day and every-year life.

Those who have watched her through the whole of this protracted trial have noticed her utter indifference to anything and everything said or suggested about her. The most terrible flagellation produced no effect upon her rocky countenance, stolid, quiet, entirely self-possessed, calm as a May morning, she sat, uninterested from the opening to the close.

Her guardians say she anticipated an acquittal, she alone knew why. When, therefore, she was informed of the finding of the court, the sentence, and its near execution, she might well be roused from the state of utter listlessness she had thitherto maintained. Weakened by continued illness, with head stunned by the sudden blow, she for a moment forgot the Surratt in the

---

59   Yes, this is how the sentence and subhead were presented.

woman, and felt the keenness of her position. Fainting, she cried aloud in the bitterness of her woe, wailing forth great waves of sorrow, she fell upon the floor and gave vent to a paroxysm of grief, partially hysterical, and wholly nervous. This was so unlike her, so entirely different from any conduct previously noticed that the officer and her attendants were alarmed for her life. They sent at once for the regular physician of the arsenal, who pronounced her system deranged and dangerously prostrated. Wine of valerian and other quieting drink was given her, and she revived, but no longer was she the Mrs. SURRATT of the court-room. She desired to see her spiritual advisers, and they were sent for. The sacred vail of ghostly comfort should not be rudely rent nor lightly lifted, but we may state with entire propriety that the miserable woman expressed the most emphatic desire for prayer and holy consolation. Desirous of clearing her mind first of all worldly affairs, she indicated the disposition she wished made of her property, and talked long and earnestly of her children and their future prospects. Toward her cowardly son JOHN she quite naturally

John H. Surratt's Jury of 1867

427

entertained feelings of deep-seated bitterness. This she in a measure overcame after having relieved her mind about him and his conduct, and finally appeared reconciled to his desertion. What the feelings of the scoundrel must be to-day we cannot well imagine. If, as Mrs. SURRATT's friends more than intimated, his testimony would save her, if, as his own offer proved, his revelations would keep her from a death of infamy, we cannot believe he will dare survive her. Suicide and the unknown possibilities of the future, would seem preferable to life and the certain remorse and disgrace attending it here.

As the night wore on Mrs. SURRATT, who had been removed from the larger room where she has been confined since her illness, began to toss uneasily on her narrow bed. She was really ill and the kind offices of the physician were frequently needed. Conscious of the approach of day, she betook herself again to the preparation of her soul for its infinite journey. She rallied mentally and physically and determined evidently to bear and brave the scaffold. Her daughter, whose faithful service has been most touching in its constancy, had done all she could. The President had been seen, Judge HOLT[60] had been visited. To both of them the most fervent appeals, inspired by a filial love as devoted as it was disinterested, had been presented, but in vain. Five of the members of the court had joined in a recommendation for commutation to imprisonment for life, and it was understood that the entire court concurred in the same, but this too was in vain. These facts the heartbroken daughter had communicated to her sentenced mother, and as she bent her head upon her neck she bathed her shoulders with tears of unfeigned grief and sympathy.

Seemingly convinced of the utter hopelessness of her situation, and apparently desirous of quieting the exceedingly demonstrative outbursts of her daughter, Mrs. SURRATT rose from her bed and again betook herself to her devotional exercises. It may seem strange that this woman, who was proven to know all about the projected assassination, who kept open house for the scoundrels who planned and the villains who did the deed, who insisted that she had never seen and never knew PAYNE, and who said, when informed of

---

60   Joseph Holt, (1807 - 1894), as judge advocate general, was chief prosecutor of the eight defendants. He was sympathetic to Southern principles but supported the Union

her sentence, "I had no hand in the murder of the President," should seem so calm and consistent in her preparation for death. Neverthless the fact is that after turning her back upon hope, she gave herself with apparent sincerity and with heartiness to prayer and communion, the effect of which it is not for us to judge.

This morning, however, the counsel of Mrs. SURRATT, Messrs. AIKEN and CLAMPITT,[61] who had determined to leave no stone unturned to effect her release, or if not that a detention in the execution of sentence, went at an early hour before Judge WYLIE,[62] of the Supreme Court of this city, and applied for a writ of habeas corpus, directed to Maj.-Gen. HANCOCK,[63] who had charge of the prison and control of the prisoners, commanding him to bring into Court the body of MARY E. SURRATT. The

READING OF THE PETITION

is as follows:

To the Hon. Andrew Wylie, one of the Justices of the Supreme Court of the District of Columbia:

The petition of MARY E. SURRATT by her counsel, F.A. AIKEN and JNO. W. CLAMPITT, most respectfully represents unto your Honor that, on or about the 17th day of April, A.D. 1865, your petitioner was arrested by the military authorities of the United States, under the charge of complicity with the murder of ABRAHAM LINCOLN, late President of the United States, and has ever since that time been, and is now confined on said charge, under and by virtue of the said military power of the United States, and is in the especial custody of Major-Gen. W.S. HANCOCK, commanding Middle Military Division, that since her said arrest, your petitioner has been tried against her solemn protest, by a military commission, unlawfully and without warrant, convened by the Secretary of War, as will appear from paragraph nine, Special Orders No. 211, dated War Department, Adjutant-General's Office, Washington,

---

61   Frederick Argyle Aiken (1837 - 1878) and John Wesley Clampitt (1839 - 1885) were Mary' Surrat's attorneys. Their primary defense was that she was a good woman, her accusers liars. When that failed, they served a writ of habeas corpus, pleading that as a civilian, she should not be under military trial. That argument, too, failed.

62   Andrew B. Wylie, justice of the Supreme Court of Washington, D.C.

63   Major General Winfield Scott Hancock (1824 - 1886) was in charge of the Old Capitol prison, its prisoners, and the court facility there.

May 6, 1865; and by said commission notwithstanding her formal plea to the jurisdiction of the said commission is now unlawfully and unjustifiably detained in custody, and sentenced to be hanged on to-morrow, July 7, 1865, between the hours of 10 A.M. and 2 P.M., your petitioner shows unto your Honor that at the time of the commission of the said offence she was a private citizen of the United States, and in no manner connected with the military authority of the same, and that said offence was committed within the District of Columbia, said District being at the time within the lines of the armies of the United States, and not enemy's territory or under the control of a military commander for the trial of civil causes, but on the contrary, your petitioner alleges that the said crime was an offence simply against the peace of the United States, properly and solely cognizable, under the constitution and laws of the United States, by the Criminal Court of this District, and which said court was and is now open for the trial of such crimes and offences. Wherefore, inasmuch as the said crime was only an offence against the peace of the United States, and not an act of war, inasmuch as your petitioner was a private citizen of the same, and not subject to military jurisdiction, or in any wise amenable to military law, inasmuch as said District was the peaceful territory of the United States, and that all crimes committed within such territory are under the constitution and laws of the United States, to be tried only before its criminal tribunals with the right of public trial by jury. Inasmuch as said commission was a military commission, organized and governed by the laws of military court-martial, and unlawfully convened without warrant or authority, and when she had not the right of public trial by jury as guaranteed to by the constitution and laws of the United States; that therefore her detention and sentence are so without warrant against positive law and unjustifiable, wherefore, she prays your Honor to grant unto her the United States most gracious writ of habeas corpus, commanding the said Major-Gen. W.S. HANCOCK to produce before your Honor the body of your said petitioner, with the cause and day of her said detention to abide, &c., and she will ever pray.

(Signed,) MARY E. SURRATT.
By FREDERICK A. AIKEN, JNO. W. CLAMPITT.

After hearing the argument, the Judge indorsed upon the petition:

Let the writ issue as prayed, returnable before the Criminal Court of the District of Columbia, now sitting, at the hour of ten o'clock A.M., this seventh day of July, 1865.

(Signed,) ANDREW WYLIE,

A Justice of the Supreme Court of the District of Columbia.

JULY 7, 1865, AT 3 O'CLOCK A.M.

The writ was then formally issued, and the Marshal of the District was directed to serve it. The news spread like wildfire, and all sorts of reports were circulated throughout the city. The hotels swarmed with talkative people, every one of whom had the latest news, and was only too ready to communicate it to his neighbor. "Mrs. SURRATT is pardoned," "She is not expected to live," "Her sentence has been commuted." Everyone had his pet theory, but it concerned Mrs. SURRATT alone -- the fate of the others seemed certain.

THE RETURN

was ordered at 10 o'clock, and at that hour the court room was thronged with people interested to know the result. The Marshal, in response to a question by the court, stated that Major-Gen. HANCOCK had not yet appeared, although it was past the hour.

After sundry criticisms and objections to the proceedings by the District-Attorney, the counsel for Mrs. SURRATT stated that if his client was guilty of any crime, she was amenable to this court, a court which was competent to take cognizance of the same, and not to a military tribunal.

The District Attorney Mr. CARRINGTON,[64] after reading the certificate of the Marshal, stating that he had served the writ on Gen. HANCOCK, at 8:30 o'clock, said that he appeared to defend the action of the Marshal by direction of the court, and he desired to report to the court, that the Marshal had done his duty.

---

64   Edward M. Carrington would later pursue every possibility of convicting Mary's fugitive son John.

The Court:

"The case is not now here on its merits. On the petition of the party this morning at an early hour, I directed this writ of habeas corpus to issue. The writ was issued and was served upon Gen. HANCOCK, who has the custody of Mrs. SURRATT, the party on whose behalf the writ was obtained. The writ required him to have the body of Mrs. SURRATT with the cause of her detention before this court this morning at 10 o'clock, he has neglected to obey the order of the court, and the question now before us is what is the court to do under the circumstances. That is the only question before the court at this time. Any discussion on the merits involved would now be out of place. The court acknowledges that its powers are inadequate to meet the military power possessed by Gen. HACOCK. If the court were to decide at this moment that Gen. HANCOCK was in contempt, the only process which it would issue, would be an attachment for the disregard of its authority; but why issue an attachment against the whole military power of the United States? This Court acknowledges that the laws are silent, and that it is without power in the premises, and therefore declines to make any order whatever. If there be a disposition on the part of the military power to respect the authority of the civil courts, they will respect the writ which has already been served; if on the other hand it is their determination to treat the authority of this court with contempt, in this matter they have the power, and will treat with equal contempt any other process which the court might order. The court therefore must submit to the supreme physical power which now holds the custody of petitioner, and declines to issue an attachment or to make any other order in this case.

After these remarks the court proceeded with the trial of Miss HARRIS, [65]which was continued until 11:30 o'clock, when

GEN. HANCOCK,

accompanied by Attorney-General SPEED.[66] The trial was at once suspended, and the Attorney-General addressed the court as follows:

---

65   An odd error. Mrs. Surratt was the only woman on trial, and there was no one named Harris.

66   James Speed (1812 - 1887),U.S. attorney general, argued that the conspirators could be tried by military tribunal because they were "enemy belliqerents."

"May it please the Court in regard to the writ of habeas corpus, directed to Gen. HANCOCK, I desire to say by way of apology for his not sooner making a return, that the process wabs not served on him until about breakfast time this morning, and that, owing to his having a great many persons to see, a great many important matters requiring immediate attention, and his distance from the court-house, he was not able to get here at an earlier hour, I wish to assure the court that no disrespect was intended to it by delay to which it has been unavoidably subjected.

The Court declined to make any order in the case.

ATTORNEY-GENERAL -- Gen. HANCOCK, in obedience to the writ, makes the following return:

HEADQUARTERS MIDDLE MILITARY DIVISION, WASHINGTON, D.C., July 7, 1865.

To Hon. Andrew Wylie, Justice of the Supreme Court of the District of Columbia:

I hereby acknowledge the service of the writ hereto attached, and return the same, and respectfully say that the body of MARY E. SURRATT is in my possession under and by virtue of an order of ANDREW JOHNSON, President of the United States and Commander-in-Chief of the Army and Navy, for the purposes in said order expressed, a copy of which is hereto attached and made part of this return. And that I do not produce said body by reason of the order of the President of the United States indorsed upon said writ to which reference is hereby respectfully made. Dated July 7, 1865.

(Signed,) WINFIELD S. HANCOCK,
Major-Gen. United States Vols., Commanding.

PRESIDENT'S INTERVENTION

EXECUTIVE OFFICE, July 7, 1865 -- 1 o'clock A.M.

To Major-Gen. W.S. Hancock, Commander, &c.:

I, ANDREW JOHNSON, President of the United States, do hereby declare that the writ of habeas corpus has been heretofore suspended in such cases as this, and I do hereby especially suspend this writ, and direct that you

433

proceed to execute the order heretofore given upon the judgement of this Military Commission, and you will give this order in return to this writ.

Signed, ANDREW JOHNSON, President.

THE COURT -- This court finds itself powerless to take any further action in the premises, and therefore declines to make orders which would be vain for any practical purpose. As regards the delay, it having been fully accounted for, the court has no fault to attach to the respondents in that respect.

ATTORNEY-GENERAL SPEED. -- It may not be out of order for me to say here that this whole subject has of course had the most earnest and anxious considerations of the Executive, and of the war-making power of the government. Everyman, upon reflection, and particularly every lawyer knows that war cannot be fought by due process of law, and armies cannot be maintained by the process of law: there must be armies, there must be battles of war; of war comes the law of war, and usage permits battles to be fought, permits human life to be taken without the judgment of the court, and without the process of the court it permits prisoners to be taken and prisoners to be held; and your Honor will not undertake to discharge them although the constitution says that human life shall not be taken, or man be deprived of his liberty or property without due process of law. Conflict of necessity comes up when war comes between the Executive and the judicial. If the war power in war does not transcend the civil, war is made for the maintenance of the civil power, that is, when peace comes, for the purpose of giving us the benefit of the civil. This country is now in the midst of a great war, and the Commander-in-Chief of the armies of the United States was slain in the discharge of his duties, and if the armies of the United States cannot, under the laws of war, protect its Commander-in-Chief from assassination, and if the laws and usages of war cannot protect by military law, its Commander-in-Chief from assassination and destruction. What has the government come to? The thing appears to me to be too plain for consideration, but as your Honor has disposed of the case, I only make these remarks for the purpose of satisfying your Honor that we have anx-

434

iously, and, I think, most naturally considered this matter, giving your Honor credit for having done what you regard to be your duty in this matter, and are very glad to hear that your Honor gives us credit for having done what we have done, and regarded to be our duty to the court. The writ was applied for and I had no authority to refuse to grant it. It is a writ dear and sacred to every lover of liberty, indispensable to the protection of citizens, and can only be constitutionally set aside in times of war and insurrection, when the public safety requires it, and in regard to offences committed in connection with the army or the militia when called into active service. With reference to the merits of this case, which has occupied so much of the attention of the public, and in fact of the whole civilian world. It would be out of place for the court to express any opinion; the case is not before it. The court can only say that it has no doubt the gentlemen connected with the government who have had the duty of conducting this trial are truly convinced in their own minds as to the manner in which they have performed their duties. I do not feel at liberty -- I could not. I dared not refuse to grant the writ. The return which has been made to the writ is from the President of the United States, and declares the writ of habeas corpus to be suspended in this case, as has been in other and similar cases, the Court has no further authority in the case. If the government desires to carry out its purpose in regard to the petitioner, the Court cannot prevent it, and I do not know that it would be possible ever hereafter to bring the case up for argument on this court, for if the petitioner be executed as designed, the body cannot be brought into court, and, therefore, there is an end of the case. The jurisdiction of this court yields to the suspension of the writ of habeas corpus from the President of the United States.

Gen. HANCOCK then asked leave to retire, which was granted, and he left in company with Attorney-General SPEED.

This settled the case, so far as Mrs. SURRATT was concerned, and word was at once sent to her that all hope was gone.

Concerning PAYNE or POWELL, as he called himself, there has been a great deal of unnecessary mystery and foolish surmisings. His name, so far as the public is concerned, is

LEWIS PAYNE

and if behind that he hid the honest name of a respectable family, the fact is one to his credit; but of that no one cares. He is dead; gone before the bar of a higher tribunal than that which last judged him, and with his future we have naught to do. The cool villainy, the absolute savagery of the fellow, has been consistent with the atrocity of his crime, until, with singular emotion, he became the apologist for his fellow-criminal, and the assailer of her son. By no means handsome, or of the romantic scoundrel stamp, PAYNE seems to have been a very common kind of person, with an exceedingly hard head and apparently no heart. No mere man would or could have deliberately cut and slashed the face of a sick and dying sufferer; it required the instinct of a demon and the temper of a brute to suggest and execute such a project. He was a species of idiot, an intelligent beast, with wit enough to understand his duty, sense enough to do it thoroughly, but unable to talk or maneuvre himself out of such a scrape as he fell into at the door of Mrs. SURRATT's house.

Throughout the trial he has been unmoved. Never sullen nor morose, he kept his eyes about him, seeing everybody and everything, but never for an instant admitting by sign or gesture that he recognized anything. The confinement didn't annoy him at all. Quite likely he would have enjoyed a night in the town, and been as ready for a spree or a murder as ever; but he rarely opened his mouth, and as rarely closed his eyes, which wandered around and around, as if in continual search for an object of rest.

In his cell, PAYNE manifested no different appearance. His conduct was the same everywhere and at all times. He was a fit tool for the hand that used him -- a reliable blade for a bloody purpose. At night he slept; in the morning he awoke early; his appetite was always good, and when the time for the meeting of the court was announced, he went along quietly as a lamb, as docile as an ox in yoke. When, therefore, his sentence was read to him, it was to be expected that his don't-care-ativeness, or stupidity, or sang froid, or whatever it may be termed, would still characterize him. He neither appeared surprised nor disappointed. Had he been pronounced "not guilty," it would have been the same -- until he was freed; then he might have developed differently, though that is mere conjecture, baseable upon no reliable data.

Doubly ironed, doubly guarded, PAYNE spent the day and night before his death. No future presented aught of hope or fear for him; no God or devil stared him in the face with searching scrutiny or tantalizing punishment. He simply felt nothing, and yet in the midst of apathy and indifference, we find him explaining that Mrs. SURRATT had nothing to do with the murder, inveighing against JOHN SURRATT as a coward and scoundrel who had deserted his mother, leaving her to die when he should fill her place, and expressing tenderest regret that any act of his should have brought her into trouble and put her life in jeopardy. It is difficult to reconcile these two phases of character, so entirely different. Common sence (sic) forbids the belief that he feigned stupidity and was in reality a man of birth and breeding, and it likewise scouts the theory that he was entitled to sympathy on account of idiocy. Declining to participate in any religious mummery, and wholly averse to any religious reality, he passed his last hours in quiet stupidity, exerting himself to please no one, caring apparently nothing, either for the people here or the probabilities of the hereafter. His body was a source of no earthly consideration. Until he died it was not his -- his keepers had it; after his death it was not his, and he did not care who had it. His friends, he said, lived in Florida. Before they could come, if they would, he would be gone, and the senseless clod which tenemented his seared soul would be en route to corruption. Why should he care? He didn't care.

One redeeming feature stood prominent. Noticing the kind consideration of Miss SURRATT toward her mother, PAYNE expressed regret that they should be compelled to part. He said he would do anything, say anything which could help Mrs. SURRATT, who was an innocent woman. He emerged from his brutism and became humane; he left his carelessness behind him and asserted the case of the mother against her recreant son; he forgot the idiot and resumed for the moment the attitude and intelligence of a man. With the clergymen he had but little to say. He seemed entirely careless as to his future, and down to the very last maintained his stolid, indifferent, hang-dog manner.

Perhaps there was more sympathy expressed for
DAVID E. HERROLD
than for any of the prisoners. He was young, thoughtless, light and trivial. He probably had never known a serious moment nor a sober thought. His following of BOOTH was very much such a companionship as a dog affords, and it seemed as if he might have been so thoroughly under the influence of that fascinating fiend as to be entirely non compos. The legal evidence against him was, however, clear and conclusive. As early as February last he was found to have been in confidential relations with the assassin, and was proved to have been present on several occasions at secret meetings with BOOTH, ATSEROTH and others of the conspirators. Once he was at Mrs. SURRATT's in company with them. He called with SURRATT and ATZEROTH at the tavern in Surratsville, and left the two carbines and ammunition which were taken away from the tavern by him and BOOTH on the night of the assassination. During their flight he acknowledged to WILLIE JETT and other rebel soldiers that he and BOOTH were the assassins of Mr. LINCOLN, and he was captured in the barn with Booth. His personal appearance was that of a boy of nineteen, dressed in a faded blue suit, in height about five feet four inches, dusky black, neglected hair, lively, dark hazel eyes, slight tufts of beard along the chin and jaws, and faintly surrounding the mouth, rather round face, full but not prominent nose, full lips, foolish, weak, confiding countenance, indicating but little intelligence, and not the faintest trace of ferocity. His sisters, who are apparently very estimable young women, labored with him, hoping to make some serious impression upon him, but in vain. He was full of levity almost to the very hour of his death. At the announcement of the finding of the court, HERROLD was unmoved. Indeed, none of the prisoners at first manifested any great concern -- HERROLD and PAYNE least of any. PAYNE was sullen and indifferent, HERROLD careless and free. After a little, when the later hours of

the night were passing silently by, he became more tractable and for the time left his habit of joking and gossiping, and when asked if he had any requests to make, desired that his body might be given to his family. With the clergyman he was ever respectful, but beyond a routine repetition of words and phrases seemed to know and care little more about the coming than the present world. Impressible to a remarkable degree, but equally elastic, he talked and wept with the ministers, but was as ready for a quib or a joke immediately after as ever. It is difficult to say he was not a responsible person, and yet he seemed more like a butterfly than a man. He was at no time manly in deportment, and his exit from this world, was in accordance with his variable temperament while in it.

GEORGE A. ATZEROTH

was a coward, mentally, morally and physically. He failed to grasp the magnitude of the conspiracy as unfolded to him by the leaders; he failed to accomplish his part of the assassination scheme, and he failed to make any one care a rap whether he lived or died. During the trial he was unconcerned; since his imprisonment, was peevish and full of complaints, and on the night before his death he was restless and uneasy. He couldn't sleep at all, and, unlike PAYNE, had no appetite. He was a poor, miserable fellow, and his death amounted to no more than did his life.

THE MORNING OF THE DAY

appeared, and with it came thousands of people from afar to witness the execution. They might as well have come to see GEORGE WASHINGTON, the one as easy as the other. As above stated, every person in any way connected with the government, was tortured and annoyed by applications for passes to the prison. This morning the crowd of besiegers again appeared before 7 o'clock, and most of them failing to receive the desired pass, the curious wended their way to the arsenal grounds, two miles distant, in the hot sun, there to renew their importunities. When we arrived at the latter place, about 10 o'clock, the streets and avenues were blocked up by hundreds of vehicles, and probably 2,000 lookers-on, whose only reward for their exposure and labor was a peep at the prison walls in the distance. Four and One-half-street, the thoroughfare leading directly to the arsenal, was strongly and thickly guarded from Pennsylvania-avenue to the arsenal lot, and at the entrance to the latter, and completely surrounding it, were numerous soldiers on guard. Entering the inclosure (sic), we found several regiments on duty -- in all, two brigades of HANCOCK's corps -- scattered here and there between the gates and the prison.

Pedestrians were flocking rapidly toward the building, and when we entered the latter, we found already several hundred persons -- a mixed assembly of civilians and military men. We learned that none of the prisoners had slept during the past night save PAYNE and HARROLD, both of whom had a sound, quiet rest of about two hours. None of them had eaten anything scarcely except PAYNE, who partook heartily of breakfast. During the night opiates had been given Mrs. SURRATT to produce rest, but without avail. The spiritual advisers and friends of the condemned left the prison shortly after 11 o'clock last night, and none returned until this morning, except Miss SURRATT, who remained with her mother from about midnight until 5 o'clock A.M. No confessions had been made. None, indeed, could have been expected from either PAYNE, HERROLD or ATZEROTH, who had already from time to time, given in the main, probably, the truthful account of their relations to the bloody tragedy in which they were participants. Mrs. SURRATT was the only one remaining who had not acknowledged the full measure of her guilt. She, it was rumored, had made a full confession to her confessor, but on inquiry we found her confession in preparation for receiving the sacrament, was confounded with an acknowledgment of guilt for publicity. She had hope up to almost the hour of her execution that her sentence would be respited, if not commuted, and she had apparently lost sight of her own interest in deep solicitude for her daughter, of whom she constantly talked, and repeatedly, frantically and with wringing of hands asked: "What will become of her -- what will be ANNA's[67] fate?"

---

67   Elizabeth Susanna "Anna" Surratt (1843 - 1904), Mary's daughter, lived in the boardinghouse on H St. She was arrested and held for a month, then released. She testified in defense of her mother.

440

STATEMENTS OF PAYNE.

PAYNE, last evening, informed Col. DODD, who has special charge of the prisoners, that so far as he knew, Mrs. SURRATT had nothing to do with the plot for assassination. Certainly she had never said a word to him on the subject, nor had any of his co-conspirators mentioned her in connection with the matter. She may have known what was going on, but to him she never disclosed her knowledge by word or act. That immediately after he had made the murderous attack upon Mr. SEWARD, he felt he had done wrong, and he had wandered around and slept in the woods that night, frequently feeling inclined to come to the city and give himself up. That when, finally, he was by hunger and loss of rest driven to Mrs. SURRATT's house he had doubts about his reception there and whether she would not deliver him to the officers of the law for punishment. Col. DODD, who has been constantly in conversation with PAYNE, recently says the latter has never varied from one straightforward, consistent story, claiming at all times that he was informed and believed that he was acting under an order from the rebel authorities, and did not, therefore, originally view his act as a murderous one. HERROLD says in the original plot to him was assigned the duty of shutting off the gas in the theatre, and he had once rehearsed the work with BOOTH; that, however, on the night of the assassination, he was only required to be in waiting near the Navy-yard Bridge to assist BOOTH in his escape.

These statements embrace substantially all the prisoners have given in the nature of confessions, other than what is found in the proofs and admissions on the trial.

DEMEANOR OF THE CONDEMNED

We were permitted to look in upon the cells on several occasions during the forenoon, and up to a few minutes before the execution. The four prisoners condemned to death were removed yesterday from the upper floor of the prison to a tier of cells on the first floor South. ATZEROTH occupied the eastern apartment, No. 151, Mrs. SURRATT the next West, No. 153, HERROLD, No. 155, and PAYNE, No. 157, thus leaving a vacant cell between each of the prisoners.

Our first observation of ATZEROTH, found him in company with the Rev. Mr. RUTLER, a Lutheran minister of the gospel. The prisoner was lying upon his bed an intent and quiet listener to the whisperings of the minister. At another time ATZEROTH seemed utterly unnerved and tossed about, frequently clasping his hands together and wringing them as in hopelessness and dispair. At noon and thereafter he became calmer and scarcely spoke or moved.

Mrs. SURRATT throughout the day continued in physical prostration, but grew calmer as the hour approached for execution. The parting between herself and daughter was borne with more fortitude than was expected of her, and whilst the latter swooned away, and was carried to an adjoining apartment senseless, Mrs. SURRATT appeared to rally in strength for the moment. Soon again, however, she lost strength, and when taken from her cell to the scaffold, she had to be almost literally lifted and borne along by the officers.

HERRODD's demeanor was somewhat after the manner he has shown from the commencement of the trial -- listlessness and lack of appreciation of his fearful position, with alternatives of serious reflection.

PAYNE was, throughout the day, quiet and firm, occasionally joining the Rev. Dr. GILLETTE in earnest prayer.

THE SCAFFOLD

In the lot south of the prison, and surrounded by a wall thirty feet high, the scaffold was erected. The structure is about seventy feet from the prison near by, say thirty feet distant, were four freshly dug graves, and beside them four large pine coffins coarsely constructed.

The scaffold was so arranged that the four condemned could be hung at the same time.

The enclosure was much larger than was stated in my dispatch of last night, and there must have been present within the lot and upon the top of the wall, which was literally packed with soldiers, quite 3,000 spectators, three-fourths of whom were soldiers.

About 12:30 o'clock, Gen. HANCOCK arrived, and remained personally inspecting all the official acts.

THE PROCESSION OF DEATH

At 1:15 the procesion proceeded from the prison to the scaffold in the following order, preceded by Gen. HARTRANFT:

Mrs. SURRATT, supported by an officer and a non-commissioned officer, and attended by Rev. Fathers WALTER and WIGETT.

ATZEROTH, attended by an officer, with whom walked his spiritual advisers, Rev. J.G. BUTLER, of the Lutheran Church, and Chaplain WINCHESTER.

HERROLD came next, attended by Rev. Dr. OLDS, of Christ Church; Episcopal.

PAYNE, attended by Rev. Dr. GILLETTE, of the First Baptist Church, of this city, and Rev. Dr. STRIKER, of Baltimore.

Mrs. SURRATT, attended by two soldiers. Her waist and ankles were ironed; she was attired in a plain black alpacca (sic) dress, with black bonnet and thin veil. Her face could be easily seen. She gazed up at the horrid instrument of death, and her lips were moving rapidly as in prayer. She was assisted upon the scaffold and seated in a chair near the drop. She gazed upon the noose, which dangled in the wind before her face, and again her lips moved as if in prayer.

ATZEROTH followed, with a glaring, haggard look. He seemed to have changed in appearance greatly since his incarceration. He, also, was assisted by two soldiers, and seemed very feeble, but appeared to rally when on the scaffold, and took an evident interest in the proceedings.

HERROLD came next, supported on each side. He seemed very feeble, but revived a little subsequently. He realized his position now, if he never did before. He was very pale and careworn. He examined the scaffold closely, upon approaching it, and especially the drop.

PAYNE came next, with his usual bold, straight attitude, looking with seeming indifference upon the instrument of death. He wore a blue shirt and straw hat. There was not firmness in his step as he marched to the scaffold.

REMARKS AND PRAYERS OF THE ATTENDING CLERGY.

The Catholic priest in attendance upon Mrs. SURRATT declined making any public remark. Dr. GILLET stepped forward and said:

The prisoner, LEWIS THORNTON POWELL, known as PAYNE, requests me on this occasion, to say for him, that he thanks, publicly and sincerely thanks, Gen. HARTRAUFT, all the officers and soldiers who had charge of him, and all persons who have ministered to his wants, for their unwavering kindness to him in this trying hour. Not an unkind word nor an illfeeling (sic) act has been made toward him.

Almighty God, our Heavenly Father, we pray thee to permit us to commit this soul into thy hands, not for any claim we have to make for it in ourselves, but depending as we do upon the merits of our Lord Jesus Christ, grant, O Heavenly Father, we beseech thee, that his spirit may be accorded an easy passage out of this world, and, if consistent with thy purposes of mercy, and thou delightest in mercy, receive him. This we humbly ask, through Jesus Christ, our Lord and our Redeemer. Amen.

Dr. OLDS, in behalf of HERROLD, followed, saying:

"DAVID E. HERROLD, who is here about to undergo the extreme penalty of offended law, desires me to say that he hopes your prayers may be offered up to the Most High God for him; that he forgives all who may at any time have wronged him, and asks of all forgiveness for all the wrong or supposed wrong he has done unto them, that he thanks the officers who have had charge of him during his confinement in prison for their deeds of kindness toward him, he hopes that he dies in charity with all the world and is convinced that his soul is in the hands of God. Amen.

Rev. Mr. BUTLER, the spiritual adviser of ATZEROTH, then rose and said:

"GEORGE A. ATZEROTH requests me thus publicly to return his unfeigned thanks to Gen. HARTRANFT, and all associated with him in this prison, for their uniform courtesy and kindness during his imprisonment. And now, GEORGE A. ATZEROTH, may God have mercy upon you. The ways of the transgressor is hard. The wages of sin is death; but if we freely confess our sins, God will in mercy pardon them. Christ came into the world to save sinners -- even the chief of sinners. Believe in the Lord Jesus Christ, and thou shalt be saved. The blood of the blessed Redeemer, Jesus Christ, cleanseth from all sin. You profess to have thus believed to have peace in your heart; and may God be with you in this hour of trial and suffering; and may you be enabled so to commend your soul to the Creator of it, that you may have peace in this last moment of life. The Lord God Almighty, Father of Mercy, have mercy upon you, and receive you into His heavenly keeping. Lord God, Redeemer of the world, have mercy upon this man. Lord God, Holy Spirit of the Father and the Son, have mercy upon him and grant him thy peace. Amen.

THE LAST FATEFUL SCENE

Gen. HARTRANFT read the order of the War Department, embracing the President's Executive Order, for the execution.

The limbs of each of the prisoners were now pinioned. The caps were drawn over their heads, Mrs. SURRATT exclaiming in a faint voice, "Don't let me fall; hold on!"

ATZEROTH exclaimed in a loud tone: "Gentlemen, take warning;" then, after an interval of about two minutes he said: "Good-by, gentlemen who are before me; may we all meet in the other world."

It was now twenty-five minutes past 1 o'clock. The officer in charge of the scaffold here made some preconcerted motions to the attendant soldiers to step back from the drop, and then, with a motion of his hand, the drop fell and the bodies of the criminals were suspended in the air.

The bodies fell simultaneously, and swayed backward and forward for a few minutes. Mrs. SURRATT, appeared to suffer very little. PAYNE and HARROLD, on the contrary, writhed in apparent agony, the first for about two minutes, and the latter for about five minutes. The muscles of their feet and hands were visibly contracted. PAYNE's hands, which were more exposed than the others, became purpled, as did his neck near where the rope was fastened. ATZEROTH's agony seemed, like Mrs. SURRATT's, to be of but very short duration.

After the lapse of ten minutes, the medical officers, Surgeon WOOD-WARD, U.S.A., Dr. OTIS, U.S.A., and Dr. PORTER, U.S.A., and Surgeon of the post examined severally the bodies, and pronounced life extinct. The ropes were cut, the bodies lowered, stretched upon the tops of the coffins, and a further and more minute examination made by the Surgeons, who state that the necks of each were instantly broken.

At about 4 o'clock the bodies were placed in the coffins and buried.

The soldiers who were required to let fall the trap of the scaffold, are of Company F, Fourteenth Veteran Reserves. They were chosen by the Commander of that regiment who, without making known what was his purpose required four able bodied men of the regiment to be selected from the left of the line, to perform a special and important duty. The selection was accordingly made before the service to be performed became known to the members of the regiment.

MUDD, ARNOLD, O'LAUGHLIN and SPANGLER[68] will probably be sent to the Penitentiary to-morrow.

---

68   Mudd, convicted of conspiracy, and Arnold, convicted of aiding and abetting, were sentenced to life imprisonment, hard labor. Pres. Johnson pardoned them in 1869. Michael O'Laughlen (1840 - 1867), who had turned himself in two days after the assassination, was convicted of aiding and abetting. He was sentenced to life, which turned out to be just two years as he died of yellow fever at Ft. Jefferson in Florida. Edman Spangler (1825 - 1875), a stagehand at Ford's Theatre, was also convicted of aiding and abetting and later pardoned by Johnson.

Acknowledgements

The author is deeply grateful to the several people who volunteered to proofread all or part of this lengthy work: Dianne Brown, Ian Cheney, Ralph Cheney, Sandra Cheney, Denise Dembinski, Frank Foley, Colette Hoffman, and Richard Waterman. Special thanks go to Joe Courtney for his encouragement and the kind words of his foreword. And of course this and many other books would not be possible without Solange Aurora Cavalcante Cheney.

Index

Harper's Weekly 280
Harris, Billy 291
Harrisburgh, Pa. 129, 190, 411
Harrisburg State House 259
Harris, Clara 26, 50
Harris, Ira 26
Harris, Walter 305
Har Sinai Synagogue 181
Hartford Courant 178, 315, 370
Hatcher's Run 14
Hawk, William Henry 25, 27, 163
Hay, John 22, 191, 193
Heartwell, Ann C. 383
Hebrews (Old Testament) 197, 300
Hendrix, Rev. T. 369
Henry I, King 252
Henry, Mayor Alexander 278
Hepburn, Sergeant 94
Herald-Tribune 237
Hernon, Jon 305
Herold, David Edgar 323–329, 340,
    344, 349, 349–351, 362, 371,
    392, 443–448
Heywood, O. 403
Higgins, Kate 384
Highland [Ohio] News 313
Hillsboro, N.C. 129
Hoge, Rev. Moses D. 333
Holt, Joseph 431
Hooker, Assist. Adjt. Gen. George H.
    181
Hooker, Gen. Joseph 99, 125, 181,
    297, 381, 408
Hooper, Samuel 276
Hopper, Major Jas. S. 381
Houbraken, Jacobus 390
Housatonic Railroad 372
Howard, Capt. L. 258
Howard, Gen. Oliver Otis 341
Howard University 341
Hunter, Sen. Robert M. T. 17
Hunter, William, Jr. 46, 290

I

Illinois State House 408
Independence Hall 277, 278, 301
Indianapolis 130, 190, 264, 301, 356,
    361, 376, 377, 381, 411
Ingersoll, Edward 322
Isaiah (Old Testament) 199, 215
Israelite Reform congregation 181

J

Jackson, Andrew 41, 55, 61, 139, 218,
    361
Jackson, Andrew Jr. 218
Jackson, Thomas J. "Stonewall" 10,
    99, 189
Jacob (biblical) 413
James, David 284
Jamestown Journal 214
Jeff Davis, Valedictory Proclamation
    of 64
Jeffersonville, Ind. 63, 234
Jernegen, Nellie 384
Jersey City, N.J. 104, 206, 265
Jett, Willie 441
Job (Old Testament) 194, 196
John Brownite 213
John (New Testament) 194, 216
Johnson, Andrew 29–30, 37–38, 49,
    52, 56–58, 77, 93–95, 123, 136,
    141, 152, 206, 291–292, 346,
    352, 436
  speech by 152–157
Johnson, Charles and Margaret 291
Johnson, Henry 305
Johnston, Gen. Joseph 8
Jones, Avonia Stanhope 35
Jones, J. Milton 285
Jones, Thomas Dow 185
Jordan, Col. Frank 258
Julius Ceasar (Shakespeare's) 151,
    233, 401

453

Glenn Alan Cheney is the author of over 25 books of fiction and nonfiction, hundreds of articles, several op-ed essays, and a few short stories and poems. His writings have covered such topics as Brazil's Estrada Real and its Quilombo dos Palmares, nuclear proliferation, atomic testing, Chernobyl, taxes, accounting standards, cybercrime, teens with disabilities, drug addiction, the Pilgrims, nuns, Mohandas Gandhi, and Central American politics. Information about him can be found at cheneybooks.com. He lives in Hanover, Conn., with his wife, Solange Aurora Cavalcante Cheney.